## MURD[ERERS]

The stories are shocking. The brutal murders of whole groups of people: entire families, offices full of co-workers, or simply customers in a restaurant who had nothing in common except their desire for lunch — and their death. The perpetrators are mass murderers, vicious killers who don't stalk and slay one victim but wantonly massacre three, four, even dozens.

Now, from the authentic files of True Detective magazine, read the horrifying stories of murderers whose lust to kill wasn't slaked until numerous victims had died: mass murderers like George Hennard, who walked into Luby's Cafeteria in Killeen, Texas and in ten minutes mowed down 46 men, women and children; Gang Lu, a graduate student whose bloody rampage through the peaceful academic halls of the University of Iowa left five people dead; and David Lewis Rice, who slaughtered the entire Goldmark family of Seattle on Christmas Eve!

## MASS MURDERERS

**PINNACLE BOOKS AND *TRUE DETECTIVE* MAGAZINE
TEAM UP TO BRING YOU THE
MOST HORRIFIC TRUE CRIME STORIES!**

| | |
|---|---|
| BIZARRE MURDERERS | (486-9, $4.95/$5.95) |
| CELEBRITY MURDERS | (435-4, $4.95/$5.95) |
| COP KILLERS | (603-9, $4.99/$5.99) |
| THE CRIMES OF THE RICH AND FAMOUS | (630-6, $4.99/$5.99) |
| CULT KILLERS | (528-8, $4.95/$5.95) |
| MEDICAL MURDERERS | (522-2, $4.99/$5.99) |
| SERIAL MURDERERS | (432-X, $4.95/$5.95) |
| SPREE KILLERS | (461-3, $4.95/$5.95) |
| TORTURE KILLERS | (506-7, $4.95/$5.95) |

*Available wherever paperbacks are sold, or order direct from the Publisher. Send cover price plus 50¢ per copy for mailing and handling to Pinnacle Books, Dept. 777, 475 Park Avenue South, New York, N.Y. 10016. Residents of New York and Tennessee must include sales tax. DO NOT SEND CASH. For a free Zebra/Pinnacle catalog please write to the above address.*

FROM THE FILES OF TRUE DETECTIVE MAGAZINE

# MASS MURDERERS

### EDITED BY ROSE G. MANSELSBERG

**PINNACLE BOOKS**
**WINDSOR PUBLISHING CORP.**

For more true crime reading, pick up TRUE DETECTIVE, OFFICIAL DETECTIVE, MASTER DETECTIVE, FRONT PAGE DETECTIVE, and INSIDE DETECTIVE magazines on sale at newsstands every month.

PINNACLE BOOKS are published by

Windsor Publishing Corp.
475 Park Avenue South
New York, NY 10016

Copyright © 1983, 1984, 1985, 1986, 1987, 1988, 1989, 1990, 1991, 1992, 1993 by RGH Publishing Corporation. For complete copyright information, see Appendix.

All rights reserved. No part of this book may be reproduced in any form or by any means without the prior written consent of the Publisher, excepting brief quotes used in reviews.

If you purchased this book without a cover you should be aware that this book is stolen property. It was reported as "unsold and destroyed" to the Publisher and neither the Author nor the Publisher has received any payment for this "stripped book."

The P logo Reg. U.S. Pat. & TM Off. Pinnacle is a trademark of Windsor Publishing Corp.

First Printing: December, 1993

Printed in the United States of America

# TABLE OF CONTENTS

**"AMERICA'S MOST HORRIFIC MASSACRE: HE MOWED DOWN 46 IN 10 MINUTES OF PURE HELL!"**
by Bill Cox — 7

**"UNIVERSITY OF IOWA'S CAMPUS CARNAGE!"**
by Gary C. King — 31

**"THE CARR'S HILL MASSACRE!"**
by Bruce Gibney — 47

**"HE TORCHED 4 OVER 'NOTHING'!"**
by Bob Coppedge — 62

**"THE CAR WAS FULL OF DEAD PEOPLE!"**
by Gary C. King — 75

**"EASTER-MORNING MASSACRE OF 5!"**
by Bill Kelly — 89

**"JUNKYARD KILLER'S SHOTGUN SPREE!"**
by Catherine Henderson — 103

**"FREAKED-OUT TRUCKER SLAUGHTERED 4!"**
by Bud Ampolsk — 122

**"MASS MURDER ON THE MISSISSIPPI COAST"**
by Gary C. King — 135

**"SALOON SLAUGHTER LEFT 4 IN GORE!"**
by Charles W. Sasser — 149

**"BAYMEADOWS MASSACRE LEFT 16 VICTIMS!"**
by Barbara Geehr — 163

**"FAMILY SLAUGHTER BY A MIXED-UP 'SOLDIER'!"**
by Gary C. King — 181

| | |
|---|---:|
| "THE GAY DRAG QUEEN AXED 4!"<br>by Bruce Gibney | 199 |
| "FRY ME FOR MY CRIMES!"<br>by Barbara Geehr | 213 |
| "SEATTLE'S BLOODY CARNAGE AT THE WAH MEE CLUB!"<br>by Gary C. King | 238 |
| "BOWLING ALLEY MASSACRE!"<br>by Bill Cox | 259 |
| "4 VICTIMS IN THE TRAILER OF BLOOD!"<br>by Bob Carlsen | 274 |
| "THE PIZZERIA BLOODBATH"<br>by Dan Buttaro | 285 |
| "5 VICTIMS OF THE TICKING TIME BOMB!"<br>by Bud Ampolsk | 312 |
| "7,000 YEARS FOR THE FREAKED-OUT GUNMAN!"<br>by Gary C. King | 329 |
| "ENRAGED LOVER MASSACRED A FAMILY OF 5!"<br>by Bob Carlsen | 344 |
| "HE BUTCHERED 3 WITH A MEAT CLEAVER!"<br>by Gary C. King | 359 |
| "THE HUNTER'S QUARRY WAS A FAMILY OF 5!"<br>by Ed Barcelo | 378 |
| "HIS TEMPER FLARED . . . AND 87 BURNED!"<br>by Bud Ampolsk | 398 |
| "4 BLASTED IN POSTAL BLOODBATH!"<br>by Gary C. King | 417 |
| APPENDIX | 433 |

# "AMERICA'S MOST HORRIFIC MASSACRE: HE MOWED DOWN 46 IN 10 MINUTES OF PURE HELL!"

by Bill Cox

Luby's Cafeteria was busy during lunch hour on Wednesday, October 16, 1991. A steady stream of customers moved along the serving line, and others were already eating at their tables in the popular Killeen Texas, eatery. A pleasant murmur of voices, punctuated by the clatter of silverware, enveloped the dining room, which looked out on an access road running along U.S. Highway 190.

Some of the crowd of diners were no doubt taking a break from their jobs or errands at the nearby shopping mall. But perhaps the main reason for the slightly larger crowd that afternoon was that it was Bosses' Day, which local employees celebrate by taking their bosses out to lunch. The cafeteria is especially favored by senior citizens, but that day's diners included business and professional types of all ages — secretaries, service trade workers, store clerks, military personnel, and public school administrators.

At 12:40 p.m., a 1987 blue Ford Ranger pickup

careened into the restaurant's parking lot, swerved around the front entrance, and gained momentum as it headed straight for the large plate-glass window to the right of the front door.

To witnesses in the parking area, it appeared as though the truck was out of control or that the man at the wheel was either intoxicated or had been stricken ill. Then the speeding truck smashed through the window, shattering glass and making a sound that some customers thought at first was a violent storm that had erupted out of the blue.

The pickup plowed over a table and its occupants before coming to a stop. Screams erupted everywhere. Those people who could were running or crawling away from the wreckage. Some were pinned under the debris, screaming in agony.

But the nightmarish tableau immediately became more horrifying. A man wearing sunglasses and brandishing a pistol jumped from the pickup, took a step forward, and shouted something that sounded like, "This is what Belton did to me!"

He swung the handgun toward a man trying to emerge from under a crushed table and fired point-blank. The gunman then turned with the weapon and began firing randomly at diners, who were still frozen in terror and disbelief. The loud shots, only seconds apart, reverberated in the cafeteria. To panicking customers trying to find cover, the surreality of the scene unfolded in excruciatingly slow motion.

The gunman pivoted and selected his targets. Witnesses noticed the look on the gunman's face: He didn't seem angry or nervous or excited; his expression was one of self-composed coldness. As he calculatedly gunned down his victims, seemingly bent on killing every man, woman, and child in the restaurant, the lone gunman kept in motion an act of carnage unparalleled in American history.

A public works employee who was pulling into the

cafeteria's parking lot was the first to call police. Speed-dialing on his cellular telephone, he reached the Harker Heights dispatcher at 16 seconds past 12:40 p.m. The call was relayed to the Killeen Police Department. Even as the man gave the alarm on the phone, he could hear shots continuing inside the cafeteria . . .

The little town of Killeen in central Texas is familiar to countless Americans. During one war or another, thousands of young soldiers have trained at the U.S. Army's Fort Hood, the nation's largest military land installation. Killeen is one of four towns adjacent to the huge base.

Since 1942, when the Army put up a camp on the rangeland around the quiet little community of 1,400 cattle ranchers, the fortunes of the Texas town—good and bad—have been linked to the Army and its wars. In that first year after the start of World War II, 70,000 troops converged on Fort Hood and Killeen in the first of many military-inspired booms. And when Killeen boomed, it did so with all the rambunctiousness of an old-fashioned oil-boom town.

In the vagaries of war and peace, Killeen's citizens and its economy knew both hell and happiness.

When Fort Hood overflowed with troops, crime, because of the commercialized vice that military towns can breed, was rampant. A paradoxical wedding between sin and economic salvation held the town in its sway, and local police fought their own war to maintain a shaky peace.

But never—even in times of war and boom that left Killeen with a violent reputation known far and wide—did anything come close to matching the hellish nightmare of October 16, 1991.

In the early-autumn beauty of that October, Killeen was basking in the glow of the good times once more. There had been a noticeable slump the previous year when Pentagon restructuring resulted in the transfer of an entire division from Fort Hood. For a while it had seemed that the base might even be closed. Then the Persian Gulf War came, and 25,000 troops left the base for the Middle East. The year that followed brought with it disruption and uncertainty for many Killeen folks. Families were separated as fathers, mothers, brothers, and sisters went off to war.

Only recently the town had welcomed home the last contingent of service people sent to the Gulf War. Families were reunited and business was on the upswing.

And then, without warning, came that terrible, never-to-be-forgotten Wednesday . . .

As the assailant unleashed his deadly fire after crashing his pickup through the cafeteria's plate-glass window, he continued to utter oaths directed at the nearby town of Belton and all of Bell County, within which both Killeen and Belton lie.

"Look at what Belton's done to me!" the gunman shouted. "Tell me, people, was it worth it? Wait 'til those f------ women in Belton see this! I wonder if *they'll* think it was worth it!"

To those crouched behind tables or sprawled on the floor hoping to get out of the line of fire, the words were the incoherent mutterings of a madman. The gunman walked and fired the gun, pausing only long enough to reload a new clip of ammunition.

As the scene was later reconstructed by eyewitnesses to the carnage, each move the gunman made brought new terror and hopelessness to his victims, both potential and actual.

Among the first victims was Olgica Taylor, who was having lunch with her daughter and 4-year-old granddaughter. The gunman walked to their table, raised the automatic pistol and shot Taylor as her daughter looked on in terrified disbelief. He turned away momentarily, then wheeled and shot the woman a second time.

He stopped in front of Mrs. Taylor's daughter, pointed the gun at her, and then hesitated. He said, "You get that baby and get out of here! Run outside and tell everybody Bell County was bad!"

The sobbing woman swept up her small daughter and ran from the building.

Outside, Ray Hardin had just driven up to drop off his girlfriend, Regina Minton, who was set to start her shift at Luby's. Minton had barely gotten inside the door when the shocked Hardin saw the blue pickup barrel through the plate-glass window.

Hardin watched in horror as the pickup driver got out and started firing into the crowd. Hardin thought his girlfriend had been hit by the truck or possibly shot, since she had just walked inside. Tossing caution aside, he ran into the cafeteria, calling her name.

Regina had come face to face with the man in sunglasses seconds after he stepped from the truck and started shooting. As the gunman looked at her and raised the gun, Regina dropped to the floor and started crawling as fast as she could. The man fired several shots in her direction. She heard bullets hitting somewhere over her head. Glass shattered and fell on her as she reached the door and crawled out. There she met Hardin, and together they dashed through the cafeteria to the food-to-go department, where Hardin spotted a telephone. He grabbed up the receiver and started to call the police when he noticed that the cold-faced gunman was staring straight at him and reloading the pistol.

As the assailant reloaded and looked around the jumble of people, he muttered again, to no one in particular, "This is what Belton done to me! Is it worth it? Is it worth it?"

Hardin dropped the phone and, grabbing his

girlfriend, ran from the building and to an automobile parts store next door. He ran inside, yelling, "Some crazy son-of-a-bitch is shooting people at Luby's! Give me a gun, give me a gun! I'll shoot him!"

But no one in the store had a gun to give Hardin.

Back at the restaurant, Bob Witherall, a telephone company employee, was standing in the serving line with his wife when the truck smashed through the window. The couple was standing toward the end of the food line. As the man started shooting, Witherral shoved his wife to the floor and crouched behind a bench beside her.

As the gunman passed the spot where the Witherrals were trying to hide, he suddenly reached over them and fired a shot into the head of another woman who was only inches from the couple. The killer's foot brushed against Mrs. Witherral as he fired the fatal shot into the other woman, saying, "Take that, you bitch!"

When the slayer walked to the other end of the cafeteria, the Witherrals and 10 other persons managed to flee through a side door to safety.

Al Gratia, 71, his wife, Ursula Gratia, and their 32-year-old daughter were having lunch at Luby's. The elderly couple had celebrated their 48th wedding anniversary on October 3rd. Gratia was a retired construction company owner and an avid golfer. His wife didn't play golf, but he liked her to ride in the golf cart with him.

Everyone said the Gratias were inseparable. When the gunfire broke out in the cafeteria, the family turned over a table and huddled behind it.

They watched in despair as the callous killer deliberately went about his business of executions, taking careful aim and firing. They noticed there were only about three seconds between his lethal shots.

Al Gratia was raging at what was happening. "I gotta do something! I have to do something. He is going to kill every one of us!"

Gratia tried to rise from behind the table several times but was pulled back by his daughter. But as the gunman came closer, the young woman was unable to restrain her father. He lunged at the stalking killer. The gunman shot him in the chest, and the courageous man fell on the floor beside his daughter.

About the time that Gratia was gunned down, someone smashed a window and people ran toward it. The daughter grabbed her mother and urged her to follow.

"Get up! Get up! We've got to get out of here!" she exclaimed to Ursula Gratia. But as the daughter ran toward the window offering an escape route, her mother crawled to her husband's side and knelt down to him. Even as she knelt, the man with the gun shot and killed her. It would be several hours before the daughter would know the final fate of her parents, who, inseparable in life, had died together because the wife would not leave her husband's side for safety.

Another victim who died in the cafeteria massacre was Army Lieutenant Colonel Steven C. Dody, who had planned to retire in two weeks. He planned to take life easy after an active career in the service, spend more time with his kids, do some fishing. When fighting in Vietnam, the officer earned the Meritorious Service Medal. Having survived that treacherous conflict, it was dark irony that he died at the hands of a maddened gunman while having lunch in a quiet suburban cafeteria.

Dr. Michael Griffith, a veterinarian in the little community of Copperas Cove, was a busy man, in his profession and in other activities. The 48-year-old veterinarian had worked with the Eagle Scouts all his life. He loved hiking and camping and working with young people in sports. He also served on his community's school board and was actively involved in the Methodist Church.

Shortly before noon on Wednesday, Dr. Griffith had just finished surgery on an animal at his clinic when a good friend dropped by and said, "Let's go to lunch."

They went to Luby's. Within minutes after their arrival, Dr. Griffith lay dead and his friend wounded in the fusillade of bullets fired by the rampaging gunman. His friends and colleagues would find it unbelievable that the veterinarian's life had ended because of a choice of where to have lunch.

Thirty-year-old Su-zann Rashott worked with her husband in the family-owned plumbing company. When it was her turn to take a lunch break on this day, she went to Luby's. That morning was the last time her husband and family would see her alive.

The toll of victims rose as three Killeen school administrators lost their lives in what would turn out to be the largest mass shooting in U.S. history. The administrators were among 15 members of the Killeen Independent School District who were present for a Bosses' Day luncheon with the director of the district's Chapter I low-income student education program.

Slain in the hail of bullets were Pat Carney, the head of the elementary school education for the school district, and Nancy Stansbury and Ruth Pujol, both administrators in the district's low-income student program. When the automatic gunfire began, Mrs. Carney was seated with her husband, who somehow managed to escape the killer's well-aimed bullets.

Also wounded were the low-income education director, who was the honored guest at the Bosses' Day luncheon, and a clerk in the school district's business office, Ms. Stansbury and Ms. Pujol were sitting at the table with the director when they fell fatally wounded.

From the count of victims, men and women, it appeared as if the killer was concentrating on women as his targets, though no one was giving thought to this possibility when pandemonium reigned in the besieged cafeteria.

Venice E. Henehan, 70, and her husband came from their home in Metz, Missouri, to Killeen. There they met their daughter and son-in-law, who they would accompany to Houston, Texas, for the weekend wedding of their granddaughter. It was a memorable time for the Henehans, who only a week earlier had celebrated their own 51st wedding anniversary.

The elderly couple and their daughter and son-in-law went to Luby's for lunch. In the few minutes after the blue pickup roared through the front window, Mrs. Henehan was killed by a gunshot and the two younger members of the party were wounded, but would survive. Mrs. Henehan's husband escaped without injury.

Zona Hunnicut Lynn and her friend, Clodine Humphrey, who lived in Marlin, Texas, had come to Killeen for a church conference. A retired school counselor, Mrs. Lynn had been second vice president of the Marlin NAACP chapter. For many years, Ms. Humphrey had been employed at the Veterans Administration Medical Center in Marlin.

As the two ladies sat quietly eating their lunch, both died in the hail of bullets from the automatic pistol of a man they had never seen before in their lives.

Usually, Tom Simmons, 33-year-old manager of the automotive department of the large chain discount store across Highway 190 from Luby's, would have been off on Wednesday.

Simmons, whose home was in Copperas Cove, had taken an extra day off the previous weekend to drive his wife and two small daughters to Brownwood for a family visit. So on this fateful day, he was working to make up for that day and was having lunch at Luby's. It was a tragic twist of fate that an extra day taken for a family trip would wind up costing him his life.

Jimmie Eugene Caruthers, 48, was employed by the Texas Department of Human Services as a contract specialist. Although his home with his wife and family had been in Austin for 26 years, he was in Killeen on business. He stopped to eat at Luby's and died in the gunman's killing spree.

Other victims who perished in the wild gunfire included a 30-year-old beauty shop owner named Sylvia Mathilde King; Debra Gray; Connie D. Miller; John Raymond Romero Jr.; Glen A. Spivey; James W. Welch and Lula B. Welch; and Juanita C. Williams.

Kreinchild Davis, one of the wounded women, would die four days later in the hospital, raising the fatalities to 23 — 15 women and 8 men. Twenty-two other customers, half of them women, were wounded in the storm of gunshots.

There would undoubtedly have been more casualties had it not been for the courage and physical resourcefulness of a burly 28-year-old employee from a nearby automobile dealership.

The heavyset auto mechanic and eight fellow employees dived to the floor when the shooting broke out. As they lay there waiting to see what would happen next, one of the men said suddenly, "He's coming our way!"

Since they hit the floor, the men had been hoping that the gunman would run out of ammunition. But they had seen with rising alarm the gunman reloading two and three times and knew he probably had a large supply of bullets. When he reloaded again and started in their direction, the mechanic decided it was time to act or probably be killed. He didn't want to go to his feet and immediately put himself in the position of a sitting duck, but he knew that as the seconds ticked by and the man with the automatic pistol moved toward them, time was rapidly running out.

Suddenly the big mechanic heaved himself up, expecting to take a bullet any second as he dashed full speed at a large plate-glass window at the back of the cafeteria. He hit the glass, and it crashed outward with his weight. In all, some 30 people, including his fellow workers, plunged through the shattered window to safety.

Using his body to break through the thick pain of glass left the mechanic with several scratches and cuts. Some cuts on his ear and one arm required stitches later on. But he was happy to be alive.

The unknown fates that decide such things spared some would-be victims while others in the immediate vicinity were shot down. One man trapped in the tumult thought at one time that his end had come, that he had "bought the farm" as Texans sometimes say laconically when referring to a burial plot.

The gunman looked directly into the man's eyes and pointed his lethal weapon at him. But at that instant a woman rose from the floor to run, and the gunman turned and fired at her. It was enough diversion for the almost-target to scramble to his feet and race to the back of the cafeteria, the opposite direction from the killer. He managed to flee out a fire exit, but he heard bullets crash into the wall over his head as he escaped.

To the people inside the building, it seemed that the bloody carnage had gone on for a very long time, but actually only minutes had passed since the gunman drove his pickup through the window and emerged shooting.

As police logs would reveal later, it was only about one minute after the public works employee who drove up on the slaughter in process and called police on his cellular phone that the first officers arrived at the scene. Two undercover officers from the Texas Department of Public Safety (DPS), working another case at a location only a short distance from the cafeteria, were in plainclothes. They were joined within minutes by a DPS sergeant and a group of officers who had been attending a seminar at a hotel near Luby's—they had even heard the shots fired by the gunman—when they received the call for help.

The officers immediately entered the cafeteria and were greeted by a scene reminiscent of Dante's *Inferno*. The dead and the dying and the less seriously wounded were scattered all over the cafeteria. Everyone seemed to be screaming. One DPS officer tried to make himself heard above the victims' wails and moans but was unsuccessful.

Within seconds they spotted the gunman—and he saw them. The gunman started shooting, and the lawmen returned his fire. The pandemonium prevented the lawmen from getting a clear shot at the killer. Some of the dying tried to reach for the officers as they made their way through the building.

In the exchange of shots, four of the officers' bullets found their mark. Badly wounded, the killer staggered in retreat to a back hallway leading to the rest rooms. As Sergeant Bill Cooper moved to within 10 feet of him, the gunman raised his pistol to his own temple, fired, and fell to the floor. A quick but cautious examination showed that the gunman was dead by his own hand.

The gun with which he took his staggering toll of lives was a 9mm Glock 17 semiautomatic pistol, which uses an ammunition clip that can hold up to 19 bullets. The semiautomatic gun is manufactured in Austria and is used as a sidearm by the Austrian Army. It has also become a popular weapon at about 4,000 law enforcement agencies in the United States.

Within a short time, the dead mass murderer was

identified as 35-year-old George Hennard of Belton, a small town about 15 miles from Killeen. As to his motive or his background, the police were as mystified as anyone else.

Apparently, the killer was carrying another semi-automatic pistol, a Ruger P89. He had three 15-round clips for the Ruger and three 17-round clips for the Glock 17 used in the shootings, said Killeen Police Chief F.L. Giacomozzi.

The cafeteria looked like a wartime battle scene. Killeen Police Officer Ricky Smith said, "I've been here thirteen years, and it's far most the worst I ever seen."

Mike Cox of Austin, information officer for the Texas Department of Public Safety, had entered the cafeteria with officers shortly after Hennard killed himself. "The scene inside is almost surrealistic, like something out of a TV movie," Cox said. "There are bodies scattered throughout the entire cafeteria. The floor is covered with broken glass, bullet holes, bullet fragments, blood."

Outside, ambulances with lights flashing and sirens wailing were arriving to haul the wounded to hospitals. Military helicopters, loaned by Fort Hood, touched down on the restaurant's parking lot and were quickly loaded with victims the ambulances couldn't manage.

Police and emergency medical workers scurried around the cafeteria, tending to the wounded. A family assistance unit, with a team of 20 Army chaplains, trauma specialists, and psychiatrists, was set up at a nearby hotel to help grief-stricken survivors and family members.

Survivors sat on the sidewalk, shaking and comforting each other. One woman tried to run back into the blood-littered cafeteria but was held back by friends.

In the meantime, print and electronic news teams

were pouring onto the site from as far away as 500 miles. TV broadcasters set up for live network coverage.

Police Chief F.L. Giacomozzi said that more people would have been killed or wounded had it not been for the speedy arrival of nearby officers who were attending the meeting at the hotel.

"The only thing that kept it from being much worse was the proximity of the officers to the scene when the call came down. Had they not arrived, it's very evident the shooting of innocent persons would have continued and the death rate would have been much higher. He wasn't out of bullets when the officers got there."

Police officials declined to identify the three DPS undercover officers because their future undercover investigations would be imperiled.

As hundreds of spectators flocked to the site, police put up wooden sawhorses and stretched yellow crime scene tape around the cafeteria and a zone about 50 yards from the building to keep back onlookers. As the hours dragged by, large refrigerator trucks were backed up to the rear of the cafeteria to haul the bodies to morgues.

Military doctors offered their services to treat the shooting casualties. The mass shooting reminded them of their all-too-recent experiences in the Persian Gulf. Some of the wounded were treated at a Fort Hood hospital.

With so little known about the mystery man who had instigated the restaurant rampage, a task force comprising more than two dozen detectives and special investigators from the Killeen Police Department, Texas Rangers, DPS agents, the FBI, and the Army was assembled to probe into the background of George Hennard.

Federal agents got busy trying to trace the two semiautomatic pistols the killer carried. Other officers began quizzing Hennard's neighbors, acquaintances, and relatives.

Foremost in the investigators' minds was the need to establish a motive for the savage massacre of innocent people, none of whom Hennard had known. Clearly, he had snapped; but, the probers wanted to know, *why* had he snapped?

The massacre of Luby's was grimly reminiscent of the tragic August day in 1966 when ex-Marine Charles Whitman climbed the 230-foot-high bell tower on the Texas University campus Austin and fired on people below for several hours before he was slain by police. The toll in that mass tragedy, only 50 miles to the south of the Killeen massacre, had been 16 dead and 32 wounded.

A more recent spree was the July 18, 1984, rampage at a McDonald's restaurant in San Ysidro, California, when James Oliver Huberty, an unemployed security guard, killed 21 people before he was slain by a police sharpshooter.

Investigators learned that Hennard had been living in a stately two-story home in Belton. The Southern-style mansion was owned by the gunman's parents. His father, a Houston doctor, and his mother, who lived in Nevada, were divorced.

Questioned by the investigators, Hennard's neighbors described him as sullen, rude, and frequently terrifying. Two sisters living in Hennard's neighborhood showed police a letter they had received from Hennard on June 6, 1991, in which he asked them for a date. In the letter, Hennard wrote, "Please give me the satisfaction of someday laughing in the face of all those mostly white treacherous female vipers from those two towns who tried to destroy me and my family." He sent pictures of himself with the letter. The sisters believed Hennard was referring to the towns of Belton and Killeen.

One of the sisters said, "He had strange ideas."

21

The sisters told police that Hennard would follow them around town, trying to engage them in unwelcome conversations. Only a week before the murder rampage, Hennard had come to the bank where one sister worked and tried unsuccessfully to talk to her.

"I would ignore him because my mother had told me to just ignore him," she said. "I just think he was obsessed."

The women related that Hennard had been following them at intervals since January 1988. His letter referred to a date when he had first spotted them at a local rock concert.

The woman's sister described Hennard as "a good-looking guy, but with scary eyes."

During the last week, they noticed Hennard following them through the aisles of a supermarket. As they started to check out, he rapidly pushed his shopping cart to the checkout and stood behind them in the line. When he went to his pickup parked beside their car on the store parking lot, he jokingly said that he had beaten them anyway.

Tracking the strange man's life, officers learned Hennard had grown up as an "Army brat," moving frequently around the country with his father, an Army surgeon, and his family. He spent some time overseas. He had been born in Pennsylvania and had observed his 35th birthday only one day before the murder spree.

Hennard had graduated from a high school in Las Cruces, New Mexico, in 1974, while his father was stationed at Fort Bliss. His senior photograph appeared in the school yearbook but no school achievements were listed. From his school days into adult life, he had been a loner with no known friends.

As far as could be determined, Hennard had not been married, the investigators said. But they were told about a mystery woman in Hennard's life, a tall blonde who drove a red Camaro.

For about three years, the woman had been an off-and-on visitor to Hennard's Colonial-style home on the quiet Belton street. Their relationship seemed to end about 8:30 p.m. on a Sunday in June 1991, when the woman and another man drove up in front of Hennard's house. Hennard and the man got into a heated argument that became so nasty that neighbors called the police.

A neighbor recalled that Hennard had raged at the blonde, saying, "You're my wife! How could you go to Killeen and dance with a bunch of GIs? How can you do this to me?" He was screaming so loudly it was hard to understand his words, the witness recalled. "He kept holding up his hands, kind of like he was going to hit her."

Although neighbors told probers that Hennard often referred to the blonde as his wife, no records of his being married could be found. According to records, Hennard joined the U.S. Navy after finishing high school and was honorably discharged in February 1977. Next he joined the Merchant Marines. There his temper and drug use got him into trouble. In 1982, the Merchant Marines suspended him for six months because of a fight on board a ship.

As a loner who found trouble everywhere he turned, a man who constantly paced back and forth unless down-keyed by marijuana, a man of volatile temper ignited over nothing, Hennard had only one place where he was at peace with himself—the sea.

But once again, his conduct had taken away that one retreat from the world he couldn't stand. Two years earlier, the U.S. Coast Guard had banned him for life from working as a seaman after he was caught with marijuana in his quarters aboard the *Green Wave*, a ship based in New Orleans.

The revocation of Hennard's license to go to sea— "pulling the ticket," as it is called—ended forever his only respite from reality.

In 1989, when he testified in front of a Coast Guard tribunal in an effort to get his license restored, Hennard admitted to a drug problem that dated back to his high school days. Mostly, it was marijuana. He told the judges that the Merchant Marines "is all I've got—it's all I know."

Hennard testified he had enrolled in a drug rehabilitation program in Houston because he realized he had to make a choice: either give up drugs or give up the sea. Unmoved, the Coast Guard upheld the revocation of his seaman's license in February 1991.

That action may have put the first crack in George Hennard's fragile mind, investigators believe.

Hennard's Houston attorney said, "The government didn't cut him any slack. He'd lost the occupation that was his entire life. You put the two together, and if he has any cracks in his psyche, you might have an explosion."

Hennard had turned to booze in recent times, former drinking buddies said. "He wasn't particular about what he drank," said one drinking cohort. "When he was drunk, that's when he'd talk crazy."

According to the autopsy by the Dallas County Medical Examiner's Office, no traces of drugs or alcohol were found in Hennard's body at the time of his death.

Hennard had one other interest—he found escape in the loud and rapid rhythm of a drum beat. He had played in a garage band when he was a teenager, but his temper had left him ostracized by the rest of the group. If he did play, he played alone.

A drum salesman who knew Hennard recalled that he had little talent but thrived on playing fast and loud, 20 or 30 minutes without stopping. "He would get really keyed up when he played."

Detectives got another glimpse into the killer's personality from a man who once worked with Hennard on a temporary construction job. The man told them that Hennard's favorite musical tune was a rap anthem called "Ain't Nothing But a Word to Me." The song describes acts of violence against women and characterizes them as "bitches."

From other sources contacted during the intensive probe, detectives heard that George Hennard did not get along with his mother. This was the woman, the sleuths recalled, who when notified about Hennard's mass killing and his own death, could only think to describe him as "a beautiful son."

From stories told by people who knew them, the mother and son relationship had not been a good one. One witness said that Hennard frequently argued with his mother and once pushed her during a squabble. The witness said that Hennard sometimes talked about killing his mother and would envision her head on the body of a rattlesnake.

"That's pretty much the root of much of his problem," said the informant. "He and his mother."

But only one summer before Hennard's massacre, officers learned, he had spent some time visiting with his mother in Henderson, Nevada, where she lived in an apartment complex. Henderson is 20 miles southeast of Las Vegas. After the summer visit, Hennard had moved back to Belton to live in his divorced parents' mansion.

It was in Henderson that Hennard had bought the 9mm Glock 17 semiautomatic used in the Luby's Cafeteria murders. He made the purchase from a mail-order gun business operated legally from a home in that town. The purchase had been made, records showed, on February 18, 1991. Hennard had filled out a gun registration form with the mail-order catalog business, then paid for the gun.

The registration form routinely went to the Henderson Police Department, which ran a criminal background check on Hennard and checked to see if the gun had been stolen. If there had been a problem, Nevada authorities explained, police would have notified the gun dealer and tried to recover the pistol.

Hennard had passed all the legal checks with no trouble. The procedure was much stricter than anything Hennard would have come up against in Texas, where guns can be bought by anyone who fills out a federal form that asks the potential buyer about any criminal history or deviant mental behavior. If the answers are negative and the buyer has a valid Texas driver's license and is at least 21 years old, he can buy any gun he wants. No background checks are done in Texas.

Records in Henderson disclosed that in March, Hennard had bought the other semiautomatic pistol at the same residential mail-order house.

Investigators came up with another interesting fact about Hennard's myriad personality traits. While visiting his mother at the Henderson apartment complex, he had befriended a neighbor woman's grandson and went swimming with the neighborhood children.

"It was frightening to think someone so calm could do what he did," the neighbor would later reflect. "I never saw him upset at any time. He was just a quiet neighbor who stuck to himself."

Another report surfaced from California, where a couple who had known Hennard described him as a heavy marijuana user who loved heavy metal music and foreign women. The husband had served with Hennard in the Merchant Marines. The couple recalled that Hennard claimed he hated his mother and all American women and bragged of relationships he had with women he encountered in South Pacific ports.

"George told me one time the only women he would ever go out with would be foreign women," said the seaman buddy's wife. "He said they knew how to behave." The ex-Merchant Marine recalled that Hennard said he hated American women because he claimed they tried to manipulate him.

The couple also thought that Hennard's loss of his seaman's card could have played a big part in Hennard's eventual Killeen rampage. "That's when he started going downhill because that was his life," said the former sailor who had served with Hennard. "He loved to be out there at sea because it is isolated and you don't have to deal with the day-to-day realities."

In Belton, the investigators obtained permission from Hennard's relatives to search the big house where he lived. If they found anything pertinent to the case, any evidence that might provide a definite motive for the mass slayings, they did not disclose it to the news media.

While officers dug for more information that might shed light on reasons for the massive killing spree, there was a development that was a bright spot in the horrible tragedy.

Although none of the Luby's Cafeteria employees had been hurt in the shootings, there was a mystery surrounding a missing 19-year-old food preparer. The manager reported him unaccounted for. There was a possibility that he had fled from the restaurant and had not returned.

Then, the day after the massacre, a worker checking through the cafeteria made a startling discovery.

The missing, six-foot-tall employee was curled up inside a 15-foot-long industrial dishwasher. The man had stayed in his hiding place throughout the night, unsure what was going on outside. It was surmised that he also might have gone to sleep. He had used his size 13 tennis shoes as a pillow.

"I was fortunate because I came out alive," he said with a grin.

It was also discovered that a missing 41-year-old employee sought refuge in a freezer and stayed there over two hours. She was treated at a hospital for exposure.

Cleanup work began at the cafeteria after it was released by police, but at this writing the chain management was not certain it would be reopened at that location.

A movie ticket stub found among Hennard's possessions was at first thought to be for a movie playing at two Killeen theaters in which a massacre by a demented gunman who then kills himself is part of the plot. A Texas newspaper ran a page-one story quoting police sources as saying that the ticket was for the movie, *The Fisher King*. But Killeen police issued a statement saying that it was uncertain what the ticket, which appeared to have Spanish words on it, was for. Police quizzed personnel at the theaters but could not confirm that Hennard had been to either one.

In the movie, the gunman is a frequent caller to radio talk shows. One night, he calls to seek advice about a woman of high social standing who had snubbed him. The show host slams yuppies as "useless," and this criticism apparently triggers the caller's shooting rampage at an upscale New York bar. In one scene, a woman is blasted and blown back through a plate glass window. After the systematic killings, the mad gunman turns the weapon on himself.

Tantalizing though the similarities between *The Fisher King* and the Luby's shootings were, Killeen police stressed after the newspaper story appeared that they had no evidence to show that Hennard had ever seen the movie.

In another development, the National Park Service in Nevada revealed it had arrested George Hennard in June 1991, after he was found drunk in the same pickup truck he would later drive through the cafeteria window in Killeen. Hennard was also fined for possession of a loaded firearm after the same two semiautomatic handguns he used in the massacre were found in his pickup by the park rangers. At the time, the guns were not impounded because they were not used to commit a crime and because Hennard told the park rangers that he had them.

"The rangers could have impounded them, but Hennard would have gotten them back at the end of June when he paid the fine," said one Park Service official.

George Hennard pleaded guilty to driving under the influence of alcohol and was fined $100 plus $10 court costs, the official said. On the firearm possession charge, Hennard was fined $50 and $10 court costs.

On October 18th, Texas Governor Ann Richards came to Killeen to join mourners at a prayer vigil for the shooting victims at the town's First Baptist Church. Prior to the service, the governor told reporters that renewed calls for stricter gun laws are "a natural aftermath of such a massacre." She repeated an earlier stand against the sale of automatic weapons.

"My own personal feeling is that I enjoy sports that involve firearms; I own them. But I think there is a very real difference—particularly when you talk to the law enforcement community—about the difference in weapons that are used for sport and weapons that are used to kill people. And that is exactly what these weapons are."

Asked how she might stand up against the strong lobbying by powerful organizations against gun control, the governor replied, "The dead lying on the floor of Luby's Cafeteria should be evidence enough that we are not pursuing a rational posture."

**EDITOR'S NOTE:**
*Ray Hardin, Regina Minton, and Bob Witherral are not the real names of the persons so named in the foregoing story. Fictitious names have been used because there is no reason for public interest in the identities of these persons.*

# "UNIVERSITY OF IOWA'S CAMPUS CARNAGE"

by Gary C. King

The macabre rumors of impending slaughter began shortly after a psychic went on national television and predicted that a massacre would occur on a New England college campus sometime around Halloween 1991. The show was hardly over when the rumors began to spread across at least six college campuses from New Hampshire to Connecticut. The prediction was particularly disturbing to those students who remembered the gruesome slayings of five University of Florida coeds in 1990. To top it off, the prediction came while the nation was still reeling over the Luby's Cafeteria massacre in Killeen, Texas, which had occurred just two weeks before.

One variation of the rumors was that Nostradamus, the 16th-century astrologer/mystic, had supposedly foreseen 15 people being brutally killed in an L-shaped building in a university setting. Another version indicated that the killings would occur on a campus with a pond and a building named for President John F. Kennedy. It was the stuff that supermarket tabloids are made of, stuff that shouldn't have been taken too seriously. The massacre was about as likely to happen as Elvis Presley returning from the dead or the Pope taking a nun for his wife—or *was* it?

"Some students thought it was hysterically funny, some thought it was ridiculous," said a spokesperson at Franklin Pierce College in Rindge, New Hampshire.

"The general attitude here is to kind of mock the whole thing," said a senior at the University of Connecticut in Storrs. "People are trying to scare each other because it's Halloween." At other colleges, however, the rumor wasn't being taken so lightly.

"We had to tell students, 'Relax, you're not going to die in your sleep,'" said a spokesperson for Wheaton College in Norton, Massachusetts.

At the University of Massachusetts at Amherst, where there *is* a pond *and* a building named for President Kennedy, female dormitory residents were so unnerved by the rumor that more than 100 of them met with the chief of campus police and pressured him into providing additional security over the Halloween weekend. Despite the stepped-up precautions, an air of unease could still be felt there.

"Who knows, maybe the University of Massachusetts was mentioned by Nostradamus four hundred years ago," said an editor of the university's student newspaper. "People here are taking this fairly seriously, especially with the mass murders that have been in the news lately."

Before the rumors could be dismissed as a Halloween prank in poor taste, however, the nation would once again be thrown into a tailspin over a bloody spree of violence and death. Little did anyone know that it really would happen on a college campus, just like the predictions said it would. But the setting for the slaughter would be more than a thousand miles to the west of New England, on a campus deep in the American heartland.

Most of Friday, November 1, 1991, had been peaceful on Iowa City's sprawling, tree-lined University of Iowa campus. Long processions of students ambled up and down the sidewalks and roadways almost hourly as they went to and from classes or veered off for study breaks and coffee at the student union. Other students, whose homes were within easy driving distance of the campus, were busy getting ready to spend the weekend with their families and hometown friends after their last class of the week. The more astute of those who remained behind in the campus dormitories kept themselves busy studying for midterms, while others less academically inclined looked forward to the Friday night "dorm parties" common to virtually every university in America. For most of the 28,000 University of Iowa students, Friday, November 1st, couldn't have been a more typical autumn day. Typical, that is, until 3:45 p.m., when the shooting began.

When Gang Lu, 28, walked through the main doors of Van Allen Hall some 15 minutes earlier, no one saw or paid any attention to the slight bulge in his jacket pocket as he made his way to the third-floor research seminar room. Lu, a slight, black-haired, bespectacled man whose English often came out in broken monosyllables, was there to attend the weekly meeting of the physics and astronomy department—or so thought the seven other scientists in attendance. Until he made his move, there was no way for any of them to discern the dark mission he had come there to carry out.

About 15 minutes into the meeting, Gang Lu, out of turn, took the floor. He was obviously nervous, and he began rambling about how certain individuals at the university had ruined his life. Now it was his turn to ruin theirs, Lu said. As Lu pulled the gun out of his pocket, he motioned for four of the students to leave the room.

"Gang Lu, don't do it" said Roger Grogan, a research scientist who had been sitting next to Lu.

Somehow Grogan knew that his words would not stop his distressed colleague.

"Leave the room! Get out, now!" demanded Lu, waving the gun. Not wanting to get shot, Grogan and the other three complied.

Grogan ran to the nearest telephone and alerted campus security to the potentially deadly situation at Van Allen Hall, but his efforts wouldn't be enough to halt the ensuing violence. It would take at least a few minutes for campus police to reach the "L-shaped" science building, too long to stop a man who had carefully mapped out his terminal plan of action.

Lu instructed Christoph K. Goertz, 47, his dissertation adviser and professor of physics and astronomy, to remain seated along with Robert Allan Smith, also a professor of physics and astronomy, and Linhua Shan, 26, a research investigator and graduate student.

"Now! You pay!" Lu began shooting, and it became clear to the victims that none of them had a chance of escaping unharmed. Lu was blocking the door, and there was nowhere to hide as the slugs of lead tore into their bodies in rapid succession. Goertz and Shan died almost instantly, but Smith, racked with unbearable pain, writhed on the floor in a pool of his own blood, waiting to die. Lu, apparently satisfied with his grim handiwork, ran out of the room and down the stairs to the second floor. He didn't have much time, and his mission was not over yet.

After reloading the gun, Lu burst through the door to Dwight R. Nicholson's office. Nicholson, 44, chairman of the physics and astronomy department, was sitting behind his desk, taking care of the last of the day's work. He was stunned and frightened at the spectacle of the raging Lu, especially at the sight of the revolver Lu had leveled at his head.

The explosions came again in rapid succession, bringing with them a wild spray of blood and tissue. Although the violence took only seconds to carry out, in Lu's mind, because his time was so limited, everything seemed to be happening in slow motion. Nicholson was likely dead by the time he hit the floor, but Lu didn't wait around to find out.

In a near frenzy, Lu ran back upstairs to the third-floor conference room after apparently recalling that Professor Smith had been writhing on the floor when he left. There were more explosions, and Smith's body arched spasmodically, literally raised inches off the floor as the additional bullets made impact. This time Smith was dead. Lu had made certain of that.

As Lu ran down the stairs again and through the first-floor hallway, the few students who were still there at that time of the day screamed at the sight of Lu's gun and moved out of his way, some dropping to the floor just in case he began shooting randomly. It was nothing less than pandemonium as the terrified students tried to determine what was happening and what they could do to help. Everything had happened so quickly that it would have been impossible for anyone to have warned Nicholson or, for that matter, anyone else. Nobody could have known where Lu was headed or who his intended victims were after he left the third-floor seminar room, and no one would have dared to follow him in order to find out. The police had already been called, and the help that they could provide, if any, was the best that anyone could have hoped for at that point.

As Lu bolted down the street, he pocketed the revolver in an attempt to avoid drawing attention to himself. To those who saw him running, he was just another student late for a class or an appointment with an instructor. Determined to complete his mission, Lu never stopped until he reached the university's administration building, Jessup Hall, two blocks from Van Allen Hall. When he entered the building, he asked to see Dr. T. Anne Cleary, associate vice president of academic affairs.

Sweating profusely as Cleary entered the reception area, Lu pulled out the revolver from his jacket pocket and leveled it at her head. Without further warning, he began firing again. After seeing Cleary's body sprawled on the floor and satisfied that his bullets had done their job, Lu turned the gun and began firing on Debra Day, an academic affairs secretary who had risen from her desk when the shooting erupted. There had been no time for Day to even think about escaping. After she fell to the floor, Lu dashed up a flight of stairs to the second floor. Seconds later, staff members heard yet another explosion reverberate through the administration building. . . .

Within a minute or two after the first shots had been heard, the second of a series of calls (Roger Grogan's had been the first) began pouring into the campus security police office and, in turn, at the Iowa City Police Department. Disturbed callers reported hearing "popping" sounds inside Van Allen Hall, and reported seeing the fleeing gunman, by now tentatively identified as Gang Lu. Fearing that the sounds had been gunshots, people had naturally been reluctant to investigate out of concern for their own safety, and were further advised by police not to do so. Within minutes, Van Allen Hall was crawling with police and paramedics. There was no sign of a gunman as they carefully made their way up the stairs to the science hall's third floor, toward the university's physics and astronomy department. It wasn't until they reached the research seminar room that they discovered the first of the carnage.

Identified at the scene by university personnel were Professors Goertz and Smith and graduate student Shan. The police and paramedics could see that the victims were dead and that each had apparently been shot at close range by an unknown caliber weapon. During all the confusion on the third floor, police were informed by other university personnel that shots had also been heard on the second floor just prior to their arrival. When they went to investigate, they found Nicholson's body lying in a pool of fresh blood near his desk.

Only minutes later, while everyone was trying to make some sense out of the unexplained violence that had occurred inside Van Allen Hall, the reports of the other shootings, the ones fired inside Jessup Hall, came in.

The police were shocked about what was happening in their normally quiet city on this autumn afternoon. Because nothing of this magnitude had ever occurred on the university campus before, they naturally chose to treat each incident as related, somehow tied together. But because of all the chaos and hysteria that had surrounded the case, the sleuths knew that it would be a while before they could get everything sorted out.

When authorities and paramedics reached Jessup Hall, they learned that two more people had been shot there but were, miraculously, still alive. They could see that Dr. Cleary and her secretary, Debra Day, had both been critically injured, prompting some to doubt that they would survive. Nonetheless, paramedics fervently treated both women as best they could at the scene, then whisked them off to University Hospital where they were taken immediately into surgery.

In the meantime, university staff members had directed police officers to the administration building's second floor where, they said, the gunman had fled. The police officers approached slowly and cautiously, their own guns drawn. But there were no sounds of movement other than their own, only deadly silence. Following a brief search, lawmen found the gunman in a room directly above the university president's office. He was lying on the floor in a puddle of blood that continued to mushroom outward beneath his head. A .38-caliber revolver lay next to his body, and officers found a .22-caliber pistol inside his jacket pocket. The .22-caliber, they noted, did not appear to have been recently fired.

The man was Asian, and he was still alive but only barely. His breathing was shallow, almost imperceptible, and he occasionally jerked and quivered in imminent death. He quietly expired as paramedics approached. It was obvious that the gunman had shot himself in the head following his 15-minute rampage. But the big question now troubling students, faculty, staff, and investigators was, "Why?" What could have possibly set off such a tragic course of events?

In their attempts to answer their question, detectives from the Iowa City Police Department and the Iowa State Police were sent to the scenes of all three shootings. In fact, all available personnel were called out to investigate the senseless slaughter that had occurred that afternoon. In addition to the detectives and countless uniformed officers, Iowa City Police Chief R.J. Winkelhake, Johnson County Attorney J. Patrick White, and a deputy county medical examiner were present at the death scenes. Campus police also assisted in the investigation.

At a hastily called news conference, Chief Winkelhake told reporters that the "shooting victims were all from the university community," and did not appear to be randomly chosen. Although he didn't yet know how many rounds had been fired, he said investigators had found shell casings "all over the place."

"Three officers went into Jessup Hall and found

the individual believed to be responsible for the shootings," said Winkelhake. "He was alive at the time but with serious head wounds."

Barely two weeks had passed since George Hennard shot and killed 23 people before killing himself inside Luby's Cafeteria in Killeen, Texas, and the last thing Chief Winkelhake would have thought was that something similarly tragic could ever happen in his town. But it had, and, although there weren't as many victims in Iowa City as there had been in Killeen, the aftermath would be just as unpleasant to deal with.

As Chief Winkelhake spoke, university staff members positively identified the dead gunman as Gang Lu, 28, a former physics graduate student. Although Lu had already received his doctorate in physics and was no longer a student there, he had maintained close connections with the university community. Detectives spent the next several hours rounding up witnesses to some of the actual shootings and former classmates of Lu's, to understand the gunman's actions.

Gang Lu, sleuths learned, was born in 1963 in the city of Beijing in the People's Republic of China. In 1985, after graduating from Beijing University, long considered China's most prestigious center of higher education, Lu came to the U.S. to further his education. He eventually earned a Ph.D. in physics in the spring of 1991. Although he had been looking for a position in his chosen field, said university officials, Lu hadn't been successful in finding permanent work and was biding his time assisting in university research programs.

Della Marshall, vice president of university affairs, told probers that Lu might have gone on the killing spree because he had been passed over for an academic honor, the university's D.C. Spriestersbach Award. The award, carrying with it a $1,000 check, is given out annually to a graduate student who has given the best dissertation in the arts and humanities, social sciences, or mathematics and the natural sciences.

"I don't know exactly what the triggering factor was," Marshall told investigators. "There's never been an incident here that compares to this." The probers asked her to do some research to try and ferret out specifically what Lu had been upset about, if anything. She was to look for notes, letters, formal complaints, anything that might shed light on the situation and particularly anything that was connected to the award.

As the evening wore on, after the crime scenes had been processed in the usual manner, the bodies were brought out in opaque "Visqueens," one-by-one, and placed inside the waiting vans. As weeping students and faculty looked on, the vans pulled away en route to the campus. The lawmen remained behind to try to piece things together, and maybe make some sense out of the sad loss of so many lives.

Roger Grogan, the research scientist at the university who had initially alerted staff and was partly responsible for notifying the police quickly and identifying the suspect, was among the many eyewitnesses who were eventually interviewed. Grogan, after partially recovering from the traumatic experience, provided detectives with one of the more vivid descriptions of the terrifying ordeal.

"I could tell what he was going to do by the way he was acting," said Grogan. "I said, 'Gang Lu, don't do it!' That's when he told us to leave. He was pretty determined. Then he stood up and started shooting," the graduate student said.

"He was seated in the seminar room in a chair along the wall and simply got up and fired his first shot and then shot the other two people," said another person.

After Lu went to the second floor and shot Nicholson, Grogan said, he returned briefly to the third-floor seminar room and shot Smith again. "I assumed he just wanted to be sure they were all dead," Grogan said.

In the aftermath of the shootings, the university community took on a somber, mournful mood. Many expressed shock over what had occurred.

"I couldn't believe it," said one freshman from Chicago. "I'm astonished that somebody could go into a mad shooting like this. I can't imagine that this could happen."

Meanwhile, according to Chief Winkelhake, detectives learned from students and professors that Gang Lu had been an excellent student. Although a loner, Lu was described as being very smart. One professor also suggested that Lu may have become distraught over not being selected for the Spriestersbach Award. He was out of work, his financial support had run out, and he needed the $1,000 provided by the award.

"It's a competitive field," said one professor. "You're talking about professionals. What was going on here was a little beyond competition," he said.

The next afternoon, Saturday, November 2nd, Dr. T. Anne Cleary died from her wounds without regaining consciousness. News of her death only served to intensify the dark mood that had already set in on campus, and the fact that Debra Day remained in critical condition did little to boost morale.

Academics alone didn't languish in the terrible loss. The world of sports also felt the impact of the university shootings, and they let the nation know it. That same Saturday night, the Iowa Hawkeyes wore black arm bands to symbolize their mourning during their football game with Ohio State University in which the Hawkeyes took a 16-9 visitor's victory.

Neither the victory nor the arm bands, however, did little to ease the pain and sorrow everyone felt.

The university's president, who was out of town when the tragedy struck, canceled his plans and turned around in mid-trip to return to the campus. When he heard of the additional death of Dr. Cleary, he ordered classes canceled for the following Monday to give the school additional time to "begin the long and difficult process of healing." When he addressed a subdued gathering of more than 200 faculty, staff, and students, he said that it would be necessary to sort out emotions and face the problem.

"We cannot make sense of this," the president said. "We are out of our depth. On Friday, the university was senselessly diminished," taken over by a "deep and terrible sadness. The injuries we have suffered are devastating." In addition to canceling classes for a day, the president ordered that all flags on campus fly at half-staff.

Over the next few days silent vigils were held all over campus, and students and faculty alike placed wreathes at the shooting sites out of respect for the victims and the memories they left behind. Also, a university-wide memorial service was held at Carver-Hawke Arena, where many wept openly.

"We all truly feel the shock and dismay, as with the families, over the loss of our loved ones," said a sophomore engineering student who presided over the memorial service. "It is midnight at the university right now," he said figuratively.

At Anne Cleary's funeral, held at St. Patrick's Church in Iowa City, someone placed two red roses in the form of a cross on her casket as family members and friends wept over her untimely death.

"Anne would be the first to scold us should we allow animosity or anger to cloud this day," said the minister. Cleary's relatives, he added, planned to send a letter to Lu's parents in China to "share with them their prayers and their hope that grief may soon give way to peace and trust." He emphasized that that was the way Dr. Cleary would have wanted it.

In an effort to ease the grief and fear that lingered, psychologists began holding workshops on the campus. Although hundreds of students and faculty members participated, the sorrow and sense of helplessness still remained.

As the investigation into Lu's motive continued, interviews with witnesses produced a picture of Gang Lu as an angry loner with an explosive temper. A physics professor recalled seeing Lu blow up several months earlier, prior to receiving his doctorate, when instructors questioned his computational techniques in a physics examination. Afterward, Lu blasted his professors verbally, charging that they had "ruined his career."

"Heaven knows, it wasn't anything of that magnitude," said a professor.

Students in China, however, speculated that Lu was emotionally unstable before he left his homeland. After arriving in the United States, some said, his condition might have deteriorated.

"Chinese who go overseas have difficulty adjusting," said one Beijing University professor. He refused to give his name out of fear of retribution from his government, which was not allowing news of Lu's rampage to appear in their state-run press. "They find it hard to feel a part of society."

"This is just too hard to believe," said another Beijing University student. "Chinese people usually are able to exercise such restraint and patience. Probably the competitiveness when he was at Beijing University placed great pressures on him, not just for a day or two, but long-term pressure."

On the other hand, fellow students in the United States described Gang Lu as brilliant, certainly not as someone who appeared to be suffering adjustment problems.

"He was at the top of the curve every time," said one graduate physics student. "I think that he thought he deserved the coveted Spriestersbach Award. He probably thought that this was all politics or something and this was sort of a brick wall that his life had come to."

Although Gang Lu and Linhua Shan hadn't always been enemies, at least not until Shan's dissertation won the award, they were described as having totally opposite personalities. Lu stayed to himself and studied, while Shan socialized and partied.

"Shan was more popular than Lu," said one student. "Lu was kind of isolated most of the time. He didn't like to communicate with other students."

Witnesses told police that Lu probably falsely perceived that Shan took his studies less seriously than himself, and as a result couldn't understand how Shan could receive the award. When Shan's dissertation was nominated over Lu's, Lu most likely felt a strong sense of embarrassment and shame. Some said that it was even possible Lu felt his loss was a failure and that he would be disgraced, and looked down upon by his family and friends.

Meanwhile, university official Della Marshall informed detectives that she had found a letter which Gang Lu had sent to the president's office prior to the shootings. In the letter, Lu complained that his dissertation hadn't been nominated for the Spriestersbach Award.

"The nature of the letter was not threatening," she told probers. But it did serve to back up their theory of motive. Marshall also said that Lu, in a formal complaint filed with the academic affairs office, had expressed anger that Linhua Shan's dissertation had instead been nominated. Shan ended up winning the award.

It became increasingly clear that the shootings, as the detectives had suspected, had not been random. Gang Lu had methodically planned and executed the murders of not only the recipient of the Spriestersbach Award, but the entire nominating and selecting panel. The investigators theorized that Lu carried his actions one step further by gunning down Anne Cleary, with whom he had filed his complaint, because he felt she hadn't acted more thoroughly on his behalf, and then shot her secretary for much the same reason.

The lawmen's theories were soon confirmed when several people came forward and turned over letters Gang Lu had written to them just prior to the shootings. There were five three-page letters, four written in English and one in Chinese, in which Lu indicated that he planned to kill members of the university's physics and astronomy department who hadn't nominated him for the academic honor. As the detectives read the letters, the motive became very clear.

"His state of mind was that of a premeditated, cold-blooded murderer," said Johnson County Attorney J. Patrick White after analyzing Lu's letters. "The letters contained information that would indicate that he had actions like this in mind."

The letters, said White, contained the names of all the shooting victims as well as some of those who were not harmed. There was also an indication that Lu planned to commit suicide after taking his revenge.

"It appears that he did make arrangements with respect to personal effects," said White.

With the discovery of Lu's letters, detectives considered the homicides cleared and the case closed. Despite the fact that the case was neatly wrapped up, with no loose ends dangling as to who committed the murders, to the victims' family members, students and faculty, justice had not been served. Nor would it ever be.

But a mystery still remains and questions will still go unanswered for eternity. Had the Halloween rumors of an impending mass murder on a college campus really been a chilling, accurate prelude to a horrible reality? Had Gang Lu's actions demonstrated that Nostradamus' prediction was on the mark? Or had Lu's actions been set in motion *because* of the circulating rumors that stemmed from Nostradamus' prediction? Had the rumors somehow influenced a mind already unbalanced? Unfortunately, no one will ever know. The answers, along with Gang Lu and five innocent people, perished on November 1, 1991.

## EDITOR'S NOTE
*Della Marshall, Roger Grogan, and Debra Day are not the real names of the persons so named in the foregoing story. Fictitious names have been used because there is no reason for public interest in the identities of these persons.*

# "THE CARR'S HILL MASSACRE!"
## by Turk Ryder

On Saturday, April 25th 1987, a resident of Oglethorpe Avenue in Athens, Georgia, got a call to check on his neighbors, retired economics professor Glenn Sutton, 82, and his wife Rachel, 78. The call came from the couple's son who was living in Las Vegas, Nevada.

"I've been trying to get hold of them since Wednesday," the son told the neighbor, "but nobody answers."

"No problem," the neighbor replied. "I'll go check on them right now."

In Athens, home of the University of Georgia, Glenn and Rachel Sutton needed no introduction. Glenn was a renowned economist who had headed the university's economics department. In 1961, he was appointed by President John Kennedy to head the U.S. Tariffs Commission, a position he held until 1974 when he returned to teaching full time. Rachel, who earned a Ph.D. from Columbia University, co-ordinated elementary school programs at the University of Georgia's College of Education and was one of the state's foremost educators.

Though they retired in 1972, the distinguished couple remained active in academic and business circles. Glenn Sutton opened a consulting firm and was in demand by companies across the country; Rachel Sutton was swamped with speaking engagements and educational projects.

The two resided in a brick, white-columned mansion on Oglethorpe Avenue, an exclusive neighborhood of estates and luxury condominiums that had once been a plantation.

The neighbor hung up the phone and trotted next door and up the driveway that wound in front of the two-story brick house. He knocked several times, but no one answered. Peering into the garage, he saw that both of the Suttons' cars were parked inside.

Perplexed, he went back to his house and called the police. "I don't know what to make of it," he said. "Both cars are in the garage, but no one answered the door."

Two patrol officers were dispatched to Oglethorpe Avenue. They tried the front and back doors and found them locked. One of the officers called headquarters with the request to contact the son in Las Vegas and get permission to force their way in. A few minutes later, they got the okay.

One of the officers got an extension ladder and they scurried up to the second-story balcony to enter the home through the unlocked window.

They checked the second story before descending the winding staircase to the first floor.

One of the officers sniffed the air, "Smell it?" he asked urgently.

His partner nodded.

They went through the living room into the formal dining room. One of the officers stiff-armed the door leading into the pantry and stopped cold. What he saw was Glenn Sutton sprawled on the pantry floor. The white of the man's shirt was soaked in blood and his thin, pale face was twisted in a death mask.

At his feet lay his wife, Rachel. Her corpse had been stuffed into a clothing bag and pushed into a corner under her husband's leg.

Both had been stabbed numerous times and had apparently been dead for days.

The officers searched the rest of the spacious and otherwise unoccupied house before retreating to the squad car to notify headquarters.

Detectives led by Chief Everett Price sped to Oglethorpe Avenue. They were followed by lab technicians and a deputy coroner.

After photographs and measurements were taken, the bodies were encased in rubber bags and taken to the coroner's office for the autopsy.

Police searched the house and examined the doors and windows. No sign of forced entry was found. It appeared that the killer had either entered the house with permission or through an unlocked door. The only door unlocked was the screen door at the back of the house.

Investigators went upstairs and peered inside the master bedroom. The bed was neatly made and there was no sign of ransacking. In another room were Glenn's plaques, awards, and memorabilia from his career in government service, including signed pictures of John Kennedy and Lyndon Johnson, his former bosses.

The sleuths went over every inch of the downstairs. From blood spatters on the walls and ceilings and from other evidence, it appeared that one and possibly both the victims were slain in the kitchen, then dragged into the pantry. After the murders, the killer apparently spent considerable time cleaning up. The hardwood floors were water-stained and a dry mop stood in one corner, indicating that he had mopped the floors before leaving.

Police were puzzled: why the effort to clean the floors? Had the killer left shoeprints on the floor or other evidence that he or she was afraid might be incriminating?

Police were even more baffled when a search outdoors led to the cars parked in the garage. Inside the trunk of one of the cars the investigators found rugs, pieces of carpet, ladies' clothing and a dishpan containing a bottle of a liquid detergent.

The rugs had come from the house; some were soaked in blood and attempts had been made to clean them. The lab later showed that 12 of the rugs were soaked with Glenn's blood, four others with Rachel's.

In the other car, investigators discovered a kitchen knife with an 8-inch blade. It was smeared with blood and matched a set of knives found in the kitchen.

"He must have come in unarmed," one of the investigators remarked.

The autopsy, conducted that evening, produced more surprises. Glenn Sutton was stabbed 13 times and died as a result of a wound to the throat. It was determined that several of the wounds were made by a large African spear, which was bloodstained and hanging from the dining room wall.

The spear wounds were postmortem—the killer had pierced the frail professor with the lethal instrument, then returned it to the wall hooks.

Rachel Sutton was stabbed six times in the back. She had defensive wounds on her arms and hands, indicating that she had struggled. She was nude from the waist down, a fact that investigators discovered when her body was removed from the laundry sack that sheathed it.

The deputy coroner found no signs of sexual assault or any physical evidence that the killer had anything in mind other than removing her slacks and panties.

The victims had been dead approximately 48 to 72

hours before their bodies were discovered.

The motive—at least one motive—for the crime was robbery. Ogelthorpe Avenue is an exclusive neighborhood with many pricey homes and wealthy owners. Even so, the killer did not get much from the Sutton estate.

A careful inventory showed that the only items missing were an Athens High School class ring, a Mercer University class ring and a Kappa Alpha fraternity pin—all which belonged to the Suttons' son.

"Wipe out a man and his wife for what?" snarled an angry detective, "A couple of class rings and a fraternity pin. You couldn't fence the stuff for more than a couple of bucks."

"This isn't the work of a pro," another detective commented. "This is more like a maniac."

If a maniac was responsible, he was adept or just plain lucky at slipping in and out of the house. Neighbors reported seeing nothing unusual in the past few days. The gardener who arrived that morning to mow the lawn had seen nothing out of the ordinary.

On April 26th, the Suttons' son arrived in Athens from Las Vegas. He told police that his father had been in failing health and had only recently been released from the hospital.

He said he'd tried repeatedly to contact his parents without success before calling the neighbor. He had no idea who would want to kill his parents or do them any harm.

Glenn Sutton ran a consulting business and kept an office in downtown Athens. In a search of his business affairs, probers found nothing improper.

"He didn't have any enemies," one district attorney's investigator noted. "Everybody seemed to like him."

As news of the killings spread, police began receiving tips, including a few "nut" calls that normally surface in highly-publicized cases. One made to the funeral home in charge of the Sutton funeral warned that the service for the Suttons would be made "unforgettable" if it took place as scheduled.

Police staked out the funeral, taking down license-plate numbers and checking mourners for unusual behavior. No problems cropped up and the funeral went on as planned.

There were also a number of calls from residents, suggesting that police check out neighbors or relatives. Except for allowing the embittered callers the opportunity to blow off a little steam, the tips yielded no leads.

One tip that did seem to have a little meat to it came from a University of Georgia coed. She'd been jogging along Sunset Drive in the Ogelthorpe Avenue neighborhood at about 8:00 p.m. on April 22nd when she looked in the backyard of the Sutton home and saw a man running toward a car with its trunk lid open.

"He looked like he was in a hurry, like he wanted to get out of there," she said. She described him as a slim, white male, possibly Hispanic, with dark skin, thick frizzy hair and clean-shaven. She didn't recognize the car or where it was from.

She hadn't thought much about it until she read about the murders in the paper and realized that the home past which she'd been jogging was the Suttons'.

The coed sat with a police artist and helped compose a sketch. It was distributed to law enforcement officers in the Athens area and issued over the police telex linking law enforcement agencies throughout the state.

But it was not given to local media for fear that it might scare away the killer or become so familiar that it would be worthless for identification purposes.

Investigators met at the Athens police station to review the evidence and consider which leads to pursue.

One thing that baffled them was the killer's decision to mop the floor and pile bloody carpeting and detergent into the Suttons' car. One officer speculated that the killer was a woman because of the cleaning.

Another thought this unlikely. "The crime was excessively violent," he argued. "The man's chest was pierced with a spear. That isn't the sort of thing a woman would do."

A third officer agreed. "The female victim was stripped from the waist down and stuffed in a bag. A woman isn't likely to do that."

The discussion got back to the carpeting. "Maybe there is no rhyme or reason to this thing," one detective said. "Maybe the guy went a little crazy after killing that couple, started stuffing the carpets in the car to get rid of them, then came to his senses and fled."

"Anything's possible, especially if you are dealing with a lunatic," another prober added.

On Wednesday, April 29th, an FBI agent went through the Sutton home to examine the scene and create a profile of the killer. Later, he told detectives that the killer apparently left the scene in a panic. He said that the compulsion for cleanliness might indicate that the perpetrator was involved in cleaning work.

"We've run into guys like this before," the agent said. "They are usually calm and appear controlled on the outside, but inside they are completely uncontrolled and can snap any time."

A bright spot in the otherwise gloomy investigative picture came from the state crime lab. The lab experts had come up with 15 prints that did not belong to the Suttons and were apparently left by the killer. These were sent to the Georgia Bureau of Investigation for comparison with prints of criminals on file. If the GBI search turned up empty, the prints would be forwarded to the FBI.

On May 11th, police got a call from a woman on Oglethorpe Avenue. She said she had just received a threatening phone call from a man who told her, "I'm going to do the same thing to your family that I did to the Suttons."

"He sounded like he meant it," the woman said. She had no idea who would make such a call or why she had been singled out.

Police installed a tap on her phone. When the man called again, they traced it to a house in Bogart. The house was placed under surveillance while detectives obtained a search warrant.

Several hours later, they stormed the house. One of the officers kicked in the door and stood staring at a frightened 16-year-old boy. The wide-eyed youth confessed to making the calls. He claimed he had read about the Sutton slayings and decided to have a little fun. "I thought it was a joke," he said lamely.

Investigators grilled the youth and checked out his story. Convinced that he had nothing to do with the killings, they released him with the admonition: "No more phone calls!"

Now police busied themselves in checking out similar crimes in other states. There was a sex slaying in Oklahoma, a homosexual slaying in Valdosta, Georgia, a mutilation rape slaying in Maryland, and a gory murder in Florida.

They also checked out leads that continued to trickle in, such as one from a woman who told police she had seen a black male jump out of a car and run onto the Sutton property.

Police traced the car tag and interviewed the driver.

"Did you run onto the property?" he was asked by

one investigator.

"Yes," came the quick reply.

"Why?"

"I had to urinate."

Also questioned were a man who said he had applied for jobs at three mental hospitals, a curious driver who asked a traffic cop if police had caught "the guy that killed that old couple," and a man who was accused of the murder by his ex-wife.

On Thursday, July 9th, the composite drawing of the man seen by the jogger was released to the media.

Calls poured in. They were checked out, including one from a caller who said the man sought was taking a French class at the university and driving around town in a Mercedes.

None of these tips led anywhere. The killer's identity remained a mystery.

On Saturday evening, August 15th, Police Sergeant Michael Turner and Officer Roger Huff were dispatched to a home on Oconee Street in the historic Carr's Hill district to make a welfare check on Ann Orr Morris, the 63-year-old wife of a retired university professor. Mrs. Morris had left home that morning to visit a friend and then her sister, Sally Nathanson, who lived at the Carr's Hill address. Her husband had called the Nathanson house several times, but received no response.

The two officers arrived at the house shortly after 11:00 p.m. They knocked on the front door but no one answered.

They walked around to the backyard. One of the officers shone his flashlight over the fence. The beam outlined something on the grass.

"My God, did you see it?" Officer Huff asked excitedly.

They both leaped the fence and rushed to where the figure of a middle-aged woman lay on the grass.

It was Ann Morris, in a pool of blood, half of her head chopped away with a hatchet.

Drawing their guns, the officers entered the back door of the house. Inside, they found more bodies. Sally Nathanson, 59, was sprawled on her blood-soaked bed. Her daughter Helen, 22, was discovered between the den and dining room. Like Ann, they had been chopped and hacked to death.

Investigators rushed to the house. A few were old pros, but nothing prepared them for the sight of the slaughter of three women on Carr's Hill. One described it as the most shocking thing he had ever seen.

In the probers' reconstruction of the crime, it appeared that Mrs. Nathanson had been killed first, then her daughter, and finally Ann Morris, who was probably attacked as she came to the back door, as she always did when she visited the Nathansons.

The motive was ambiguous. The victims in the house showed signs of possible sexual assault, yet they had not been raped.

Over $150 was missing from Ann Morris' purse and the house showed evidence of ransacking, but robbery didn't seem to fit either.

As a detective remarked, "You don't kill people like this for a few bucks."

Some detectives commented that the brutal attack on these three women reminded them of the Sutton case. Others disagreed. Unlike the Sutton case, no meticulous clean-up attempt had been made.

In an interview with Ann Morris' husband, a lead surfaced when police learned that three cars should have been parked at the house.

A gray 1984 Dodge Diplomat belonging to Helen Nathanson was missing, the investigators determined.

A radio alert was immediately placed on the vehicle.

Several hours later, Officer Kirk Graham was cruising Moreland Avenue in east Athens when he spotted a gray Dodge parked in front of a wood-sided house. He checked the license plate—it was the car wanted in the Carr's Hill murders.

Two men in the front yard told the officer the car had been parked since early that morning. They didn't know who it belonged to. They suggested that the officer talk to the next-door neighbor. "He got a bike and he rides all the time," one of the men said. "Maybe he saw something."

Graham knocked on the door of the house and a teenager answered. He was Clinton Bankston, 16. He said he didn't know anything about the car. "It don't belong to me or my mom," the youth said. He talked in a rush and looked away from the officer as he spoke.

"What's the kid so nervous about?" Graham wondered.

He looked Bankston over and his eyes fixed on a key chain hanging from the teenager's belt. At the end of the key chain was a Chrysler car emblem.

"Are those your keys?" he asked.

"Yes," the youth answered.

"Come with me," Graham asked. He took the boy into custody and put him in the back seat of the cruiser while he radioed headquarters.

At length, Sergeant W.J. Smith arrived. He questioned the youth and asked him where he got the vehicle. The kid replied that he got it two days ago from a friend of his named Chris.

"Chris wanted to leave it here," he said.

Smith spotted a set of house keys in the boy's pocket—keys to the Nathanson residence. He ended the interview and took the youth to the station.

Juvenile authorities were contacted, as well as Bankston's mother. A video camera was set to record the teen's statement.

Bankston told investigators that he had gone to the Nathanson's house on Carr's Hill at the urging of his friend Chris Ward. He said they went there to "take some stuff" and that things got out of hand when Chris started killing people with a "sword-ax" he'd brought to the house.

Bankston described the horrific murders of the three women in detail but insisted he'd had nothing to do with them.

In response to a question about the attack on Helen Nathanson, Bankston declared that his only part in the crime was moving rugs around. "I didn't kill nobody. I just moved rugs and stuff 'cause Chris said he can get rich like this."

The detectives looked at each other. The rug-moving had taken place during the Sutton murders four months earlier, not at the Nathanson house.

They knew they had solved the four-month-old case.

Police learned that Bankston had spent Friday night, August 14th with his grandmother, but he'd left on his bike early Saturday morning. The next time she saw him was on Saturday at lunchtime when he drove up in the Dodge. "He said that the car belonged to his friend Chris."

Bankston was booked into county jail, charged with the murders on Carr's Hill. He was later charged with the murders of Glenn and Rachel Sutton after his fingerprints matched those found in the Ogelthorpe Avenue home.

Now police launched a massive search to find the mysterious Chris Ward. Bankston described Chris as Caucasian, 5 feet 10 inches tall, 150 pounds, with blond hair. He said he and Chris had been good friends for years.

But his mother and grandmother didn't know Chris Ward. Nor did classmates at Athens High School, from which Bankston had dropped out in his freshman year.

Bankston did have a former friend named Chris, but he looked nothing like the Chris Ward he'd described. Police ran computer checks on Chris Wards and on registered owners of Pontiac Trans-Ams, which Chris was supposed to drive.

Nothing clicked.

The sleuths began to wonder if Chris Ward existed. They wondered if Bankston had invented a friend to help explain the five murders. "Sometimes they have to invent an imaginary friend," an investigator remarked. "It is like they need one because they can't really accept what they did."

The shy teen struck the probers as something of an oddball. In their background investigation, the detectives learned that Bankston idolized rock singer Michael Jackson and was particularly taken with the "Thriller" album. Like his rock idol, Bankston often wore makeup and eye shadow to school, broke into song and "moonwalking" dance steps.

Teachers described him as a passive student who didn't really have any friends. "Clint could very well be the type to make up a person because he really didn't have any friends," one teacher said.

The shy lad had now been thrust into the limelight as the suspect in two of the most shocking murder cases in Athens history.

Psychologists were called in to examine the teen and determine if he was mentally capable of understanding the charges against him, and if he could stand trial. They discovered that Bankston was a mass of contradictions: a youth with a borderline I.Q. who wished he was white, yet who blamed whites for the premature death of his dad, whom he idolized.

"He may have drawn a connection between the victims and the loss of his father and displaced upon them that homicidal rage," a psychiatrist with Piedmont Psychiatric Center offered.

"Confused sexual identity . . . kid on the edge . . . inappropriate laughter . . . inclined to be moody . . . never seen anyone quite like him before . . . oddball" were comments that found their way into the reports about the suspect.

Bankston's quiet nature made him appear an unlikely suspect. In courtroom appearances, he rarely looked anyone in the eye and had the look of someone lost and alone, like a little puppy eagerly searching for its master.

Investigators were not taken in by the placid, harmless demeanor, however. They had been to Carr's Hill and Ogelthorpe Avenue and seen his handiwork firsthand. They advised jailers to use extreme caution when dealing with Bankston.

The advice was well-taken. In October 1987, Bankston made a telephone call from the jail. A few minutes later a deputy noticed that the keys to two jail doors were missing.

He searched Bankston's cell and found the keys.

When questioned about the keys, the teen got up from his bunk and declared, "I'm leaving now."

He was quickly subdued.

From then on, the jail's most celebrated inmate was kept under close observation.

In January 1988, jailers confiscated a letter Bankston had passed to a trustee in which he described how he was going to kill a jailer and escape.

"The deputy comes on during our shower times and phone call times," Bankston wrote. "That's when I can kill him. Also get me some scissors. One would be okay. Flush note down the toilet when you get finished reading it."

Bankston was scheduled to stand trial in May 1987. At his arraignment, District Attorney Harry Gordon promised he would seek the death sentence.

A guilty verdict was almost assured.

Because of the death penalty issue, Clarke County Judge Joseph Gaines appointed two of Athens' most prominent attorneys Edward Tolley and Don Wells, to represent Bankston. In a preliminary hearing, the two lawyers successfully obtained a ruling that Georgia law prohibits the execution of a person under the age of 17.

Bankston had been 16 when arrested.

D.A. Gordon was appalled. If ever a case merited the death sentence, he said, this was it. His outrage was shared by most of Athens' citizens.

There was nothing they could do, however. On May 12, 1987, Clinton Bankston pleaded guilty to five counts of murder and was sentenced to five consecutive life sentences.

As he had in previous courtroom appearances, he showed only mild interest in the proceedings.

He is currently serving his sentence at the state prison in Alto.

EDITOR'S NOTE:
*Chris Ward is not the real name of the person so named in the foregoing story. A fictitious name has been used because there is no reason for public interest in the identity of this person.*

# "HE TORCHED 4 OVER 'NOTHING'!"

## by Bob Coppedge

In the wee hours on the morning of August 22, 1991, Newport, Tennessee, resident Mike McClain was having trouble sleeping. First there had been a rapping sound and a loud voice in the hall outside his small apartment. Then, when he had barely dozed off, he heard his neighbor, Pat Southerland screaming from her one-room apartment, "Fire!"

McClain sniffed the air. Smelling smoke, he quickly roused himself, went to the window and climbed out. He then shimmied down some electrical wires onto some pipes and made his way to a telephone.

The Newport Fire Department answered the call with two engines and 10 men. They had no idea what lay ahead of them when they answered the 3:09 a.m. call to Woodlawn Avenue. When they arrived, they found a man standing alone in the middle of the street who showed them the way to the fire. Smoke was coming from the building and they heard what all firefighters dread to hear—people might be trapped inside.

The building housed a cafe-lounge on the ground level and eight apartments upstairs. A separate entrance led up to the apartments, where the fire and smoke seemed to be concentrated.

The firemen, wearing airpacks, entered the smoke-filled stairwell and quickly extinguished the blaze. Once they were in the building, they heard individual smoke alarms going off all over the place. The alarms were later found lying on the floor melted.

The firefighters had contained the fire with little structural damage to the building, but the blaze had taken a much grimmer toll — a toll on which no dollar amount could be placed.

In the first room to the right at the top of the stairs, the firemen found the body of a resident in the bathroom shower stall. Water was still running in the sink. The man's body was immediately removed and Fire Chief Roger Butler was notified that a fatality had occurred in the fire.

The firemen checked the other rooms and found three more bodies. Of the eight rooms, five were occupied and only Mike McClain had managed to escape the carnage.

Chief Butler told his crew to leave the other bodies until investigators arrived and made their observation. The bodies were removed from the building between 3:00 and 7:00 a.m.

Tennessee Bureau of Investigation (TBI) Agent David Davenport and Newport Criminal Investigator Jimmy Gregg arrived at the scene and began searching for the cause of the deaths and fire. State Fire Investigator Roy Shinall, notified by the Cocke County Sheriff's Department, arrived from his home near Gatlinburg about an hour after the first body was removed.

First indications were that the fire that caused the deaths of four people was deliberately set. It was not just arson probers were dealing with. It was murder. The task of determining for certain whether or not the fire was deliberate fell on the shoulders of State Fire Investigator Roy Shinall. Arguably the more difficult task fell on the shoulders of the other officers, who had to find the person who started the fire. Arson is one of the hardest crimes to prove without a witness who saw the arsonist actually strike the match.

The positions of the bodies indicated that they had died from smoke inhalation.

The first victim removed from the building was identified as 60-year-old Sam Frazier. Blind since birth, Frazier had lived alone in the room for at least 10 years. He was probably the best known of the four victims because of the years he had spent entertaining and promoting country music in the state. His room was the first on the right at the top of the stairs. Charles J. Roberts, 68, occupied the room next to Frazier's. His body was found between his bed and the north wall. Patricia Southerland, 34, lived in the third apartment. Her body was found in her doorway. McClain, who had escaped through the window, occupied the last room on the right side.

Ada Ruth Gregg, 33, the only resident on the left side of the hallway, was found lying on the floor next to her bed.

The four victims had apparently woken up and attempted to flee the building but apparently died of smoke inhalation, Chief Butler said. All four bodies were taken to a nearby city morgue for autopsies.

"It didn't take twenty gallons of water to extinguish the blaze." Chief Roger Butler told newsmen. The main problem, he said, was the smoke. Fuel on the carpet in the hallway created a blanket of smoke throughout the upstairs. "Breathing this smoke is much more dangerous than, say, wood smoke," Butler added.

No one could have survived the noxious fumes. Apparently, Southerland had opened her door and was unable to make it back to her room. All that saved the lone survivor, McClain, was that he went out the window and did not open the door.

Officers spent most of the day at the scene retrieving items to send to the crime lab for analysis. The outside door to the entrance was marked with deep scratches, indicating that it had been forced open. Mike McClain told officials that shortly before the fire, he heard someone in the hall rapping on the doors. Then he heard someone saying, "Ada, you better give me that knife or I'll take a warrant on you." A few minutes later he heard Southerland yell, "Fire!"

"Someone threw an accelerant on the carpet and doors," TBI Agent Davenport said. He pointed out the charred holes in the carpet at the start of the hall just off the top stair landing.

The probers' big break came from one of their own. Early in the night, at about 12:20 a.m., a man had contacted the police department and reported that someone had his knife. Officer Lynn Shults went to the address given, the bar and grill below the apartments, to try to settle the dispute. The man, Carey Caughron, claimed that Ada Gregg had his knife, which he described as a family heirloom, and said she wouldn't return it to him. Caughron said he and Gregg had been talking in the bar and he was showing her the knife. Suddenly, she grabbed it and took it upstairs to her room, locking the door and refusing to come out.

Shults and the operator of the cafe tried to get Ada Gregg to come out and talk to them. After some persuasion, she finally emerged, and while Caughron waited outside, she spoke with the officer and cafe manager.

The woman insisted she didn't have the knife even after the officer placed her in the patrol car and started toward the courthouse in an attempt to scare her into giving it up. Ada Gregg started crying and swore up and down that she did not have Caughron's knife.

"I didn't have anything I could charge her with," Shults told his colleagues now working the arson-homicide, "so I took her back to the apartments."

Shults said he advised Caughron that he could go to the courthouse the next morning and swear out a warrant against Gregg for theft. Caughron told him, "I don't need a damn warrant. I'll take care of it my own way." The knife was later retrieved from a ledge outside Gregg's window.

It was about 2:30 a.m. when Officer Shults responded to a call about a wreck in west Newport that he noticed a bronze Mustang parked near the bar and grill. When he returned about an hour later, he saw the commotion at the bar and grill. The bronze Mustang Shults had seen in front of the bar and grill belonged to Carey Caughron.

At 5:00 a.m., the Mustang was observed about half a block from the bar and grill. Caughron was a passenger in the car, which his relative was driving. Both were taken to the courthouse and questioned. The relative said they were driving around, saw the excitement at the bar and grill, and had stopped. The relative did say that Carey got out of the car in front of the bar and grill earlier. Carey Caughron was charged with public intoxication and held in jail. The relative was never charged and was released about noon.

Officer Shults observed that Caughron had apparently changed his clothes since their earlier encounter, and he reeked of a peculiar odor. "Once I got him in the police car, I could smell singed hair," Shults said.

State Fire Investigator Ray Shinall examined the burned building and found evidence that it was deliberately torched. A strong odor of accelerant hung in the air. The speed at which the fire raged led Shinall to believe that the accelerant had been gasoline. He found evidence that fuel had been poured on the floor in front of Sam Frazier's apartment. The trail led to the apartment Ada Gregg occupied and on down the hall to the other apartments, then down the stairs, where it was ignited. In the hall where the fire started, probers found a cap similar to one from a car's gas tank. Sleuths also removed the downstairs door to the stairwell. The door bore tool marks that the crime lab might be able to match with the object used to pry the door open.

The detectives impounded Caughron's bronze Mustang, and then a search warrant was obtained to make a search of Caughron's residence. The car's gas cap was missing, and the one found in the building appeared to fit it. A screwdriver that could possibly have caused the gouge marks on the door was also found in the car.

At Caughron's home, the officers seized a pair of men's jeans, boots, and a watch, all of which Fire Investigator Shinall believed had gasoline on them. These items were tagged and sent to the crime lab for positive identification.

Agent Davenport outlined in an affidavit the findings to support a warrant charging Carey Carl Caughron with first-degree murder. The suspect had been held in custody since 5:00 a.m. "He was too drunk to talk to this morning," Agent Davenport said.

Caughron was arraigned at 9:00 p.m. before General Session Judge Marcus Mooneyham, less than 24 hours from the time the fire alarm was sounded. During the short arraignment, Caughron said he was disabled and under treatment at Cherokee Mental Health. Judge Mooneyham said that arrangements would be made for Caughron to receive his medication.

The court appointed attorneys to represent Caughron, and his bond was set at $500,000—

$100,000 for each count of first-degree murder and $25,000 on each of the four counts of aggravated arson.

During the arraignment, Caughron said, "Everybody upstairs threatened to kill me, and I've not done a thing."

Sheriff Tunney Moore indicated that he was concerned with Caughron's safety in the Cocke County Jail. "I will keep him separate, but I would feel better if he were in the Sevier County Jail."

The relative with Caughron when he was picked up for public intoxication said the suspect was not drunk. "He hadn't been drinking for eight months," the relative said. "They were looking for a brown car and so they stopped us. They jerked me out of the car and handcuffed me and questioned me," the relative maintained. "The boy's not done it."

The relative expressed fear that bad publicity about Carey's brother, Gary Caughron, would harm Carey's case. Gary Caughron was on death row after a conviction for a torture-murder of a Sevier County woman.

"Gary was charged with something he didn't do," the relative said, claiming that he had been railroaded, and now Cary was being framed.

The relative said the only thing the officers had was the argument between Caughron and Ada Gregg, one of the victims. They had been "friends for years. He wouldn't kill nobody. He wouldn't hurt a cat or dog," the relative maintained.

The autopsy reports confirmed the officers' first observations—the victims had all died from smoke inhalation. The lab reports stated that the accelerant used had been gasoline, and that the clothes confiscated from the suspect also had gasoline on them.

The state crime lab report stated that there were not enough marks on the door to determine if tools confiscated from the suspect's car had been used to break in the door.

Caughron was admitted to the Middle Tennessee Mental Health Institute for an evaluation of his mental state. After 30 days of observations, doctors determined that Caughron was mentally competent to stand trial. The doctors believed Caughron was faking an illness and was trying to gain something by presenting himself as more impaired than he really was.

The November session of the Cocke County grand jury indicted Carey Carl Caughron on four counts of first-degree murder, four counts of felony murder, one count of aggravated arson, and one count of attempted first-degree murder. Lesser charges of public intoxication and resisting arrest were handed down in separate indictments.

Defense attorneys were denied a motion to exclude the death penalty under a state law forbidding imposition of the death penalty on a defendant with a low IQ.

On Tuesday, June 23, 1992, jury selection began with Judge Rex Henry Ogle presiding. District Attorney General Al Schmutzer and Assistant Ed Bailey would present the state's case. Public Defenders Ed Miller and Susanna Laws would represent the defendant. The state was asking for the death penalty, and the jurors were questioned closely about the case. It was shortly after 3:00 p.m. that a jury of seven women and five men were selected with two women alternates.

Schmutzer told the jury the state's case was based on circumstantial evidence, that there were no actual witnesses, but, he continued, "A case can be just as strong with circumstantial evidence as with direct evidence."

Defense Attorney Miller said that his case would be a straightforward not guilty plea combined with an insanity defense. He said the defense wasn't sure a crime had even been committed and "was not conceding this man is guilty." But because of the defendant's mental condition, he said, he was obligated to raise the insanity defense.

D.A. Schmutzer used the investigators and Mike McClain to lead the jury through the search for what occurred on August 22nd, and how in the end, it all pointed to Carey Caughron. The most damaging testimony probably came from Investigator Shinall, who told the court of his findings at the scene, which were later confirmed by the lab.

"Everything I found was consistent with gasoline in this area [around the stairwell]. There was nothing that was consistent with any other cause, such as accidental or the weather," Shinall said. "This was an intentionally set fire." He added that when Caughron was being processed on August 22nd, he noticed the odor of singed hair about him.

The defense called relatives and friends of Caughron to explain why and how his clothes had gasoline on them.

They testified that while Caughron was working on a car that day, he had used gasoline to "prime" the carburetor and it backfired.

Caughron testified that he had siphoned gasoline again that day. He had siphoned gasoline from his car to his truck to drive to town. Even so, he had run out of gasoline on the Greeneville Highway.

A man took him home and he got his car and started out again when the car ran out of gas at about the same spot. He was helped by another person the second time. Each time he siphoned gas, Caughron said, he didn't use a funnel but just poured it in, spilling as much as he got into the tank. Caughron said he was alone when he ran out of gas.

A Good Samaritan who lived near the Greeneville Highway testified that he had helped a man who had run out of gas on the morning of the fire. He couldn't identify the man but said a woman and children were in the car.

Caughron said he and a relative returned to town and saw the fire. They circled around the block to see what was going on, and the police pulled them over.

The defense introduced testimony that revealed the defendant had fallen from a motorcycle while riding with another person. Also, during Caughron's childhood, he was struck and knocked down a stairway. After this, Caughron would have to be told when to eat, and at other times, he wouldn't even blink when someone talked to him.

Doctors testified that injuries caused from these incidents could contribute to organic brain syndrome, which can cause behavioral disorders, including schizophrenia.

According to a clinical psychologist, Caughron was "in an active psychotic state" in January 1990 and was taking medication for his condition. One symptom was that he heard the voice of his late father telling him he was looking after Caughron and his family. Caughron also explained that the medication "makes me sleep and helps me with my voices at night."

Caughron denied that he had anything to do with setting the fire that took four lives. However, he remembered the argument he had with one of the victims over a knife, and of driving around Newport on the morning of the fire. But he could not remember anything about setting the fire. During cross-examination by D.A. Schmutzer, Caughron repeatedly would answer, "I don't remember," or "I don't know," to questions about the events of August 22, 1991.

Caughron did admit that he purposely tried to do poorly on mental evaluations because, "I thought they were trying to railroad me." The defense had subpoenaed a doctor to testify to Caughron's impaired mental condition shortly before and at the time of the fire. The doctor, however, did not show up in court. The defense attorney said the doctor was his main witness, or at least his second most important witness, and "without his testimony, we cannot continue." When the doctor's office was contacted, it was learned that he was in Washington, D.C., and the secretary didn't know how to get in touch with him.

State investigators contacted the doctor later in the day and learned that he would be available to testify the following afternoon. The doctor, a psychiatrist, arrived at the courthouse shortly before 1:00 p.m. on Friday. The doctor testified that he had examined Caughron two months before the fire and found him "extremely spacy." Caughron was hearing voices and had reported a 15-year history of alcohol and drug abuse. The psychiatrist had prescribed an antipsychotic drug for the patient, but Caughron had never had his prescriptions refilled.

A neuropharmacologist testified that if a person suddenly stops taking the medication, the psychotic symptoms could actually worsen into a condition known as "supersensitivity psychosis." That condition, the expert testified, could have caused the defendant's behavior.

Called as rebuttal witnesses by the state were doctors who found Caughron capable of standing trial. They told the jury of their observations and how they interpreted them.

A ward nurse from the Mental Health Institute told the jury that Caughron, who had apparently been unable to add seven and three when interviewed by the doctor, had played cards with other patients. "He was playing spades," the nurse said. "He was winning."

A social worker testified that at one point,

Caughron told her he was "playing crazy" so he wouldn't get the death penalty.

After five and a half hours of deliberations, the jury returned with a guilty verdict on four counts of first-degree murder, four counts of felony murder, and one count each of aggravated arson and attempted first-degree murder.

The same jury then heard witnesses in a hearing sentence to determine if the defendant would receive life or the death penalty. Caughron's attorneys, in a plea for Caughron's life, told the jury, "He was unable, due to his mental limitations, to understand the consequence of his act. He thought the people would leave and he would find the knife. He didn't think beyond that."

With a breaking voice, Defense Attorney Miller stated that his client was sorry. "This is someone who has never been in the game," Miller said. "He's never had a chance."

"We have sympathy for these victims but whatever you do today, it will not bring back those victims."

D.A. Schmutzer argued that Caughron had gone home after his argument with Gregg, siphoned gasoline from the truck, returned to town and set the fire, drove back home, changed clothes, and returned to the fire scene. "For anyone to do all that, there's no question that this defendant knew what he was doing.

"These four victims had a family. They had a life. They had a hard life, too. They had found themselves, for whatever reason, living over a beer tavern on skid row. They had lives that this man snuffed out for no good reason."

The seven woman, five-man jury deliberated for two hours and gave Carey Carl Caughron four life sentences.

In an unusual move, the jury presented a written recommendation "that the four life sentences run consecutively and not concurrently."

Judge Ogle followed the jury's recommendations on the life sentences and sentenced the defendant to 25 years each on the other two charges. He then turned to Caughron and said, "This jury . . . has given you the benefit of their grace. There was more than enough proof in this record to support a death sentence. You are a lucky man."

Caughron spoke to the jury, "I'd like to thank the jury for giving the life sentences."

Both the prosecution and defense said they were satisfied with the verdict.

"This was a very conscientious and hard-working jury who did a good job in a hard trial," D.A. Schmutzer said. "They did what they thought was right and I have no problems with that."

Defense attorneys said they were pleased with the life sentences, but were not pleased with the verdict and said there would be an appeal.

Caughron's family members didn't think he had done any of the things he was accused of doing. "He was just at the wrong place at the right time as far as I can see," one relative said. "It could have happened to any of us."

"I think that justice was done, but I hope he has to serve every day of it," said one victim's relative. "At least they get to see him."

EDITOR'S NOTE:
*Michael McCain is not the real name of the person so named in the foregoing story. A fictitious name has been used because there is no reason for public interest in the identity of this person.*

# "THE CAR WAS FULL OF DEAD PEOPLE!"

by Gary C. King

Except for the sound of the wind whispering through the tops of the tall fir trees and the occasional bird or animal noises, the woods of the Willamette National Forest near the Mount Washington Wilderness Area were quiet, offering a tranquil retreat for anyone venturing in by choice. The forest trails are a haven for hikers and nature enthusiasts, and the rushing waters of the McKenzie River are a real treat for thrill-seeking rafters.

It is no wonder that most of the sounds are those of nature's. However, on late Friday afternoon, November 15, 1985, the tranquility was broken by the manmade sound of an automobile traveling down a remote, seldom-used private road which connects to a main road that leads to and from the small community of McKenzie Bridge, Oregon, a mountain hamlet located several miles east of Eugene. Soon voices could be heard, laughing and carefree, and the barking of a friendly dog became distinctly audible.

The laughing soon ceased, however, and an altercation that led to coldblooded violence began. Although the shouting match of the participants occasionally vented out of the dwelling, which was an old schoolbus that had been converted into a home it is likely the arguing was only heard by the participants themselves. And maybe the forest animals, since it was miles to the nearest residence.

Like the laughing, the arguing and shouting suddenly ended when one of the participants aimed a small-caliber gun at 26-year-old Dwayne Denney's head. A noticeable tic, likely caused by fear or perhaps anger, or both, manifested itself in one of Dwayne's eyes as he stared down the barrel of the pistol, and he began to grimace when the man with the gun began to squeeze on the trigger. Suddenly the gunman moved the pistol's aim slightly to the left and fired once, deliberately missing Dwayne's head.

As the gun recoiled, Dwayne's eyes grew wild, taking on a fierceness that bordered on rage. Nearly deafened by the blast, he shrieked, but did not back away. It may have been merely a warning shot for Dwayne to back off, or it might have been intended to instill further terror in his mind, a sort of mental torture prior to carrying out the final act. Whatever the reason for the violent hostility, Dwayne foolishly began shouting again.

"Well, after that, what are you going to do?" Dwayne asked, taunting the man with the gun. "Kill me?"

"Yes," answered the man without hesitation. With devilishly quick responses he lowered the pistol and fired a single shot directly into Dwayne's forehead. When the bullet hit its target, Dwayne's body lurched backward, and a spray of blood and tissue flew out of his head.

Dwayne's female companion, 26-year-old Debbie Frederickson, screamed and briefly kneeled over Dwayne's motionless body before attempting to flee. But the killer's reflexes were too quick for her and the third shot from his pistol hit her in the back of the head and she, too, went down.

The killer then turned and walked quickly outside to take care of Debbie's 7-year-old boy, Kenny Rogers, and his dog, both waiting patiently in a 1972 American Motors Hornet parked nearby. The boy undoubtedly heard the shots, but he likely had not understood what had occurred. If he had been aware of the bloody carnage that had just taken place inside the bus, he probably would have climbed out of the car and run for his life into the woods.

The killer, his breathing rapid, approached the Hornet, all the while keeping a tight grip on his gun. He could see the boy, cold and afraid, hugging his dog inside the darkened car. Innocent and trusting, the little boy looked up and attempted a smile through the window at the man and likely wondered why his mother and her boyfriend had not come out instead.

Before the boy had a chance to speak, though, the killer fired a shot through the passenger window, putting a bullet in young Kenny's forehead.

At that same instant, Kenny's dog jumped out through the shattered window and headed into the forest, frightened away by the gunshot. The killer reached through the shattered opening and fired another bullet into the child's head, just to be sure. The youngster slumped over in the car seat and bled profusely from his wounds. Unfortunately for the helpless little victim, death did not come quickly.

As the boy lay dying in the front seat of the Hornet, the killer and his female companion returned to the bus and dragged Dwayne and Debbie outside and loaded them into the back seat of the car. Attempting to cover their tracks as completely and carefully as possible, and afraid that the victim's dog might somehow find its way home, the killer's female companion sought out the animal. When she finally found the dog wandering about the woods and won his confidence, she beat it to death with a baseball bat and climbed into the Hornet. They then drove east to Oregon 126, the main highway that links Eugene, Oregon, with the central part of the state, to dispose of the car and the bodies.

As the killer began to drive away he sensed movement beside him. It was the boy, and he clearly wasn't dead yet. Deciding he would fix that, the driver coldly and unhesitatingly drew out his pistol and fired another slug into the youth's head. The boy lurched once, then again lay motionless in the front seat.

A short time later the killer turned off Oregon 126 onto a side road and, after deciding the area was appropriate for disposing of the bodies, he ran the Hornet head-on into a tree. Immediately after impact he again sensed movement beside him, and again he fired a shot into young Kenny's head. As he and his companion left the vehicle, the killer heard Debbie move in the back seat. He aimed the gun at her head and fired once more. After her body jerked from the impact of the bullet she lay motionless, leaving the killer satisfied that his actions had been successful. He and his companion then began their hike home.

The following day, Saturday, November 16th, was Sally Dennison's and Ray Nichols' day to go hiking and white-water rafting. Longtime friends, Sally and Ray had hiked up, over, and through some of the most popular trails in the Pacific Northwest. Experienced, they knew where to go and see all types of wildlife and spectacular scenic views, and it was a rare occasion that they finished their explorations without an abundance of outstanding photographs that would make those found between the covers of travel and nature magazines often appear amateurish.

On this particular autumn day, Sally and Ray, accompanied by a few fellow hikers and friends, decided to venture into the Oregon Cascades, a group of mountains which run north and south through the center of the state. It was early when they arrived at the Willamette National Forest at a location near the Three Sisters Wilderness Area (named after three peaks) and the Mount Washington Wilderness Area. They parked their vehicles at an area well below the summit of McKenzie Pass and unloaded their gear.

The rippling white waters of the south fork of the McKenzie River could be heard in the distance, and a heavy mixture of mist and clouds hung in the tops of the tall fir trees on this brisk, chilly morning, serving as a kind of forest shroud. Although cold, the air smelled clean and fresh, and the group of hikers set off on a day-long trek they were sure to remember for years to come. It was a day of hiking and rafting that started off not unlike many others they'd ventured on, but it was one that would end unlike all the others they'd been on, complete with sinister overtones and bullet-riddled bodies.

It was approximately 1:30 p.m. when the hikers and rafters came across the crashed Hornet on Deer Creek Road, an old logging road, just off the McKenzie River National Recreation Trail. Curiosity and concern prompted Sally and Ray to leave their group and take a closer look.

Sally's shrieks echoed through the forest when she peered into the driver's side window and found the body of the young boy in the front seat of the Hornet and the body of the man in the back seat. Her screams brought the others in her group running to see what the fuss was all about and, after seeing the blood and the lifeless bodies, they understood.

As the hikers stared in awe and horror, they heard a low, moaning sound that came from nearby. When they fanned out to find the source of the sound, they soon found Debbie Frederickson propped up against the base of a tree near the passenger side of the car. Her face, neck, and shirt were covered with blood, much of which was dry by this time, but because of the bright crimson wetness on the side and back of her shirt they could tell that she was still bleeding. When asked what had happened, she appeared disoriented and could not provide any details, leaving the hikers to wonder if her injuries, as well as those of the man and the boy, had been caused by an automobile accident.

The hikers made Debbie as comfortable as possible and administered what first aid they could while two others rushed off to highway 126 to flag down a car that could take them to a telephone where they could call for help. A short time later an Oregon state trooper arrived at the remote location.

Because of the severity of Debbie's wounds she was rushed to McKenzie-Willamette Memorial Hospital in Springfield, near Eugene, and additional troopers were dispatched to the Deer Creek Road to further assess the situation and take a statement from the hikers.

The hikers' statement told the troopers very little except, of course, how they came upon the bodies. Examination of the bodies, however, told the troopers they were definitely dealing with a case of homicide, and not an accident, as the hikers had first believed. Close observation revealed the bullet wounds in the boy's and man's heads. Likewise, when Debbie Frederickson arrived at the hospital, even though she was still unable to talk, it was confirmed that she, too, had been shot.

Due to the nature of the case, OSP Homicide Detective John Wood and David Codding were quickly dispatched to the scene from OSP's Eugene office. They were accompanied by several assistants, the OSP crime lab, and a deputy medical examiner.

The bodies were cold to the touch, Wood and Codding noted, and appeared to have been there for several hours. Likewise, the car's engine was cold, adding credence to the theory. They speculated that the victims were shot at a different location and transported to the scene where they were found after death. But this was merely conjecture on the detectives' part at this point and not a result of evidence or eyewitness reports.

After the bodies were thoroughly photographed by the photographic unit they were removed from the car, then examined at the scene by the deputy medical examiner, who told the detectives that it appeared the victims had been shot at close range, a determination he made from the presence of powder burns on the skin. He said that it appeared the man had been shot once, but that the boy had likely been shot several times. Following the preliminary examination, the bodies were loaded into the medical examiner's vehicle and taken to the Lane County Morgue in Eugene.

As a matter of thoroughness, casts were made of the tire tracks found in the vicinity of the car, even though there was little doubt that the tracks belonged to the Hornet. The tracks led off of the main road onto Deer Creek Road, right up to the point where the car stopped when it impacted with the tree. The work of preparing the casts was done so that the door leading to any doubt that the tracks were the Hornet's later could be firmly closed.

Aside from the tracks there was little evidence of significance found in the vicinity of the vehicle, and it appeared that most of the evidence would be found inside the car itself. This included a large amount of blood and blood spatters, indicating that at least some, if not all of the shots had been fired inside the car. The detectives reasoned that if there had been any shooting at another location, as they suspected, there would likely be good evidence found at such a location, too.

In the meantime; the two dead bodies were positively identified as 7-year-old Kenny Rogers and 26-year-old Dwayne Denney. Their relationship was not immediately known, but within hours detectives had determined that Kenny and his mother, Debbie Frederickson, lived with Denney in the community of Blue River, near McKenzie Bridge.

At the hospital, Detective Wood interviewed Debbie prior to her going into surgery, but he said she still appeared disoriented and still couldn't believe that she'd been shot. The motive for the shootings still had not been determined at this point, he said.

"It appears to be an attempted triple homicide," said Wood. "The murderer probably felt they were all dead when he left." Wood added that Debbie had been shot in the back of the head and had suffered superficial wounds to her forehead and to her right thigh from two other gunshots.

During surgery, doctors removed a small-caliber bullet from Debbie's brain. She was left partially disabled and listed in serious but stable condition afterward. News of her condition was not made public for fear that the killer might try to find her and finish her off and, as an added precaution, an armed guard was posted outside her hospital room.

The autopsies revealed that young Kenny had been shot four times at point-blank range, and the slugs removed were later determined to have been .25-caliber. The same caliber slug was removed from Dwayne Denny's body, and serology tests revealed the presence of alcohol and methamphetamines in his blood. There were also recent needle marks on one of his arms, indicating that he'd injected speed shortly before his death.

Was this possibly a drug-related crime? And if so, had Denney been attempting to make a buy when he was killed? The track marks on his arms indicated that he'd been using drugs for some time. But was he dealing in drugs, too? The detectives felt they could get their answers from Debbie, as soon as she was able to talk. In the meantime, they had other leads to run down, including going over Denney's Hornet with a fine-tooth comb.

There were several latent fingerprints found inside the Hornet and these were lifted for later analysis. Because the crimes involved multiple gunshots, particularly because several were fired inside the car, crime-lab technicians did a blood-splatter analysis to determine the positions of the victims and the killer. Even though powder burns indicated the victims were shot at close range, blood spatter analysis could, hopefully, determine the velocity of the bullets and the angle in which the bullets struck the victims, ultimately demonstrating how the gun was held by the killer. Such findings are often useful in determining the degree of intent.

After the news of the shootings broke in the Eugene area, followed by a plea for public assistance and the fact that there had been a survivor, the OSP office in Eugene was contacted by a witness. The witness, Rita Simms, told detectives that a man by the name of Humberto "Zeke" Zalaya, 50, had committed the killings of Kenny Rogers and Dwayne Denney and attempted to murder Debbie Frederickson. Other details of the witness' statement were not made public at that time, but a source close to the investigation said the theory that the shootings were drug-related had been correct.

As soon as she was able to talk, detectives interviewed Debbie Frederickson who, although still unable to believe that she had been shot, confirmed much of what witness Rita Simms had told police. Debbie said that on the evening of the shootings she and Denney, along with her son, drove to Zalaya's schoolbus home located in McKenzie bridge to buy drugs, as they had done at least once a month for the past six months.

On that fateful evening, Debbie said, she and Denney left her son and his dog in the car and entered Zalaya's bus. Inside was Zalaya, his wife and their five children, and Rita Simms. After purchasing a small amount of methamphetamines from Zalaya, the adults injected it. A short time later an argument broke out between Zalaya and Denney; Denney had insisted that Zalaya sell him some more drugs. Zalaya refused, and became angry when Denney refused to leave until he received more drugs. Prior to the fatal shooting, Debbie told detectives, Zalaya fired a warning shot at Denney.

Following a background check on their prime suspect, the detectives learned that Zalaya was an ex-con who had served time in three California prisons on a variety of charges, all felonies. He was described by prison officials and others who knew him as having a high-strung personality, cold and calculating. They learned from additional witnesses that he was a small-time dealer in Oregon who made a living selling relatively small amounts of marijuana and methamphetamines. He was being treated for a liver ailment at the time of the shootings, and he often traded his prescription Dilaudid, a strong pain-killer, for speed. Little else was known about Zalaya at this point in the case.

Armed with arrest and search warrants, detectives and troopers stormed Zalaya's bus home. However, Zalaya and his family weren't there when the lawmen arrived. While the detectives made inquiries as to where the suspect might be, criminalists went ahead and processed the bus and the surrounding area for clues.

A short time later, according to OSP Trooper Mike McCullough, Zalaya and his wife were located by police after detectives reportedly received a tip by informants. They were staying at the residence of acquaintants in Springfield. After police quietly surrounded the residence, Zalaya was taken into custody without incident for questioning in the McKenzie Bridge murder and was lodged in the Lane County Jail in Eugene. His wife, Leslie, 35, a substitute schoolteacher, was also arrested because of her alleged presence during the commission of the crimes in question. The couples' five children were taken into custody by the Oregon Children's Services Division. Zalaya consented to interviews with detectives and was questioned thoroughly.

According to State Police Sergeant Kenneth Chichester, Zalaya said he and the victims were acquainted with each other, partially confirming earlier reports from Rita Simms and Debbie Frederickson. Because of the time frame that was developed from information obtained from Zalaya, the witnesses, and the autopsy reports, Chichester said that the victims had been left at the remote site for 15 to 16 hours before they were discovered by the hikers.

After a careful review of the evidence so far obtained, Zalaya was charged with two counts of aggravated murder and one count of attempted murder. He was also charged with being an ex-convict in possession of a firearm. He was held without bail. His wife, Leslie, was charged with two counts of first-degree kidnapping of Debbie and her son, Kenny. Her bail was set at $10,000 and she was released after posting $1,000, the required 10 percent.

After repeated grilling by the investigators, Zalaya finally confessed to the crime, much to everyone's surprise. His confession was tape-recorded and videotaped. In the videotaped reenactment of the crime, Zalaya explained the argument between himself and Dwayne Denney over drugs. He said that as the argument intensified, Denney began threatening him, his wife, and one of his children. Zalaya said that at one point, Denney grabbed one of his children. After he pulled out his gun and shot Denney between the eyes he said he shot Debbie as she attempted to flee from the bus. He said he then decided he had to do something about the boy, Kenny, a first-grader, who was waiting in the car outside.

"He was like, afraid, but I couldn't understand why he was afraid of something if he wasn't in the house," Zalaya told detectives, explaining his perceptions of the boy's feelings when he went outside to shoot him. In his gravelly voice, Zalaya said he raised his pistol and fired, hitting the boy in the forehead. He said he reached inside and shot the boy again, to make sure he was dead.

"I had no choice," said Zalaya. "It was him or me. I know that if I leave a boy around that's heard shots . . . I didn't want to shoot him." He then explained how he and his wife dragged the victims out of the bus and loaded them into the backseat of the Hornet. When he climbed inside to drive away, said Zalaya, he sensed movement and fired another slug into the boy's head. He and his wife then drove the victims east on Oregon 126.

"I'm wondering where in the hell I'm gonna take this car," said Zalaya. "What am I gonna do with the stupid car full of dead people?" After pulling onto the logging road, Zalaya said he decided to run the Hornet into a tree. He said he then felt something move beside him again, and he again fired another shot into Kenny's head. He said he also heard Debbie move in the backseat, and he likewise shot her again. Thinking they were all dead, Zalaya said he and his wife began walking home. He said he threw his .25-caliber pistol into the white water of the McKenzie River, (the authorities were never able to recover the gun).

"In looking back at it," asked Detective David Codding, "would you have done anything different now?"

"No," answered Zalaya gruffly, "No. Nothing."

In spite of the confession, Zalaya pleaded innocent to the charges in Lane County Circuit Court. Court-appointed Defense Attorney Steve Chez said a defense of mental disease or defect might be used. His trial was set for June, 1985. In a non-jury trial before Circuit Judge Gregory G. Foote, the prosecution presented its case against Zalaya through expert testimony of crime-lab technicians, detectives, medical examining experts, the videotaped reenactment of the crime and confession, and an eyewitness.

Rita Simms, the eyewitness, repeated for the judge that the adult victims, Dwayne Denney and Debbie Frederickson, had gone to the Zalaya bus to buy drugs. After the purchase was made, Simms described how Denney demanded more drugs and refused to leave the bus until he got them. It was then, she said, that she, her son, Debbie, and the Zalayas' five children watched in stunned disbelief as Zalaya shot Denney between the eyes and then turned the gun on Debbie and fired.

In arguing that Zalaya suffered from an extreme emotional disturbance at the time of the shootings, co-Defense Attorney Jack A. Gardner said that it was Zalaya's "background in prison, the small quarters of the bus, his confrontation with Dwayne Denney and, unfortunately, the narcotics ingested by the defendant, (which) all acted . . . to produce a result in his mind, right or wrong." The defense further contended that Zalaya accidentally shot the child while he was trying to shoot their dog, which was in the car with young Kenny.

After viewing the videotaped confession produced by the prosecution, Judge Foote said that he accepted eyewitness Rita Simms' account of the ordeal rather than that of the defendant.

"I find that Dwayne Denney did not seize the defendant's child (as Zalaya had claimed during the confession) . . . that there was an argument that escalated, but that the argument involved only Dwayne Denney and the defendant," said Judge Foote. Foote said that Zalaya was definitely not suffering from an extreme emotional disturbance when he shot the young child. "The court finds that that was essentially a coldblooded, premeditated, execution-style killing," he said. Foote immediately issued guilty verdicts on both counts of aggravated murder.

On Tuesday, August 20, 1985, Judge Foote sentenced Zalaya to two consecutive life terms for the shooting deaths of Dwayne Denney and Kenny Rogers, imposing a mandatory minimum prison term of 30 years on each of the murder charges. Foote also sentenced Zalaya to 20 years with mandatory minimum term of 10 years for the attempted murder of Debbie Frederickson. He also imposed a five-year "enhanced" penalty because a firearm was used to carry out the crime. In meting out the sentence, Judge Foote said it was apparent to him "that the defendant continues, even at his mature age, to have an explosive volatile personality that is easily ignited."

Leslie Zalaya's trial began in mid-November, 1985, and much of the same evidence that was presented at her husband's trial was presented at her jury trial. Charges against her had been changed to include aggravated murder, felony murder, attempted murder, hindering the prosecution of her husband, and two counts of kidnapping. The prosecution also contended that she helped her husband try to hide the victims' bodies in the remote area where they were found.

In spite of her husband's testimony on her behalf, in which he maintained that her only involvement was after the shootings when she beat the victims' dog to death with a baseball bat, Leslie Zalaya was convicted of manslaughter, first-degree kidnapping, and hindering prosecution in her husband's case by burning certain evidence. She was sentenced to 10 years in the Oregon Women's Correctional Center.

Debbie Frederickson eventually recovered from her injuries and, after living with her relatives for a while in California, she moved to Montana.

On Sunday, April 5, 1987, Humberto "Zeke" Zalaya died in the Oregon State Prison infirmary where he had been hospitalized since February 5th for treatment of what was believed to have been cancer to the liver.

## EDITOR'S NOTE
*Sally Dennison, Ray Nichols, Debbie Frederickson and Rita Simms are not the real names of the persons so named in the foregoing story. Fictitious names have been used because there is no reason for public interest in the identities of these persons.*

# "EASTER-MORNING MASSACRE OF 5!"

by Bill Kelly

GLEN AVON, CA.
MAY 25, 1989

The temperature that muggy April day hit the high 70s and the humidity in Glen Avon, a rural ranch community near Riverside, California, was testing the stamina of joggers. At quitting time, city personnel headed for the suburbs, scurrying home to T-shirts and briefs, backyard barbecues and pool lounging. As the sun settled behind the mountains and suburbia quietly settled in for a night of comfy recreation, Riverside city slowly came to life.

At daytime, the city is a driving metropolis with workers and shoppers shouldering and shoving their way along crowded streets. At nighttime, another form of hustling takes its place.

Significant attention has been given to Riverside's "night-lifers" recently by the Riverside Sheriff's Department, and formidable improvement has been made. Still there remains a sizable faction of "night people" who are nourished by the vices of man.

Impenetrable to boosted foot and motor patrol, drug traffic and prostitution flourishes like stubble in the city, but hardly openly. The unlawful transactions in drugs and sex take on a ritualistic air as the night people slither about the shadowy city.

Beat officers and undercover agents work like beavers

to contain this disgraceful practice, but, simply, the laws of supply and demand make their efforts more or less futile.

In fact, the citizens as well as the police, are usually gratified when the night breed keep to themselves and victimize one another. Usually, the public will only scream when an "innocent bystander" succumbs. Therefore, John and Jane Doe pay little attention to crime among the lawless. Only the most blatant or tawdry among this element rates mention in local newspapers.

As most of Riverside and its adjoining rural communities slept during those muggy morning hours of April 3, 1988, an item worth mentioning was evolving.

At 5:30 a.m., Easter morning, Carrie and Pete Zona were fast asleep. Suddenly Carrie shook her husband. "Pete," she whispered. "Wake up. I heard gunshots!"

Pete rubbed the sleep from his eyes, and at his wife's urging, walked out onto the porch of his mobile home. It was as quiet and peaceful as an oxygen tent. He was ready to go back in the house when he spotted a man scurry from the mobile home across the street, jump into a white pickup truck and squeal down the street in classical gangster-movie style.

Once inside, Pete picked up the phone and dialed 911. "What's going on?" his wife asked.

"I don't know," Pete answered. "But it don't look right to me—some fellow just took off in Ron's pickup."

Police responded quickly and by 5:50 a.m., prowl cars were swarming over the mobile home park and lined down the 4400 block of Tyrolite Street.

Police had received several calls that something was afoul at the Holliday mobile unit. One caller even said that before the gunshots she had heard a woman screaming, "Don't! Please don't!"

Sergeant Dan Borden was one of the first to arrive at the scene. His backup arrived on his heels. With guns drawn, the officers entered the mobile home, a double-wide, three-bedroom residence, located at the rear of a white stucco home.

All of the lights were on inside the house. In the middle of the living room was a woman who was bleeding profusely from the face and stomach. She was still alive, but plenty scared. Moving forward into other areas of the modest home, police discovered blood everywhere: on the floors of the living room, the kitchen area and the hallways leading to the bedrooms. They also found four blood-soaked bodies strewn about. Two pre-school children were found unharmed in a back bedroom of the 40-foot-long mobile unit. The children, age three and two respectively, were picked up by relatives who lived nearby. The two-year-old clutched a stuffed Easter bunny that was sodden with blood.

A neighbor who had called the police, and who had wandered inside to see what all the fuss was about, nearly fainted from the shock of seeing the lifeless forms that were once her friends. She could see that Calleen and Ronald Holliday were both dead. She could also see that their houseguests, David Kelley and Jennifer McCaughan were dead and couldn't bring herself to go near the bodies.

Sergeant Borden picked up the phone and dialed headquarters. He asked for a patrol supervisor and an on-call homicide team. He told the dispatcher to send an ambulance and to notify the coroner that it would be a while before he could have the bodies.

Within minutes, an ambulance arrived and whisked the wounded woman away to Riverside Hospital. She could not talk. She had been shot in the face, and a bullet had apparently lodged in her lower jaw. A bullet had also passed through her body into her hand. That she was alive at all was a godsend.

Deputies from the Glen Avon and Riverside County Sheriff's Department began taking brief statements from the neighbors who had gathered outside the Holliday home. Crime scene investigators sealed off the residence to protect any evidence that might be valuable to the district attorney's office. Other deputies acted as sentries until personnel from the Department of Justice crime laboratory in Rubidoux arrived, took photographs, dusted the place for fingerprints and bagged evidence.

The probers set about the task of ascertaining the dimensions of the crime scene. Once established, great consideration was taken not to contaminate it or otherwise disrupt anything; it would have to be processed accurately and methodically. Every officer was ordered not to smoke, run any water or use the bathroom, for fear of contaminating the crime scene.

The interior of the mobile unit was a bloody mess. The floor and carpets beneath the bodies were soaked. Crimson splatters garnished the walls in the rooms where the shootings had occurred.

It appeared that each of the victims had been shot several times by a small-caliber weapon, an observation Sergeant Borden jotted down in his notebook. The four victims were identified as Calleen Holliday, 23, and her husband, Ronald, 28, of the Tyrolite Street mobile home; David Kelley, 28, of Galena Street, Glen Avon; and Jennifer McCaughan, 20, who lived with Kelley. The 18-year-old woman who had been shot in the jaw, was identified as Nancy Brown, a family friend.

It appeared that the McCaughan woman had sustained a fearsome beating prior to having been shot to death. The medical examiner jibed with investigators' opinions, but cautioned them that he couldn't confirm his opinion until after he'd performed a definitive autopsy on McCaughan.

A cursory inspection of the house showed that a safe was wide open. One of the detectives was overheard telling his superiors that it "appeared" the place had been rummaged through. Drawers had also been dumped and numerous items were overturned. It was difficult initially to determine whether anything had actually been taken from the residence, Sergeant Borden said. He explained that such a determination would not be made until a full inventory of the victims' property could be made by the victims' relatives or friends.

Since a search warrant had to be obtained, it was 13 hours before the bodies could be removed from the unit. Borden explained that the victims' bodies had to be photographed and sketched in the position in which they lay. Blood samples had to be taken from the victims and the adjacent areas that were literally saturated in gore. Areas of the carpet were cut for further analysis. Crime lab technicians searched inside for trace evidence, such as clothing fiber and hair, and outside for footprints or something the killer could have dropped in his flight.

Fingerprint technicians spent 10 hours dusting for latent prints in all likely and unlikely places. They collected some excellent specimens. Whether or not they could place the killer at the scene would remain to be seen.

After a methodical search of the outside property, the probers failed to come up with the gun used by the killer, prompting them to believe that the killer took the murder weapon with him for disposal. However, detectives did recover several .22-caliber spent casings, perhaps the most phenomenal evidence collected from the crime scene.

Usually, a killer will either drop the murder weapon at the scene, in a state of panic, or dispose of it nearby because he or she wouldn't want to be picked up with the weapon on their person. With this in mind, detectives spent countless hours searching the property next to the Holliday residence. Having failed to recover the weapon, they resigned themselves to the fact that the killer had taken the gun with him when he fled.

Additional scrutiny in the hours that followed revealed that nothing of value had been taken from the mobile unit. This prompted the homicide sleuths to theorize that the killer had simply rummaged through the place, overturned items and dumped drawers to make it look like a robbery. If that conjecture proved correct, what then was the killer's motive? With robbery debatable, the crimeflouters wondered if this was a crime of passion or maybe even a crime of revenge.

As the probe continued, sheriff's department detectives worked fastidiously, trying to ferret out clues that could lead them toward a suspect while the trail was still tepid. They interviewed friends, acquaintances and relatives of the five victims. They were able to come up with a feasible explanation of what had happened leading up to the calamity that Easter morning.

Among the things they found out was that the four who died were longtime friends. Just about every weekend the foursome partied together with backyard barbecues, beach parties or stay-at-home get-togethers. The foursome had spent the evening of April 3rd partying, first at Kelley and McCaughan's house, and later at the Hollidays' trailer.

The mobile home sat on a terra firma street in a semirural area 50 miles east of Los Angeles. A hand-painted sign outside identified the property as Lorrue Kennels. Calleen Holliday helped her mother groom and board dogs while Ron worked as a freelance carpet layer.

They were drinking tequila when Calleen Holliday phoned one of Kelley's four siblings around midnight. One relative of Kelley's said that although she could tell they had been drinking, each one of the four she talked to didn't seem drunk.

Kelly's relative described David as an outdoors man who excelled in basketball at Jurupa Junior High and Rubidoux High. She described him as an easygoing guy, who never bothered anybody.

At 17, David Kelley had a part-time job as a drywall hanger while attending high school. One day he sliced off the tip of his index finger with a power saw. The kids at school started calling him "stubby." Embarrassed over his disfigurement, he dropped out of school.

Other family members said David was always getting hurt and had recently been involved in a serious auto accident. Another relative said the association between the four friends who were murdered was closer than sardines in a can.

"They were always together," another relative said. "It seems befitting they should have died together. I think that's the way they would have wanted it."

As the hunt for the killer continued, police discovered yet another pitiful circumstance. The tiny, three-month-old, premature daughter of Jennifer McCaughan and David Kelley was battling for her life in Riverside County General Hospital. The infant had been held only once in her mother's arms, and never would be held again. She was surviving on a respirator and was facing a painful and uncertain future.

Meanwhile, a bulletin had been issued by the Riverside County Sheriff's Department for Ronald Holliday's white pickup truck — the one the killer had evidently fled in. Riverside County Sheriff Cois Byrd had the teletype division run a backward search of Ronald Holliday's name to learn the year, make and license number of any vehicles registered to him.

Within minutes, the dispatcher called Sheriff Byrd with the license number and vehicle identification number. Byrd had the teletype operator phone the dispatch center and the truck description was immediately flashed over the airwaves.

Officers were instructed to stop the pickup and check for ownership. They were also told to use extreme caution. Meanwhile, the pickup was put into the nationwide stolen vehicle network.

While this was going on, Sergeant Borden was at the hospital, glumly checking on Nancy Brown. She was being kept under close guard and her whereabouts were a close secret, especially to the press. Despite having been shot in the mouth, Nancy was able to communicate with the officer.

As she mumbled, the loose threads of the mystery were gathered up one-by-one, woven neatly into place. A few hours later, Sheriff Cois Byrd announced to reporters that the murder investigation had suddenly developed new leads.

"We're dealing with one subject of interest," he said. He declined to reveal any specifics, including the identity of the subject or whether he was a real suspect.

In keeping with decorum conceived by Sheriff Byrd, he and the entire homicide team were briefed by Sergeant Borden as to the progress on the case. Borden had the team's unified attention as he walked through the scene.

It was a story right out of a soap opera.

According to Nancy Brown, Ron Holliday and Brett Alexander Hale worked together as carpet layers. She said Ron was allowing Hale to stay at his home for the past couple of weeks until he could get on his feet.

Brown said she had nothing to do for Easter weekend and remembered that the Hollidays and their two friends, McCaughan and Kelley, always had something going. Brown decided to drop in on them. Hale was there. Everyone was drinking, laughing and having a good time. There were also drugs. Brown said she inhaled three lines of "speed" (a reference to amphetamines or methamphetamine) and drank a tequila "slammer." Hale, Brown said, drank the most and injected himself with speed.

She said that after Hale had wolfed down at least two six-packs and had injected himself with speed, she heard gunshots.

"I turned my head, and when I turned my head I got shot," she said. Brown said when she looked up she saw Hale standing in the middle of the room with a smoking pistol.

After she had taken a slug in the mouth and one in the stomach, Brown said, she heard Calleen Holliday scream, "Brett, no!" Then two more shots rang out. As Brown lay bleeding on the living room floor, she heard a door close and a truck start up and drive away.

Authorities went public, saying they were now looking for Brett Alexander Hale for questioning in the shooting spree at the Tryolite Street mobile home. They even went so far as to call him a suspect and a warrant was issued for his arrest.

The search for Hale went into high gear as sheriff's deputies and detectives made inquiries among his haunts. However, Hale never showed up at these locations, prompting lawmen to believe he had fled the vicinity.

On Tuesday, April 5, 1988, Colton police received a call from a rancher. He said he and his hired hands had stopped off at a topless bar in a semirural area east of Los Angeles, about 10 miles from where the slayings had occurred. It was here they spotted the white pickup truck that had been flashed across TV screens that morning. They said the driver was acting suspiciously. His description fit the man the announcer had said was wanted for questioning in the Glen Avon slayings: six-foot-tall, about 220 pounds, dark piercing eyes, black, curly hair and a mustache.

Police cars raced toward the vicinity where the suspect had been spotted, and a helicopter and dogs were also summoned. It seemed as though the whole assortment arrived together.

However, the bushy-haired suspect did not linger in that dreary place for long. At the sound of sirens echoing in the distance, he took off on foot, across a desert patch, like a rabbit responding to the word "hounds."

When police arrived, several witnesses pointed toward the desert, as mysterious and silent as a dark theater.

"He went that way," the caller told the officers. And, in lickety-split, several hard-breathing patrolmen frantically darted toward the moisture-starved shrubs. A helicopter hovered overhead, leveling an eye on the frontier below.

Dark clouds were wiping up spilled sunlight as the forces of the law plunged after the suspected killer. Shouts of excited men and barking hounds reverberated through the valley. A group of wild ponies tore down the valley in panic. The ponies were stamping and whinnying in fright.

Suddenly someone shouted, "Here he is!" And the suspect crawled out from a patch of brush near a riverbed. His hands wee high. Meekly, he said, "Don't shoot! I give up."

Deputies moseying around the riverbed found a .22-caliber pistol that the suspect had apparently tossed away as lawmen were closing in.

With Brett Alexander Hale in the Riverside County Jail, Sheriff Byrd noted that homicide investigators still wanted to learn exactly why he had unloaded a murderous blast upon the only people who had been good to him.

"We're trying to determine what caused this young man to discontinue his normal pattern," Byrd confided. He added that detectives were still trying to check on the credibility of the witnesses who had already given statements.

On Tuesday, September 13, 1988, five months after he was locked up in jail in Riverside, 29-year-old Brett Hale appeared in Riverside Municipal Court before the honorable Judge Timothy J. Heaslet. Hale was charged with felony, murder.

Relatives and friends of the victims packed the courtroom as Judge Heaslet announced that he had heard enough evidence to convince him that Hale should return in two weeks for further proceedings.

Following his preliminary hearing, Hale, clad in brown slacks and a tan and brown sweater over a sky-blue shirt, was returned to the Riverside County Jail. His attorney, Public Defender Richard Cleary, said that his client was being held without bail.

Numerous legal lulls brought the case to trial on March 23, 1989, before Judge Patrick F. Magers.

Prosecutor Danuta W. Tuszynska opened the state's case by informing the court that she would not ask for the death sentence, although "this is one of the worst massacres in county history."

Her first witness was Nancy Brown, now 19, who had survived the vicious attack. She told jurors that the group had been drinking and watching a rock-n'-roll videotape when all hell broke out. She was sitting with Jennifer McCaughan, talking, while Ron Holliday and David Kelley talked nearby. Calleen was in the kitchen preparing a snack. Hale was seated in the love seat in the living room, alone. She said the Hollidays' two-year-old daughter was asleep in a living room chair with an Easter bunny her parents had given her earlier. They had just finished taking videotapes of the little girl with the bunny.

Brown testified that she, Ron Holliday, Kelley, McCaughan and Hale had just finished taking methamphetamine, or "speed," when she was shot. "I seen Brett standing with a gun like this" by the love seat.

The next thing Brown remembered was hearing Calleen Holliday begging for her life in the kitchen: "Brett, no!" Then there were more shots.

After Hale fled, Brown said that although she was bleeding from the face and stomach, she managed to pick up the phone and dial 911. "Hurry," she cried. "He might come back!"

Then she looked up. The Hollidays' little two-year-old was standing there with her stuffed bunny in her hand. "It was covered with blood," Brown recalled.

The girl had apparently slept through the massacre, but now she was standing in the kitchen, over the dead body of her blood-drenched mother. "Mommy," she begged, "get up."

After presenting experts on the effects of "speed," Brett Hale took the stand in his own defense. He said that after taking the drug it took only a few minutes before he killed his four friends. He testified that he had injected himself with a half-gram of speed and wanted to kill himself, but opted to take the life of his companions instead. He said he remembered shooting them all once, but did not remember reloading and shooting them again. "I loved them," Hale said. "They were my best friends."

Hale told the court that he first began using marijuana at age 13, and by the time he was 15 he took speed almost every day. He dropped out of school in 1975 before he could finish 10th grade.

Contending that there were no arguments before the killings, Hale testified that the entire group was drinking and taking drugs throughout the weekend party. He said he took speed about 20 times, wolfed down "junk food," fries, tacos, hamburgers and didn't sleep a wink.

"Everything in my life was in the dumps," Hale told the court. "I kept wanting to get my act together but I kept falling back. I couldn't pay my bills. I had no money."

He said he walked into another room, where Ronald Holliday kept a pistol. He used a syringe to inject all the speed he had left in his arm. The drug, mixed with a dozen beers he had downed, made him feel even more depressed.

"I was thinking about killing myself . . . I got the gun off the shelf and I held it in my hand . . . I sat there. I was going to do it right there in the room . . . then something snapped . . . I walked into the living room and opened fire. Ron, my very best friend, was first . . . I wasn't thinking of anything that I'm aware of . . . I had no feelings at the time, no bad ones."

A coroner took the stand and testified that Hale had shot each victim once, reloaded two times and then shot them again. He said the Hollidays were shot through the heads; David Kelley in the heart and head, and Jennifer McCaughan in the throat and face.

The prosecution produced a witness who said that a week before the massacre, he was chatting with Hale and watching a television show about Charles Manson, the convicted mastermind behind the grisly murders of Sharon Tate and six others in 1969. The witness said Hale turned to him and said, "Manson is my hero."

The prosecution alleged that 15 shots were fired from the .22-caliber magnum pistol that Hale had tossed in the shrubbery just before he was captured.

"This man is guilty of first-degree murder," the prosecutor told the court. "These acts are not the product of a chaotic mind. They were the acts of a cold-blooded killer."

She said Hale was thinking clearly when he disconnected the video player before fleeing in Ronald Holliday's pickup truck. And, he was thinking clearly when he changed his bloody clothes at a relative's house and abandoned the truck near the Santa Ana riverbed. Hale was also thinking clearly, Prosecutor Tuszynska said, when he tried to cover up his tracks so the hounds couldn't pick up his scent.

"And when he tossed away the gun, he was clearly thinking," Tuszynska remarked, staring straight at the defendant, who sat with his head bowed slightly.

A psychologist testifying for the prosecution said that someone suffering from drug-induced impairment would recall either all or none of the events of the killings, not just selected portions as Hale had.

The witness said he had investigated 400 homicides in which speed was involved. Killers on the drug usually used force far beyond what was actually needed to kill, he testified.

The defense argued that the murders were not premeditated, and therefore were second-degree murders. These findings would not only spare Hale from the death sentence, which the prosecution was not seeking, but would also spare the killer from a sentence of life in prison without parole.

After a six-week trial, the panel returned with a first-degree guilty verdict. On May 25, 1989, Riverside Superior Court Judge Patrick F. Magers sentenced Brett Hale to the maximum: three separate 25-years-to-life terms, a life term, an additional five years and, finally, a life term without parole.

Hale took his punishment without showing any emotion. As he was being led from the courtroom in shackles, a relative of David Kelley's elbowed her way to him and calmly asked: "I just wonder why, Brett? Why did you have to kill?"

The prisoner stared at her blankly. He never answered. He was quickly led away to solitude, where man is least alone.

EDITOR'S NOTE
*Carrie and Pete Zona and Nancy Brown are not the real names of the persons so named in the foregoing story. Fictitious names have been used because there is no reason for public interest in the identities of these persons.*

# "JUNKYARD KILLER'S SHOTGUN SPREE!"

## by Catherine Henderson

When Michael Schilling drifted into West Virginia, he was AWOL from the army base at Fort Benning, Georgia. He told relatives that as a Special Forces soldier, he was afraid that one day he might be forced to kill someone.

Schilling hoped to enroll in a computer training course at the Charleston Jobs Corps. Although that never panned out and his stay right outside the city limits of St. Albans, about 15 miles west of the capital city, lasted only two months, Schilling did meet 19-year-old Bonnie Sanson Pauley.

From the Charleston program, Schilling transferred to a Job Corps program in Maryland, where he decided that nursing was a better career. But he missed Bonnie. In January 1988, Schilling returned to West Virginia and moved in with Bonnie and her family. Nearly a year had passed since he had first come to the Mountain State.

Schilling wrote and called his relatives down south frequently. He said he planned to marry Bonnie and take her to North Carolina.

Meanwhile, Schilling stayed with Bonnie and her clan as a member of an extended family living together in what would become known as the infamous Compound. Their two rundown mobile homes and a dilapidated camping trailer huddled together as if each needed to lean on the other in order to continue standing.

Landfill would be a more accurate description of the area surrounding the trailers. To say it was a yard would suggest far more civilization than was apparent anywhere among the piles of bottles, tin cans, useless appliances, broken toys, clothes, and debris of almost every type imaginable. Starving dogs were chained and tied across the expanse of plowed-up mud. Abuse and neglect had honed Caesar, an irascible mutt with a good dose of rotweiler in him, into a formidable guard dog.

Less than a quarter of a mile away was an abandoned junkyard that for years had been the focus of public ire. The city had no authority to make the owners either clean it up or close it down. Just several yards outside the St. Albans' line, it came under county jurisdiction and, for numerous reasons, the five-mile strip between the two towns of St. Albans and South Charleston was largely ignored. The brutal murders of a mother and her two children there prompted locals to call the stretch Murderers' Row, usurping its previous title, Badlands.

Eventually, state regulations required the eyesore to be fenced in and hidden from public sight. But hemmed in by the railroad from behind and the busy four-lane in front, space was at a premium. Before long, carcasses of cars were piled on top of other cars. It was a vertical system of storage, and a precarious one at that. There were more community complaints. Cars were towering above the fence. Eventually the junkyard was deserted, at least to the daylight observer.

Like everywhere else along this strip, night activity in the junkyard picked up considerably. Skittering rats and vicious, glinty-eyed possums were frequent visitors.

So were Michael Schilling, Billy and Otis Sanson, Bonnie Pauley's brothers who lived in the Compound, and Mark McCallister, who had moved in about five years earlier when he and Bonnie were junior high school sweethearts. When their romance had ended, McCallister stayed on, taking up with a relative of Bonnie's who neighbors say talked about marrying McCallister.

The human beings foraged in the junkyard for copper. Since nobody came around anymore and nobody seemed to care who did, the brothers and their helpers could work at their leisure — strip as many cars as had something to offer, then resell what they managed to appropriate. It was illegal, but then so were a lot of other goings-on around the junkyard. The job was dangerous, but the pickings were easy. Moreover, they didn't need many tools, just some pliers, and they brought a nice, red-handled pair with them.

Arguments were routine and fights frequent, often over Mark McCallister's sexual liaison with Billy and Otis' relative, who was old enough to be his mother. Billy Sanson just flat out didn't like Mark. One neighbor would recall that Billy would order Mark to move out; then, just when Mark had gathered up all his clothes, Billy would say he was only kidding. Although only 5 feet 8 inches tall and 155 pounds himself, Billy still towered above the frail, small McCallister. Billy said himself that one time he had blacked both of McCallister's eyes. Whatever the reason, Mark McCallister always got the worst end of every fracas.

By February 1988, Michael Schilling's communication with his family stopped. They wrote letter after frantic letter, even addressing the last several "To Whom It May Concern." No response was elicited. It was October, and still there was no word from Michael. His family filed a missing-person report with the Kanawha County Sheriff's Department and with the West Virginia State Police. Schilling had been missing almost a year, they said.

Bonnie Pauley was also concerned about Michael's disappearance, but she got on with her life. She met 22-year-old Jimmy Price, who lived nearby. Neighbors described him as good-hearted: "He'd do anything to help you." Jimmy and Bonnie began dating just a few months after Michael Schilling disappeared. As soon as Jimmy could find a job, he and Bonnie planned to get married. Until then, he needed money. So he took up where Schilling left off—accompanying the Sanson brothers and Mark McCallister on their nocturnal raids in the junkyard.

Hardly seven months had passed since Michael Schilling's disappearance, when Jimmy Price suddenly turned up missing, too. On November 5, 1989, Bonnie Pauley left the trailer, telling friends that she was going to find out what had happened to Jimmy.

The Compound seemed to attract transients, temporary lovers, and live-ins who cemented casual acquaintances into camaraderie with liberal doses of alcohol and marijuana. Visitors stopped for a few days, stayed a while longer, and then drifted off. Their relatives might have been concerned when they lost contact, but that was hardly cause for suspicion.

Two missing persons, however, weren't the switch that finally threw the spotlight on the Compound. A relative, tired of seeing animals abused, sick, and dying, called the Kanawha-Charleston Animal Shelter and reported what was happening.

Shelter officials investigated the matter. The director found sick dogs, all covered with parasites, all with no water or shelter. Most of the dogs were starving. The director issued a warning: the group had two weeks to clean up their act or else.

Two weeks later, the director returned. Nothing had been done. A month passed and still there was no change. Each time she came, she was told that they were waiting for their welfare checks. "Besides," bristled Mark McCallister, "we have other bills to pay." Bonnie Pauley chimed in her agreement.

The "family" certainly wasn't starving, but living conditions inside the trailers weren't much better than those the animals had to endure outside. Even Billy Sanson found the place disgusting. People said he wasn't like the others. He had ambition. He had even recently held a decent job. Much of his time he spent away from the Compound. The constant bickering and squabbling drove him crazy.

Now Billy began to clean up the place, picking up trash, even putting down new carpet. He and Mark started building a room onto one trailer.

On November 10th, the animal shelter director returned with Corporal Akers of the Kanawha County Sheriff's Department. Akers had warrants for the arrests of Billy and Otis Sanson, Mark McCallister, and Bonnie Sanson Pauley. Bonnie was nowhere to be found, however. Relatives at the trailer who had continued to cash her welfare check said she had Jimmy Price had moved to Texas.

The animal shelter director removed from the camping trailer 16 dogs, two cats, an aquarium filled with goldfish, a white rat, a rabbit, a land turtle, a water turtle, a dead mockingbird in a cage, a dead kitten, and a dead puppy. As many dogs were left as were taken. Those that remained seemed to be in better shape. An animal cruelty hearing was scheduled.

Two months passed and the Compound seemed to have quieted down. On Saturday night, January 7th, Billy and Otis Sanson decided to go clubbing at one of the strip joints that lined the highway less than half a mile up the road. The brothers were leaving about midnight when they ran into a friend. "They asked me to go next door [to another strip club] and drink a beer," the friend would later recall. But he told the brothers he didn't feel like drinking and went on home.

That same night, the manager of another club reported that Mark McCallister had come in about nine or ten o'clock looking for Billy Sanson.

Finally, the brothers called it a night and Otis Sanson went back to the camping trailer to read the Bible. Those who knew Otis said that he talked scriptures a lot but didn't take it very seriously.

Around 2:00 a.m., a relative saw McCallister helping Billy unload his van. The pair had a new stash of hubcaps. Shortly afterward, McCallister joined Otis in the camping trailer.

Four days later, on Tuesday, January 10, 1989, a phone call to 911 put the animal cruelty case on a remote back burner. Metro logged the message at 3:25 p.m. The voice on the other end was hysterical. Billy Sanson had been murdered. The caller was a relative of Sanson's who claimed to know.

It was almost quitting time, so Corporal J.W. Johnson, chief of detectives of the Kanawha County Sheriff's Department, sent a detective who lived in that direction. Not knowing any details, Johnson told him, "Back up road patrol and see what they've got."

Road deputies who had already arrived on the scene radioed back to Corporal Johnson that there was a lot of blood inside one of the main mobile homes. By this time, Johnson and Detectives R.J. Flint and R.L. West were already on their way to the scene.

St. Albans police directed traffic and held back the constantly growing crowd. The family was sequestered in one of the trailers.

Although the deputies' first report had described blood in the mobile home, it was the camper that attracted their attention. An electrical cord connected it to the main trailer, so obviously someone was using it. Then why, the investigators wanted to know, was the door not only locked but also nailed shut? It didn't take much force on the flimsy door to pop it open. Deputies knew immediately what they had. "The stench of death was overwhelming," Detective West later commented.

In the middle of the floor was a pile of debris, mostly couch cushions from the roll-out bed. The smell was coming from underneath.

Corporal Johnson, ready with the camera, snapped a shot of the whole scene, removed one cushion, and snapped another photograph. He lifted up the second cushion and out popped a human hand. "We got something here," he called to Detective Flint, who was outside the door.

Systematically, Johnson removed the rest of the cushions. It was Billy Sanson, apparently dead several days and still dressed in his party clothes, which consisted of a leather jacket, sweater, and green sweat shirt. His gray sweatpants and white undershorts had been pulled down to his ankles. Blood from a gaping hole in the back of his head matted his longish brown hair. A shotgun blast had fractured his skull in numerous places, fractured the bones in his face, and had partially destroyed his eyeballs.

Billy Sanson was pronounced dead at 3:45 p.m., less than 20 minutes after the 911 call had come in. The caller had also reported one more thing: Mark McCallister was the one who'd done the shooting.

With the crime scene secured and the body transported to the medical examiner's office for autopsy, all deputies and backup from the state police, St. Albans PD, and Charleston PD spread out searching for Mark McCallister, who was on the run, but with nowhere to go.

Overhead, the whirling blades of a state police helicopter fanned the area. Apparently, McCallister was heading south, behind the Compound near the railroad tracks, to a small patch of woods. He then moved west along the tracks, where he stopped at an auto body shop and spray-painted his bright red hair black. So much for a disguise.

Witnesses reported seeing McCallister moving toward the strip joints. It was 6:30 p.m., already dark in the short daylight of January, as Corporal J.W. Akers, Deputy D.A. Brick, Sergeant R.W. Long, and Corporal D.W. Jenkins with his dog Shadow from the Charleston PD cruised along Route 60.

There, in the parking lot of one of the clubs, stood Mark McCallister. Deputy D.A. Brick swung the cruiser in as Corporal Akers and Sergeant Long jumped out and grabbed McCallister. A screwdriver was protruding from his pocket. McCallister made a desperate grab for it. The dog Shadow snarled a convincing warning as Corporal Akers disarmed McCallister. "Before he knew what was happening, we had him up against the car, patted down, cuffed, and on his way to headquarters," Corporal Akers would later say.

Detective Flint remained at the crime scene to finish sketches while Detective West and Corporal Johnson returned to take a statement from the suspect. Corporal Akers sat in.

Mark McCallister had been advised of his right to remain silent, but Johnson wanted to be sure he comprehended. To Corporal Johnson's questions, "Do you understand what you are under arrest for?", McCallister replied, "First-degree murder."

Sleuths learned that Mark Southern McCallister, born August 6, 1969, had barely reached the eighth grade when he dropped out of school. His school record was troubled and even contained a psychiatric evaluation. At best, McCallister was limited and barely literate. Corporal Johnson frequently simplified his already carefully phrased questions.

"Now something happened there at the house—somebody was shot—right?" asked Johnson.

"Yeah," responded McCallister.

"Who was shot?"

"Billy Sanson and Jerry Sanson."

Lawmen Johnson, Akers, and West exchanged looks. There were two people shot? Until this point, Johnson had been talking about only Billy Sanson, who was the reported victim, and Johnson had not yet mentioned where the body had been found. Now Johnson mentioned the camper. McCallister looked puzzled. Corporal Johnson tried again.

"Mark, why did you put Billy in the camper?"

McCallister shook his head. "I didn't put Billy in the camper," he said.

"Well, who the hell is in the camper? We found a body in the camper," Johnson said impatiently.

"Oh," McCallister said helpfully. "That's Jerry." Apparently, McCallister sometimes called Otis Sanson by his middle name, Jerry.

"Then where's Billy?" asked Corporal Akers.

McCallister had a sudden lapse of memory. "I don't know," he replied.

"That's bull," challenged Akers.

"All right, all right, all right! I killed both of them," the suspect admitted.

"Then where's Billy?"

"He's in the box."

While Johnson and Akers continued to question Mark McCallister, Detective West once again rounded up a team of officers and headed back to the crime scene. Johnson radioed Detective Flint. "We got another one. Look near a chicken coop," he told Flint.

Following McCallister's directions, the sleuths headed to the back of the Compound to search an abandoned pen that had once contained dogs, chickens, and any number of things. According to McCallister, "Nobody went back there anymore." Dragged up alongside the pen and back under an overhang from the adjacent shed was a large cardboard box, much like one that a refrigerator would be packed in. The box had been sealed shut with duct tape.

Deputies ripped open an end. They found the real Billy Sanson wrapped in a blanket decorated with a blue and gold liberty bell. Sanson was wearing a dark brown M*A*S*H T-shirt, and, as had been with his brother Otis, his clean blue undershorts had been pulled down to his ankles.

Apparently, Billy had been hit full force in the face with a shotgun blast from a distance of no more than three feet. At 9:00 p.m., Billy Sanson was pronounced dead and transported to the M.E.'s office. Inside the mobile home, police seized a 16-gauge Winchester shotgun covered with rust.

In the meantime, Mark McCallister freely continued to relate his story. About 2:00 a.m., Sunday, he said, he and Otis had been playing around with the shotgun, when it accidentally went off. "Otis just happened to be standing in front of it," McCallister said.

"So you shot him in the back of the head?" one of the investigators asked.

Apparently the discrepancy eluded McCallister. "Yeah," he muttered.

Seeing what he'd done, McCallister panicked. "When I get scared, I do stupid things," McCallister said. He said he tried to drag Otis Sanson out the door, intending to put the body out back in the shed. "That's how his pants got down," McCallister felt compelled to add. The shotgun had belonged to Otis, who stored it in the camper. According to McCallister, they had planned to go hunting or shooting rats. After shooting Otis, McCallister went to the main trailer. He knew if Billy found out what he'd just done, "Billy would beat me and call the law. I thought he would kill me." So McCallister reloaded his shotgun and stepped inside the door.

Billy, who was asleep, rose up. "What the hell is going on?" he demanded. It was the last time Billy would intimidate little Mark.

McCallister swung the muzzle directly into Billy's face and blasted away. It was approximately 3:00 a.m., and the shotgun blast reverberated throughout the trailer. McCallister's lover got up, peered in, cried a little, and, according to McCallister, never looked into the room again.

At 200 pounds, Otis Sanson had been nearly impossible for the diminutive Mark McCallister to budge, much less drag, and Billy, although considerably lighter, was still a load. Nonetheless, McCallister dragged him out onto the porch, but he saw that dawn was just at the horizon. So "I drug him back in and went to sleep out there."

Hours later, McCallister's lover found him curled up on the porch, at which point he aimed the gun at her and warned her that if she ever told anybody, he would hurt her, too. In the meantime, he tied her up with electrical cord. "Keep quiet," he ordered, waving the gun at her.

Then he left.

Although bound and threatened, the "victim" was outside walking around, neighbors later reported. For the next two days, Billy Sanson lay undisturbed in the bedroom, blood all around him.

Eventually, McCallister returned to the trailer. On Tuesday at about 3:00 a.m., two full days since the shooting, he dragged Billy, already boxed, to the back of the lot.

Since hearing the shotgun blasts, relatives in the other trailer had been watching out the windows. McCallister felt certain no one would know what was in the container. By that afternoon, the observers were certain that they knew what had happened. It was their call that had brought the deputies to the scene.

Mark McCallister, charged with the murders of Otis and Billy Sanson, acquired two court-appointed attorneys. Although his confession helped the state's case, overwhelming evidence seemed to indicate that the trial would be speedily concluded — or so everyone thought.

In the meantime, McCallister's grandmother, 64-year-old Charlotte Ruby Ferrell, who lived near the Compound, hadn't been seen for several days. Her family was concerned and asked the deputies to investigate.

Corporal Akers, who had been specifically requested by the Criminal Investigation Unit for just this case and was still available, took the call. Investigators collecting evidence from the crime scene had called it a day when Akers and Sergeant Sherri Lanham arrived at the Ferrell house. It was Thursday night, January 12th.

Upon finding the front door locked, the relatives had peered in through the windows. They could see that the place had been ransacked; drawers were pulled out and their contents dumped on the floor. Akers tried a window. It was stuck tight. A screwdriver on the hasp of the door, however, worked just fine.

Akers and Lanham forced the door. As they entered, they noticed that the house reeked of the musty smell that accompanies dampness. A heaviness in the air, more like dread and sorrow, seemed to add to the already stale interior.

Corporal Akers noted the sheets and blankets heaped up on the bed. "I just knew she was under there," he later said. When a routine search of the rest of the house produced nothing, the sleuths returned to the bedroom. Turning back one cover at a time, they gingerly lifted the bedclothes. That's when Akers found a foot.

Charlotte Ferrell had been shot in the right side of her head. A gaping wound testified that a shotgun had been held just inches away from her. Still wearing a white cardigan sweater and a tank top, Ferrell's body was nude from the waist down. She had been wrapped in blankets, sheets, and curtains. Apparently, the dampness inside, combined with the swaddling effect of the bedclothes, had caused the body to mildew. "This was the first time I ever saw a body do that," Corporal Johnson commented later on.

Charlotte Ruby Ferrell, who had often taken her grandson to buy clothes and frequently picked him up from school, was pronounced dead at 9:08 p.m. The medical examiner estimated that she had been murdered on January 6th and thus had been dead for six days.

Deputies soon learned that McCallister and Billy Sanson had cashed Ferrell's Social Security check at a local bank. Billy Sanson's fingerprints were found throughout the Ferrell house. Missing items from the scene such as a coffee pot, toaster, portable television, and even towels were recovered at the trailer where Mark McCallister was staying.

McCallister and Billy had apparently found just a few dollars in cash. The Ferrell's cache of money, which they knew was there somewhere, had been overlooked. The sleuths found it slipped between the mattress and box springs in a red-zippered pouch. It contained nearly $1,300. Apparently, Charlotte Ruby Ferrell had died concealing what was probably the sum total of her life savings.

Even the seasoned deputies found this murder particularly troublesome. "I was an undertaker's apprentice for years," Corporal Akers later remarked, "but the senseless and brutality of this old woman's death haunted me."

Sheriff Art Ashley felt this was his low point. "To see this poor old innocent lady, who was not going to cause anybody any harm, have a gun put right to her head and her brains blown out, was beyond belief. They didn't have to kill her—they didn't even have to hurt her! She was harmless."

Since Mark McCallister had confessed to murdering the Sanson brothers and had now received counsel, he was saying nothing. Deputies had believed that the Sansons were his only two victims. Charlotte Ferrell's death had come as a complete surprise, but it gave new meaning to the three people still missing. Perhaps they hadn't left the Compound after all.

Corporal Akers was assigned to try to locate Bonnie Pauley, Michael Schilling and Jimmy Price and to track down every possible place they might have gone or any relative they might have visited. All efforts seemed to point to the fact that the threesome had simply vanished.

Deputies obtained a search warrant for the entire Compound. They also notified the animal shelter director to return to the scene and pick up the remaining dogs, who were guarding their meager existence with all the ferocity they had had beaten into them.

Backhoes, shovels, sledgehammers, and a team of deputies began a grid search, turning up the entire area. Personnel from the medical examiner's office, firemen, and paramedics all stood ready. The plowed-up ground yielded at least 100 skeletons and carcasses of dogs—even one of a horse—but no human remains.

Then, the police received an important tip. Apparently, Mark McCallister had been seen "fooling around" across the highway at an old abandoned motel.

Twenty years earlier, the establishment was notorious

for its by-the-hour rates. It was a rough, seedy, and mysterious place. Teenagers whispered about it, and some of the finer gentlemen from near as well as far didn't want to see it closed down. The cabins followed the slope nearly to the river, and a parking lot dropped down in back to conceal the cars. Eventually, business slacked off when clients and workers discovered that society was changing. Such goings-on didn't have to be negotiated in quite so much secrecy or in nearly as much squalor.

For years, the place sat abandoned, falling in on itself. But the rooms, or what was left of them, literally overflowed with lavatories, toilets, pinball machines, bottles, and clothing. Detective Flint entered one room and found clothing piled to the top of his head. "There could've been bodies everywhere and we would've missed them. It was a trash pit," he later reported.

Divers were sent into the water behind the motel to search the bottom of the Kanawha River and the surrounding banks. They came up with nothing.

It was time for assistance from another type of expert. From Rockville, Maryland, a woman and her female German shepherd PC of Mid-Atlantic DOGS (Dogs Organized for Ground Search) were flown in. Six-year-old PC started sniffing through the old motel. Wherever she hit, searchers dug. Scents of humans were everywhere. Trained to sniff out the odor of any decomposing human corpse — as opposed to a tracking or trailing dog, which follows the scent of a specific missing person — PC knew precisely what she was searching for.

Because the motel sat on an incline, the front appeared to be only one story, but a basement provided a bottom entrance, or more correctly, an exit. A flight of concrete stairs led down into the winding, twisting labyrinth of rooms, an eerie shell of misery and ruin. "Every time I kicked in a door, I expected a body to fall right down on my head," Corporal Johnson said later.

In front of the steps was a discarded wooden pallet from some type of heavy-duty packaging, which Corporal Akers stood on to push in the basement door. PC had hit on this exact spot during her first trip through the rooms, and now, after half a day's work, she returned to the pallet. The dog's discriminating nose told her—this was it!

Corporal Akers lifted the pallet. Underneath was a sheet of plywood. He hauled it aside. Beneath that was a rolled-up blanket with something inside that looked like garbage tied up in a trash bag, the same type of bag that the lawmen had found with other bodies. As Akers opened the sack, the stench hit him in the face. He hollered his discovery.

By the time Corporal Johnson, who was about 50 feet away, had picked up his radio, he got a whiff. "Get somebody over here, we've found it," he said.

Detective Flint had remained in the Sanson-Ferrell Compound. Now he came charging across the four-lane, deputies and medical assistants hot on his heels. Searchers grabbed for masks and a quick smear of menthol salve under their noses. The stench indicated they had finally found Bonnie Pauley.

She was clothed in a lacy white blouse and white bra. The rest of her nude body was wrapped in a blue and red bedspread. Bonnie had been beaten, her right jaw had been broken, and her face and scalp showed greenish-black discoloration. Perhaps she had been raped, but it had been too long to tell. Apparently, a blunt-force injury to the face had been her first trauma, followed by a shotgun blast to the back of her head. From the condition of Bonnie's partly mummified body, the M.E. determined that she had been dead about two to three months.

By now, visual identification was impossible, but relatives agreed that the two red hearts with "KS" and "Tammy" on her right arm and "Love" on the left arm with "Rock and Roll" down below it were Bonnie's tattoos. Like the previous victims, except for Charlotte Ferrell, Bonnie had marijuana in her system. She may have been shot where she lay, or she might have been moved.

At 99 pounds, Bonnie Sanson Pauley wouldn't have been all that heavy.

Deputies now turned their attention to the junkyard. Two months earlier, Corporal Akers had worked a burglary near this same area and had found a library card with Michael Schilling's name on it. "At the time, I didn't think much about it," Akers recalled later, "but now I just had a bad feeling about that junkyard." PC and her owner were brought back from Maryland.

Sheriff Art Ashley, only 10 days into his newly elected position when the Sanson brothers were murdered, was determined "to search every square inch of the three acres and every one of the eight hundred cars."

"Again," Corporal Johnson later recalled, "people were telling us things." One witness related an incident that had happened back in May. Mark McCallister and Otis Sanson had gone into the junkyard with Michael Schilling, but McCallister came back by himself. According to the witness, when McCallister returned to the trailer, he ran in, took a shower, and changed clothes. After a while Otis came back and seemed to be upset about something, although the witness never found out what it was. This was the last time the witness ever saw Michael Schilling alive.

Accompanied by PC, deputies began popping car trunks and opening cars with jimmies and power tools. "We opened everything in there, but couldn't find a thing," said Johnson.

Rumors were flying. Lawmen were told to look in the blue car, this car, that car. By now, the searchers had been digging and sifting through the incredibly foul debris for nearly 20 days. They were cold, exhausted, and skeptical, but clamp-jaw determined.

Suddenly, in the dark, PC hit on a Cadillac. Detective Flint pried open the trunk. When the seal cracked, "the smell came flying out." there, somewhat mummified, were the remains of Jimmy Price, clothed in a blue nylon parka with a West Virginia emblem and a white shirt that prophetically read, "Tell Them I Am Surfin'." His blue jeans had tears around the hips and legs, possibly from animal bites.

Price, too, had been hit in the back of the head with a shotgun blast. Some of the wadding with pellets had exited through his left eye, and the force had fractured his skull in numerous places.

Like Bonnie Pauley, Jimmy Price was beyond visual identification. But his relatives knew that the Viking head with a hatchet and sword on the right arm and the hooded robe with a devil's pitchfork on the left arm were his tattoos. James E. Price Jr. was declared dead at 9:48 p.m. on January 30th. According to the M.E., he had been dead since October. He, too, tested positive for marijuana in his system.

Although sleuths now knew that they would find one more body, they called it a day. "Each time we found a body, we called it quits for the day. Everyone was totally worn out and the tension was enormous," Corporal Johnson later said.

Prisoners from the jail began phoning Sheriff Ashley. They had something he might like to know. Apparently, Mark McCallister had become quite a celebrity and had regaled his fellow inmates with all the particulars and stories only he knew. Although characterized by some as limited, McCallister could remember each spot where he'd stashed the bodies.

"Check the blue car that is on top of some others. There should be gas tanks laying around," the prisoners reported to Ashley.

PC leaped and scrambled up stacks of cars, many as high as four decks, with Corporal Akers right behind. The cars rocked and swayed dangerously, shifting first this way, then that. Footing was wherever they could find it on the slippery metal.

PC had it. It was a car several over from where the prison informants had directed. Michael Schilling lay in the front passenger seat of a once classy Thunderbird, gas tanks piled on top of him to hide the body. Beside him lay a pair of red-handled pliers.

Blue jeans, white socks and tennis shoes, and a black short-sleeve sport shirt held together the skeleton, all that remained of Michael Schilling. Only dental records could identify him. Like the other victims, he'd died from a shotgun blast. Michael Schilling was pronounced dead at 3:45 p.m. on January 31st, cause of death—multiple wounds to the head. The M.E. estimated that he had been killed on June 7, 1988.

Mark Southern McCallister, now 21, was charged with six counts of first-degree murder. He pleaded guilty to two counts—the deaths of the Sanson brothers—and was sentenced to two consecutive life sentences without parole on December 20, 1990.

McCallister wasn't through yet, however. He requested that Kanawha Circuit Judge Andrew MacQueen reconsider the sentence and grant him mercy because of his young age and limited education.

MacQueen replied, "This case was and is an extremely perplexing one because of the many mysteries that remain unsolved. McCallister admitted to two of the killings, but denied being involved in the other four."

Did McCallister have help? How did he, at only 5 feet 4 inches tall and 130 pounds, manage to lift Michael Schilling's body to a hiding place that was at least eight feet off the ground?

At the time of his arrest, McCallister was carrying a piece of identification from each of the six victims. "We didn't think much about it at the time, but when we found all the bodies, it became different," said Corporal Akers.

"I am thoroughly convinced that Mark McCallister had a hand in killing all those people," said Sheriff Ashley. "But I am also thoroughly convinced that he did not do it by himself."

Mark McCallister is currently serving his life sentence at the West Virginia State Prison in Moundsville. Although the files of Charlotte Ruby Ferrell, Bonnie Sanson Pauley, Michael Schilling, and James Price are still officially open, they are a part of the only serial murder case in the history of West Virginia.

# "FREAKED-OUT TRUCKER SLAUGHTERED 4!"

by Bud Ampolsk

As the recent presidential campaign switched into high gear, the issue of "family values" came to the fore, and with it, the attendant matter of child care. After Vice President Dan Quayle fired his salvo at the CBS television sitcom *Murphy Brown*, decrying what he perceived as the glorification of unwed motherhood and chastising Hollywood's TV and film industry for contributing to the decline of the American family, Arkansas Governor Bill Clinton also took up the family-values theme in his acceptance speech for the Democratic presidential nomination at his party's convention.

One of the points made by Governor Clinton was that if he was elected to the nation's highest office, his administration would sock it to deadbeat fathers who welshed on their responsibility to support their children. "Take responsibility for your children," he warned, "or we will force you to do so." His stress on the words *responsibility* and *force* suggested that harsh federal penalties would be sought for those fathers who skip out on their child-support obligations.

Meeting child-support payments can, of course, be a sore point for those who may feel they are being unfairly saddled with responsibility, or others who are having a tough time making ends meet. Sometimes, when hard-pressed by the authorities to make their payments, some of these fathers can become downright belligerent, even violent toward social workers who are assigned to carry out the requirements of the law.

In this instance, in mid-October of 1992, violence turned into multiple murder in the small town of Watkins Glen, situated in the Finger Lakes region of northwestern New York State.

The seat of Schuyler County, Watkins Glen sits at the southern end of Lake Seneca in a picturesque area which, in October, attracts large numbers of weekend tourists who come to take in the beauty of the fall foliage and the pristine landscape. The residents of Schuyler County, aware of the closely contested baseball League Championship Series and the coming World Series face-off between the Atlanta Braves and the Toronto Blue Jays, anticipated a steady flow of winter hot-stove visitors to the Baseball Hall of Fame at nearby Cooperstown. This expectation, coupled with an early drop in temperatures that gave promise of a favorable ski season, foretold continuing chimes of cash registers ringing happily away.

The general upbeat mood of the region was reflected by those who worked in the compact county seat facilities located in Watkins Glen, a tiny town with a year-round population of 2,200. Most of the county offices are housed in a small red-brick building next to the Schuyler County Courthouse on the town's main thoroughfare.

Until now, security had never presented any problem for officials. There was an easy come-and-go attitude. No armed guards kept vigil in the hallways. No ominous metal detectors commanded the entrances.

Of those who had business with county employees, no one had ever caused trouble in the past. There was never any reason to anticipate that anything would shatter their efficiently quiet routines. The mere fact that the building also housed the Schuyler County Sheriff's Office and other administrative units was enough to maintain a friendly and businesslike climate throughout the working day.

Even when disagreements occurred, they were usually defused quickly by an understanding and neighborly staff. County employees prided themselves on not being overbearing and impersonal bureaucrats. More often then not, a smile and a kind word provided the solution to almost any situation.

Such was the approach of 60-year-old Florence A. Pike, the supervisor of the Schuyler County Support Collection Unit. A woman with a ready sense of humor, she had a reputation for being unflappable in the face of irate or unruly visitors.

On Wednesday, October 14, 1992, a small flare-up took place. Pike later told a relative of hers that during the day, a heavyset middle-aged man came to the office to discuss a child-support delinquency situation with her. Declaring that he could not pay the amount in question, the man said that if the county persisted in forcing him to come up with the arrears, he would kill himself. The relative later told an acquaintance that Pike had not taken the threat seriously.

At about ten o'clock that Thursday morning, October 15th, Florence Pike was in her office on the second floor of the county building. Also there were 48-year-old Nancy J. Wheeler, a senior account clerk, and 28-year-old Denise M. Van Amburg, a part-time clerk. In another office across the hall was 54-year-old Phyllis Caslin, an investigator for the support group.

No one knows whether the four social workers were aware of the beefy man carrying a duffle bag and briefcase as he climbed the stairs toward the offices. Obviously, there was nothing about him that aroused the suspicions of anybody else who might have passed him on the street or in the hallways of the county building.

Suddenly, the peace was shattered by the staccato, rapid bark of semiautomatic small-arms fire coming from the second floor.

In a flash, Schuyler County sheriff's officers were on their feet and racing towards the sounds of gunfire. Their first move was to evacuate other workers who might become targets for the unknown shooter. As the employees fled the building, Deputy Sheriff Alfred J. Foote led his fellow officers to the second floor. There, the lawmen came across a shocking sight. Four women—three in one office, the other in the office across the hall—lay dead. All had been cut down by a hail of slugs.

While some of the sheriff's officers remained with the victims, Foote and the others began a search of the surrounding corridors, hoping to flush out the unidentified shooter. Tension etched the faces of the searchers—they had no way of telling what had set off the killer's rampage and what he might do if he was cornered.

When the lawmen actually came upon the gunman, he was standing in a corridor, gun in hand. He was not pointing the weapon at any of the advancing officers, however. The gunman was holding it against his own head.

Deputy Sheriff Foote recalled the harrowing 10 minutes that followed: "We had a conversation. We asked him his name and he told us. [The man identified himself as 50-year-old John T. Miller of North Ridgeville, Ohio.]

"We asked him if we could get him some help." Foote continued, "and he said, 'No, nobody can help me now.'"

At this point, Miller was very calm. The deputy sheriff later described him as having been even somewhat cooperative. Miller assured the lawman that "he had hurt everyone he wanted to hurt." In fact, the gunman was quite solicitous about the other county workers who had been thrown into a state of near hysteria by the cold-blooded executions carried out scant minutes earlier.

Miller told Deputy Sheriff Foote not to worry about evacuating any other office employees. "He told us people didn't have to hurry, they could take their time, that he had done what he came to do."

Foote noted that the only time the slayer showed any rage was when he spoke of the child-support payments sought by the county social workers. "He said the people here ruined his life, that he couldn't get a job, or a wife, because he owed so much money," the deputy sheriff later reported.

Then, as Foote and another deputy looked on, Miller carefully put down an envelope which he said contained a letter that would explain what he'd done. Then he walked around once in a tight circle. As the officers watched in shaken disbelief, there was one last sudden burst of gunfire as Miller shot himself.

An ambulance was immediately called and the mortally wounded Miller was rushed the three miles to Schuyler Hospital, where he was pronounced dead at 10:41 a.m.

At this point, the deputy sheriff did not disclose the contents of the handwritten note. He did say that it did not mention Miller's plan to shoot the four women.

With the blood toll standing at five, the unnerved lawmen soon became aware that as terrible as the massacre had actually been, it might have been worse. Their search of one of the bags Miller had been carrying revealed that it was filled with ammunition.

What remained now was the mystery of who John T. Miller was, and what had led up to the mass killings.

Schuyler County Sheriff Michael J. Maloney began sifting through piles of court and social department records to piece together the terrible saga of a trucker-turned-mass murderer.

What the sheriff learned was that Miller was the man who had visited the Schuyler County Social Services Department the previous day, on October 14th, and had warned Florence Pike that he intended to kill himself.

Maloney's investigation suggested that despite the apparent wantonness in the slayings of the four women, Miller had been highly selective in picking his targets. The killer had encountered another county worker in the hallway, but he'd told her to leave the area without trying to harm her.

The sheriff also noted that after the killer had shot his victims, he had been confronted by two deputies outside the social workers' offices. Miller had attempted to leave by a stairway, but he'd found it blocked off by a state trooper and a Watkins Glen police officer.

Information about the actions and attitudes of the dead gunman during the last days of his life began trickling in from locales in Ohio, as well as Watkins Glen.

A friend and co-worker of his reported that the last time he saw Miller had been on Monday, October 12th. "He came in that morning about seven-thirty a.m., and was a little upset because they had garnisheed his wages on Friday," the friend said. "As far as I know, it was the first time they had done it. He told us it was for child support and that the child wasn't his."

A company official reported that Miller earned from $500 to $700 a week and had been employed by the firm since August 23, 1988.

Miller's domestic troubles had begun following a liaison in 1966 with a 19-year-old Schuyler County part-time babysitter who worked for one of his relatives. In October of that year, she realized that she had become pregnant.

The woman confronted Miller, telling him that she didn't want to bear the child. "I was drunk and crying," she later said about the episode. "He was scared and he said, 'Don't hurt yourself, and don't hurt that child.'" Despite those noble sentiments expressed by Miller, the woman said, he refused to take any financial responsibility for the child.

The woman sued Miller in family court to get help with her hospital bills. In late 1966, Schuyler County

Judge Liston Coon ruled that Miller was the father and ordered him to pay $20 a week in child support.

Miller made one payment and then fled from his Schuyler County residence to Wichita, Kansas. A New York State warrant was issued for his arrest.

Meanwhile, the county officials were not about to let a newborn child suffer. When the baby girl was born on April 14, 1967, the county began issuing food stamps and rent-supplement payments to the mother. About four years later, the welfare authorities placed the child with a foster family. The state continued making welfare payments to the foster family; thus, it was to the county that Miller owed the back child-care support.

Sheriff Maloney well recalled Miller's first arrest in Schuyler County in December 1970. At that time, the sheriff apprehended Miller on the outstanding warrant in Miller's former home in Montour Falls, a town near Watkins Glen, while the fugitive was there on a trip from Wichita.

In commenting on the arrest, Maloney said about Miller, "He was arrogant. I remember it twenty-three years later."

The sheriff noted that Miller had stubbornly refused to make the child-support payments. As a result, he served a six-month term in the county jail.

The scenario was repeated in August 1976. Once again, Miller had traveled from Wichita to Montour Falls on a visit. For a second time he was arrested and he spent six months in jail rather than settle his debt.

After the 1976 jailing, Miller's rap sheet showed two subsequent arrests in 1978 and 1980. Miller served no prison time in the county jail on those arrests, however.

There was no evidence that poverty was the motivating factor in Miller's refusal to comply with the child-support ruling. A relative of his noted that during the 1970s, when Miller traveled to Montour Falls from his homes—first the one in Wichita Falls and later the one in Ohio—he had been doing well enough to afford a new pickup truck and a house trailer. He had also bought a younger relative a new pair of contact lenses as a present, according to the male family member.

In 1982, Miller found himself in deeper trouble with the law, this time in Brook Park, Ohio. A 911 call brought Brook Park officers to the home of Miller's girlfriend, where Miller was alleged to be in the process of beating her up.

When the officers entered the girlfriend's house, Miller bolted to an upstairs bedroom. With the cops on his heels, Miller let his temper get the best of him. He drew a Ruger .44-caliber magnum revolver. With their own lives now endangered, the officers scuffled with Miller and succeeded in disarming him. But the situation became far more complicated for Miller when the lawmen discovered a cache of two large-caliber pistols and a Browning 12-gauge shotgun in the house.

According to Thomas Dease, Chief of the Brook Park PD, Miller was sentenced to two years' probation on the charges arising from the violence and gun possession, with a proviso from the judge that Miller undergo psychiatric treatment.

In 1988, things were looking up for the embattled trucker. In an interview for a job with an Ohio transportation company, Miller kept quiet about his checkered past, which included his various involvements with the police. He got the job and was soon hauling loads of pizza flour from Cleveland to Philadelphia, Albany, and other points east.

His employer found no problems with Miller's on-the-job performance. When informed of the Watkins Glen killings, an executive of the firm sketched a picture of a man who was entirely responsible and reliable while at work. The executive described the trucker's favoring of neat flannel shirts and blue jeans held up by suspenders. Miller had been a meticulous note-taker on his road trips, the executive said, and had built up an exhaustive file of the warehouses and loading docks to which he delivered his cargos. Miller's yearly income averaged out between $25,000 and $35,000.

While 1988 might have appeared to be a good year for the heavyset trucker, other events were taking place hundreds of miles away from Miller's home in North Ridgeville, Ohio, that would set the stage for the Watkins Glen tragedy.

In Washington, D.C., that year, Congress was expending a great deal of effort to reform the administration of the national welfare laws. After endless committee hearings and extensive floor debate in both the Senate and House of Representatives, the Family Support Act of 1988 was passed.

One of the law's key provisions authorized welfare authorities to automatically deduct money from the paychecks of delinquent parents who failed to comply with court-ordered support payments. Another provision gave the law sharper teeth by allowing government agencies to use Social Security numbers in tracing the deadbeats. In 1989, using the new powers granted to them, the Schuyler County authorities succeeded in tracing Miller to North Ridgeville. By now, according to their reckoning, the trucker owed more than $8,000 in unpaid child support.

Law enforcement officials said that the Schuyler County Welfare Department was able to garnishee Miller's tax returns and recover $1,660.

In August 1992, the welfare authorities went after the still-outstanding $6,780 by garnisheeing Miller's wages from his transportation-company employer. The first payroll deduction showed up on Miller's paycheck on Friday, October 9th. The amount was $51.

At the transportation company headquarters on the following Monday, Miller told friends and his employer that he "was going to New York to straighten the situation out."

One co-worker said of the conversation with Miller, "As far as I know, it was the first time they had done it, and he was a little upset. He told us it was for child support and the child wasn't his."

Official computer records showed that an order had been filed on September 22, 1992, in Ohio's Cuyahoga Domestic Relations Court to garnishee Miller's wages at the rate of $221 per month.

As the investigation into Miller's last days went forward, Schuyler County Sheriff Maloney revealed that he had requested the aid of the state police in the probe because all four of the women victims were close friends of his.

As Watkins Glen residents slowly began to recover from the shock of the massacre, some members of the tightly knit community tried to express their feelings of outrage and grief.

A woman employed as a Schuyler County probation officer set the theme when she commented. "You don't expect anything like this to happen in this small and rural and backward county." The probation officer had come to Watkins Glen three years before, after having served in the same capacity in Orange County, about 50 miles north of New York City, where crimes of violence were more frequent. She articulated her Schuyler County neighbors' fears for the future when she added, "They don't have that sort of thing here—didn't."

A man who lived across the street from the county building in which the victims were slain was overwhelmed by how they had been trapped at their desks because of their cramped offices. "You didn't have to be an expert shot to shoot anyone in that office," he observed. Then, expressing a sense of personal loss, the man focused on the four victims. "They were lovely ladies," he said. "They were the last people you would expect to be hurt in that fashion."

A woman who worked at a market across the street from the scene of the quadruple murders described the pandemonium immediately following the first sounds of gunfire. "A lady came running out of the county office building and said she saw a man with a gun and heard gunshots."

Bursting into tears as she gave her account, the market employee said, "This doesn't happen in Watkins Glen. It's a tourist town. It's always happy-go-lucky people around here."

Veteran State Trooper Gene A. Chisolm surveyed the stricken Watkins Glen residents as they milled around Sheriff Maloney in the county office building parking lots while network video crews recorded the scene for the evening news programs.

"There are many other incidents like this on television," Chisolm said. He was referring to the widespread practice of community grief-counseling at scenes of disaster. "It's second nature to do stuff like that." Such counseling was taking place in a basement office of the red-brick government building.

Even longtime peace officers like Sheriff Maloney found it difficult to keep from giving vent to their emotions. As ashen-faced townspeople surrounded him in the parking lot, Maloney told reporters, "In my thirty years as sheriff, I've never seen anything as horrible as this."

Meanwhile, Michael Moran, a spokesman for the Civil Service Employees Association which represented the four slain welfare workers, pointed out that these murders were not an isolated happening. "As freaky as something like this is, it's not totally uncommon," Moran said. "Social workers are harassed and threatened all the time. It's a lot more dangerous job than the public realizes."

Those who mourned the dead women wondered whether there might have been any way of spotting the killer before he'd begun his murderous spree. But those who'd had contact with him since his arrival in Watkins Glen on October 13th said they'd noticed nothing about Miller that marked him as a mass killer.

Indeed, the owner of the motel in which Miller had

registered at 6:00 p.m. that Tuesday evening reported, "There was nothing unusual about him. No red flag went up in my mind."

Nor did Miller do anything to call attention to himself between his arrival and the massacre.

Keeping his cool as the lethal hour approached appeared to be part of Miller's overall plan of vengeance. At least that was the implication of the week-long probe Sheriff Maloney conducted into the gunman's activities.

Maloney said his eight-day probe showed conclusively that Miller had never planned to return from Watkins Glen to his home in North Ridgeville, Ohio. The lawman noted that on October 13th, Miller had purchased a one-way bus ticket from Cleveland to Elmira, New York, which is 20 miles away from Watkins Glen.

When Miller arrived in Watkins Glen, he told both a taxi driver and the owner of the motel that he was in town because his truck had broken down on the road.

"I think he basically planned the whole thing to bring attention to himself and the child-support issue," said the sheriff. "My guess is, he planned to do it [the killings] Wednesday and then changed his mind."

Maloney also said that the Lama 9mm semiautomatic handgun used by Miller had been purchased from a sporting-goods store in Litchfield, Ohio, in 1980. The purchase was apparently made after Miller was placed on probation for the domestic dispute during which he'd pulled a gun on Brook Park police officers in 1982. In that incident, Miller had been convicted of a felony, and Ohio law bans convicted felons from possessing handguns.

Meanwhile, Schuyler County officials were taking steps to protect government workers against a recurrence of the mass murders that had taken place in Watkins Glen. Deputy Executive Thomas J. Santulli said that as of Monday, October 25, 1992, all visitors to county buildings would have to pass through metal detectors. In addition, all buildings would henceforth have only one entrance, compared to the five entrances previously kept open.

"There's always the element of risk out there—that'll never change," Santulli said. "We're just trying to make it a better situation."

Sheriff Maloney reported that the renovations to provide only one entrance had already been made in the building where Miller killed the four women. Two deputy sheriffs were now assigned to patrol the area and to monitor visitors.

"We feel safer with sheriff's deputies here," said an employee of the county's Public Health Office. "But you don't go through an experience like last week and not be worried."

# "MASS MURDER ON THE MISSISSIPPI COAST"
## by Gary C. King

It was hot and muggy in Nicholson, Mississippi, on Saturday, September 15, 1990. The mercury approached a hundred in much of the state, but down south, particularly in Pearl River County next to the Louisiana border, the high humidity of the Gulf Coast made it seem even hotter. By nightfall it began to cool down a bit, but it was still sultry and uncomfortable. It wasn't a good time to begin a major murder investigation; but, then, there really isn't any good time to start a murder probe.

It had been a busy evening so far at the Pearl River County Sheriff's Department, and one of the deputies on duty that night, puffing on one cigarette after another, didn't expect things to slow down much as the evening wore on. It was, after all, a Saturday night, and the department had already been called out to settle more than its share of bar fights, domestic squabbles, and robberies. Things could, in all likelihood, only get worse.

It was only minutes before 9:00 p.m. when the call that would ultimately prove to be the worst of the evening came in. At first this latest call had seemed simple enough. It was from a relative of the local Frierson family who said she was worried because she hadn't been able to reach them by telephone all day. There was supposed to be a Frierson family reunion for 200 family members the next day, and the relative had last-minute details to discuss. But the Friersons, who lived just off Mississippi Highway 607 in the community of Nicholson, weren't answering their phone. It just wasn't like them. The relative asked the sheriff's department to send someone out to check on them.

A team of deputies arrived a few minutes later at Ray Merle "Smokey" Frierson's small brick home, located on the northwest corner of a NASA buffer zone near the Hancock County line. Ray Frierson had lived there with his wife Mollie since 1973. They liked it there and were well known and well liked throughout the community.

Except for the sounds of crickets and an occasional passing car on Highway 607, everything was quiet!—almost too quiet—as the deputies stepped out of their patrol cruisers. The night's stillness was made even more eerie by the incessant insect sounds and by the sight of occasional lightning bugs blinking their tails in the pitch black. Making the deputies feel even more ill at ease, no one came outside the house to find out why they were there. Nothing moved in or around the house.

One of the deputies knocked loudly on the door. Nobody answered. The lights stayed dark inside the house. After several repeated attempts, all futile, the lawmen decided that they had better go inside. Gaining entry through an unlocked door, the deputies began turning on lights as they slowly went from room to room.

When they reached the front bedroom, the deputies reeled back in horror at the atrocity that lay in front of them. An older man, whom the deputies believed to be Ray Frierson, and an older woman, whom they believed to be his wife Mollie, were lying sprawled on the floor, covered in blood. A young boy lay nearby, also covered with blood.

After regaining their composure, the deputies carefully checked the victims for signs of life. They found none. The deputies cautiously retraced their steps out of the bedroom, not wishing to disturb anything of evidentiary value.

Before leaving the house, however, the deputies checked the other rooms. It was possible, they reasoned, that additional victims might be in other areas of the house. Speculating that the perpetrator might also still be inside, they drew their guns as a precaution.

They soon learned that their reasoning about possible other victims had been correct. In the second bedroom, they found the partially clad body of a woman, whom they believed to be in her late 30s or early 40s, spread-eagled on the floor. Noting that the victim's clothing had been ripped or forcibly removed, the investigators strongly suspected that she had been sexually assaulted, either before or after she was killed.

After making certain that there were no other bodies and that the perpetrator was not on the premises, the deputies cleared the house and reported their grim findings to headquarters. Pearl River County Sheriff Lorance Lumpkin was located and notified of the carnage at the Frierson residence. He instructed that the area be sealed off from all unauthorized personnel and identified as a crime scene. Lumpkin arrived a short time later, accompanied by a medical examiner, a deputy district attorney, and a crime scene technician.

Each of the victims, Sheriff Lumpkin observed, had been shot more than once and in different parts of their bodies. The older man appeared to have been shot in the back of the head at close range. Tissue, blood, bone, and possibly brain matter had been dispersed about the room as a result of the force of the blast, some of which had traveled several feet from the body. The older woman had been shot in the face, resulting in severe disfigurement. It also appeared that she had been beaten on the head.

The boy, whom the sheriff believed to be in his teens, had also been shot in the head, but with a small-caliber weapon. He also had other wounds to his body, primarily bruises and abrasions. The female victim in the other bedroom had been shot in the abdomen and head, also with a small-caliber weapon.

During a preliminary examination of the house, Lonnie Arrinder of the Mississippi State Crime Laboratory discovered two bloody footprints in one of the bedrooms. There was so much blood in the bedrooms that Arrinder couldn't help but wonder why there weren't more bloody footprints. He also found a 20-gauge shotgun and a .22-caliber rifle on the premises. The shotgun had blood and possible tissue fragments adhering to its stock and barrel. Arrinder theorized that it might have been used to beat one of the victims, most likely the older woman, in addition to shooting her and others. He also found scattered about articles of bloody clothing, which he carefully placed in paper bags so that the bloodstains could dry.

After the scene was carefully photographed, crime lab technicians collected blood and other bodily fluid samples, which they carefully marked according to source and location. They also vacuumed for trace evidence of hair and clothing fiber, using separate filter bags for each location, and searched for identifiable latent fingerprints.

During the evening, deputies ferreted out important information from several of Ray Frierson's relatives. As a result, they eventually had enough information to positively identify the bodies. The bodies in the front bedroom were identified as 61-year-old Ray Frierson, 56-year-old Mollie Frierson, and 13-year-old Joshua A. Morrell, the Frierson's stepgrandson.

The body in the second bedroom was identified as 38-year-old Pamela Ann Howard. Pamela and Joshua, family members said, were relatives who had lived with the Friersons for some time. Relatives claimed that Pamela and Joshua were both retarded, one of the main reasons that Ray and Mollie had taken them in. Sheriff Lumpkin was also told that yet another relative, 17-year-old John Morrell Frierson, nicknamed "John Boy," lived in the house. No one, however, knew where he could be found. If being a Saturday night and John Boy being a teenager, the lawmen surmised that he was out partying with his friends.

As the lawmen continued questioning family members, they learned that John Boy and Joshua were brothers and that Ray and Mollie Frierson, who had adopted him eight years earlier after his mother was murdered, were John Boy's stepgrandparents. According to police sources, his mother's body had been discovered in the central part of the state, but her murder was never solved. Pamela Howard was John Boy's and Joshua's aunt.

With the help of relatives, a sketchy inventory of the Friersons' possessions was obtained. Afterward, the detectives determined that the only thing of value that was missing was Mollie Frierson's 1988 Ford Escort. Because very little money was found in the victims' clothes or inside the house, the investigators also suspected that cash may have been taken, but they didn't yet know how much, if any.

With the missing car, an obvious lack of cash on hand, and the possible rape of Pamela Howard, Sheriff Lumpkin and his detectives felt that they had established clear motives for the murders. The strongest motive of all, however, appeared to be the elimination of witnesses. All of the aforementioned were aggravating factors that could bring a death sentence for the perpetrator if convicted of the crimes.

According to Sheriff Lumpkin, certain signs indicated that Pamela Howard had been raped and Mollie Frierson sodomized after having been shot. However, the sheriff wouldn't elaborate on the specific reasons leading to this conclusion.

When the criminalists no longer needed the bodies at the crime scene, morgue drivers placed the corpses inside body bags and removed them one at a time to a waiting van. As a small gathering of onlookers watched from behind barriers, the van left for the morgue where definitive autopsies would be conducted.

While sheriff's investigators and crime lab technicians searched for clues and collected evidence at the crime scene over the next several hours, the sheriff and several deputies questioned the victims' acquaintances and relatives in search of clues to the killer's identity. It wasn't long before their efforts paid off. One person in particular provided information that ultimately broke the case wide open.

Two days before, the informant told the investigators, Mollie Frierson had expressed concern for her safety, telling a family member that she was afraid John Boy was "going to kill them all." John Boy, sleuths were told, drank to excess. His drinking sometimes made him violent and abusive, and family members suspected that he also used drugs. Mollie had even told a family member that she planned to take John Boy to a drug and alcohol rehabilitation center following the family reunion—if, she added ominously, she "made it through the weekend."

Investigators in any homicide case always start out looking "close to home" for suspects, and now Sheriff Lumpkin believed he would have to look no further than John Boy Frierson to find the family's mass murderer. John Boy, he believed, had both the motive and the opportunity to carry out the killings. The evidence, he hoped, would rule him in or out as a suspect.

Lumpkin and his deputies worked fervently as they gathered leads from John Boy's friends and acquaintances on where the teenager might be. By the early-morning hours of September 16th, while crime lab technicians continued working at the Frierson house, deputies traced John Boy to a girlfriend's apartment just outside Picayune, a town only a few miles north of Nicholson. Deputies quietly surrounded the apartment complex, then moved in to make the arrest.

Frierson was there, all right, but they didn't have to worry about him putting up a fight. He wasn't in any shape to make a break for it. When the deputies made their presence known, John Boy staggered into their midst, making no effort to flee. He appeared to be heavily under the influence of drugs and alcohol. The deputies arrested him at his girlfriend's apartment without incident. He was taken to the Pearl River County Jail where he was booked on suspicion of murder in connection with the deaths of his family.

Shortly after the suspect's arrival at the jail, Sheriff Lumpkin and Deputy Joe Stuart took Frierson into an interrogation room. The youth looked pale, tired, and weak. He was apparently coming down from his alcohol and drug-induced intoxication. After deciding that he had sobered up enough to be fully aware of what was going on, the probers read their suspect the Miranda rights again, after which Frierson agreed to give them a statement. As Sheriff Lumpkin asked questions, Deputy Stuart took notes.

Surprisingly, according to Lumpkin and Stuart, Frierson admitted that he had shot his relatives. He said he was "mad at the world" because Ray Frierson wouldn't allow him to go raccoon hunting. Frierson said he took $200 from a purse and wallet that was in the house, but he denied raping his grandmother and aunt. Afterward, Deputy Stuart typed up the youth's statement and provided a copy to the district attorney's office.

Meanwhile Dr. Paul McGarry, a New Orleans pathologist, was brought in to conduct the autopsies. A pathology assistant prepared the corpses for the postmortem examinations, which included running an ultraviolet light over the bodies of the female victims in search of semen. Semen appears as bright white under the ultraviolet, thus facilitating its collection by the pathologist. Semen was detected on Pamela Howard's body, and vaginal swabs were taken. Additional swabs were obtained from other parts of Pamela's and Mollie's bodies, just in case trace amounts of semen had been overlooked. These would be combined with acid phosphatase, a sensitive enzyme that turns pink when mixed with semen. Following the autopsies, Dr. McGarry reported his findings to Sheriff Lumpkin and Assistant District Attorney, Buddy McDonald.

Pamela Howard, said Dr. McGarry, had been shot once in the abdomen and four times in the head with a small-caliber weapon. The presence of semen and signs of violence other than the gunshot wounds led Dr. McGarry to believe that Pamela had also been raped.

"Was sexual battery inflicted prior to death?" asked the assistant D.A.

"Yes, it was," Dr. McGarry replied.

The pathologist explained that he had collected and preserved from the victim's body semen that could be used for deoxyribonucleic acid (DNA) testing. The seminal fluid samples were air-dried and frozen and sent, along with a sample of John Frierson's blood, to a court-recognized DNA diagnostics lab.

Dr. McGarry found that both Ray and Mollie Frierson had been shot at close range with what he believed to be a 20-gauge shotgun. The pathologist said that Ray had been shot in the head three times with a small-caliber weapon, but it was the shotgun blast to the back of Ray's head that had caused his death. Ray was already dead when the shots with a small-caliber weapon were inflicted, said McGarry.

The pathologist determined that Mollie Frierson had sustained a gunshot wound to her chin and had subsequently been beaten on the head with a weapon consistent with the shotgun found at the crime scene.

McGarry said Mollie had received five powerful blows to the head. The approximate time of the victim's death was sometime on the morning of September 15th.

McGarry said that Joshua Morrell had been shot three times in the head with a small-caliber weapon. Also present on his body were several bruises and abrasions, primarily on one of his arms, an elbow, and a shoulder, all of which the pathologist characterized as defensive wounds. He said that the wounds were probably caused when the boy held up his arms as he tried to fend off the attack.

Meanwhile, a DNA diagnostics laboratory in Maryland began processing John Frierson's blood and the seminal fluid found on and inside Pamela Howard's body. Using conventional serological typing methods, the lab first determined that the blood type of the semen found at the crime scene was of the same blood type as John Frierson's. Had the blood and semen been of different types, Frierson could have been eliminated as the suspect. He was not so lucky.

Next, DNA was extracted from the semen collected from Pamela Howard's body and from Frierson's blood samples. The DNA strands were then "cut" into small fragments by an enzyme and compared. The result, according to the scientist who conducted the DNA typing, provided an autoradiograph, a genetic "print" as unique to each individual as a set of fingerprints. As was expected by the investigators, the DNA extracted from Frierson's blood and from the semen found inside Pamela Howard's vagina matched.

Adding fuel to the case against the suspect, according to Lonnie Arrinder of the Mississippi State Crime Laboratory, the two bloody footprints found at the crime scene matched John Frierson's footprint.

Meanwhile, according to Pearl River County Justice Court Judge Richard Cowart, authorities began receiving a number of threats against Frierson's life.

People were outraged over the senseless, brutal murders that had been committed in their community, and some were determined to do something about it. Residents couldn't understand how someone could have so ruthlessly murdered such a nice couple as Ray and Mollie Frierson and their family.

As a result of all the threats, when Frierson made his first court appearance, he was taken to the Justice Court building in an unmarked police car and was required to lie down in the backseat. He was ushered by several armed deputies into the courthouse through a side door.

Despite the apparently irrefutable evidence stacked against him, Frierson pleaded innocent to four counts of capital murder and asked for a jury trial. Defense Attorneys Rex Jones of Hattiesburg and William Ducker of Poplarville were appointed to represent him. The judge set Frierson's trial for the following August, and he continued to be held without bail.

Shortly after Frierson's arrest, the question of his ability to stand trial and assist in his own defense was brought up. At the request of the defense team, Frierson was sent to the state mental hospital at Whitfield where he underwent extensive psychiatric examinations. After subjecting him to a battery of tests and interviews, psychologists and psychiatrists at the hospital determined that he was, in fact, competent to stand trial.

Although Frierson was a juvenile at the time of the slayings, the prosecution sought to have him remanded to adult court over the objections of his defense team. If he was prosecuted through the juvenile system, prosecutors argued, he would be released on his 21st birthday. The severity of the crimes, they argued, demanded a more severe punishment. A judge agreed, and Frierson was ordered to stand trial as an adult.

Because of the publicity and the charged emotions

surrounding the murders, Frierson's trial was moved to Natchez, a town several counties west in Adams County. Jury selection began on Monday, August 12, 1991. After a jury was seated, Judge R.I. Pritchard III ordered that the jury members be sequestered throughout the trial because of the extensive publicity.

Dressed in a black, short-sleeved shirt and blue jeans, John Frierson appeared to be in a somber mood as he was led into the Adams County Chancery courtroom. His legs were shackled for added security, and spectators were required to pass through a metal detector before entering the courtroom.

The jury was led step-by-step through the case by Assistant District Attorney Buddy McDonald, from the time the bodies were found, through the evidence gathering and DNA testing, and finally to Frierson's confession to Sheriff Lumpkin and Deputy Joe Stuart.

At one point Dr. Paul McGarry, the New Orleans pathologist who had performed the autopsies on the victims' bodies, explained the details of the deaths and the manner in which all the victims were killed. McGarry used sketches to show jurors the points where bullets and shotgun pellets had entered the victims' bodies. Gruesome color photographs showing how the victims were found were also introduced as evidence. Tearful family members were present in the courtroom. Occasional gasps could be heard from spectators who managed to glimpse the photos as they were passed between attorneys, judge, and jury.

Later, the deputies who found the bodies described the locations and manner in which the bodies were found. Sheriff Lorance Lumpkin and Deputy Jo Stuart also testified that Frierson agreed to make a statement confessing to the murders after his arrest. The two lawmen said they believed Frierson was fully aware of what was going on when they read him his Miranda rights and when he made the incriminating remarks.

One of the most dramatic moments of the trial came when Frierson took the witness stand in his own defense. Because the state's case against Frierson was so strong, the best defense strategy seemed to be to simply put the defendant on the stand and try to gain sympathy from the jury. Defense Attorney Ducker asked Frierson if he had anything to say to the jury.

"I'm sorry," said Frierson as his voice broke. Speaking softly into the microphone between sobs, Frierson said that the day of the murders seemed like a dream to him. He said he didn't remember giving a statement to the lawmen. He said that he had been under the influence of drugs and alcohol before he was arrested and had remained intoxicated for a while after his arrest.

Responding to questions from Defense Attorney Rex Jones, Frierson said he could only remember "bits and pieces" of his arrest. He said he didn't remember telling the officers that he had shot his relatives, took $200 cash, and stole his grandmother's car. He said that he had a long history of alcohol and drug abuse problems, and that he had only been "straight" for the few months after his arrest.

In closing arguments, Jones maintained that Frierson's drug, alcohol, and emotional problems had in effect turned him into a "walking time bomb" that detonated on the morning of the slayings. Jones argued that Frierson never received the drug and alcohol rehabilitation when he needed it most. "He was a ticking time bomb. The Mississippi juvenile system failed.

"There was an explosion," said Jones. "I don't think he intended to rob them, and I don't think he intended to commit sexual battery. After hearing the evidence, I think he killed them, but I don't think he did it while in the commission of other crimes."

Co-counsel Drucker then literally begged the jury to spare Frierson's life, contending that the defendant might be able to turn his life around and do something constructive someday. He suggested that Frierson might be willing to participate in a prison program in which inmates held talks with teenagers warning them about the dangers of drug and alcohol abuse.

In rebuttal, Assistant D.A. McDonald pointed out for the jury that the defense never questioned the DNA testing or other evidence of sexual assault on Pamela Howard, which he said "spoke the loudest.

"I cannot look at the photographs of the four victims here and feel that the system failed John Frierson," said McDonald. "If this is not capital murder, there has never been capital murder in the state of Mississippi, and there will never be capital murder in the state of Mississippi." He urged jurors to sentence Frierson to death.

On Thursday, August 15, 1991, the jurors announced after three and a half hours of deliberations that they had found John Morrell "John Boy" Frierson guilty on four counts of capital murder. They were, however, unable to agree unanimously on whether to sentence Frierson to death by lethal injection or to life in prison. As a result, Fifteenth Judicial Circuit Court Judge R.I. Pritchard III was bound by Mississippi statutes to sentence Frierson to life in prison for each of the four counts.

Frierson, with his chin resting in his hands, remained emotionless and without expression.

"I didn't know what to think," said Defense Attorney Ducker afterward. "I am just very thankful that's the way it came out. The boy did a very terrible thing and he'll be punished for it for a long time, but I don't think we're in the business of killing seventeen-year-olds."

"We're disappointed," said one of the several family members of the victims who had been in attendance for the entire trial.

"We wish the jury would have been able to return a death sentence verdict," commented Assistant D.A. McDonald.

John Boy Frierson is now serving his life sentences at the Mississippi State Penitentiary. Unless his convictions are overturned on appeal, Frierson will not be eligible for parole for 40 years, until the year 2031.

# "SALOON SLAUGHTER LEFT 4 IN GORE!"

## by Charles W. Sasser

Police in Tulsa, Oklahoma, said the rising crime rates west of downtown and north of the Arkansas River reflected the effects of urban blight on the city's older neighborhoods. The scarred gray face of the New Ferndale Lounge at 1216 West Archer Street was crisscrossed with chains and studded with iron bars as each in a progression of owners attempted to keep out local burglars. Crime stats indicated the tavern had been burglarized 10 times in recent weeks.

Otherwise, police said, the New Ferndale Lounge was a quiet neighborhood bar where working people went for suds and pretzels and snooker after the five o'clock whistle blew. It was, that is, until early Sunday morning, October 14, 1990.

Shortly after 1:00 a.m., three patrolmen were rendezvousing at a convenience store a half-block west of the lounge to exchange information about a crime when they were interrupted by a man and a woman who came running up the dimly-lighted street shouting for help.

"They're all dead!" the woman reportedly screeched. "Hurry!"

The inside of the lounge, police would later comment, looked like the aftermath of a combat raid. Bodies were strewn everywhere. Some country and western singer wailed out of the jukebox, something about mama and booze and cowboys. Thick odors of cigarette smoke, beer, urine, and blood commingled in the close atmosphere.

Officers noted that the shooting must have just occurred. The blood smell was still strong and fresh, and two of the bodies on the floor were emitting feeble groans and twitching spasmodically. A check of the other two bodies revealed that they were freshly dead and still warm. Each of the four victims, officers determined, had been shot in the head with a single, small-caliber bullet.

Police immediately summoned Emergency Medical Services and detectives. By the time homicide Sergeant Wayne Allen arrived at the scene, the two surviving victims were on their way to the hospital. They were identified as the barmaid, Carol McDaniels, 42, and her live-in boyfriend, Timothy Sheets, 39. Detectives soon provided names for the two dead men: Steve A. Smith, 34, and Tyrell L. Boyd, 27. The four had been found sprawled on the floor in their own blood at the base of the bar, which formed a rough horseshoe against the west wall.

"The victims had had little time to react," Sergeant Allen explained. "I think they were taken totally by surprise."

An Emergency Medical Technician (EMT) said Sheets "grabbed my arm real tight" when paramedics began working on him to save his life, but he was unable to name his attacker. Carol McDaniels reportedly complained that her arm hurt, although like the other three, she had been shot in the head. She relapsed into gurgling sounds, also unable to shed light on the nature of the brutal assault or its perpetrators.

Police were left with two dead people, two wounded,

and an open cash register. Sergeant Allen remarked that the motive for the crime appeared to be robbery, but he knew you could never be sure. Appearances were sometimes deceptive, either unintentionally or on purpose to cover some sicker, more sinister motive. It was difficult to believe robbers would coldly proceed to execute four people over a few hundred dollars.

Sergeant Allen assigned on-site Homicide Detective Ken Makinson, assisted by Detective Mike Cook, to handle the principal investigation.

"Three hundred fifty dollars," said the current owner of the bar. "That's about what's missing from the cash register. . . . I told all my girls that anytime anybody tried to rob the bar, you just give them whatever they want. I told them their lives are worth more than money."

"It's unusual for an armed robbery to have this much violence," said Lieutenant Jack Putnam, "but people do get murdered for small amounts of cash. People will kill you for fifty dollars."

While crime scene forensics experts organized the time-consuming task of gathering, identifying, tagging, and analyzing physical evidence, Detectives Makinson and Cook supervised a neighborhood canvass for witnesses. They questioned Candy Bryant and her boyfriend who had discovered the crime and run up the street to summon patrolmen.

According to police accounts, Candy Bryant was one of the barmaids at the New Ferndale Lounge. She worked Saturday night until approximately 10:00 p.m. when Carol McDaniels agreed to come in and take her place. Candy wanted to attend a party at another bar. Around midnight, Candy and her boyfriend decided to return to the New Ferndale, arriving there at almost exactly 1:00 a.m., apparently only minutes after the bloodbath occurred.

"That could have been me shot instead of Carol," Candy realized, stunned.

As for physical evidence at the crime scene, detectives said, there was almost nothing that might be considered a clue. Canvassing detectives were also running into the same brick wall. A regular bar patron supposedly informed police that everything at the tavern was peaceful when he left at 12:30 a.m. A minister working until 1:00 a.m. at his church just down the block said he neither heard nor saw anything unusual.

There was only one sliver of light breaking through the darkness surrounding the case. According to Sergeant Wayne Allen, a local woman claimed to have seen a man enter the bar alone a few minutes before 1:00 a.m. That was too close to the estimated time of the massacre for him not to have been somehow involved.

"If you have five people in an enclosed space and four turn up shot," a detective reasoned, "it's likely the fifth one did it."

There was only one problem. The witness' sobriety came into question. Was the woman too drunk to recognize the man, or to even know what time it was when she saw him? Still, she was the only thing police had going for them. The vivid description she gave of a tall, dark, young man indicated she might have seen something worth pursuing.

More than 24 hours passed while police concentrated their search on the only suspect they had. During those critical hours, the release of a ballistics report indicated that all four victims had been shot by matching .22-caliber bullets. That seemed to add to the single witness' credibility, whether or not she was drunk.

Also during those 24 hours, the condition of the two surviving victims in Intensive Care deteriorated. Police were told that it might be days or weeks before the survivors would be able to provide any information . . . if they lived.

In the meantime, Detective Makinson and Cook patiently ferreted out several other patrons of the New Ferndale Lounge who admitted to being in the bar from midnight on. None of them knew anything about a solitary male such as the one described by the drunken witness. However, one or two of them recalled that there had been at least six people in the tavern as late as 12:30 a.m., 30 minutes before the slaughter began.

Four of the people were to become shooting victims. The other two had been in the lounge much of the evening drinking and playing pool. They were strangers described as a tall white man and a shorter one, both in their early 20s. The tall one was angular and unshaven with longish light brown hair and a knife slash of a mouth. The short one was dark and baby-faced with pouting lips that made him appear slightly effeminate.

Maybe robbery hadn't been the motive after all. Maybe something else happened. Only the two survivors in Intensive Care and the suspect or suspects knew what that "something else" might be.

Police broadcast an APB (all points bulletin) on the pair. If nothing else, they were witnesses.

Monday afternoon, October 15th. Detectives corralled the suspect the drunken woman supposedly had seen entering the bar before the mass shooting. Jackson Polk denied knowing anything about the crime, insisting that while he sometimes frequented the lounge, he had not been anywhere near it at the time of the execution.

The female witness stared at a lineup consisting of Polk and five other men. After a while, she reportedly turned away and shook her head.

"The man I seen ain't there," she said.

"It just wasn't the right guy," said Lieutenant Jack Putnam. "We thought we had something but we didn't."

Tuesday, October 16th. Early-morning hours. A lone black man armed with what might have been a .22-caliber revolver robbed a convenience store one-half block west of the New Ferndale Lounge. He became another possible suspect, although an unlikely one.

At 10 o'clock that same morning, Timothy Sheets died, raising the death toll from the lounge shooting to three. Carol McDaniels still remained in critical condition.

"He was just an ordinary kid trying to make a living and he was in the wrong place at the wrong time," a relative said of Sheets. ". . . But to think it was for so little money."

Plainclothesmen under the command of Homicide Sergeant Wayne Allen continued to probe the backgrounds and lives of the four victims, trying to determine if some motive other than robbery existed. Other detectives chased the holdup man from the convenience store robbery. Detectives Makinson and Cook were busy running down a lead of their own.

It wasn't much of a lead at first. A woman leaked word to police that she had seen a Ford belonging to a local thug named Johnny Davis parked in front of the New Ferndale Lounge late on Saturday night. So far, Davis had escaped police questioning.

As police scoured the city for Davis, another piece of information found its way to Detective Makinson's case file. Davis had supposedly been with a couple of friends that night, one of whom was tall and the other short and "kinda sissy-looking."

That roughly matched the descriptions of the two strangers seen in the bar. So far, so good.

Makinson and his partner, working from tips, traced Johnny Davis to an auto repair place on the corner down from the lounge. Davis assumed the roles of the three famous monkeys who heard no evil, saw no evil, and spoke no evil.

"I was awful drunk that night," he kept saying, according to detectives. "I don't remember a lot."

"Maybe we can find something to jar your memory," the sleuths promised.

Cook and Makinson were both veteran detectives, good street men who would pick up a clue or tidbit of information and keep at it until they had wrung it dry. Playing a hunch that there was more to Johnny Davis than he let on, the detectives kept after his backtrail. And their determination began to pay off.

"Johnny told me them two guys had a gun that night," an informant confided in the plainclothesmen. "He ought to know. He said he sold it to them."

That was the most important clue to have surfaced in nearly three days. So back to Johnny Davis went the officers.

"Maybe this will jar your memory. You sold a gun . . ."

That jarred Davis' memory all right. Davis immediately admitted to owning a Ruger .22-caliber pistol, which he had sold several days prior to the murders.

"I sold it to Jerry," he confessed.

"Jerry?"

"A tall guy. Said he was just out of the penitentiary."

"You were with him last Saturday night?"

"Yeah. But I left early. He and the other guy, David, were still at the bar when I left."

"Did they have the gun?"

"Yeah. But I'm not sure they had anything to do with the shootings. I don't think they did."

Makinson would sum it up later: "I think Davis knew all about it. But all we had to go on at the time were hunches and a lot of circumstances pointing to two strangers in a neighborhood bar. It was clear what we had to do—find Jerry and his partner David and see what they had to say."

"We got to the point where there were just six people left in the bar . . ." said Sergeant Wayne Allen. "It's like working a jigsaw puzzle."

Tuesday, October 16th, began eventfully with the convenience store robbery near the murder site and the death of the shooting's third victim. It was destined to become even more eventful.

Developing information gleaned from Johnny Davis

and the female informant whose tip had led to Davis, Detectives Makinson and Cook soon compiled names and personal data on two men believed to have been the fifth and sixth persons at the New Ferndale Lounge on Saturday night-Sunday morning.

Department of Corrections (DOC) records disclosed that the shorter of the two men, 25-year-old David Keith Lawrence, was an ex-convict with three prior felony convictions — two in 1988 for burglary and embezzlement, the last in 1989 for burglary of an automobile. Street word had it that Lawrence lived with a woman in the Osage Hills Apartments, a low-income government housing project on North Osage Drive.

"Find him," was the command that Sergeant Wayne Allen passed on to his detectives.

The taller man was also an ex-convict. Jerry Lynn McCracken, 23, had been sentenced to five years in prison in 1989 for knifing three people in a Lawton, Oklahoma, bar fight while he was stationed there with the U.S. Army. DOC said he had been released in July 1990 on what is termed "pre-parole."

A convict on pre-parole is still considered to be an inmate. His restrictions are supposedly more strict than a regular parolee's, although an observer of the system is hard put to detect a difference."

Sleuths traced McCracken to a rented room at a halfway house on North Boulder Avenue. Subsequent news reports quoted the house administrator describing McCracken as a man "bound for hell . . . with a chip on his shoulder. . . . He was very rebellious . . . he didn't want his privacy invaded. He's fallen in with a bad crowd."

The administrator added that McCracken frequently violated house rules, such as signing out before leaving. Apparently, he had not signed out on the night of the massacre at the New Ferndale Lounge. At least twice during the three months that McCracken had been out of prison, the administrator had reported him to his parole officer. The first time was for suspected drug use when the house proprietor smelled marijuana in the convict's room; the second time was for congregating in a nearby vacant lot to get drunk with other convicts.

The administrator complained bitterly that McCracken's parole officer had not investigated either charge.

"I'm not surprised," the administrator said with a sigh upon learning that tenant McCracken was a murder suspect. "I've had that old sick feeling."

McCracken's roommate, another ex-con named Bob Doth, reportedly shed additional light into the probe. Doth characterized McCracken as "a guy with a quick temper . . . [But] I don't understand this whole deal. He was supposed to find out Thursday if he was going on parole or not. He was planning to go to Tennessee for thirty days."

"Do you know anything about a gun he might have had?" detectives asked the halfway-house resident.

"He flashed a twenty-two pistol," came the recorded response. "It wasn't the first he had."

Posted on the wall above McCracken's bed at the halfway house was a caricature of himself in prison stripes with a ball and chain on his leg. It was captioned: "If you don't like it, git out of my cloud, dude."

Police were about to swarm all over Jerry Lynn McCracken's cloud.

Shortly before noon that Tuesday, Detective-Lieutenant Jack Putnam reportedly spotted David Lawrence striding down North Osage Drive near the apartment he shared with his girlfriend. Minutes later, Lawrence found himself snugly handcuffed and on his way downtown to police headquarters where Putnam, backed up by Detectives Makinson and Cook, machine-gunned him with questions.

Accounts of the police interrogation describe how Lawrence resisted only temporarily before suddenly opening up like some punk kid caught shoplifting red-handed. Lawrence did, Detective Makinson said, what most criminals did under such circumstances—he blamed his accomplice. Police knew the routine. There was no honor among thieves and killers.

"Jerry did it!" the baby-faced ex-con cried. "He shot all of them. I was there, but I didn't know he was really gonna do it . . . I have a conscience. I'm not a murderer."

Detectives taped David Lawrence's confession. He stated that McCracken and he arrived at the New Ferndale Lounge at about 7:30 on Saturday evening, October 13th. They brought along a bottle of whiskey, and, chasing their swigs from the bottle with beer, they proceeded to get drunk. McCracken also carried his pistol stuck under his belt.

The drunker they became, Lawrence said, the meaner McCracken grew. They were soon talking about robbing the tavern, stealing a car, and taking off cross-country on a crime spree.

"I thought he was just joking," Lawrence insisted.

Around 1:00 a.m., there were four people left in the bar other than Lawrence and McCracken. McCracken got up and went to the toilet; he swaggered back to the bar and stood alongside Lawrence. Without further fanfare, McCracken produced his pistol, jumped back, and pointed the gun.

"This is a robbery!" McCracken yelled. "Get your hands on the bar! I want all the money!"

No one resisted. Carol McDaniels, the barmaid, followed orders and emptied cash register receipts onto the bar. McCracken was wired hot like the coil on an old Model-T Ford. Across the horseshoe bar from him, Steve A. Smith reached for his back pocket apparently to surrender his wallet. McCracken's deadly gun leveled at him.

An instant later the shooting started. The massacre began.

"It was like he got started and couldn't stop," Sergeant Allen later explained to the press.

McCracken shot Smith in the face. The man toppled off his bar stool, already dead. McCracken shot Tyrell Boyd in the back of the neck; Boyd also died before he hit the floor.

Next came Timothy Sheets. A blood trail on the floor marked the spot where Sheets had tried to crawl across the floor.

Carol McDaniels, behind the bar, was the last to fall, with a single .22 slug to the skull. She remained alive, but surgeons were warning police not to count on her as a witness.

Their suspicions now reinforced by direct evidence, the Makinson-Cook detective team descended upon Tulsa in an intensive two-hour manhunt. It led them to the lot of a pipe drilling firm on South Norfolk Avenue. Jerry McCracken supposedly worked there occasionally as a day laborer.

"He was unloading a truck," Makinson would recall. "I think he knew what was up and was expecting us. He was unarmed. He just kind of gave up."

Cops knew the routine all right. When the interrogation began, McCracken allegedly took the same course of action as David Lawrence—he blamed his accomplice.

"David's lying," McCracken reportedly insisted. "I didn't shoot them. David shot all of them."

The story McCracken told and testified to in court was essentially the same as Lawrence's, the only exception being that the star of the drama, the gunman, depended upon who was doing the talking. There the two ex-cons were, each pointing the finger at the other.

"It seemed like a dream," said McCracken, according to court transcripts. "I can't believe I was there. I wish I was at another place."

Afterward, the two men fled the tavern with about $300 cash, a pack of cigarettes, and two empty beer pitchers and mugs to keep police from finding fingerprints on them. On foot, the pair ran the several blocks to the apartment that Lawrence shared with his girlfriend.

"You went back with the murderer?" an incredulous Chief Prosecutor Tom Gillert later asked McCracken, obviously not believing his story. McCracken's lawyer was asserting that the only thing McCracken did wrong was to "associate with ex-cons."

"He [Lawrence] didn't shoot me," McCracken replied. "I was afraid when he shot the people, but not after."

"Under the law," Detective Makinson explained, "it doesn't make any difference which one actually pulled the trigger. They're equally guilty."

"It's the most inept, cruelest massacre that can happen," Chief Prosecutor Gillert commented. "When those two people came out of [the bar], they were both guilty of first-degree murder."

On Thursday, October 19th, Gillert charged each of the two ex-convicts with three counts of first-degree murder, armed robbery, and shooting with intent to kill. He amended the charges on Monday, October 23rd, after Carol McDaniels died over the weekend.

The charges now read four counts of first-degree murder. It was the largest number of victims stemming from one Tulsa homicide case that police could remember.

Although the "whodunit" might have been solved, Detective Makinson pounded the streets for days afterward building corroboration for the case, seeking out additional witnesses, and attempting to gather supporting evidence.

Regular bar patrons of the New Ferndale reportedly identified both suspects in a lineup as the strangers they saw in the bar the night the slaying occurred. Detectives Makinson used clues from the suspects' statements in his search for the murder weapon. He started at a dumpster on North Boulder Avenue and, finding it empty, made his way to a church not far from the halfway house where McCracken had lived. There, while not recovering the weapon, he seized ammunition that reportedly matched the type used in the mass slaying and which McCracken had allegedly hidden there.

McCracken reportedly told fellow jailmates that he had made it impossible for police to ever be able to find the gun.

In May 1991, David Keith Lawrence pleaded guilty to murder and robbery and agreed to turn state's evidence in order to avoid the death penalty. The recent execution of Charles Troy Coleman had made the death penalty a real threat in Oklahoma for the first time in over 20 years. Lawrence accepted life imprisonment plus 20 years and took the witness stand against Jerry Lynn McCracken in September 1991.

McCracken's attorney argued that David Lawrence, not McCracken, was the triggerman.

"In his aggressive, drunken state . . . he shot and he kept shooting until he shot everyone in the bar," the attorney said. "When Mr. Lawrence came out with a gun, he went nuts and killed four people. He did what many small men do when they drink too much — he grew from a small man to a big man."

"I'm here to keep from dying," Lawrence snapped from the witness stand. "But I'm not lying."

It is an affirmation of the American judicial system that juries have a way of reaching the truth most of the time. It took only 90 minutes for the jury to reach a decision on Friday, September 21, 1991. They found McCracken guilty of being the gunman in the brutal mass slaying and recommended that he be put to death for the deaths of the four patrons of the New Ferndale Lounge.

Jerry Lynn McCracken currently waits out appeals on death row at the Oklahoma State Penitentiary in McAlister. David Keith Lawrence is serving his life sentence at the same maximum security facility.

**EDITOR'S NOTE**
*Candy Bryant, Jackson Polk, Johnny Davis, and Bob Doth are not the real names of the persons so named in the foregoing story. Fictitious names have been used because there is no reason for public interest in the identities of these persons.*

# "BAYMEADOWS MASSACRE LEFT 16 VICTIMS!"

## by Barbara Geehr

At 10:44 a.m. on Monday, June 18, 1990, emergency calls began coming in on Florida's Jacksonville Sheriff's Office lines in rapid-fire order. Dispatcher Robynn Owens fielded the first one—a call from a woman who did not identify herself. In a barely audible voice over the sound of gunshots, the woman said, "This is the GMAC loan office in Baymeadows. Somebody's in here with a shotgun, shooting everybody."

Owens, immediately alert, asked, "Is it a man? A woman? Who is it?"

"A black man," the caller responded.

"Stay on the line while I notify patrol units," the dispatcher instructed her. "Don't hang up. Okay?"

"I gotta go," the woman caller whispered.

Those three words are believed to be the last ones ever spoken by the unidentified caller, for even as Owens was ordering patrol units to the General Motors Acceptance Corporation office, she heard five distinct gunshots over the emergency line. Then the line went dead.

Dispatcher Cynthia Weatherly answered the second call, which also came from inside the GMAC loan office. A male caller who also did not identify himself, whispered excitedly, "There's a man with a gun in here!" A dial tone abruptly cut off the connection. Weatherly tried to get the man back, but all she could raise was a busy signal.

A third caller, who identified himself as a GMAC employee, said he was calling from an office in another building in the complex. "There's a man with a gun inside the GMAC office, and he's firing at everyone in the office," he told Melissa Feagin, the dispatcher who answered this emergency call.

"Officers are already on their way," Feagin said. "Can you describe this man? Can you tell me what he's wearing?"

"He's a black male—he looks like he's in his forties and he's wearing a blue jacket. I don't remember anything else—except the gun he was using. It looks like a twenty-two automatic rifle."

"Where is the man now?"

"He's still in there. I'm still hearing shots. He's still shooting at everybody."

"Hold on," Dispatcher Feagin told him. Then she informed patrol units en route to the GMAC office that the suspect was still inside the GMAC office, was still armed and still firing shots. She relayed the brief description of the gunman that she had just obtained.

Getting back to the caller, she asked him what else he could tell her. "Do you know how this man got into the office? Did he drive up to the building in a car, or what?"

"I don't know," the caller answered. "I was at my desk. I heard two shots. I looked up. There was this guy with a rifle, and he was shooting. I ducked behind my desk, which happens to be at the front of the room. He wasn't firing in my direction. I managed to sneak out behind him. I came over here to a neighboring business to call the emergency number. That's everything I know—a black guy came into the office and he started shooting."

"Okay, officers are on their way," Dispatcher Feagin assured him.

The fourth call came in on Dispatcher Cynthia Weatherly's line. "Listen," an unidentified male said, "get the police to GMAC right away." Weatherly recognized the voice as that of the man who had called from inside the GMAC office a few minutes before and had been cut off.

"The police are already on their way," she said. "They'll be there any minute. Has anybody been killed?"

"Yes, yes!" he said. "Everybody is being killed!"

"Can you tell me anything about this gunman? The kind of weapon he's using? The kind of clothing he's wearing?" Weatherly asked.

"He's a black male, and the rifle he's carrying looks like an AK-forty-seven. All I remember about his clothing is, he's wearing a hat."

"A hat? What kind of a hat?"

"I don't know."

"Has he got a mustache? A beard? Is he wearing a mask or anything like that? Do you have any idea who he is? Did you see the vehicle he drove to the office park in?"

"No, no, no!" the caller answered. "Listen—this guy is walking around, shooting." The caller's voice lowered to a less-audible whisper. "It looks as though he's starting to head in this direction."

"Are you in a safe place?"

"No. Listen, you better send the SWAT team."

"They're also already on their way. Is this guy anywhere near the spot where you're at?"

There was no answer."

"Sir? . . . Sir, can you talk?"

From that point on, Dispatcher Weatherly heard only gunshots . . .

When sheriff's patrol and investigating officers reached the crime scene at 10:49 a.m., they could hardly believe what they saw. Eight GMAC employees lay dead beneath their desks, three other employees and two customers had been seriously wounded; and the unknown gunman himself was stretched out on the floor at the back of the room. Apparently, he'd committed suicide. The rifle he'd used to carry out the bloody rampage and the revolver he'd taken his own life with, both lay beside him.

Investigators cleared and secured the building and called rescue units and the medical examiner to the scene. Then they tried to reconstruct what had happened in the 11,000-square-foot open office. At the time the shooting started, more than 80 employees had been working at their flat-top, row-lined desks, and two customers had been standing at the collection counter at the front of the room, preparing to make payments on vehicles financed through the loan company.

Based on statements given by the survivors, investigators learned that the gunman, a "fortysomething" black male carrying a semiautomatic rifle, had walked through the front door of the building and immediately opened fire. He shot the two customers at the collection counter and then methodically began going through the open room, firing away at the horror-struck employees.

Seeking safety, the workers dropped to their knees and began crawling from desk to desk. Several made it to a storage room, others to the exit door at the back of the room. As luck would have it, the door was stuck. A 49-year-old woman, who had worked at GMAC for 21 years, got up from her knees and slammed her body at the door again and again until it finally opened. "Come on!" she'd yelled to her co-workers and led several of them to safety outside.

Inside, the gunman began stalking the employees who had sought cover underneath their kneehole desks. As he made his way from the front of the room to the back, he stuck his rifle under desks at random, pumping bullet after bullet into whoever happened to be hiding there. By the time he reached the back of the room, 11 more victims lay dead or wounded. Then he abruptly dropped his rifle, pulled a revolver out of his pocket, and shot himself in the head.

"I couldn't believe what was happening," a woman whose desk was at the back of the room told the investigators. "The man walked in the front door and never said a word. He just immediately started shooting. When I heard the shots, I looked up, and when I saw him standing there with a rifle, I—like 'most everyone else—got under my desk.

"My first thought was that it was a robbery and to stay down. But the shots continued, and they kept getting closer and closer to where I was. He shot the two people under the desks in front of me. Then he shot the supervisor in front of them.

"After that, he shot the three people behind me. I was sure I was next. But then he dropped his rifle, pulled a revolver out of his pocket, and shot himself. Suddenly, everything became stone silent. There was not even the sound of a ringing phone."

The first paramedics and firefighters to reach the Baymeadows office park set up a parking area around the corner from the GMAC building for all the emergency equipment that would be arriving. Then the rescue teams entered the building where, as a first order of business, a veteran paramedic walked among the 13 people who had been gunned down and made the difficult decision as to which ones would receive medical treatment and which ones were beyond help of any kind.

Once the professionals began patching wounds, administering fluids intravenously, and comforting the victims who were being prepared for transport, the veteran paramedic realized that additional help was needed. He summoned three more rescue units and another fire unit to the scene.

The GMAC employees found dead at the scene were Denise Sapp Highfill, 36, of the leasing department; Drew Woods, 38, a credit representative; Lee Simonton, 33, a customer-relations manager; Barbara Duckwell Holland, 45, of the finance department; Cynthia Perry, 30, of the general office; Janice David, 40, a supervisor in the claims and collection department; and Sharon Louise Hall, 45, whose position was not given.

The two customers slain were 42-year-old Julia White Burgess, who was at the office to make a payment on a pickup truck, and 24-year-old David Hendrix, who was also making a payment on a vehicle financed by GMAC. Hendrix had been shot several times and was critically wounded, though still alive at the time of his transfer to the Baptist Medical Center. There, it was discovered that his wounds had collapsed both lungs, and he died on the operating table, bringing the death toll in the bloody massacre to nine.

Between 11:04 and 11:25 a.m., two helicopters and two ambulances transported the four seriously wounded victims to Jacksonville area hospitals. From that point on, the lives of all four were in the hands of the trauma surgeons and their medical teams.

During the time that rescue workers were administering aid to the wounded, the investigators tried to identity the gunman by searching the pockets of his jacket and pants. They found no identification, but plenty of ammunition for both the Universal .30-caliber clip-fed semiautomatic rifle he used in the slayings, and the .38-caliber Rohm revolver used to kill himself. They also found several rifle clips—some empty and some full—throughout the office.

Duval County Medical Examiner Peter Lipkovic and members of his staff arrived at the scene and removed the bodies of the gunman and his victims for autopsy. The M.E. later reported, "The gunman died from a single gunshot wound fired into his head from his own thirty-eight-caliber revolver. We found no trace of medication, illegal drugs, or any other substance which could have affected his judgment. He was not a drug-crazed addict. In fact—except for the gunshot wound—his autopsy proved to be one of the most normal I've ever done."

The autopsies completed on the victims showed that all had been killed with a clip-loaded semiautomatic .30-caliber rifle. "And all were shot two to four times, mostly as they crouched beneath their desks," M.E. Lipkovic added.

The bloody rampage, which quickly became known as

the Baymeadows Massacre, raised the number of worst massacres in the United States over the past 50 years to 16. In Duval County, Florida, the killings were the worst in that county's history. They were even worse than the one on a spring night in 1983 when a resident of the Palms Hotel became so unhappy over a rent dispute with the management that he set the hotel on fire, killing seven people.

As horrifying as the Baymeadows Massacre was, the Duval County investigators soon discovered that it was but the final act of a bizarre shooting spree that had actually begun in a rundown northside Jacksonville neighborhood just after midnight on Saturday.

An unemployed Vietnam veteran, 39-year-old Louis Bacon had become the first victim at 12:50 a.m., while he was standing at the corner of Moncrief Road and West 23rd Street, talking with a couple of other men with whom he had reportedly been drinking and using cocaine. That night being exceedingly hot and humid, the men were wearing light shirts, shorts, and sneakers.

One of the witnesses later described what happened: "A black man, carrying something in a pink blanket, walked straight up to Bacon like he was out looking for him. He pulled a thirty-caliber rifle out of the blanket and fired a bullet straight into Bacon's chest. The bullet hit so hard it blew Bacon right out of his sneakers and he didn't hit the ground until three feet away."

"The gunman's glasses fell off when he fired the shot," another witness said, "but he didn't stop to pick them up. He left them and the pink blanket right there on the sidewalk. But he kept hold of the rifle. Then he just walked away, going down Twenty-third Street. Nobody went after him because he was armed. Me and another guy called an ambulance, but it didn't do no good. The bullet had gone straight into Bacon's heart, and he was dead before the ambulance even got there."

A few minutes later and two blocks away, the same gunman, now driving a 1977 green Buick, apparently spotted his next target—30-year-old Doretta Drake. Drake, who was also said to have been drinking and using cocaine, was talking with two women friends in a vacant lot on Myrtle Avenue.

As one witness put it, "An old green Buick jumped onto the curb in front of the vacant lot, hitting a woman who happened to be standing there. She wasn't hurt, though, because when the car hit her, it somehow threw her onto the hood, and she just sort of rolled off onto the sidewalk.

"The driver got out of the car and said, 'Excuse me.' The woman was so scared, she took off running. The guy then pulled a rifle out of the car, took direct aim at Doretta Drake, and shot her square in the head. He then calmly put the rifle back into the car, got in himself and drove on down Myrtle Avenue and turned onto Twenty-second Street."

There, the investigators learned, the gunman stopped to ask a teenage couple for directions. Before pulling away, he shot the youth and his girlfriend in the shoulders. They were rushed to a nearby hospital. Both survived. Doretta Drake, however, died at University Medical Center two hours after being shot.

Duval County Sheriff Jim McMillan theorized that the fatal shooting of Louis Bacon and Doretta Drake in the predawn hours of Sunday stemmed from arguments over the "services of a prostitute." It was noted that though both Bacon and Drake had criminal records, neither of these victims had ever been arrested on any kind of charges related to prostitution.

All four of the Sunday predawn shootings took place within 10 minutes. Still the reign of terror was not over. Shortly after 1:00 a.m. on Sunday, a man fitting the description of the gunman—but now dressed in blue jeans, a blue shirt, and a cap—walked into a convenience store on Jacksonville's north side and picked up a package of luncheon meat and a loaf of bread. Then, pulling a pistol out of his jeans and holding the clerk at bay, he demanded all the money in the cash register. "I don't have anything to lose," he told the clerk as he grabbed the cash and calmly walked out of the store.

Although the investigators did not immediately learn what the gunman did for the next 24 to 26 hours, they were quickly able to link Sunday's predawn shootings and the convenience-store robbery seven or eight hours later to the Monday-morning massacre at GMAC. They recovered the 1977 green Buick used in the Jacksonville shootings in the Baymeadows office park, the building complex where the GMAC loan office was located.

On the passenger-side seat, they found a loaded 9-millimeter pistol, two clips, and 51 cartridges. On the floor lay a paper napkin imprinted with the logo of the northside convenience store, and hidden in the trunk were 12 pieces of blue nylon rope, neatly cut into 24-inch pieces. That made the investigators believe that the gunman might have originally intended to take hostages when he entered GMAC and opened fire.

On Tuesday, ballistics experts at the Florida Department of Law Enforcement (FDLE) in Jacksonville reported that tests showed bullets recovered from the bodies at both the Jacksonville and Baymeadows murder scenes had been fired from the same rifle—the .30-caliber semiautomatic recovered at the scene of the massacre.

The detectives had little difficulty in establishing the identity of the gunman. A check with the U.S. Bureau of Alcohol, Tobacco and Firearms showed that all three of the recovered weapons—the rifle used in the massacre, the revolver with which the gunman shot himself, and the loaded 9mm pistol found in the 1977 green Buick—had all been registered to 42-year-old James Edward Pough.

The sleuths learned that the rifle—a high-powered weapon often used for shooting deer—had been purchased at a Jacksonville pawnshop about two months before the shooting. The .38-caliber revolver used by the gunman to take his own life had been registered 11 years before. The 9mm semiautomatic pistol found in Pough's Buick, along with a veritable arsenal of other weapons, had also been registered in his name over the years.

The investigators were also able to verify the gunman's identity by questioning the witness to the northside Jacksonville shootings and the residents of that area, where Pough had lived for 10 or 12 years.

Whereas the identification of the gunman in both shootings had been made in a relatively easy manner and Sheriff McMillan had developed a possible motive for the murder of Louis Bacon and Doretta Drake, finding the motive for the massacre at GMAC was to prove a far more difficult matter. As burial services for all the victims and the gunman himself got under way, the investigators began delving into every aspect of James Edward Pough's life.

Born in 1948 as the first of what would become a family of nine children, Pough grew up in a Jacksonville area of now vacant land behind the downtown campus of Florida Community College. Investigators and probation officers of the 1950s remember the neighborhood as one of "high crime and high delinquency." Nonetheless, the sleuths learned, the boy grew up in a religious atmosphere and attended church regularly.

Childhood bouts with asthma may have helped to make Pough dependent on—as well as devoted to and protective of—his mother. When his father left the family in 1959, the then 11-year-old did everything he could to help her. Pough was completely devastated when she died in 1984 and, up until the time he took his own life, he regularly visited her grave behind Florida Community College.

Pough, given the nickname "Pops" early in life and called that by practically everyone ever since, attended a vocational high school but dropped out in his sophomore year. Due to his childhood problems with asthma, he was declared medically unfit for military service in the Vietnam War. At age 18, he went to work as a common laborer, and he remained a common laborer for the rest of his life. He did his job well, however, and was considered to be highly dependable.

A supervisor at the mechanical contracting company where Pough was working at the time of the massacre told the detectives that it was hard for him to believe the killer they were asking about was the James Edward Pough the crew knew as Pops. "Pops was a good worker, a most dependable guy," the supervisor said. "He was on the job from seven in the morning until three-thirty in the afternoon five days a week and earning union scale. That came to four hundred bucks a week."

The supervisor described Pough as one of the best and most dependable workers in the 300-member Local 301. "We personally observed Pops and his work habits on other union jobs before we hired him. We actually requested him by name, which is something we don't ordinarily do. We never had a problem with him. He never missed any time from the day he started—until the Monday morning of the massacre, that is."

"What happened then?" one of the detectives asked.

"He telephoned to say he wasn't coming in."

Investigators learned from another company employee that January of 1990 had been a bad month for Pops. "His wife left him, and he gave up the Pontiac Grand Am he'd had for only a few months," the co-worker explained.

"Do you happen to know why he gave up the car?"

"He was finding the monthly payments too high to go on carrying."

Another co-worker recounted what he considered a puzzling incident which had taken place about two months before the massacre: "Pops was all upset on this particular day, and he actually begged me to pray for him. When I asked him why, he said, 'I'm going in there and never coming out.' I couldn't get him to tell me where."

Family members agreed that Pough's life had been

"work and home, work and home, and almost nothing else." One relative told the investigators, "He stayed by himself a lot. He didn't seem to want or need any friends. After he got married, he became even more reclusive."

His neighbors described Pough in much the same way. One of them said, "He'd always stay to himself—he never had any visitors. He'd see a neighbor, he'd speak, and then get in his car and go to work. He'd come home, he'd speak, and then go right upstairs to his apartment."

Other neighbors offered similar descriptions of Pough: "He was a nice person—he minded his own business." "He stayed in his own house a lot, but he was always nice whenever you saw him." "There were no misunderstandings, no trouble." "He was never seen carrying a weapon." "We don't know what happened to him. He was nice. He would talk nice to you." "You wouldn't expect nothing like this from him." However, the Duval County court records painted a somewhat different picture of James Pough, whose brushes with the law began the year he turned 17. He was arrested twice in 1965 on charges of vagrancy. In 1966, he was again arrested two times—once for attempted robbery and once for assault to murder. In the latter case, he attacked a 47-year-old construction worker with a two-by-four because the man owed him a quarter. There is no clear record as to whether Pough spent time in jail on any of those charges.

In July 1969, Pough was arrested on a gambling charge and paid a $10 fine. Three months later, he paid a $75 fine for brandishing a knife in a threatening manner. The following year, he was arrested but not prosecuted for auto theft and vagrancy-prowling by auto. Two years later, he was charged with the murder of his best friend, David Lee Pender.

Homicide Sergeant Paul Short remembered the Pender case well. "On Saturday nights in 1971," he recalled, "the hot spot on what was called The Strip was this nightclub on Avenue B, near West Forty-fifth Street. Saturday-night shootings there were common and often led to a slab at Duval Medical Center.

"Pough and Pender were there with their girlfriends on the night of May eighth. Somewhere around closing time, Pender called Pough's girlfriend a bitch, and all four of them got into a heated argument which spilled out onto the street. Pough grabbed a thirty-eight-caliber pistol out of his girlfriend's purse and shot Pender in the arm, the chest, and the head. Pender was dead on arrival at Duval Medical Center, and Pough was charged with murder.

"By the time the case got into the court system a month later, the charge had been changed to manslaughter. Eventually, Pough pled guilty to aggravated assault. The judge withheld adjudication of guilt and put the defendant on probation for five years. As a condition of the probation, the judge ordered that Pough, henceforth, not have any firearm or dangerous weapon in his possession at any time."

One of Pough's relatives, reminded about the Pender murder, told the investigators, "Pops was never the same after that. He couldn't get over the fact that he had killed his best friend. He used to have nightmares about it. It was like he had lost a part of himself."

The last of the official record showed that Pough had been taken to court twice in 1977 on bad-debt charges. In January, the first creditor won a judgment for $919; in June, Pough settled a bad debt in the amount of $207.

In August 1982, a warrant was issued charging Pough with unemployment compensation fraud. The warrant was never served, however, due to an error in Pough's address in the files of the unemployment compensation office.

In January 1990, Pough's wife left him and filed a petition seeking protection. According to the terms of the petition, Pough was not to talk to her, write to her, or call her on the telephone for a year. He was also to stay away from where she worked and lived. The court granted that injunction three months before the Baymeadows

Massacre.

When investigators questioned his wife about her reasons for leaving Pough in January, she answered, "He kept getting more and more violent and I kept getting more and more scared . . .

"Actually," she explained, "I'd really made up my mind to leave following two incidents in which Pops held a rifle to my head and threatened to kill me. The final outburst wasn't even half as bad as those two times—he just threw a glass at me. But that was the last straw. I left and filed a petition to keep him away from me. The court granted the petition in March."

A female friend, who had previously lived in the same neighborhood as the Poughs, backed up Mrs. Pough's story about her husband's violent outbursts. "Yes," she said, "Pops did have lots of violent outbursts, and most of them were directed at his wife—probably because she was the only one he ever let around him.

"But I always believed there was a reason Pops' temper got so bad—like something must have happened to hurt him in his early lifetime. I know that after his momma died, he often said he didn't have anything to live for. He also used to say that when he left this world, he was going to take someone with him. Losing both his wife and that Pontiac Grand Am in January may have been more than he could handle. He loved them both. They gave him a feeling of self-esteem.

"What I'm trying to say, I guess, is I don't want you to walk away with the idea that Pops wasn't generally a nice person, because he was. But you just didn't cross him—he really did have a very bad temper."

As for Pough's lifestyle at the time of the massacre, he was living alone in a four-room second-floor apartment in a rundown cinderblock duplex in Jacksonville's Moncrief Park—a high crime area where, only the year before, police had answered 1,243 calls for crimes that included homicide, rape, robbery, assault, burglary, theft, stolen cars, and narcotics and weapons violations.

Pough was the only tenant in one of three duplexes standing side by side and enclosed by a padlocked barbed-wire fence. During the 11 years he lived there, he had installed burglar bars over the entrance door and the windows of his second-floor apartment. The windows on the lower floor of the house were covered with plywood.

The outside of the house might not have been very pretty, but the inside was different. Pough had purchased furniture and appliances on a four-year installment plan and tried to make the apartment "homey." He had a television set in every room and slept on satin sheets.

When the investigators first inspected the apartment after the massacre, however, they found that it had been ransacked. The only things left were a rusty weightlifting bench, four bags of garbage, two pictures of Jesus Christ, and a calendar on which two dates were circled in red. One was May 8th, the date on which Pough had shot and killed his best friend, David Pender, 19 years earlier. The other was June 18th, the date of the Baymeadows Massacre. Pough had apparently set the date for what was to be his final mission in life.

The investigators knew that now was the time to zero in on James Edward Pough's relationship with GMAC, the car-loan company which had financed his purchase of the white Pontiac Grand Am. Information gathered from official records, from people involved in the transactions, and from various members of Pough's family showed that, in December 1988, James Edward Pough went to a Pontiac dealer on Jacksonville's Atlantic Boulevard to trade in his old car for a newer one. He was immediately attracted to a snappy-looking used Pontiac Grand Am with an odometer reading of 49,158 miles and a price sticker of $11,988.

A relative of Pough's said, "Pops told us right away he knew he had to have that car and would do anything to get it. He began negotiating on the price."

The dealer's records showed that after deducting an allowance for Pough's trade-in and adding the sales tax, the price of the car would be only $10,368. "Pough then wanted to know the best financing deal he could get," the Pontiac dealer recounted. "I took down credit information, contacted the GMAC loan office in Baymeadows, and came back with its offer. Beginning in February 1989, Pough would start making payments of three hundred and fifty-two dollars a month for fifty-four months."

The dealer pointed out that the amount of the monthly payment included an 18 percent interest charge and brought the actual amount being paid for the Pontiac, after deduction for trade-in and addition of sales tax, to $19,037—almost twice the amount of the price on the windshield sticker.

"But Pough didn't seem to care," the dealer said. "He loved that car and he took the deal."

Members of Pough's family made similar comments: "Pops knew he would have a hard time paying for that car, but we figured he would find a way. We were really happy for him. He'd worked so hard all his life, we thought he deserved a nice car."

In the beginning, Pough apparently did find a way to meet the monthly payment of $352. He began driving three co-workers to and from the job, charging each of them $15 a week. The monthly income from that service paid approximately half of the monthly note on the vehicle; Pough was able to pay the other half from his own salary. But the car-service arrangement eventually broke down and Pough found himself with only his own earnings to meet the $352-a-month note.

Pough made what was to be his last payment on the note in November 1989. In January 1990, he bought the 1977 green Buick that he later used in the Jacksonville street murders and the Baymeadows Massacre. In March, he received the first of two notices from GMAC. It declared that his Pontiac Grand Am had been sold at auction for $5,400, and included a bill for $6,394 now owed to GMAC for "the service contract fee, the auction fee, the repossession and reconditioning fees and late charges."

On April 6th, Pough received a second notice demanding the money due.

In the predawn hours of Sunday, June 17th, James Pough shot and killed Louis Bacon and Doretta Drake and wounded two teenagers. Six hours later, he robbed a convenience store at gunpoint.

The detectives had long wondered what the gunman had done in the hours between the convenience-store robbery at 9:00 a.m. on Sunday and the GMAC slayings which had begun shortly before 11:00 a.m. on Monday. By now, they had more or less reached the conclusion that Pough had spent the time alternately sleeping and working on his diabolical plan for the next day. And they were probably right — except for one brief span of time.

It was barely past eight o'clock on that Monday morning of June 18th, when a security patrol supervisor at Florida Community College's downtown campus noticed a man standing near the entrance to the main building. He knew the man, for he had seen him there many times before. That man was James Pough, otherwise known as Pops. Pops had visited there often because, from there, he could see his old neighborhood. He could even see Dew Drop Street, the street on which he had grown up. But most of all, Pough could see the St. Joseph Missionary Baptist Church, where his mother's funeral services had been held and where her body lay buried in the adjacent graveyard.

The patrol supervisor watched as Pops stood at his mother's grave, staring silently, and then, just as silently, walked away. How could the security man have known at that moment that Pough would next telephone his job supervisor to say he would not be in that day because he "had something to do." How could anyone have foreseen that by 11 o'clock that morning, James Edward Pough would shoot nine people to death, gravely wound four others, and then fire a fatal bullet into his own head at the back of the 11,000-square-foot office?

In August, investigators closed the case on the Baymeadows Massacre, one of the 16 worst in the country, the very worst in Florida and, according to the final line of the closing report, the most senseless in criminal history. The final line on that report states: "No motive exists for Mr. Pough's acts."

# "FAMILY SLAUGHTER BY A MIXED-UP 'SOLDIER'!"

by Gary C. King

SEATTLE, WASH.
JUNE 10, 1986

It was December 24, 1985, Christmas Eve, at the Charles Goldmark home, situated on a bluff overlooking Lake Washington in the fashionable Madrona area of Seattle. While others were busy doing their last minute shopping, the Goldmarks were at home preparing for a party for their closest friends and relatives, to be held later that night. Charles, 41, was busy wrapping the last of the gifts to go under the tree while his wife, Annie, 43, ironed clothes in their upstairs bedroom. The couple's children, Colin, 10, and Derek, 12, were busy playing in another part of the house. They were all enjoying the Christmas spirit and doing their own thing that day.

Goldmark, a prominent Seattle attorney who specialized in civil law, had invited numerous people to his traditional Christmas Eve dinner party, and this year's bash showed signs that it would outdo all previous ones. The party was scheduled to begin at 7:00 p.m., but the first guests arrived a few minutes late at 7:10 p.m.

The Goldmark home was darker than it should have been when Peggy O'Leary and her family walked up the front steps carrying gifts, mostly for the two kids, Colin and Derek. Peggy excitedly rang the bell, but there was no answer. She repeated the attempts again and again, each time with the same results.

She wondered what had happened. Where were the Goldmarks? It wasn't like Charles and Annie to plan a party, invite guests over and then not be home. Just as she and her family decided to leave, they heard noises from inside the house. They were sounds of agony.

Peggy pounded on the front door and called out Charles' and Annie's names, but her efforts ended in failure and frustration as she was unable to gain entry to the house or get someone to answer the door. All the while, however, the sounds of agony continued.

Terrified for the Goldmarks' safety and well-being, Peggy O'Leary went to the nearest telephone and called a friend of the Goldmarks, Mark Adams, who had an emergency key to the house. Fortunately, Mark had not left for the party yet. He told Peggy he was on his way and would bring the spare key to the Goldmark home.

He arrived minutes later. As he let himself in through the front door he, too, heard the agonizing cries. He followed the sounds upstairs, turned on the bedroom light and could not believe the horror before his eyes.

Charles Goldmark was lying on the floor next to the bed, bloody from head to foot, making guttural sounds. One of his arms extended behind his back up onto the bed where Annie lay, also covered in blood but quite still. One of Annie's arms extended behind her back, and Mark Adams could see that her hand was bound to Charles' arm with a pair of shiny handcuffs. Lying behind the bed were the two boys, Colin and Derek, also bound together and covered with blood. Sick to his stomach, Mark ran out of the room and called the Seattle Police Department and emergency medical personnel.

Annie Goldmark was pronounced dead at the scene, apparently from having suffered stab wounds and severe blows to the head. Charles, Colin and Derek, however, were still alive, and they were rushed by ambulance to Harborview Medical Center. They, too, appeared to have been beaten with a blunt object and stabbed.

Seattle Police Homicide Lieut. John Gary, assisted by Detectives Earl Davis and John Boatman, headed the investigation into the brutal assault on the Goldmark family. They were accompanied by King County Prosecutor Norm Maleng and Deputy Prosecutor Bill Downing among others, including a person from the King County Medical Examiner's Office and technicians from the Washington State Police Crime Lab. The house was completely sealed off, and as guests arrived for the party, they were told the grim news and turned away.

The investigators noted there were no signs of forced entry into the Goldmark home, which prompted them to theorize that the perpetrator either had been known to the family or had been allowed inside after using some kind of ruse. It was possible the perpetrator had pulled a gun or other weapon when one of the occupants answered the door. In any case, the detectives initially noted there were no signs of theft or disorder aside from the attack that left one person dead and three others critically wounded on Christmas Eve.

Lying on the floor near the bed, which would have been in close proximity to the victims, was a long bloody kitchen knife and a bloody steam iron. There was tissue and matter present on the pointed tip of the iron, which prompted the detectives to theorize that it had been used to inflict the blows to the victim's skulls. Although there was a tremendous amount of blood on the floor, the investigators noted that no footprints had been made in the blood, which indicated the perpetrator had been very careful. For that reason the sleuths believed he wore gloves and doubted that fingerprint analysis would yield anything significant.

Peggy O'Leary and Mark Adams explained to the investigators how they gained entry to the Goldmark home and found the victims. He told the sleuths that he was the first one to go inside, but that he had no idea what had occurred until he went upstairs.

"I turned on a light in the (upstairs) hall," Adams told Detectives Davis and Boatman. "There was a beam of light (shining) into the bedroom. I saw a stark naked body, white in the light . . . Then I saw Chuck lying on the floor . . . He was moaning and yelling."

The investigators worked inside the Goldmark home throughout the night and Christmas day, processing it for clues. A group of 25 investigators fanned out in the affluent neighborhood, questioning neighbors about suspicious persons, vehicles and/or activities in the area on the day of the attack. The only thing unusual, the sleuths were told, was a young man seen loitering in the neighborhood that afternoon. He was described as being in his mid-to-late 20s, with neatly trimmed dark hair. He was wearing an open jacket, a sweater, and a stocking cap. Neighbors said that he appeared lost or perhaps disoriented. After "extensive canvassing of the neighborhood," according to Lt. John Gray, only a few tentative clues had been produced. Unfortunately there were no screams, gunshots or other loud noises that could help pinpoint the time of the attack.

"It's a real whodunit," said Gray, who added that no potential motive had been arrived at. The brutal attack was senseless, he added, and appeared to be random.

In the meantime, after undergoing extensive surgery for "bad head injuries," Charles Goldmark and his two sons were placed in the intensive care unit at Harborview Medical Center where they were listed in critical condition. Doctors said the victims' prognoses were not good.

Meanwhile, an autopsy was performed on Annie Goldmark's body by Dr. Corinne Fligner, a forensic pathologist with the King County Medical Examiner's Office. Dr. Fligner told the detectives that Annie suffered a severe stab wound to the neck that severed her spinal cord and paralyzed her limbs. She had sustained a five-inch-deep wound to her left chest. It was likely that Annie died instantly, said the doctor. Either of the stab wounds would have caused death, and her skull had been fractured by repeated blows from the tip of the steam iron found in the bedroom.

Following the analysis of blood taken from Annie Goldmark's body, a chemist reported to the investigators that chloroform was present. As a result of the startling discovery, the detectives reasoned the attacker subdued his victims with the chemical prior to carrying out his bloody deed.

"We have every reason to believe everyone was unconscious when they were attacked," said Deputy King County Prosecutor Bill Downing, "and that no one knew what was happening to anyone else."

As the investigation continued, the detectives probed into the victims' backgrounds in an attempt to uncover a possible link, no matter how remote or unlikely, they might have had with the perpetrator. The probers learned that Colin and Derek attended a private school near their home. Charles Goldmark was an experienced mountaineer, and the family loved the outdoors. They hiked, skied and fished together every chance they got, which proved somewhat difficult at times because of Charles' busy professional schedule.

Annie, the detectives learned, was a native of France but attained her U.S. citizenship. She was well-educated, fluent in four languages, and was politically active with the Democratic party. She was also active in the community but was described by those who knew her well as a devoted and loving mother and wife.

Charles was a partner with a downtown Seattle law firm. A 1965 graduate of Reed College in Portland, Oregon, Charles Goldmark went on to receive his law degree from Yale University. He was active in student government at Reed, and held a position within the National Student Association. A confirmed Democrat, Goldmark was a leader of presidential candidate Gary Hart's 1984 Washington State campaign.

On the surface there didn't appear to be anything in the Goldmark family's background that could help the detectives. But as they probed deeper, the sleuths learned there was a darker chapter in the family history that most would have preferred to leave buried.

What the detectives uncovered was that in the early 1960s Charles Goldmark's father and mother were accused of being communist sympathizers. Goldmark's father had been a Washington State legislator who had served several terms, but lost his campaign for re-election in 1962, largely because of the alleged communist activities. Goldmark's parents were eventually exonerated of the charges when they filed and won a libel suit against the Washington State newspaper that had published the accusing articles, but not before their reputations had been severely damaged. Although the detectives found the information particularly interesting, it appeared doubtful that any of it could be tied in with the violent Christmas Eve attack.

As the probe widened, investigators were sent back into the Madrona neighborhood where they covered a six block area in search of additional clues. Crime lab technicians continued to process the Goldmark home for clues, but police officials declined to reveal what additional evidence had been uncovered. The only information released at that time was done so by Seattle Police Chief Patrick Fitzsimons, who said the attacker had worked alone and the killings did not appear random after all. He declined to elaborate on that latter point, but said his detectives were continuing to run down leads and actually had a line on a suspect.

The next day, however, before the investigation had advanced much further on its own merits, the police received a tip from a member of the Duck Club, an ultra-conservative organization based in Florida (but with a Northwest chapter). As it turned out, the tip blew the case wide open.

According to the member, Max Taylor, who said the Duck Club's membership is anti-socialist and anti-communist, an acquaintance by the name of David Rice came to visit him on Christmas day and boasted that he had "dumped the top communist." Taylor told police that when Rice appeared at his door he asked if he could stay for a few days while he wrote a confession to a crime that he had committed.

"He sat in a chair for a few minutes," related Taylor. "and then said, 'I've got to talk with you.' We went into the kitchen, and he said. 'The cops are after me. They could be arriving any minute. I've just dumped the top communist. There were four involved.' "

The new information was quite a surprise to the investigators, particularly the communist angle and especially after they had previously discounted such avenues of investigation. However, the detectives wasted no time in getting to Taylor's apartment to interview him further.

"He (the caller) was acquainted with the suspect," said Chief Fitzsimons. "(However,) there does not appear to be any personal connection between this man and the Goldmark family."

When the probers arrived at Taylor's apartment, they learned that the suspect lived nearby. As a result, they set up a stakeout as they prepared to make the collar, all the while pressing Taylor for as many details as they could about David Rice.

Taylor told them that Rice had been brought to a couple of Duck Club meetings by his girlfriend, Margo Cobb, but that Rice had not been admitted to the actual meetings. Taylor said all he knew about Rice was that he was an unemployed steel worker who had moved to Seattle from Durango, Colorado. Taylor added that Rice had been in the city for approximately 3½ years.

As the detectives were concluding their interview with Taylor, they spotted Rice coming out of the nearby building where he lived. The identification was confirmed by Taylor, and Rice was arrested on the street. He offered no resistance, and was booked into the King County Jail on suspicion of murder, attempted murder, assault, and burglary.

Meanwhile, the sleuths obtained warrants to search Rice's apartment. The search turned out to be fruitful, and much evidence was collected. Among the items taken from the small dwelling were a pair of blood-soaked gloves, bloody clothing and keys to handcuffs that fit those which bound Annie and Charles Goldmark. They also found a toy pistol, a bottle of chloroform and notes that linked Rice to the Goldmarks. There was an abundance of anti-Semitic literature found in the apartment as well as communistic and Judaic writings.

In the hours that followed, Seattle police confirmed that Rice's description matched that of a man seen asking directions to the Goldmark home a short time before the attack, which enabled detectives to place the attack within 2 1/2 hours of the time the victims were discovered. During that same investigative time span, detectives had been notified by a bank official that a man had attempted to use one of Charles Goldmark's credit cards at 7:38 p.m. on the night of the attacks to withdraw money from an automatic teller machine. Because the user had not known the secret code number for the card, a photo had been taken by a hidden camera. The photograph was of David Rice.

Rice's only known criminal background, the detectives learned, involved two misdemeanor charges of lewd conduct that stemmed from acts of indecent exposure in Seattle in 1984. At the time of the Goldmark attack, Rice had not been tried on either charge.

With the insurmountable evidence against the suspect continuing to grow, King County District Judge Barbara Taylor Howard ordered David Rice held without bail. Rice did not immediately enter a plea to the charge of aggravated murder.

The following morning, at 2:05, ten-year-old Colin Goldmark died at Harborview Medical Center of wounds attributed to the Christmas Eve attack that claimed his mother's life. His father Charles and his brother Derek remained in critical condition in the hospital's intensive care unit.

In the days that followed, Seattle detectives worked round-the-clock to obtain as much information as they could about David Rice, much of which they obtained from acquaintances, relatives and a former girlfriend. Much of what they learned painted a bizarre picture of the suspect.

According to those who knew him, David Lewis Rice, 27, was driven by voices of imaginary beings from another planet. He also feared a communist invasion of the United States, and carried with him a blueprint for an underground shelter that would save 1,500 people from an impending nuclear holocaust. "He was to build the shelter to save the world, basically," said his former girlfriend, Margo Cobb. Cobb told the authorities that as time went on she came to believe that he was mentally ill. His condition worsened in 1985 to such a degree that she felt he could no longer tell right from wrong. "I was concerned about the delusions of grandeur," she said, and his increasing preoccupation with weaponry and a communist takeover of the United States.

Meanwhile, there was little change in the condition of the surviving Goldmark family members. Both the father and son were kept alive by respirators, and officials said that "both are still very, very critical . . . Derek is a little worse off than Charles, but both are in very critical condition."

Shortly before 10:00 a.m. on Thursday, January 9, 1986, Charles Goldmarks' fight for life ended when he died from the massive head wounds he'd sustained. Derek died from his wounds three weeks later on Thursday evening, January 30th.

David Rice was charged with four counts of aggravated murder. A conviction on these charges is punishable by death. The court appointed Tony Savage, a veteran "Perry Mason" type lawyer, and William Lanning to defend him. He pleaded innocent by reason of insanity. Because of the evidence against Rice, as well as statements he made to police after his arrest (which weren't made public until the case came to trial), William Lanning said his client "doesn't dispute any of the facts . . . We're not looking for a not-guilty verdict . . . I'm looking to save his life."

"It is my judgement that there are not sufficient mitigating circumstances to merit leniency," said Prosecutor Norm Maleng at a news conference, "and I am therefore filing a notice of our intent to seek the death penalty in this case." Maleng assigned Deputy Prosecutors William Downing and Robert Lasnik (who teamed a few years earlier to successfully prosecute the Seattle Chinatown Massacre case in which 13 people were murdered) to prosecute the case against David Rice. It would be a dramatic trial, one that King County residents would not quickly forget.

Amidst defense contentions that Rice suffered organic brain damage from injuries received as a child, damage that might have affected his mental abilities, David Rice underwent extensive psychological examinations prior to going to trial. Defense Attorney Lanning asked for neurological exams because Rice had been cut at the age of four when he crashed through a plate glass window and because he hanged himself at the age of eight after an argument with a family member.

After five examinations by a court-appointed clinical psychologist, it was determined that Rice suffered "schizoid and paranoid features" and frequently thought "friends" from outer space told him to do certain things but was otherwise legally sane, both at the time of the examinations and at the time of the Christmas Eve attack.

"The point is," wrote the psychologist, "that Mr. Rice did not cook up this (communist) stuff by himself, out of touch with reality," but in fact had been given his first information by members of a right-wing club who (mistakenly) identified the Goldmarks as leading communists in the area.

At his trial, which began in May before a packed courtroom of spectators, David Rice appeared relaxed as he was led handcuffed and shackled into the courtroom of King County Superior Court Judge Jim Bates. He sat quietly during opening remarks, and often took notes on a yellow legal pad.

"Slaughter was decreed" by the defendant, said Deputy Prosecutor Bill Downing, "because of his need for cash and as a target for his unfocused anger." In his 30-minute opening statement Downing said Rice chose Goldmark as a target in an effort to obtain cash because he thought Goldmark was "a prominent figure in the local Communist Party . . . He was wrong as wrong can be." Downing also told of another Seattle attorney who had been targeted by Rice, identified in Rice's notes, but said Rice backed down from the potential attack because he found the attorney's neighborhood too confusing. Downing said Rice then decided on Goldmark, whose neighborhood was easy to enter and leave.

"What you're dealing with is not a mentally responsible man," countered Defense Attorney Tony Savage, who conceded that details of the killings as outlined by the prosecution were "tragically true." Savage then told the jurors that Rice had been involved with right-wing extremists for months, and "became more and more enmeshed in this . . . His mental illness provided fertile ground to the point that these beliefs became real—at least to him," including a belief that a communist army was poised on the Mexican border waiting for orders to invade the United States. "He considered Mr. Goldmark a communist," added Savage. "He was going to get information from him to lead him up the ladder of the communist conspiracy . . . It is our contention that the defendant was and is mentally ill to the point that this has to be taken into consideration."

During the early stages of the trial, the jury heard testimony from the Christmas Eve dinner party guests who found the Goldmarks in their upstairs bedroom. They also heard testimony from police officers, detectives and medical and crime lab personnel. One of the first witnesses was a court-appointed clinical psychologist who extensively examined David Rice.

Although the psychologist concluded that Rice was legally sane, he added that the defendant was deeply disturbed and suffered from "grandiose ideas that he is meant to help a core group of people survive the coming nuclear war." He suggested to the jury that the attacks may have been triggered by a political pamphlet Rice had read, which stated that 30,000 to 50,000 foreign soldiers were poised at the nation's borders awaiting word from the Federal Reserve Board to enter and take over. The psychologist said Rice told him he hadn't planned to kill Goldmark but went to the Goldmark home to obtain cash and interrogate the lawyer about "the communist conspiracy" because Goldmark was "the highest obtainable target I could reach."

Another witness was Margo Cobb, Rice's former girlfriend who was also a member of the ultraconservative Duck Club. Cobb said she recognized that Rice was disturbed and had attempted to get help for him from a friend whose specialty was using hypnosis in therapy. But the therapy sessions were sporadic at best, she said. Cobb also conceded that she took Rice to two Duck Club meetings, but said Rice remained outside the meeting room. Although she admitted that some of the right-wing, anti-Semitic books found in Rice's apartment came from her own apartment, where Rice often stayed, Cobb said they didn't really share or hold the same political beliefs.

"I remember that we did not talk about politics very much. He talked about weapons and explosives, and he did talk about the impending communist invasion that's supposed to be happening sometime soon." Cobb said that beginning about August 1985, "there was some intimacy" between herself and Rice, but that the relationship did not work out.

"You cut him off sexually?" asked Deputy Prosecutor

Downing.

"He didn't seem to understand when I said to back off and give me my space," responded Cobb, who added that Rice told her he loved her and insisted that she marry him. Cobb said she continued to see Rice out of kindness and because of a fear she held that he might die without attention from her. Cobb said she liked Rice, but added that he was recuperating from a failed marriage that yielded him a child and that she simply did not want to remain involved.

"Did he ever tell you about the black box in his head?" asked Defense Attorney Tony Savage on cross-examination.

"Yes, he did," replied Cobb, about three to four months after the start of their relationship, about the same time he began talking of his shelter plan. "What he basically said . . . is that problems he could not solve or deal with, he would put them into this black box (in his head). Which was just another something that alerted me that he should be looked at."

At another point in the lengthy trial, prosecutors played tapes of a confession Rice made to police after his arrest and presented a written confession which was found in his apartment.

"I have a great concern for human life," Rice said during one of the tape interviews. "One of the things I hoped to achieve was to save a lot of lives at the expense of a few others. To sacrifice a few for the greater number . . . The evidence against the communists is well-documented. People say that Jews are behind the communists, but I don't think that is as well documented . . . I considered myself a soldier in the fight against communism and, sometimes, soldiers have to kill."

In the interview, Rice said at one point that he would have had some "definite changes" in his plans if he had known that the two Goldmark children were at home. "I would have kept his family out of it. The kids were not my enemy. They weren't anybody's enemy. They weren't supposed to be there . . . I didn't expect them to be there, and if I did expect them (to have been there), I wouldn't have been there . . . (But) they had already seen me—it was too late . . . I know now that what happened was a big, terrible blunder. What I have done was against my principles."

At one point Rice said that his new, post-arrest belief that Goldmark was not a communist after all has made him "feel bad about him, too . . . It's kind of hard to handle . . . I actually try to think about it as little as possible."

When asked by police during the interview if he had thought he could fulfill his political goals as well as his financial ones by killing the Goldmarks, Rice answered, "Yes. I assumed he (Goldmark) would have an amount of cash on him. I didn't know how much, but I figured it would be enough to get me by."

It was pointed out by the prosecution that Rice had obtained only $14 from Goldmark.

In a "To Whom It May Concern" letter written by Rice and found by police during the search of his apartment, Rice wrote: "I'm the person you want in the Goldmark killings. I know what I did was a terrible thing and that is why you see me as I am . . . I guess I should tell you why I did this so you won't have to ask anyone else: My life is a mess. It has been since my wife left. (Margo) has been trying to help me out, but I'm afraid that she isn't able to do much for me. I'm too far gone."

In another letter, written to Margo Cobb, Rice said: "I am fighting a losing battle against a very powerful force—evil. This is Satan's world now. The enemy's grand finale is almost upon us—the extermination of all existence. We are going to have to destroy the complex system he has built." The letters were passed around for the jurors to see.

In a videotaped interview, Rice told another psychologist that Charles Goldmark's passiveness allowed him to enter the residence by posing as a deliveryman. Once inside, he used a toy gun and chloroform to subdue his victims.

"If he had told me to get out of his house, that's exactly what I would have done," Rice said in the videotaped interview. He also said that Goldmark's obliging, conciliatory attitude may have been a wise approach in certain threatening situations, "but in my circumstance, it was just the opposite—it was the wrong thing to do." Rice added that he was uncomfortable with the insanity plea "because I knew what I had done . . . I told the cops when I first came in that, if at all possible, I want the death sentence."

During closing arguments, Prosecutor Robert S. Lasnik described Rice as more cunning than crazy, "more disturbing than disturbed, more determined than deranged, and more reprehensible than irresponsible."

During the prosecution's 70-minute closing argument, co-Prosecutor William Downing said the state had provided "more than enough evidence" that the Goldmarks' slayings were premeditated, committed in the course of a robbery or burglary and carried out to conceal Rice's identity. Both are necessary elements for the jury to reach a verdict of aggravated first-degree murder. Downing reiterated that the Goldmarks were chosen as victims because of an "offhand remark" by a member of the ultraconservative Duck Club concerning Goldmark's father and the incident that occurred more than 25 years ago.

"It was a plain, old-fashioned mistake, not a delusion," said Downing, referring to the remark Rice heard about Goldmark's father and then "twisted it to serve his own purposes." Downing added, however, that Rice's primary motive was money. Both prosecutors asked the King County Court jury to find Rice guilty of four counts of aggravated first-degree murder.

"This man has a mental disease, a mental defect," said Defense Attorney Tony Savage in his closing arguments to the jury. "There is the root of the problem . . . Whatever he was thinking, he did not have these people (the victims) in mind. He was looking for the father (the elder Goldmark) . . . He was at war against communism.

"Is the defendant a danger to society?" asked Savage. "Yes," replied the lawyer to his own question. "And he probably will be for the rest of his life." Is it likely that Rice would repeat his crimes? the lawyer asked. Savage said jurors should say, "absolutely yes," but added that they should find him innocent by reason of insanity.

On Thursday, June 6, 1985, David Lewis Rice was found guilty of four counts of first-degree aggravated murder for the fatal bludgeoning and stabbing of the Goldmark family. As Rice was led from the courtroom, he said, "The scum lied," referring to Prosecutor William Downing. "He said that I lied to save myself, when in actuality the lie was to kill myself."

"We are very satisfied that the jury has seen things the way we feel they should be seen," said Downing of the verdict. He declined further comment because of the pending penalty phase of the trial.

Defense Attorney Tony Savage said he was "disappointed" that the jury hadn't found Rice innocent by reason of insanity, and added that the verdict was "not unexpected. They (the prosecution) had better facts than we did." Savage added that Rice "is a very sick man," and that "whatever happens, he should not be released."

During the penalty phase of the trial, in which the same jury was responsible for deciding which punishment Rice should receive — death or life imprisonment without possibility of parole — Prosecutor Downing referred to "the care the defendant took to wear gloves" while committing his crimes. Downing also said that, in spite of the tremendous amount of blood inside the Goldmark home, "there were no bloody footprints . . . the defendant had taken care not to step in any of the blood and leave bloody footprints." Downing showed the jury again the photo of Rice attempting to use the automatic teller machine after the vicious attack had occurred. "Here he is, taking care of the Number one purpose of that evening—getting some cash."

During his presentation to the jury, Deputy Prosecutor Lasnik reminded the jury of the horrible events that occurred in the Goldmark home on Christmas Eve 1985. He described how Rice used chloroform on Charles Goldmark, then on his wife, Annie, and finally on Colin and Derek. Lasnik said the children's last thoughts on this earth were the terror in that bedroom. "That is what you have to keep in mind . . . This is one of the very few crimes that screams out for the death penalty."

"The death penalty is repugnant," said co-defense counsel William Lanning. "It's as morally wrong for two million people to put a man to death as it is for just one person . . . No one at all can question that he is mentally ill . . . Except for the defendant's mental condition these crimes would never have occurred . . .

"Next year, or 10 years from now," continued Lanning, "when you are cloistered in your own home in the dark of night, if at that time you will have a reasonable doubt whether David Lewis Rice should have been put to death, David Lewis Rice is entitled to that doubt now and at this time."

On Tuesday, June 10, 1986, after only six hours of deliberations, the jury voted unanimously that Rice should be executed for his crimes.

"It was obvious he had money in mind," said the jury foreman after the verdict had been read. "If the death penalty doesn't apply to this case, what kind of crime does it apply to?"

The last person executed in Washington State was Joseph Chester Self, who was hanged in 1962. The jury's verdict against Rice made him the 8th person to face death in a newly enacted death penalty statute.

# EDITOR'S NOTE
*Margo Cobb, Peggy O'Leary, Mark Adams and Max*

*Taylor are not the real names of the persons so named in the foregoing story. Fictitious names have been used because there is no reason for public interest in the identities of these persons.*

# "THE GAY DRAG QUEEN AXED 4!"

by Bruce Gibney

CHINO, CALIF.
MAY 15, 1985

The U.S. Coast Guard cutter plowed through the choppy seas off the Santa Barbara, California coast.

It was a few minutes past 5 o'clock on Saturday morning July 30, 1983. A thick fog still hung over the blue green waters, pierced only by illumination from the cutter's bank of searchlights.

On board, washing down sea sickness pills with cups of coffee, were heavily-armed members of the Santa Barbara Sheriff's Special Weapons Team.

They were on board at the request of the Coast Guard who had received a frantic call for help at 4:30 that morning.

It was placed by a woman who said she had been raped by a crewman from a sailboat that was moored near theirs in Pelican Cove.

The victim's husband had been passed out when the assault took place. Now awake and enraged, he wanted to take the law into his own hands, the woman said.

Not wanting to take unwarranted chances, the Coast Guard had contacted the sheriff's office.

At daybreak, the cutter entered Pelican Cove and churned towards a 32-foot sailboat that was moored

100 yards off shore.

The cutter was 150 yards from the boat, when a black man, naked to the waist, tangled matted hair hanging in pigtails to his shoulders, leaned over the railing.

Spotting the cutter, he leaped over the rail and swam madly for a dinghy moored nearby. The dinghy was no match for the cutter and was pulled over before the half-naked black man had a chance to row to shore.

Dragged aboard and put in handcuffs, the suspect was taken to a holding room until he could be returned to the mainland.

One of the crewmen asked his name.

"Angel Jackson," the man replied immediately.

It was a lie.

And once his real name was learned, the story of the early morning arrest would make the front pages and nightly news programs from coast to coast.

Chino, California is a bucolic farming community 30 miles southeast of Los Angeles. Ranch homes dot the rolling hills and, despite the presence of a minimum-security state prison and a camp for juvenile delinquents in the immediate area, the feeling of isolation and serenity is so pervasive that residents rarely lock their doors.

That all changed, however, after a man called the San Bernardino Sheriff's Office Sunday morning June 5, 1983.

He was in shock but coherent. The man said he had gone to the home of his friend, Frank Douglas Ryen, to pick up 11-year-old Christopher Hughes, who spent the night at the Ryen home. Hughes was a relative of the man.

When he got there, Christopher was dead and so were Frank Ryen, Ryen's wife, 41-year-old Peggy, and their daughter, 10-year-old Jessica. Only an eight-year-old family member showed signs of life. He was unconscious, his throat slashed ear to ear, but his heart was still beating.

Deputies and paramedics rushed to the isolated ranch on the 3600 block of English Road in the Chino hills, west of the Corona Freeway.

The lawmen who first arrived in the driveway of the spacious ranch-style home were no strangers to the grim realities of their work. Neither were the seasoned paramedics. Violent death was an everyday fact of life in their professions. But nothing in the past had prepared them for the sight that greeted their eyes inside the ranch house.

Frank and Peggy Ann Ryen were in their bedroom hacked and stabbed repeatedly.

Ten-year-old Jessica was found in her bedroom, while Christopher Hughes was sprawled in the hallway. Both had been stabbed and axed.

San Bernardino County Coroner Brian McCormick said they were the "most gruesome, senseless homicides I've seen since being associated with this office. The killer or killers thrust sharpened objects — axes, hatchets, screwdrivers or ice picks — more than 20 times into each of the four victims."

The eight-year-old boy, who was the lone survivor of the massacre, was secured on a gurney and flown by chopper to Loma Linda University, where the emergency room staff worked frantically to save him.

Meanwhile, two teams of homicide detectives from the sheriff's station in San Bernardino were dispatched to the ranch house. Before the day was over, 35 detectives were searching the ranch and going door to door down English Road.

In their search, investigators did manage to find bloody footprints in the victims' house and a shed outside the house, where sleuths believed the killer changed clothes. They also found blood samples which were later tested and found not to be from the victims.

By evening, a few things were clear. The location of

the bodies, the fact the victims were prepared for bed, and the physical condition of bodies indicated the slaughter had commenced around midnight.

The detectives theorized the first victim was Frank Ryen, followed by his wife and then the children, who might have been awakened by screams and had been trying to escape when assaulted.

The killer or killers had then fled in the Ryens' 1977 Buick station wagon, which had been parked in front of the house when Christopher Hughes was dropped off the night before.

Police issued an APB on the missing station wagon, with the advisement that the vehicle was wanted in a murder investigation and peace officers were to use extreme caution when approaching occupants of the vehicle.

Meanwhile, detectives searching the Ryen ranch found evidence the killer or killers had spent several hours and possibly longer in a small, unused house that was down the hill from the Ryen property.

Bloodstains were found on the wall and near the entrance to the shed. And in one corner, lawmen discovered bloodstained clothing that had apparently been changed after the slayings.

The part owner of the house identified a bloodstained hatchet, which was found near the murder scene and stained with the survivor's blood, as one that had been left in the shed. He also said that he had kept a large hunting knife and ice pick in the house, and that these items were now missing.

A pathologist told sleuths these instruments could have been the ones used to make wounds in the victims' bodies.

San Bernardino Sheriff Floyd Tidwell called a press conference Monday afternoon. It was jammed by three dozen reporters from newspapers and television stations from as far away as San Francisco.

"Do you have a motive?" one reporter asked. "Nothing that could explain this," the sheriff replied. "This is utterly senseless."

"Did the survivor see the killer?" another asked.

"We don't know," the sheriff responded. "We don't know what the hell he saw, or if he will remember anything."

The sheriff explained the youth had been bludgeoned in addition to the knife wounds he sustained. The youth was rendered temporarily silent after undergoing a tracheotomy to help him breathe.

He said the boy's vocal chords had been severed and that detectives would try to communicate with him with a device that when held to the throat amplifies voice sounds.

"You have to remember that the boy is only eight and has been through a lot," the sheriff said.

Another reporter thrust his hand into the air. "Do you have any suspects?" he asked.

"Maybe," came the reply.

Tidwell explained his investigators were seeking two men and a youth who fled last week from Chino detention facilities. The sheriff admitted, however, that the three were "not good suspects" and that all leads in the case so far were "weak."

The sheriff added that his men were checking out other leads, including the report that three men—white or Latino—drove up to the Ryen home Saturday afternoon in a blue vehicle.

The sheriff said a burglary last May 7th at the Ryens' Santa Ana chiropractor's office was also being looked into to determine if it had anything to do with the murderous attack.

Santa Ana police had arrested three suspects in the burglary. Two were in jail, but the third was being sought on a warrant for failure to appear for arraignment the week before the Chino massacre.

The day after the press conference, a 17-year-old youth was arrested in the City of Industry. The youth had escaped from the Boy's Republic, an institution for disadvantaged youths, which was located one mile from the Ryens' home. The boy was one of three escapees police had wanted to question.

Two days later, an escapee from the minimum security wing of the California Institution for Men at Chino was arrested in nearby Westminister.

Police questioned both men closely. Those interrogations and the inmates' willingness to take polygraph examinations and assist in the investigation cleared them as suspects in the Ryen murders.

That left one escapee to find: a 25-year-old drifter named Mark Watson. Watson had been convicted of burglary in Los Angeles and transferred to Chino. He was kept in a medium security wing until his fingerprints were checked for identification with the FBI and he was evaluated by prison officials.

Through a clerical error, however, Watson was transferred to a minimum security wing on June 1st. The next day he walked away from his work duty station and disappeared. Prison officials were not immediately concerned. Watson did not have a history of violence and was not considered dangerous.

But Watson was not who he said he was. The real Mark Watson was back in a minimum security facility in Pennsylvania. The man using his name was a former prison inmate of Watson's, Kevin Cooper.

And Cooper had a history of violent, irrational behavior. He had been arrested for rape, had a history of drug use, and had been institutionalized in mental hospitals for the criminally insane. Detectives tied Kevin Cooper to the Ryen murders after an inmate came forward and said he had issued Cooper a pair of Pro-Keds high top tennis shoes so he could play basketball.

"If somebody wants to be on our team, we want to give them the best shoes," the inmate told sleuths. "These were the best for our floor."

The prison-issued shoes had a one-of-a-kind tread that matched bloody tread prints which had been discovered in the bedroom of the Ryen home and shed. The bloody prints were made by a size 10 D shoe—the same size as Kevin Cooper's.

Two detectives flew to Pennsylvania. They learned that Kevin Cooper was an adopted child who was born and grew up in Pittsburgh, where, according to relatives, he was a slow learner and "always a problem in school."

Allegheny County psychological records described Cooper as a man who was sane until an overdose of unidentified drugs made him psychotic.

The psychotic episodes were infrequent, but when they occurred, Cooper could be very, very violent.

A former girlfriend learned this the hard way. She told police she had a five-month relationship with Kevin Cooper that ended in June 1982; and, at one point, the two took out a marriage license.

According to the woman, the wedding bells were muted when Cooper, in a psychotic rage, burst into her house, punched and kicked her senseless, then held a knife to her throat and raped her repeatedly.

The girlfriend broke off the engagement. Deep down she knew it probably would not have worked anyway.

Part of his problem was his sexual identity. "Kevin is gay," she told lawmen.

Lawmen weren't surprised. They learned that while at Chino, Cooper hung around with inmates who were effeminate homosexuals or transvestites.

And while in Los Angeles County Jail on burglary charges, he had listed himself as a homosexual and was placed in the special section reserved for homosexuals, transvestites and sex offenders.

San Bernardino detectives, with the aid of their Los Angeles counterparts, obtained a list of inmates who were on the "fruit wing" when Cooper was incarcerated there.

Those still incarcerated were eliminated from the list, while those who had been friendly with Cooper and had been released were questioned.

The manhunt heated up on June 11th, one week after the Chino slayings, when a patrol officer in Long Beach spotted the Buick station wagon belonging to the Ryen family. It was parked in a lot at a local church in Long Beach.

Interviews with church officials revealed the car had been parked there for about a week. Criminalists went over the car inch by inch. It had been wiped clean of prints. But on the seat, technicians found shreds of tobacco that under a microscope matched tobacco found in the hideout house. The brand was sold only to prisons and was standard issue at the Chino prison.

San Bernardino detectives, aided by Long Beach police and vice detectives, questioned homosexuals and transvestites for information about Kevin Cooper's whereabouts.

They received plenty of help from the gay community since the last thing the homosexuals wanted was a dress-wearing psychopath in their midst.

Long Beach police received dozens of calls from homosexuals who said they had seen a transvestite matching Cooper's description hanging out in area bars.

But they never caught Cooper. The closest police came was a 30-year-old transvestite who met Cooper while both were in jail. He told police that Cooper had spent a "night or two" with him in Long Beach after the murders.

The transvestite told detectives Cooper did not say anything about the murders and there was nothing in his demeanor or actions that suggested he had committed a crime or was wanted by police.

"We stayed together for a couple of days and then he split," the transvestite recalled. "He said he might go to

Los Angeles, but I don't know where he is."

There were more sightings, including the one made by an Orange County sheriff's deputy who made a routine traffic stop and noticed the driver looked similar to Kevin Cooper and was wearing a dress.

The dress-wearing driver, however, was identified as someone else and was released.

More time passed. The 35 detectives assigned to the case the first day of the investigation had dwindled down to four. Tips were phoned in daily and had to be checked out. And the APB had to be updated each day, but it was mostly a waiting game.

Then, at 4 o'clock on Saturday morning July 30th, a frantic call for help was received by the U.S. Coast Guard Station in Santa Barbara, 130 miles north of Los Angeles.

It came from a woman aboard a sailboat moored off Santa Cruz Island who claimed she was raped.

A U.S. Coast Guard cruiser, with the Santa Barbara Special Weapons Unit aboard, was dispatched and three hours later a suspect was in custody.

The woman who had radioed the distress call was taken by helicopter to a Santa Barbara hospital where she was treated for physical injuries suffered during the rape.

She was visited by a sheriff's detective investigating the case.

"What happened?" he asked.

The woman explained she had been raped by a man named Angel Jackson who was a crewman on a 32-foot boat moored nearby.

She related that, on Thursday evening, she and her husband had dinner on the 32-foot sailboat with the boat's owner and his family.

The woman said Angel paddled over to their boat the next morning and offered to show them San Clemente Island.

"We were very comfortable with him," the woman's

husband said. "He seemed like a nice, talkative individual. He even brought us cookies that he had made."

The three returned to the boat and partied all afternoon and night.

The woman said Angel was friendly and fun until her husband passed out. Then he whipped out a knife and threatened to kill her if she didn't do what he wanted.

"I tried to scream," she said, "But he put his hand over my mouth and said he'd kill us both if I tried to fight and didn't do what he wanted."

The woman relented. "He kept saying, 'Don't give me no trouble, girl.'"

After the rape, Angel stayed on board and ate three baked potatoes she had cooked that night before returning to his boat. The woman said she then passed out and she and her husband woke up about 4:00 o'clock and called the Coast Guard.

An examination at Goleta Valley Hospital showed injuries consistent with rape. She also had scratches where the knife had been pressed against her neck.

Angel's boss was questioned and he was as surprised as anyone. "I've known Angel for two months, since we picked him up in Mexico," the skipper told probers. "He has been nothing but a good guy to me and my family. I can't believe something like this could happen."

He said he had planned to take his 32-foot sailboat to South America but bad weather forced him to seek refuge in Esenada, Mexico, about 60 miles south of San Diego.

While waiting for repairs, he met the man who called himself Angel Jackson.

"I was walking down the street in Ensenada and he was walking in the other direction," he recalled. "He asked if I knew any place he could get work. I needed an extra hand and I told him he could work for me in exchange for room and board. He said great."

Angel stayed with the family for two months. He took the forward bunk which was separated from the main cabin where the family slept and was directly over a storage area that held firearms.

"He knew where the guns were," the skipper said. "He could have shot us any time he wanted. But we never had reason to think he wished us ill will."

They left Ensenada June 11th and sailed south. Bad weather again made them turn back and this time they decided to go back to California and attempt the South America trip another time.

They arrived in Pelican Cove in late July. A week later, Angel was arrested for rape.

"I am still amazed this happened," the skipper told sleuths. "Angel has always been a straight guy with us."

The skipper was to be amazed again when he learned the identity of his new crewman.

While in custody, a sheriff's deputy noticed the rape suspect's physical similarity to Kevin Cooper, whose face stared out from wanted posters plastered on every wall of the station house.

To prove the point to other deputies, the deputy took one of the posters from the squad room and showed it to them.

"It does look like him," one of the disbelievers said.

One of the detectives investigating the rape was notified. He went into the interrogation room where Angel Jackson was sitting and told the prisoner he looked a lot like the wanted man.

"Are you Cooper?" the detective asked.

The suspect shrugged.

San Bernardino was notified and a set of prints were sent over the telex. The prints were a perfect match. Angel Jackson was California's most wanted fugitive, Kevin Cooper.

On July 31, 1983, a chained and manacled Kevin Cooper was brought to the San Bernardino County central jail where he was greeted by a jeering crowd of vociferous spectators, some holding crude signs demanding his immediate execution. He was booked on suspicion of murder and held without bond in one of the isolation wards, reserved for inmates considered high security risks.

On August 19th, rape charges were filed against Kevin Cooper in Santa Barbara. Three months later, beginning Nov. 9th, Cooper began his preliminary hearing in San Bernardino court. Two months and 87 witnesses later, he was ordered to stand trial for the Chino murders.

Outside the courtroom, Dennis Kottmeier, the district attorney of San Bernardino County, who had decided to prosecute the case himself, told reporters that he would seek the death sentence.

A trial date was scheduled for April, 1984. But on March 13th, Superior Court Judge Richard C. Garner ordered Cooper's trial moved to San Diego County because of extensive publicity.

After the usual delays, the trial got underway October 23rd, before Judge Richard Garner, with Dennis Kottmeier and John Kochis as co-prosecutors and David Negus as the defense attorney.

The trial lasted five months and included more than 700 exhibits and 143 witnesses. Occasionally tedious, frequently riveting, the real life courtroom drama was a contrast in styles.

Dennis Kottmeier was mild mannered, almost dispassionate in his presentation. Conservatively dressed in a dark sports coat and white shirt with knotted tie, he presented the evidence and testimony as if each were a piece of a jigsaw puzzle.

In contrast, David Negus fit the stereotype of the disheveled public defender, earning the name, "Columbo" from at least one juror, as he paced the courtroom, running his hand through rumpled hair.

Unlike his appearance, however, Negus paid close

attention to evidence and testimony.

Carefully detailed charts and photographs belied his apparent disorganization, and he often referred to statements made more than a year ago to catch inconsistencies in court testimony and to discredit witnesses.

His lengthy — some said tedious — examination of witnesses prompted the judge to suggest that "we should penalize you five dollars for every ten minutes you make us wait so we can all have a party when this is over."

If tiresome, his efforts were effective. The thrust of the defense was there was no direct evidence linking Kevin Cooper to the murder and that he was on trial because the D.A. needed a scapegoat.

Negus admitted Kevin Cooper had been hiding out in the unoccupied house near the Ryen house after he escaped. But Negus claimed Cooper did not see the Ryen family or even go into their house.

Kevin Cooper had already left the ranch and was on his way to Mexico when the family was slain, Negus contended.

Negus, however, was unable to sway the jury, who took five days to review the exhibits and testimony before returning a verdict that Cooper was guilty of four counts of murder and one count of attempted murder.

Cooper, neatly attired in a dark sport coat and white shirt opened at the neck, patted his attorney on the back and said, "That's okay, you did your best."

However, a litany of key pieces of evidence was presented by the prosecution: a bloodstain found in the hall of the Ryen home was Cooper's type. The shoe prints found in the bedroom of the murder house and the hideout house had been made by Cooper's prison-issued shoes. Last of all, there was the bloodstained hatchet found outside the murder house, which was determined to have come from the hideout house.

During the penalty phase, jurors learned of Cooper's lengthy rap sheet, frequent forced stays at state mental hospitals, and the rape of his fiancée.

Negus told jurors that the marriage was probably called off because Cooper was not ready to settle down.

Jurors again returned to their chambers to determine the punishment for the crimes Cooper was convicted of. This time the vote was harder because the death penalty was invoked.

As one juror said later, "It may be you are sure beyond a reasonable doubt that he did it and find him guilty. But when you reach the penalty phase, is that enough to sentence him to death?"

The answer: yes.

Three and one half days later, the jury recommended that Cooper die in the gas chamber for murdering the four Chino Hills residents.

Cooper received the verdict without outward show of emotion. He was led quietly back to his jail cell.

By law, his case will be automatically appealed to the State Supreme Court. Until it is reviewed, about five years from now, he will be kept in a private cell on Death Row at San Quentin Prison.

EDITOR'S NOTE:
*Mark Watson and Angel Jackson are not the real names of the persons so named in the foregoing story. Fictitious names have been used because there is no reason for public interest in the identities of these persons.*

# "FRY ME FOR MY CRIMES!"

## by Barbara Geehr

In Jacksonville, Florida, in the early-evening hours of January 12, 1986, the owner of Window Decor, an interior decorating shop on the west side of the city, sensed something was wrong when he telephoned the store from his home and got no answer. Though it was a Sunday, the shop was supposed to be open until 8:00 p.m. The lone employee, 27-year-old Thomas Underwood, had always been highly dependable. If he decided to close early because of business being slow, he would have telephoned to make sure it would be okay.

The owner drove over to the Crossroads Shopping Center where Window Decor was located. Pulling in, he could not help observing—as he always did—how rundown and nearly deserted the area had become. What had once been a thriving shopping center was now a row of empty stores, bracketed at one end by a grocery and, at the other, by his own little shop.

Parking in front of the store, the owner observed that Underwood's 1983 Buick was not there, yet the store lights were still on. Believing the employee would never drive off leaving the business unattended and the lights on, the owner became more uneasy. He got out of his car to check the shop's front and back entrances. Both were securely locked. Peering into the store through the front window, the owner saw, stretched out on the floor near one of the window displays, what was unmistakably the body of Thomas Underwood. He hurried over to the store at the other end of the shopping center and called the Jacksonville Sheriff's Office.

Patrol officers and Homicide Detective John Bradley arrived at the scene within minutes. The owner unlocked the front door and, as the group of lawmen entered, the owner recounted to Bradley why he had come to the shop and how he had seen Underwood stretched out on the floor through the front window.

Detective Bradley's superficial examination of the body showed the victim had been shot once in the head at close range and that all the pockets in his clothing had been emptied. "Robbery appears to be a possible motive for the slaying," he commented to the store owner. "Does anything appear to have been taken from the shop?"

"Not that I can see right at this moment," the shop owner answered, glancing around the room. "Nothing seems even to have been disturbed."

"Okay, then," the detective said. "You may as well go home. If we need you for anything, we'll get in touch."

After the store owner left, Bradley called the medical examiner's office to have Underwood's body removed for autopsy. Then he called the Florida Department of Law Enforcement (FDLE) to have its mobile crime laboratory come to the scene and process it for evidence. He also assigned officers at the scene to neighborhood interviews. "I don't know what you'll come up with," Bradley told his crew. "The grocery's the only other business still operating in this forsaken shopping center. Still, you never know. Someone in the area somewhere may come up with something that will give us a lead."

With these matters taken care of, Bradley returned to headquarters and put out a BOLO on Underwood's late-model Buick. Three days later, it was found in a deserted area not far from the shopping center where the Window Decor clerk had been slain. The vehicle had been doused with gasoline and set afire; it was completely burned.

By this time, the medical examiner had determined that Underwood was killed by a single shot fired into his head at close range. Ballistics experts stated the weapon from which the fatal bullet had been fired was a 12-gauge shotgun. But from that point on, the investigation went nowhere. Processing of the crime scene turned up nothing in the line of physical evidence, neighborhood interviews produced no leads, and follow-ups on tips led only to dead ends.

Nonetheless, as the days, weeks, and months wore on, Detective Bradley remained confident that he would one day bring the case to a successful close. "We all know there's always somebody out there somewhere who knows something," he reminded his fellow investigators, who chided him about the lack of progress in the investigation. "One day, that person is going to telephone this office and tell me something that will lead me to Underwood's killer. Take my word for it."

Bradley's prophecy would come true, but two years would pass as he waited.

In Jacksonville, on Saturday, August 6, 1988, it was 10 minutes before 2:00 p.m. when a dark-colored sedan pulled off Normandy Boulevard onto a narrow dirt road leading through the woods at the edge of Donut Lake to a restful retreat at the end. Soaring temperatures and high humidity made the afternoon fit for neither man nor beast, and the two men sought refuge in the hideaway at the end of the little-used road.

The men had gone only a quarter of a mile into the wooded area when they observed tire tracks off the road on the right. Then they saw smoke. They stopped and got out of their vehicle to investigate. Following the tire tracks into the woods, the men came upon a smoldering body wrapped in what appeared to have been a bedspread. They hurried to the nearest phone they could find and telephoned the Jacksonville Sheriff's Office.

Responding officers found the corpse so badly burned that it was not even possible to identify its sex. It seemed likely the victim may have been killed somewhere else, wrapped in the bedspread, transported to the woods, and set afire there. After the fire investigators determined that the body had been doused with a flammable liquid before being set afire, the remains were transported to the medical examiner's office.

With only a bedspread-wrapped body burned beyond possible recognition and a set of tire tracks to work with, detectives knew breaking the case was going to depend on help from the public. Despite heavy media coverage, nearly three weeks passed before the hoped-for tip came into the sheriff's office. Sergeant Steve Weintraub fielded the call, which turned out to be from a 16-year-old girl who did not want to give her name.

"I've thought about making this call for a couple of weeks," the teenager said, "and I think you ought to know this is a very hard thing for me to do. It could also get me into a lot of trouble, so I don't want to be contacted or hassled in any way after I tell you what I know."

Sergeant Weintraub promised both anonymity and freedom from hassle by investigators. He then asked exactly what it was the caller knew.

The caller replied that she didn't know the full name of the victim whose burned body was found in the woods near Donut Lake, only that he was called Dwayne. She also stated that 28-year-old Michael Durocher was in some way involved in Dwayne's death.

"Do you know where Durocher lives, how we can reach him to ask a few questions?" Weintraub asked.

"Yes. His pickup truck is outside a one-story green house on Wilson Boulevard right now, so he's probably there." The teenager gave the house number.

"Could you at least tell me how you happen to know these things?" Weintraub asked.

The teenager answered, "Because I'm his girlfriend, and he told me." She then abruptly hung up the telephone.

The name Michael Durocher rang no bells for Sergeant Weintraub at that moment, but he didn't want to take the time to check criminal records. He considered it a stroke of luck to have received at least the first name of the unidentified body found near Donut Lake and to have been given the name and whereabouts of someone said to be involved in the killing.

Accompanied by Detective Frank Japour, Sergeant Weintraub drove in an official vehicle to the Wilson Boulevard address. He was glad to see a pickup in the driveway. "I hope that pickup is Durocher's," he said to Japour, "and that Durocher is still here."

When the investigators walked up to the front door of the green, single-story house and knocked, they got no response. After repeated unanswered knockings, they returned to the sheriff's vehicle and, on the portable telephone there, obtained the phone number for the Wilson Boulevard address. A call to that number proved more productive.

The person answering the phone said he was Michael Alan Durocher. In the give-and-take conversation that followed, Sergeant Weintraub explained that a tipster had given the sheriff's office information that Durocher had been involved in the killing of the person whose burned body had been found near Donut Lake and that he and Detective Japour wanted to talk to him about it.

Durocher, who, Weintraub thought, sounded as though he'd been drinking heavily, insisted he didn't know what the detective was talking about. He kept demanding the name of the tipster and making a strange comment. "Give me the name of the tipster; that will help me decide whether to kill myself," Durocher said again and again.

Weintraub turned the telephone over to Detective Japour. "Maybe you can do better with this guy than I can," he said. "We need to get him to come outside."

However, Japour was unable to make any more headway with Durocher than Weintraub had. After an hour of futile conversation, during which Durocher kept saying he had a shotgun and would kill himself before he would be taken alive, Detective Japour put down the phone. "We've got to call in the Special Weapons and Tactics team," he said.

The SWAT team reached the scene at 4:00 p.m., the time for the start of rush-hour traffic. Sheriff's investigators sealed off Wilson Boulevard in the Fouraker Road area. They also evacuated the occupants of neighboring homes while SWAT members slipped into nearby backyards, took positions on the roofs of the next-door houses, and surrounded the one-story house where Durocher was holed up with a shotgun. They called for Durocher to come out, unarmed and with arms raised. They called and called again several times over several hours.

The only time the lawmen caught sight of the self-imprisoned man was when he asked for a pack of cigarettes. Detective Japour tossed one into the front yard of the house, and a man the investigators believed to be Durocher slipped out the front door, grabbed the cigarettes, and then ran back inside. He was dressed in jeans, wore neither a shirt nor shoes, and carried a shotgun in one hand.

Three hours into the tense standoff, a sudden rainstorm sweeping through the neighborhood drenched SWAT members and sheriff's investigators and didn't do much to allay their growing impatience. Not until 8:00 p.m., four hours after the standoff began, did Michael Durocher surrender. Sergeant Weintraub and Detective Japour took him to the sheriff's office where he waived his Miranda rights and willingly related the events leading up to the killing of 38-year-old Edward Dwayne Childers, now identified as the person whose burning body was discovered by two men investigating smoke in a wooded area near Donut Lake.

According to Durocher's statements, four people were living in a house owned by Nancy Adams—Nancy,

George Hennard, who killed 23 people in Killeen, Texas.

Luby's Cafeteria, site of Hennard's massacre. Hennard drove his pickup truck through the front window before beginning his killing spree.

Gang Lu, University of Iowa physics student and mass murderer.

Gang Lu's victims: Professor Christoph Goertz, Associate Professor Robert A. Smith, Professor Dwight Nicholson, associate vice president of academic affairs, student Linhua Shan.

After shooting three people in a drugged rage, Humberto "Zeke" Zalaya confessed to police, he wondered, "What am I gonna do with the stupid car full of dead people?"

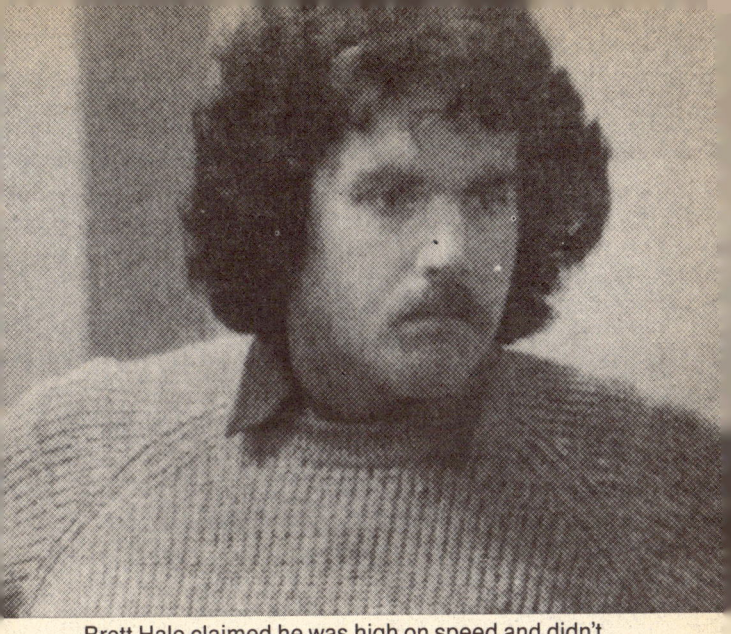

Brett Hale claimed he was high on speed and didn't mean to kill four people, whom he called "my best friends."

Calleen Holliday and Jennifer McCaughan were two of Hale's victims.

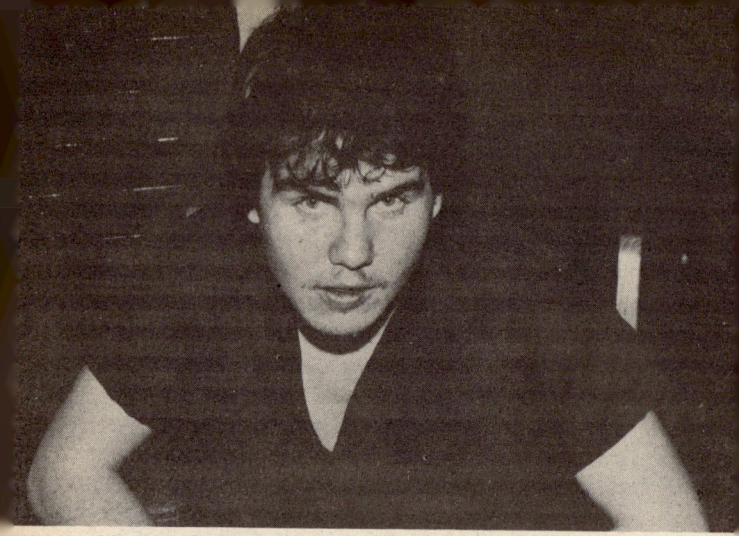

Mark McCallister killed six members of his "extended family" who lived in a huddle of three campers in West Virginia.

Without police dog PC, police might never have found the bodies of McCallister's victims amidst the debris of this junkyard.

The hammer used to bludgeon Edward Dwayne Childers to death had been washed and left casually in the sink.

After being arrested for the murder of Childers, his roommate Michael Durocher confessed to even more hideous crimes.

Thomas Wyatt (*above*) and Michael Lovette (*right*) received three death sentences for the three murders they committed at a pizzeria in Vero Beach, Florida.

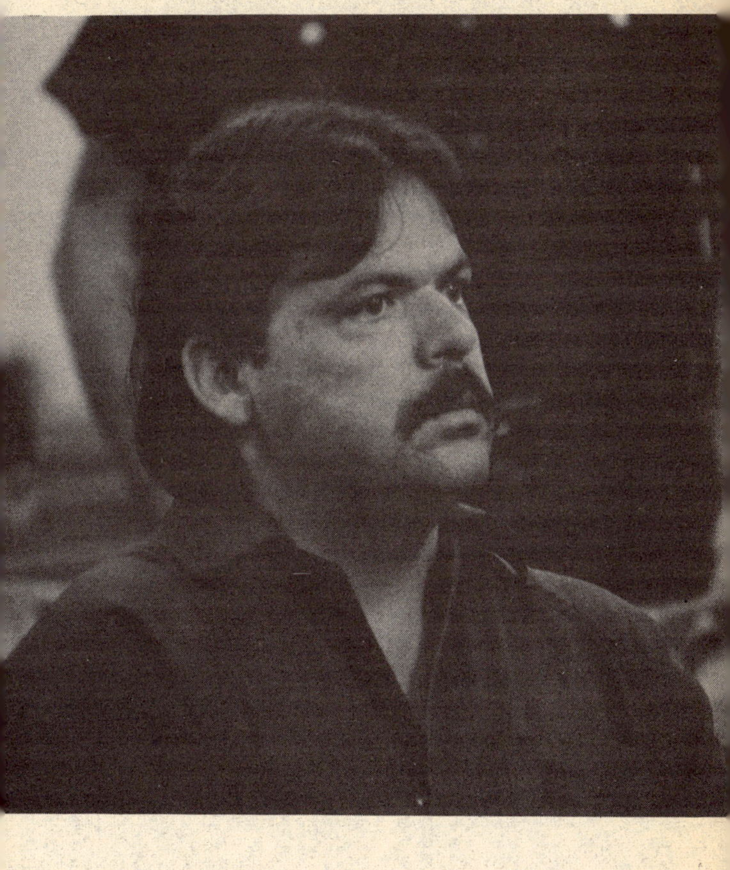

When police responded to an emergency at this quiet house in Long Island, New York, they found six shooting victims.

The only family members missing were Marion Brooks and her son Andrew. Marion's body was found six weeks later.

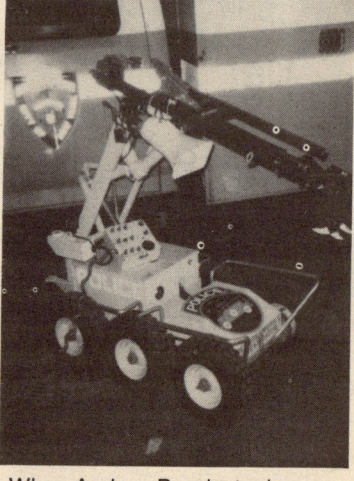

When Andrew Brooks took hostages in another house, police sent in a remote controlled robot with a closed circuit camera to pinpoint the gunman's location.

17-year-old Chou Aing was babysitting her little cousins Kiry and Chantha when they were attacked.

Their cousin Narin Aing was convicted of the murder.

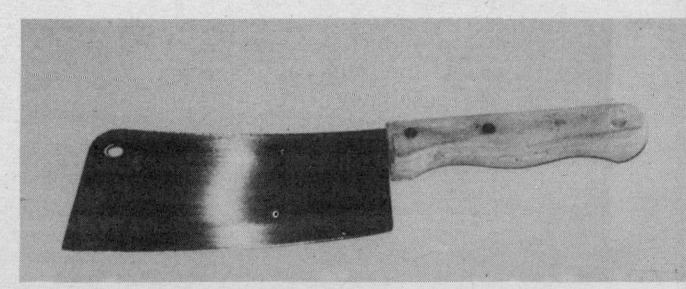

He had used a knife and this meat cleaver to deliver over 100 wounds to his three victims.

Dwayne, Larry English, and himself. "Nancy and Dwayne had a problem," Durocher explained. "He was sponging on her, taking advantage of her. He was making long-distance calls on her telephone and stealing things from the house. He was trying to steal her flea-market business. They had a big argument, and Nancy told Dwayne he had to get another place to live. She was going out, and if I remember right, she told him to be out before she got back the next day.

"Now, this was a Friday night," Durocher continued, "and we'd all been drinking. Dwayne was already drunk and went to sleep on the couch in the living room. Larry and me weren't ready to go to sleep. We sat there, drinking and talking, and we got really pissed off about how Dwayne had been taking advantage of Nancy. We also got pissed off because he owed both Larry and me two weeks' salary—which was around four hundred dollars apiece. We kept talking about how he made a lot of promises he didn't keep, and we decided to bump him off."

"Just like that? You mean while Dwayne was right there in front of you sleeping on the couch, you and this Larry talked about killing him?" Sergeant Weintraub asked incredulously.

"Yeah. And we also talked about how we should do it. At first, Larry wanted to borrow my shotgun and shoot him; but as we got to thinking about it, we decided the sound of the gunshot would be sure to wake up the neighborhood. We then discussed choking him or cutting his throat, and then figured that would make too much of a mess. We even discussed breaking his neck."

"What did you finally decide?" Sergeant Weintraub asked.

"After looking at all the options, we decided the best, fastest and least painful way to kill him was to beat him over the head. Larry found a problem with that: He said we didn't have a club. I told him not to worry about that, because I had a hammer in my truck."

Weintraub asked if the hammer became the murder weapon.

"Yeah," Durocher answered. "I went out to my truck, brought the hammer back and handed it to Larry. I didn't want to watch the actual killing, so I went to my room and closed the door. I turned my radio on. In a couple of minutes, I heard a thud and gasping. I figured Dwayne had got the first blow and couldn't breathe. I turned the volume on my radio up. I didn't want to hear any more."

"Did you return to the living room to see what happened?" Detective Japour asked.

"No. I really didn't want to see. I just went to bed and didn't come out of my room until I got up at eight o'clock the next morning. Larry was half-asleep in a living-room chair. He told me we had to get rid of the body. The spread on the couch where Dwayne was lying was full of blood, so Larry just wrapped the body up in that. We carried it outside and put it in the back of my pickup. Larry said it was up to me to get rid of it. He said I could dump it in the woods off Normandy Boulevard, near Donut Lake."

Sergeant Weintraub wanted to know why the body was burned and where the gasoline with which it was doused had come from.

"We didn't want anybody to find any fingerprints, so we agreed the best thing was to burn the body. I got a two-gallon can of gas from the laundry room of the house before I drove out by the lake. I backed up into a wooded area there, pulled the body out of the truck, poured the two gallons of gasoline over it and lit it with a piece of paper.

"After that, I drove back to the house and woke Larry up. I told him what I'd done. He noticed some blood on the couch, so he put a different spread over it. I put the empty gas can back in the laundry room. Larry washed off the hammer and I put it back in the truck."

"What time was it when all this was going on?" Japour asked.

"I am not sure of the times these things happened."

"Okay," Weintraub said. "What this adds up to is you're admitting you furnished the weapon for the murder but denying you did the actual killing."

"It's the truth about what happened."

"I think it's a lie," Weintraub retorted.

At this time, the sergeant charged Michael Alan Durocher with first-degree murder in the beating death of Edward Dwayne Childers. He set the time of the killing as between nine o'clock on the night of Friday, August 5th, and Saturday afternoon of August 6th. At first appearance the following morning, Circuit Judge J. Kesler ordered Durocher held without bond and appointed a public defender to represent him.

Physical evidence recovered from the house where the killing took place included a videotape, a tape recording, bloody couch cushions, empty gasoline cans, and a supply of gasoline. Durocher's fingerprints were lifted from one of the empty cans.

Sergeant Weintraub now delved into the suspect's family background and checked criminal records. He learned that Michael, born in January 1960 in nearby Orange Park, had grown up in a working-class home. A tall, wiry youth, Michael first expressed his own feelings of violence at the age of 12 when he threatened to use a rifle to protect a relative from another family member's physical abuse. At that young age, also, he began experimenting with drinking and drugs.

Michael's parents divorced when he was 13, and his mother had to sell their home and move into an Orange Park apartment complex which housed low-income families. There, Michael grew up fast. At age 14, he was picked up by Orange Park police as a runaway.

At 15, Michael was drinking regularly, smoking marijuana, and using other drugs with the older boys who hung out at the apartment complex. At 16, he dropped out of Orange Park High School, was again picked up as a runaway, and was arrested for shoplifting.

In August 1979, the youth, then 19, was arrested for burglary; a year later, for possession of marijuana and grand theft. A month after the grand theft arrest, he was charged with armed burglary, for which he began serving a two-year term on June 6, 1980. He was later transferred to a Jacksonville work-release center, from which he escaped briefly. Officially released from prison in 1982, he began working as a carpenter.

"Not a pretty picture," Sergeant Weintraub commented to Detective Japour as they reviewed the findings.

"But an increasingly common one," Japour replied.

Durocher was not a troublesome prisoner, but he was a talkative one. To the half-dozen investigators who had occasion to interview him, he repeated certain key statements again and again. "I'm not going to take the heat alone," he would say. "I'm going to bring somebody else down with me. . . . It wasn't my fault. . . . The only thing I want is not to get the total blame."

On September 8, 1988, a Duval County grand jury indicted Michael Alan Durocher for the first-degree murder of his housemate, Edward Dwayne Childers. At the trial, which began on January 6, 1989, jurors returned a verdict of guilty as charged and recommended a sentence of life in prison. Judge David Wiggins set a sentencing date for January 30, 1989.

About this time, Larry English was charged with a felony in a different judicial circuit. The case was resolved with a plea bargain.

If Michael Durocher had been talkative before his trial, he now became even more so while awaiting sentencing. To other prisoners he not only repeated the old statements he'd made to investigators but, for the inmates' benefit, added a few new ones. Of special note were ones to the effect that he had killed Childers, had killed others, and would now kill himself because he knew he "wasn't going to get out."

As is common in prison populations, a few of the listeners, opting for special considerations in their own situations, relayed the new statements to sheriff's office investigators.

The fact that Durocher said he had killed others became of special interest to Detective John Bradley, who, in three years, had not unraveled the mystery of the murder of Thomas Underwood, the clerk at Window Decor, the interior decorating shop at the Crossroads Shopping Center. Though Durocher's statement wasn't quite the same thing as the telephone call from a tipster that Bradley had never stopped believing would one day come to his desk, he decided it was certainly something to check out.

On January 23rd, exactly one week before Michael Durocher was to be sentenced in the Childers case, Detective Bradley went to have an exploratory talk with him. Up front, the detective put the purpose of his visit on the line: he said he wanted to find out what Durocher knew about the January 1986 murder of Thomas Underwood at Window Decor.

Durocher said, "I'm sure you know a jury returned a guilty verdict on me in the Childers case a couple of weeks ago and recommended that the judge sentence me to life in prison. I feel sure the judge will follow that recommendation when he hands down the sentence next week. Well, I don't want to spend the rest of my life in prison. If I tell you about Underwood, will you promise to get me the death penalty for that killing?"

"I will do everything in my power to see that you get whatever penalty the case warrants," Bradley replied. "However, it is the judge who determines penalties."

"If I get the death penalty, I may reveal something else to you."

"Let's stick with the Underwood case for the moment."

Durocher then recounted his actions on the Sunday

afternoon of January 12, 1986. He explained that he needed money, so he went into Window Decor with the idea of robbing the place. He said he was armed with a 12-gauge shotgun to show he meant business. "But the clerk," he explained, "whose name I didn't know until I read it in the paper the following afternoon, wasn't cooperative. I really had intended just to rob the guy, but after thinking about it, I decided to go ahead and kill him. I fired one shot into his head at pretty close range."

Durocher said he then went through the victim's pockets, took his money—which was about $40—and his car keys. "After that," he continued, "I locked the place up and drove away in the guy's late-model Buick. I picked up a can of gasoline, poured it over the vehicle, and set it on fire."

"What about the shotgun you used? What happened to that?" Bradley asked.

"It was a twelve-gauge Mossberg. I sold it to a friend."

"I'd like to recover it."

Durocher supplied the name of the person who had purchased the shotgun. Then at Bradley's request and with a waiver of Miranda rights, he willingly put into writing his confession to murder, armed robbery, auto theft, and arson. Bradley charged him on all four counts.

The next week, on the very day Circuit Court Judge David Wiggins was to hand down Durocher's sentence in the Childers case, the convicted killer sent for Detective Bradley. During their talk this time, he made the revelation he had hinted at in their previous conversation. He now said he had killed three other people.

"Okay," Detective Bradley said. "Tell me about it."

Durocher stated, "I shot my girlfriend Grace Reed and her two children, Candice and Joshua. Candice was five years old; Joshua was only six months. He was also my son."

"Then Candice was not your daughter?"

"No. Grace already had Candice at the time I met her. She'd been married briefly to some guy from Michigan."

Michael Durocher then related that over the Thanksgiving holidays in 1983, Grace Reed and the two children, who were living in New Jersey, came to Jacksonville, Florida, where he was working. "We all went to visit a relative in Orange Park over Thanksgiving. After we left there the next day, Grace and me got to arguing. It ended with me shooting all three of them, the two kids first and then Grace. I buried their bodies in Green Cove Springs."

"That was in 1983?"

"Right. A little more than six years ago."

"Exactly where in Green Cove Springs did you bury the bodies?" Detective Bradley asked.

"I'm not going to say right now," Durocher replied.

"What happened afterward?"

"Nothing, really. Her family didn't even file a missing-person report until a couple of years later. Clay County investigators asked me a few questions. I told them Grace and me had argued, that she'd picked up the kids and left in a huff, saying only they were going back to New Jersey. After a while, things just sort of died down."

"Are you willing to put all this in writing?" Bradley asked.

Durocher said he was and, after being Mirandized, he wrote a confession.

When he finished, Detective Bradley pointed out that the case was under the jurisdiction of the Clay County Sheriff's Office. He would telephone to advise investigators there of the developments.

"What I did to Grace and the kids has haunted me for over six years," Durocher said. "It looks like my day of judgment has finally come. I might as well get everything over with at one time."

"Well, you'll get your sentence on the Childers case today. You'll be facing an indictment on the Underwood case soon, and the Clay County Sheriff's Office will undoubtedly reopen the case involving the disappearance of Grace Reed and the children."

Later that day, Judge Wiggins, following the jury's recommendation, sentenced Michael Durocher to life in prison, with a mandatory 25 years, for the first-degree murder of Edward Dwayne Childers.

On February 16th, another Duval County grand jury indicted the now-convicted killer for first-degree murder and armed robbery in the Thomas Underwood case. Charges of grand theft auto and arson were dropped.

With a life sentence in the Childers case and an indictment in the Underwood case, Durocher appeared to become depressed and morose. He showed no interest in helping his attorneys prepare a defense for the Underwood slaying and robbery. He repeatedly stated that he wanted the death penalty.

On February 21st, Durocher's attorneys, while preparing an insanity defense, filed a motion requesting the appointment of an expert to determine whether their client was insane at the time of Underwood's killing and whether he was competent to stand trial. They maintained that Durocher's reason for confessing the killing to Detective Bradley was his wish to die. "He is totally unwilling to assist in preparing a defense," the motion stated.

In April, Judge Wiggins ordered psychiatric evaluations of the defendant. Resultant reports, received in May, noted three previously ordered court evaluations of the subject: The first, in 1976, followed Durocher's arrest on a charge of shoplifting; the second, in 1979, followed a suicide attempt after being arrested for robbery; the third, in 1984, followed another suicide attempt after an arrest for burglary. Durocher told one psychiatrist his reason for both suicide attempts: "I felt like I was getting a bum deal in life."

Concerning the present evaluation, the psychiatrists

explained Durocher's reason for confessing to Detective John Bradley about the Underwood murder and robbery. "Since he had already been given a life sentence in the killing of Childers—which he still maintains is something he didn't do—he said he believed he would be better off just getting his life over with. Accordingly, he wrote the murder confession and also promised further revelations to Detective Bradley if Bradley would work toward getting him the death penalty.

"The patient now asserts the Underwood murder confession was a lie, that he made it to manipulate, to be sure he would get the chair. In retrospect, he now regrets having done that, though in a sense, he thinks being dead would be better than being in prison where, he says, he has to watch his back and sleep with one eye open every night.

"He cites his experience in prison as one in which he is surrounded by guards indifferent to his conditions and by acts of violence. He insists the only violence he has ever committed has been toward himself. He has stated, 'The system just wants to write me off as a casualty, a big loser.' "

In summation, the report stated: "The patient is a twenty-nine-year-old white male, recently convicted of the first-degree murder of Edward Dwayne Childers and who now repudiates a confession he gave to another murder, that of Thomas Underwood. He is currently lucid, well oriented, shows excellent reality testing and is of average native intelligence. His cognitive facilities are intact. He seems mildly depressed."

The psychiatric experts found the patient's character disorders mixed and noted he had a history of substance abuse.

They concluded: "In our opinion, the patient merits adjudication of competence to proceed to trial and does not meet the criteria for commitment to a mental institution. It is further our opinion that he was not insane at the time of the Underwood crime but able to understand the nature, quality, and wrongfulness of his acts."

On June 7, 1989, Duval County grand jurors found Michael Alan Durocher guilty on the two counts with which he was charged: murder in the first degree in the shotgun slaying of store clerk Thomas Underwood and robbery of the victim while armed. The following day, they recommended a sentence of death in the electric chair. Judge Wiggins, at sentencing, followed the recommendation; Durocher was then transferred to death row at Florida State Prison in Starke.

During the time between Durocher's sentencing in the Childers case and his transfer to death row for the Underwood killing, Captain Jimm Redmond of the Clay County Sheriff's Office, upon information received from Duval County Detective John Bradley, had reopened the missing-person file on Grace Reed and her two children.

According to the original report, the 21-year-old woman was last seen alive the day after Thanksgiving 1983 when she and her two children left the home of one of Durocher's relatives in Orange Park with Durocher. Under questioning, Durocher had stated that Grace and he argued and she left in anger, saying she and the children were going back to New Jersey. He'd neither seen nor heard from them since.

Captain Redmond's first step in reopening the case was to pore through every paper in the voluminous file to learn everything he could about Grace Reed. According to statements from members of her family, Grace, the eldest of three children, grew up in a modest, split-level home in Paulsboro, a blue-collar community in Gloucester County, New Jersey. At age 13, Grace ran away from home but returned after an absence of only a few days.

In high school, the teenager showed a talent for art, much of which focused on rock music and rock stars. In the school yearbook for 1976, the year in which she graduated, Grace noted her likes as Johnny Winter, Kiss, and shiny, glittery clothes. Among her dislikes were getting out of bed and "people who try to tie you down and run your life." "Oh, wow!" was her favorite expression.

In the late 1970s, Grace married a man. They set up housekeeping in Michigan. Though the marriage lasted only a short time, Candice was born of it. Shortly after having the baby, Grace left her husband, returned to Paulsboro, and got on welfare.

Why Grace Reed became involved with Michael Durocher apparently puzzled everyone in their family. Such statements as "She was very naive. . . . She didn't think highly of herself. . . . She was always attracted to lost-puppy types" appeared frequently in interview reports.

Apparently, Grace began corresponding with Durocher when he was in prison on a grand-theft charge. "I believe it was her naive faith in people that led her to Michael," a family member said. "A friend told her he was in prison on a trumped-up drug charge and needed someone to write to him because he was lonely. Grace was always drawn to anyone with a sad story to tell, probably because she'd known hard times herself. A romance developed through their exchange of letters.

"When Durocher was released from prison in 1982, Grace and Candice, who was four, went to Orange Park to meet him — face to face, at last. A short time after that, he traveled to New Jersey to visit them there. I doubt Grace was really in love with Michael; she may have felt sorry for him and mistaken that for love."

The relative continued, "Anyway, their relationship brought them a son in the spring of 1983. They named him Joshua Michael. I saw him once before I joined the Army. When I returned to Paulsboro on leave just before Thanksgiving of that year, I found the apartment Grace and I had shared padlocked. Grace and the children had gone to Orange Park to visit Durocher.

"I reported back to duty and got stationed overseas. I didn't get back to the States until 1985. I still didn't find Grace. I contacted [a family member] who by this time had moved to California. We compared notes. We decided to report Grace and the children missing after we contacted Durocher and learned he'd neither seen nor heard from her since Thanksgiving of '83."

From an interview report in the file, Captain Redmond learned that one of the Clay County detectives on the case had talked with the Paulsboro chief of police, who identified himself as a friend of the Reed family. The investigator wrote, "The chief described Ms. Reed as like a flower child of the '60s. He said she always tried to see only the best in people, that she was the kind of person who would take a wet dog out of the rain and feed it, even if it meant she didn't have anything for herself."

Plainly, Captain Redmond decided, the initial investigation had gone nowhere, partly because Durocher's story had seemed believable, partly because it seemed likely that Reed and her children had departed both the county and the state, partly because no response from anywhere had ever been received on the numerous local and multi-state BOLOs put out, and partly because no evidence of foul play had ever been found.

Redmond closed the Reed file and began an investigation of his own. He obtained Durocher's criminal record and talked with the death row inmate's family. Its various members, loyal to one of their own, would only offer excuses for Durocher's many brushes with the law, though one did admit that Durocher had told him about killing Reed and the two children.

No one knew, or could even guess, however, where the bodies were buried, and Durocher was still withholding that information. Since, under Florida law, a person can be convicted of first-degree murder without a corpus delicti, Captain Redmond went ahead and charged Michael Durocher with the November 1983 slaying of Grace Reed and her two children.

On January 10, 1990—six years and two months after the slayings occurred—a Clay County grand jury indicted Durocher on the three first-degree murder counts. The setting and resetting of trial dates followed, due to prosecutors and defense attorneys alike needing more time to prepare their cases. What everyone involved hoped would be the absolute final trial date was set for October 22, 1990. As that date drew close, Durocher was moved from death row at the Florida State Prison to the Clay County Jail.

There, on the afternoon of October 15th, exactly one week before the scheduled trial, Captain Redmond convinced Durocher to reveal where the bodies of Grace Reed and her two children were buried. The prisoner gave the location as south of Green Cove Springs, along U.S. 17, about three miles south of Clay County Road 209. He described the site as having been covered with pine trees at the time of the murders. "But since then," he said, "all those trees were cut down to give the land a chance to grow back. There's nothing there now but palmettos and underbrush."

At nine o'clock the following morning, Captain Redmond and a crew of Clay County sheriff's detectives began digging in the cleared timberland. At 2:30 p.m., they came upon the bodies of the two children buried in a shallow common grave about 200 yards in from the highway.

The remains of the five-year-old girl, clothed in a dress and tennis shoes, lay atop the decomposed body of the six-month-old boy, who was dressed in a sleeper and baby shoes. The body of their mother was not found, but detectives theorized she had to be buried somewhere nearby.

Once the children's remains were transported to the medical examiner's office for autopsy, the search for Grace Reed's remains continued until dark. It was resumed throughout the following day with negative results. At that point, Captain Redmond called the search to a halt. "Before we go any farther," he said, "we have to get more specific information on exactly where Grace Reed's body may be located."

The grisly discovery of the children's bodies was followed by equally grisly reports from the medical examiner and a forensic anthropologist. The medical examiner found that the five-year-old girl had been shot in the head at close range with a shotgun, but he was unable to state the cause of death of the six-month-old boy. A forensic anthropologist, however, was able to determine that the boy had died from stabbing. The findings, coupled with the fact that Grace Reed's body had yet to be found, prompted cancellation of Durocher's October 22nd trial date, and a new date being held in abeyance.

Again, Captain Redmond went to talk with Michael Alan Durocher, who was still being held in the Clay County Jail pending the setting of a new trial date. Durocher appeared relieved upon learning that the bodies of the two children had been unearthed.

Redmond said, "If we can now find the body of their mother, I feel sure the Reed family will see that all three of these innocent victims will get a fit and proper burial."

Durocher willingly gave more explicit information as to where Reed's body was buried.

"I believe it would be a good idea for you personally to show us exactly where you buried Grace's body," the captain said.

Durocher agreed to do that. With the first light of day on October 22nd, he accompanied Redmond and a team of detectives to the area where the bodies of the two children had been unearthed.

Digging was renewed. At 9:10 a.m., Reed's skeletal remains were recovered from a shallow grave 32 feet from where the bodies of her two children had been found the week before. A corroded shotgun shell found near the body led Captain Redmond to theorize that the mother and children had been killed at the burial site.

"It appears the slayings may have taken place right here on the grounds where we're standing," he said to

Durocher. "You've already confessed to the triple slayings. Why don't you go ahead and explain how everything happened? You'll feel better, once you get it off your chest."

Durocher seemed eager to take advantage of the opportunity to explain. He said, "It was a suicide pact. Grace and me decided to kill ourselves and the children."

"When was that decision made?" Redmond asked.

"The day after Thanksgiving, six years ago. After we left my [relative's] house where we'd spent the holiday. Grace and the kids had driven down from Jersey in a rented car. It was no great and sudden decision. We'd talked about it before."

Durocher then related how he, Grace, and the children first stopped at the house where he was living to pick up his shotgun and then at two other places to pick up a bottle of whiskey and a shovel. "We were going to shoot and bury the kids first," he explained. "We drove around for a while and finally spotted this place. It was an isolated spot and covered with pine trees back then. We stopped by the edge of the woods."

Durocher paused briefly. When he started talking again, Redmond found him sounding more like the observer of a scene taking place before him than like a participant in it. Durocher said, "Grace, Candice, and me got out of the car, leaving Joshua, who was sleeping, on the car seat. Grace told Candice we were going on a picnic and to walk toward the woods. As soon as Candice started walking ahead, I pulled the shotgun out of the car, fired it, and killed her."

"How far from you was she when you fired the shot?"

"I was standing about fifteen or twenty feet behind her. I just raised the gun up and fired. The one shot dropped her."

Captain Redmond asked what happened after that.

"The sound of the shot woke Joshua up. Grace lulled him back to sleep and then placed him down on the ground. I shot him there."

"And after that?"

"Grace was crying, so we got back into the car, drank whiskey, and talked for a while. Then she asked me to kill her because she couldn't bring herself to do it. She said she would come back and haunt me if I didn't hold up my end of the suicide pact and kill myself after killing her."

Durocher said that after killing Grace, he found he was unable to turn the gun on himself. "I buried all the bodies and then took the shotgun and all the things belonging to Grace, the kids and myself which were in the car and dumped them into a swamp near the Clay-St. Johns county line. I later set fire to the car Grace had rented to make the trip from New Jersey to Orange Park."

Captain Redmond drove Durocher back to the Clay County Jail and then returned to his office. Discussing Durocher's account of the slayings with a fellow investigator, the captain said, "I wonder how much of Durocher's story is true. For one thing, he said he fired the shot which killed the little girl from a distance of fifteen or twenty feet; the medical examiner stated the fatal bullet was fired at close range.

"For another, the forensic anthropologist determined stabbing—not a bullet from a shotgun—caused Joshua's death. And for still another, I doubt there was ever any such thing as a suicide pact. From all the information we've gathered, I don't believe Grace Reed was the kind of person who would ever consent to any harm coming to her children. I think it's more likely Durocher planned to get rid of Grace and the two kids long before they ever came to Orange Park for the Thanksgiving weekend visit."

The captain notified Grace Reed's family about the unearthing of the remains of Grace and the children and related Durocher's story about a suicide pact leading to the killings.

"No way!" one of Grace's relatives retorted. "Grace adored her two kids. She would never have agreed to Michael killing them. She would have scratched his eyeballs out first!"

The medical examiner's report confirmed that Grace Reed, like her five-year-old daughter, had been killed by a bullet fired from a shotgun at close range. Evidence recovered at the scene indicated it was more likely the woman had been kneeling in the dirt of her own grave, pleading for her life, when she was killed rather than sitting in a rented automobile, begging Durocher to kill her because she was unable to kill herself.

With the discovery of the bodies of Grace Reed and her two children, December 3, 1990, was set for Durocher, already indicted in the triple slaying, to stand trial. He decided to plead innocent, and his court-appointed public defender entered a not-guilty plea.

That prompted the assistant state attorney who prosecuted Durocher in the murder of Thomas Underwood to comment, "I don't know what motivates Durocher. He talks to investigators for a while, then tells them to go away and then initiates contact again. He's kind of paved his own way to another death sentence this time. At the same time, he won't plead guilty but goes through a whole procedure as though he were innocent and fighting for his life. He gives the prosecution the ammunition it needs to prosecute him successfully and then tries to dodge the bullets."

Prosecutors let it be known that although Durocher was already on death row for the Underwood killing and armed robbery, they intended to seek the death penalty for the slaying of Reed and her children. The lead prosecutor said, "Our policy is to seek the death penalty even though it has already been imposed in another case because so many death sentences are overturned."

The public defenders said their case would be based on Durocher being innocent of the crimes by reason of insanity. "A psychiatrist has evaluated the accused as a self-appointed mythical character living in his own fantasy world," stated a spokesperson for that office.

With the trial date being six weeks away, Durocher was transferred from the Clay County Jail back to death row at Florida State Prison. As the trial date drew near, prosecutors and public defenders, at the end of November, asked for a postponement. They needed more time, they said, to interview witnesses and prepare their cases. Circuit Judge William Wilkes reset the date for March 4, 1991.

At jury selection on the appointed day, Durocher, now 31, appeared relaxed and even smiled every now and then as prosecutors and public defenders selected seven women and five men, along with two female alternates, to hear the case.

In opening statements, Assistant State Attorney Laura Starrett, seeking the death penalty, disputed Durocher's story that the killing of Grace Reed and her two children resulted from a suicide pact. "A different set of events drove Durocher to the killings," she contended.

Describing the defendant as a cold-blooded, ruthless killer, Prosecutor Starrett said, "Mrs. Reed and her children weren't just murdered; they were executed. You have before you a man who has killed again and again. How can anyone deserve to die more than someone who has killed five people?"

Testimony from Clay County sheriff's investigators, the medical examiner, the forensic anthropologist, and several other professionals disputed Durocher's story that the killings resulted from a suicide pact made by Ms. Reed and himself. Evidence was presented indicating the killings had been preplanned.

In the middle of the third day of the trial, Durocher suddenly forbade his counsel from presenting to the jury any testimony or evidence in his behalf. He interrupted the proceedings by standing up and saying, "Let's skip the rest of this trial. I plead guilty to all three of the murders I am charged with. I understand my legal rights and I am waiving them. I know pretty much all there is to know about them."

Judge Wilkes directed the stunned jurors to deliberate immediately on a penalty. In Florida, first-degree murder is punishable only by death in the electric chair or life in prison with no chance of parole for 25 years. In handing down the sentence, a judge is not bound by the jury's recommendation.

It took the seven women and five men less than 35 minutes to recommend unanimously that Michael Durocher be given three death sentences — one each for the November 1983 murders of Grace Reed and her two children.

Chief Assistant State Attorney John Delaney said it marked the first time in the Fourth Judicial Circuit that a jury ever recommended three separate death sentences in one case. The circuit covers Duval, Clay, and Nassau Counties.

On March 22, 1991, Judge Wilkes, calling the three murders "more heinous and cruel than what would be used to destroy an animal with rabies," sentenced the confessed killer to three additional death sentences in accordance with the jurors' recommendation. Durocher expressed no emotion when Judge Wilkes handed down the sentences. Under Florida law, all death sentences are automatically appealed.

EDITOR'S NOTE:
*Nancy Adams and Larry English are not the real names of the persons so named in the foregoing story. Fictitious names have been used because there is no reason for public interest in the identities of these persons.*

# "SEATTLE'S BLOODY CARNAGE AT THE WAH MEE CLUB!"

## by Gary C. King

SEATTLE, WASHINGTON
OCTOBER 25, 1983

At approximately 12:30 a.m. on Saturday, February 19, 1983, three young men walked nervously through Chinatown in Seattle's International District, on the south side of the city. They passed by the Kingdome, then the James Street train station, as they turned onto South King Street and headed towards Maynard Alley, site of the Chinese Wah Mee Club, a private drinking and gambling establishment. Gambling, of course, is illegal in Seattle, but it is common knowledge to many that private club games are usually played in Chinatown with stakes sometimes as high as $10,000, $20,000 even $30,000! It was precisely that kind of money which attracted these three young men early that Saturday morning.

The Wah Mee Club (meaning "beautiful place" in Chinese) is located in Maynard Alley, just a few steps off King Street. There are no signs identifying it. The entrance is enveloped on both sides by garbage cans and dumpsters, and to an unknowing passerby, the entrance just looks like the back door to some establishment, perhaps a restaurant. It's certainly not an appealing area by day, even less so by night unless, of course, you had specific business there and were not alone.

The three young men who went there on the morning of February 19th knew precisely where they were going, and they did have specific business, although it was of a different nature than usual. They wanted money all right, but they wanted to take it from patrons and the "house" bank by armed robbery. Having already decided they would leave no witnesses, the three men entered the Wah Mee Club with guns drawn.

There were 14 patrons in the club that fateful morning, 13 men and one woman, most of whom were sitting on wooden stools that were situated around the club's curved bar. Most of the gamblers were restauranteurs from the area who had closed their tills and had gone to the club for some friendly gambling and drinks, activities which had gone on since the 1940's when the club was formed. Never in the club's history had anything so tragic, so devastating, so bloody occurred as that which was about to happen on the morning of February 19, 1983.

The three men ordered the club's patrons and employees to lie face down on the floor in a semi-circle. They were gagged, hog-tied (hands behind their backs tied to their feet) and robbed of all their cash. Then they were each shot at close range as they lay there helpless, some more than once. Their merciless killers backed out the door from which they entered, and escaped into the darkness of the night. The incident was the worst mass killing in the history of Washington State, and was ranked as one of the nation's worst.

One victim begged one of the killers to bind his hands loosely. Apparently, due to the man's physical condition, the killer complied with his pleading, evidently feeling that he couldn't pose a threat to their plans. However, miraculously, that victim escaped death and was able to loosen his hands after being shot in the neck and chin. The man then crawled to the alley, where he alerted a passerby to the tragedy that had occurred.

When Seattle police units arrived, they were horrified by the sight of people lying on the floor, either dead or dying. "They didn't miss," remarked Detective Gary Fowler, referring to the killers hitting their targets. It was a ghastly sight, and most of the cops and medical personnel were sickened as they checked the victims for survivors. Unfortunately, all but three were dead, and two of those three died a short time after arriving at Seattle's Harborview Medical Center.

According to Officer Gary Flynn, Seattle Police Department public information officer, the victims had been bound with nylon cord and had been shot with small caliber weapons. The victims had been found in three closely connected rooms of the club.

"I saw an enormous number of human beings that had been shot in the head and were lying in a gross pool of blood," Flynn told reporters. The sole survivor, according to Flynn, had improved from critical to serious condition at Harborview Medical Center where he was being kept under heavy police guard. Because of heavy sedation, Flynn said, the survivor had been unable to give police a complete story of what had happened.

According to Seattle Police Chief Patrick Fitzsimons, the perpetrators of this most heinous crime evidently were known by the proprietors of the Wah Mee Club because they were allowed entry through the locked door after a doorman observed them through a peephole. Since there was no money found inside the club, Chief Fitzsimons said detectives were assuming robbery was the motive. "We're looking at this as an isolated, unique situation at this time," said Fitzsimons.

After the bodies had been removed and were taken

to the morgue, detectives and crime lab specialists remained at the scene throughout the entire next day and evening gathering evidence. They collected blood samples, and even sifted coagulated blood in search of bullet and bone fragments. They also scraped dried blood off the floor and spatters from the walls, and fingerprint technicians went over practically every inch of the club in search of identifiable prints. They left with many good specimens, although they suspected most of the prints belonged to the club patrons.

On Tuesday, February 22nd, Dr. Donald T. Reay, King County Medical Examiner, released details of the autopsies performed on the victims of the massacre. "They were bound with synthetic cord, very loosely tied with no strong knots present," Reay determined. "There were no bruises and there were no rope burns. There was no sign of a struggle."

Reay said that the 13 victims had been shot a total of 29 times (not including the survivor), 12 of whom had been shot on the side or on the top of their heads as they lay face down on the floor, hog-tied. Twenty-eight of the shots had been fired from two to ten feet away, and the other shot was fired at very close range, as close as 12 inches, leaving considerable gunpowder residue. Reay said he had been unable to determine if all the victims had been shot by the same gun and was not sure if the shots had been fired from a rifle or a handgun. He said all the shots were of small caliber.

According to the medical examiner, nine of the victims had been identified: John Loui, Dewey Mar, Gim Lun Wong, Chong L. Chinn, whose ages he did not release, and Jean Mar, 47; Wing Wong, 59; Moo Min Mar, 52; Hung Fat Gee, 50; and Henning Chinn, 52. Four of the victims, aged 30 to 70, were not identified immediately and tentative identifications were not available.

In the meantime, the probe continued as police

scoured Chinatown in search of witnesses, with two squads of detectives and countless officers working around the clock. "So far," said a police spokesman, "we have not found anyone who saw somebody leaving the Wah Mee Club."

Police theories were beginning to circulate, among them, that the killers were known there and were willingly admitted, as previously pointed out. The cops also speculated that the victims most likely thought they were merely going to be robbed when the perpetrators showed their guns, and decided to cooperate to avoid getting shot. Little did the victims know that they'd be shot—one at a time.

Meanwhile, all of Seattle's Chinatown was shocked and outraged at the senseless carnage that took place early on the morning of February 19th. Citizen speculation ranged from talk about the tong gang wars, to revenge of gambling losses. Nearly all expressed anger and sorrow mixed with confusion. Nearly everyone police talked to in Chinatown knew about the illegal gambling club and the fact that it had been bankrolled by rich businessmen desiring high-stakes gambling. "They were playing some of the highest stakes in Chinatown," said one man who police interviewed. "You could make a $1,000 bet there, and some people lost $20,000 or $30,000 in a single night."

"It just can't be a robbery," said another man who did not wish to be identified, explaining that there likely was not enough money in the place to justify killing 13 people, his view obviously opposite from the previous man police talked to. "I imagine that it's a place for the older generation folks who've gambled for a long time and who gamble all over the district."

"I didn't hear anything and neither did my dog," said another person police interviewed who lived adjacent to the Wah Mee Club. "I was home all evening, watching television. I'm a TV freak. It's a sound building and I didn't notice anything unusual in the area. But I don't know what they usually have because I don't generally go down there at night."

"They were good people," said a female relative of two of the massacre victims, crying as she spoke. "They were very generous. I can't realize that other people would kill them. I just don't know how to explain how good they were."

"The club's been there for a long time," added another relative of two of the victims, who didn't wish to be identified. "Back in the old days, it was really wide open, but it's been really low key lately. I thought they had closed it down." The relative had his own ideas about the robbery-massacre.

"I think most of the people there were in the restaurant business," he added. "Usually they were all the same people. I think there must have been a lot of money down there that night for some reason. I wouldn't be surprised if they had over $70,000 there, maybe more, I mean in the pockets of those people." He also said that he didn't think the robbers planned to kill the victims, stating that the perpetrators may have been wearing masks. He said he felt that at some point one or more of the gunmen was recognized, prompting the slaughter.

"I couldn't believe it," he added. "I couldn't believe it until I went down and saw the bodies. They (Chinese) don't do that. It just doesn't happen. I mean, what is this? I still don't believe it. I'm still not sure it happened."

In the wake of the Chinatown killings, many people criticized the police department for not putting a stop to the illegal gambling, saying that if not for the gambling the killings would not have occurred. But, unfortunately, the critics of the police didn't stop to think about the obstacles that are put in their way, primarily by the Chinese community itself.

"They've been in operation for over 25 years," explained Chief Fitzsimons, "so there are chronic problems that we deal with as well as we can when the situation allows." He also said that gambling in Chinatown is difficult to control because of the tight security at the clubs, all of which are private.

"There are certain behaviors," said Police Officer Gary Flynn, "and gambling is one of those that are accepted by the Chinese community, *their* community, and accepted almost with a fervor in some areas."

As one group of detectives continued their search for eyewitnesses, another group continued a search for clues. Countless hours were spent inside the Wah Mee Club as investigators crawled on their hands and knees scraping coagulated, sometimes completely dried, blood samples from the floor in search of clues, in particular bullet fragments. Many hours were spent by homicide sleuths pounding the pavement in Seattle's Chinatown, asking probing questions when and where appropriate. But the answers they were receiving were not, so far, bringing them any closer to a suspect in the state's worst mass murder case.

However, police soon obtained their "lucky break" in the case when the massacre's lone survivor told detectives he knew at least two of the men who committed the barbarous acts of violence at the Wah Mee Club. The survivor told the cops information that put them onto "Bennie" Ng (pronounced "ing") and "Willie" Mak, two young men who had been to the club on more than one occasion. The survivor also told the cops there was a third man involved, but he could not identify him. Police pleaded with the public to help identify the third man.

"We need cooperation and information," urged Seattle Mayor Charles Royer, "on this outrageous, once-in-a-century crime." The plea for help was made at a meeting of the Chong Wa Benevolent Association, a group of Chinese community and family groups, and was directed at the 10,000 Chinese believed to live in Seattle. Seattle Police Chief Patrick Fitzsimons was also present.

"We need your help in trying to find out who may have been with those two men in Chinatown," said Fitzsimons, "particularly on that evening." As the pleas for help in identifying the third suspect were being made, detectives were closing in on Ng and Mak.

Police reports formally identified the two suspects as 20-year-old Benjamin K. Ng and 22-year-old Kwan "Willie" Mak, both born in Hong Kong and presently living in south Seattle. Police records further showed that Ng had been arrested two years earlier as a suspect in a shooting which sent four Chinese youths to the hospital. However, charges were dropped for lack of evidence.

When police went to Ng's residence where he lived with his girlfriend, he was quietly taken into custody as search and arrest warrants were served on him. When Detective William Baughman "Mirandized" Ng, the suspect acknowledged that he understood his rights and for what he was being arrested, but denied shooting anybody.

When asked about his whereabouts on the evening of February 18th and early on the morning of February 19th, Ng purportedly told Baughman that he stayed late Friday evening (the 18th) at a video arcade, playing games until nearly mid-night. He then told detectives that he drove along Interstate 5 from midnight until about 1:30 a.m., at which time he returned to his girlfriend's apartment and watched a late night movie on television. He said he then went to bed.

During the search of Ng's girlfriend's apartment, police found money on the bedroom dresser. Ng told them it was "my money as a dealer at the Hop Sing Club," but when detectives uncovered a shoebox full of cash totaling more than $10,000, Ng had no explanation. In addition, police ferreted out two .38-caliber handguns, .38-caliber ammunition and a rifle.

Meanwhile, Kwan "Willie" Mak was similarly being arrested by detectives at his residence and charged with the Chinatown massacre. Both men were booked into jail. During interrogation, Mak purportedly told detectives, "I did all the shooting," but later retracted the statement.

In the meantime, crime lab technicians reported that two .22-caliber handguns were believed to be the murder weapons, neither of which had been recovered. However, lab tests revealed that one of the bills found in Ng's bedroom had a clear fingerprint of one of the victims found shot to death at the Wah Mee Club.

In a press release issued on February 25th, police revealed the items found during a search of Mak's residence. Among the items taken into evidence were two rifles, two shotguns, a loaded .357 magnum, ammunition, a gym bag with two additional handguns inside (caliber not revealed), paper money in various denominations in both U.S. and foreign currency, and suspected narcotics. Additionally, detectives discovered a piece of white cord inside a car parked at Mak's residence.

Moreover, in light of the evidence and the method of operation of Washington State's most heinous crime, police listed Ng and Mak as suspects in a similar, as yet unsolved murder of two Oriental women in Seattle's Beacon Hill district July 16, 1982. They had both been shot to death, and police believed robbery was the motive. However, Ng and Mak have not been charged with that crime and must be presumed innocent.

In the days and weeks that followed the Chinatown massacre, there was an intense feeling of uneasiness in the International District of Seattle. When this reporter visited there, people would look and follow, always suspicious of my every move. It was clear that outsiders were not welcome, and residents were reluctant to discuss the brutal murder case. Those who were willing to talk about it, did so evasively, dodging direct questions by merely expressing anger and condemning the act. A few expressed opinions that if the killers were convicted and did not get the death sentence, they would not live long anyway. It was indeed an eerie place to be at that time, and the feelings the residents held were not likely to quickly change.

On Wednesday, March 30th, nearly a month and a half since the Wah Mee Club shootings, police announced that they had identified a third suspect in the massacre. Charges filed that same day in Seattle District Court identified the suspect as 26-year-old Wai-Chin "Tony" Ng, also a resident of Seattle and reportedly an immigrant from Hong Kong. He is no relation to Benjamin Ng.

"We now have all the principal suspects in the crime identified," announced Maj. Dale Douglass, chief of Seattle Police Department's criminal investigation unit. However, "Tony" Ng was not in custody, and he had not been seen since the morning of February 19th. One of Ng's relatives said that he may have returned to Hong Kong, and some of his friends said he may have traveled to San Francisco or Vancouver, British Columbia. Police in those cities have been notified that Seattle District Judge Philip Y. Killien has issued a no-bail warrant for Ng's arrest.

Wanted posters describing "Tony" Ng as a murder suspect in the Chinatown massacre were put up all over the city, printed in English as well as Chinese. The wanted posters were placed in store and restaurant windows, stapled to telephone poles and glued onto concrete walls. They were found in downtown shops, offices, bus and train stations. No matter where one decided to go in Seattle, it was likely they'd see at least one of the wanted posters.

According to detectives pounding the streets, several good witnesses had turned up. According to one witness, whom police would not identify for reasons of the witness's personal safety, Benjamin Ng was seen sitting in a restaurant across the street from the Wah Mee Club with two other people shortly before the slayings occurred.

"He was sitting in a booth with two friends," police reported the witness as saying. "I don't know them. They sat, and they leave. I can't say anymore."

Sources close to the investigation also reported that additional witnesses claimed to have seen Benjamin Ng walk from the restaurant and enter the Wah Mee Club a short time before the killings occurred. Still yet another witness claimed to have seen Kwan "Willie" Mak standing outside the club as police arrived on the scene after the slayings.

"The word is that Mak was bowling with some friends in the early morning hours after the murders," said an informed source, "and they all went down to the Wah Mee Club and watched police taking out the bodies. Mak left when word got around that one of the victims was still alive."

Rumors were running rampant throughout Chinatown that a tong war had broken out, that the murder suspects had been hired to "rub out" rival tong members. Both Benjamin Ng and "Willie" Mak were members of a tong organization, the Hop Sing Tong, which swiftly and emphatically denied any involvement in the killings.

"It was strictly a robbery and people should not believe it could possibly have been linked to anything more," said a tong spokesman in an attempt to quash the rumors. "The tong did not send the two. Hop Sing members and leaders are among the most grieved and embarrassed over what happened and are attending funerals of the victims."

Meanwhile, a Chinese benevolent organization announced that it was now offering a $30,000 reward for information leading to the arrest and conviction of "Tony" Ng, still at large, and anyone else who might have been involved in the mass slaying. So far, however, the reward offer has not brought any substantial results in the case.

King County Prosecutor Norm Maleng announced that his office would seek the death penalty against the suspects, who have both pleaded innocent to the charges levied against them. Both have been held in private jail cells, without bail.

In the wake of the trials of the much publicized case, feelings of bitterness, hatred and revenge were running high in Seattle's Chinatown. "If they (suspects) go free, somebody will kill them," remarked one International District shopkeeper. "You can't blame the families for wanting revenge. Even if they go to jail, they'll all be killed."

"The rumor is that some members of the families of the victims don't want the killers put to death," said a relative of one of the victims. "They want them to get off so they can get them themselves!"

Benjamin Ng was the first to go on trial for the February 19th massacre, and jury selection for prosecutors and defense attorneys was no easy chore due, mainly, to pre-trial publicity. "I can't overstate how gruesome the facts of this case are going to be," said John Henry Browne, Ng's attorney. Browne previously defended mass-murderer Ted Bundy.

"The state will introduce gruesome photographs and chilling testimony and will paint a picture of a real disaster," Browne told a group of potential jurors. "If you find Benjamin guilty, can you put aside your emotional response to the fact that 13 people are no longer living and give consideration to the evidence you hear?" The question was asked with regard to the penalty phase of the trial, during which jurors must decide if Benjamin Ng would receive the death penalty or a sentence of life imprisonment if convicted. Following several days of repeated grilling, a jury was finally seated and the much awaited trial of Washington State's worst mass killing got underway.

Amid tight security, in which each spectator was screened by a highly sensitive metal detector like those used in airports, the first Chinatown Massacre trial began to a packed courtroom. Countless spectators were turned away because of lack of seating, which was limited even for reporters.

During opening statements, Defense Lawyer John Henry Browne acknowledged that Benjamin Ng was involved in the bloody, heinous crime, but denied that his client shot anyone. He stated that Ng's part consisted primarily of hog-tying the victims and robbing them.

On the other hand, however, the prosecution contended that Ng, along with two accomplices, bound and robbed the 14 victims, then, on their way out of the club, stopped, turned and systematically fired 32 shots in an attempt to eliminate all of the witnesses. However, one survived, the prosecutor said, and would testify against the defendants.

"As the three men reached the door," said Bill Downing, deputy King County prosecutor, "they stopped, turned and with guns drawn, the shooting began, guns firing rapidly, bullets blasting throughout with deadly accuracy." Downing said that Ng and his accomplices wanted some money and decided to obtain it by armed robbery in a plan that would leave no witnesses. "Unexpectedly," said Downing, "the defendants' plan is being defeated because of the miraculous escape of the 14th victim."

Downing explained to the jury that the 14th victim was an old man, who had been shot in the jaw and the neck, able to free himself and make into Maynard Alley and summon help because he had persuaded one of the robbers not to tie his hands and feet so tightly. "No need to tie so tight," Downing quoted the witness as saying to his attacker. "I am an old man."

Downing told the jury that the witness would testify, however, that Mak was "in charge," and said yet another witness would testify that Mak purportedly told him of a plan he'd made to rob the Wah Mee Club and kill anyone who resisted or caused trouble. It had earlier been reported that Ng would attempt to blame the shootings on Mak, and that Mak would do likewise to Ng. It was for that reason the two trials were separated as opposed to having one trial for both defendants.

"There is no question Benjamin tied up these individuals," said Defense Lawyer Browne, "but Benjamin did not shoot that night." Browne told the jury that no blood had ever been found on Benjamin's clothes, and a witness was produced who testified that on several occasions in 1981, Mak discussed plans to rob another private Seattle club, the Gim Lun Club. According to Mak's alleged plan, the victims would be tied up and shot to death, so no witnesses would be left to testify against him. According to the witness, Mark purportedly said a .22-caliber handgun would be used since it wouldn't be as noisy as a larger weapon.

Under questioning by Browne, the witness told the court that at first he hadn't taken the robbery-murder discussions seriously, but as time went on he knew they meant it. "Why did you think they were becoming more serious?" asked Browne.

"Because they just wanted to go ahead and do it," replied the witness. "I wanted nothing to do with it because I had my own business. I don't need that kind of money."

"Did Mak ever indicate or say that he would kill the victims if his accomplices refused?"

"Yes," replied the witness, who added that Benjamin Ng had very little to say during any of the meetings where robbery was discussed.

Benjamin Ng sat still with a grim look on his face as he listened to testimony from Dr. Donald Reay, King County medical examiner, and Dr. Harry Bonnell, a deputy medical examiner. "Many of the victims died within a couple of minutes," explained Reay, as he described how several of the bullets shattered as they hit bone, literally spraying tiny slivers into brain tissue. Both medical examiners said they doubted any of the victims could have survived. Reay's testimony indicated that the killers would have had to walk through the clustered victims, perhaps even stop over some of them, as they fired their weapons into their victims' brains.

The courtroom fell deadly silent for several minutes as the jury was shown gruesome photographs of the Wah Mee Club victims, lying clustered together in a semi-circle, hog-tied, large pools of blood near their heads.

The jury heard testimony from the prosecution's star witness, the lone survivor of the massacre. The witness told the jury that Mak and the third man, the one who is still at large, arrived at the club first. Benjamin Ng showed up a short time later. Approximately eight people inside the club were ordered to lie on the floor and were then hog-tied by Ng and the third man. Ng had brought an ample supply of nylon cord inside with him, and as additional persons entered the club that night, they also were ordered to lie down and were hog-tied.

At one point, the witness said, one of the victims, Dewey Mar, asked the robbers if they were after money. "Shut up," Mak purportedly told him. "You're not supposed to say anything."

"Mak acted like a leader," said the witness in less than perfect English. "He had gun, he stood watch over people all the time while others (tied) up victims." When the shooting began, recalled the witness, all three robbers had drawn their guns. "I saw all three guns pointed."

"Tat-tat-tat-tat, just like a firecracker, not too loud," said the star witness. "I saw fire come out of guns. More than one gun fired. I saw bullets flying around, and one gun doesn't do that much. At least they had two of them firing at the same time. I was in the first round to get hit. I got hit, one was in gum, one was in neck. Blood was coming out."

"How many fired their guns?" the witness was asked.

"All three of them," he replied.

"I don't think he's lying," said Defense Lawyer Browne. "He's just confused."

Deputy Prosecutor Bill Downing told the court that he was not sure just how many guns were fired at the Wah Mee Club the night of the slayings, stating that ballistics evidence had found that at least two were fired with a possibility that a third gun had been fired. The prosecutor stated that it wasn't necessary in this case to prove Benjamin Ng actually fired one of the guns; the state only had to prove that Ng knew of the plan to rob and kill anyone inside the Wah Mee Club early on the morning of February 19th.

The prosecution's star witness stated that while he was hog-tied on the floor after the perpetrators had already robbed the victims, he turned his head and looked back over his left shoulder to see why they were still in the building.

"I don't think it was good at all," said the witness, "because they took all the money and they don't leave. Either they are waiting for somebody else or they got more to do," he had reasoned. It was about that time that the shooting began.

"Was there screaming?" asked Bob Lasnik, deputy prosecutor.

"No, not at all," replied the witness, "just hard

breathing." The witness told the jury that he lost consciousness, but soon awoke and heard either Ng or Mak ask if there were any more bullets. He said he fell unconscious again, but said he awoke when he thought he heard someone knocking loudly at the door of the club. "At that time I still hear hard breathing, somebody still alive." He explained that he had been able to free himself of his bindings and make it to the door, where he met someone who called police. Had he not been able to free himself, it was said, he would have drowned in his own blood.

"Do you see the person with the gun in court?" Lasnik asked the witness.

"Yes," he replied as he pointed at the defendant, Benjamin Ng.

Ng was convicted of aggravated first-degree murder by the eight-man, four-woman jury, who also would decide whether he would receive life in prison or the death sentence.

"All right! All right!" screamed a relative of one of the victims.

"He killed both my parents," said another relative of the victims. "I hope he gets the death sentence. That's when justice will be done."

"I hope he gets hanging or lethal injection," added one of the spectators. "Life in prison wouldn't satisfy me."

By September 20, 1983, the jury for the trial of the second defendant, Kwan Fai "Willie" Mak, had been seated. The trial was similar to Ng's, except that prosecutors would attempt to portray Mak as the mastermind of the crime, the schemer of the whole thing. On the other hand, Mak's defense was that he was guilty only of robbery for taking two guns from two of the victims, and he would attempt to blame Ng for the shooting by painting a picture of Ng as being violent due to brain damage.

"I left the Wah Mee Club prior to anyone being

shot," said Mak in a statement. "I left because Ben Ng was acting strangely and appeared to have abandoned the plan which we made prior to entering the club. I was concerned that he might shoot somebody, but I did not interfere because I was frightened that he would turn on me and shoot me. I left the club and heard what appeared to be gunshots."

But according to a report written up by Sgt. Joe Sanford, Mak purportedly stated that "I did all the shooting," a statement he later retracted. Mak also claimed at one point after his arrest that his main reason for going to the Wah Mee Club that night was to "rough up" a rival tong leader, and that he didn't expect anyone to be killed. He remained calm after his arrest, Sanford said, until he learned there was a survivor. "At that point he appeared afraid; he was shaking, he lost a little bit of his composure. Up until that time he was a cool individual," testified Sgt. Sanford.

Unlike Ng, Mak took the witness stand in his own defense, and attempted to pin the massacre on Benjamin Ng. Mak said that Ng had a blank look in his eyes, a look he had seen on other occasions. Mak said that on October 22, 1981, when he and Ng and another companion were disposing of a stolen safe by dumping it into Lake Washington, Ng "lost control" and chased and shot an elderly jogger by the name of Franklin Leach, who happened upon the trio as they were disposing of the safe. Mak also said he observed the blank look in Ng's eyes when Ng allegedly shot and killed a barking dog that had been annoying him.

"What did Ben do at the Wah Mee Club?" asked Mak's attorney, Jim Robinson.

"He look pale," replied Mak, "especially the expression from his eyes, is no expression. It's scary when you look straight to the eye. He was running around the place (the club) looking for a towel. I sense something not right. I think, 'What's he gonna do? What's gonna happen? I was a little bit scared, it's not a good feeling." Mak said he crept out the door, his gun in his holster. When he got outside, he said, that's when the shooting began.

Mak also told the jury that following his arrest, Sgt. Joe Sanford yelled at him. " 'We know you did it,' " Mak quoted Sanford as saying. " 'There's 13 people dead and you're trying to play games with me.' " Mak also said Sanford informed him that he would receive a reward if he identified the third man involved in the slayings.

At one point in the trial, Sgt. Sanford testified that Mak admitted all to him. " 'There is no third man. I did all the shooting,' " Sanford quoted Mak as saying.

"Did you ever tell Sgt. Sanford that you did all the shooting?" asked Mak's attorney, Jim Robinson.

"No," Mak replied.

A friend of Mak's testified that two weeks prior to the Wah Mee Club massacre, Mak purportedly discussed robbing the patrons and the bank of a gambling club, and killing all of the patrons to eliminate any witnesses.

" 'You have to tie up the victims or wear masks,' " the witness quoted Mak as saying.

"What if you don't wear masks?" asked King County Deputy Prosecutor Bill Downing.

"Have to kill, they can recognize us," the witness testified. The witness further stated that's when he decided he didn't want any part of it and dissociated himself with Ng and Mak.

Towards the end of the trial, Prosecutor Downing accused Mak of trying to bluff his way out of the murder charges against him by shifting the blame and "tailoring his story to fit the evidence."

"Do you know what poker-faced is?" Downing asked Mak. Downing explained to him, with a hint of contempt and sarcasm in his voice, that to be a good poker player you have to be able to bluff your way through a lousy hand to win.

"No," Mak responded. "It takes best hand to win. When you bluffing, you don't get away with it."

"This is the day of judgment for Willie Mak," said Deputy Prosecutor Bob Lasnik. "Now he must pay for the lives he stole and the lies he told."

During closing arguments, Prosecutor Downing recalled that Mak's story had been contradicted by several witnesses, that blood matching one of the victims had been found on items of clothing belonging to Mak, that a holster belonging to one of the murder weapons had been found at one of his relative's residence, and that he had been pointed out by the state's star witness as being the leader of the whole affair.

"He's a cool-headed, cold-blooded young man capable of committing such an atrocity and not batting an eyelash," declared Downing. "This case does boil down to credibility. You must decide if the defendant is being straight with you, or if his story is the fiction of a desperate and manipulative mind. It's up to you to say the cold-blooded acts of this schemer, this manipulator, are exactly what the law calls aggravated murder in the first degree."

The six-man, six-woman King County Superior Court jury returned a verdict of guilty of 13 counts of aggravated first-degree murder against Willie Mak.

On Thursday, October 6, 1983, Mak was sentenced to death for his part in the Chinatown massacre. If the sentence is carried out, he will have a choice of hanging or lethal injection under Washington law.

On Tuesday, October 25, 1983, Benjamin Ng was sentenced to 14 consecutive life terms for the Wah Mee Club slayings. Ng was also charged with first-degree murder in the October 22, 1981 shooting of Franklin Leach as he jogged around Lake Washington. If convicted of the charge, Ng could receive a maximum sentence of life in prison. As for the shooting deaths of two Beacon Hill women found shot to death in July, 1982, no charges are planned at the present time, according to King County Prosecutor Norm Maleng. "While there is evidence to implicate both Mak and Ng in these horrible murders, we simply do not have sufficient credible evidence to justify filing charges at this time," explained Maleng.

"I regret what has happened," Ng told King County Superior Court Judge Frank Howard at his sentencing. "I'm sorry for the families of the victims. And I'm sorry for my family, what they have had to go through."

The third suspect in the Chinatown massacre, Wai Chu "Tony" Ng, remains at large.

# "BOWLING ALLEY MASSACRE!"
## by Bill Cox

History has etched memories of violence on Las Cruces, New Mexico. Today a modern city of 56,000 residents and home of New Mexico State University, the beautiful southwestern city lies between the rugged Organ Mountains on the east and the Rio Grande River on the west, in the heart of Mesilla Valley.

Here, Apache Chief Geronimo once rampaged in a slaughter of the innocents and outlaw Billy the Kid once gunned down a gambler in the nearby historic village of Mesilla. For nine months, Mesilla was Confederate Headquarters for the Arizona Territory during the Civil War. Here stands the adobe wall ruins of the only remaining station on the famed Butterfield Stagecoach Trail. Kit Carson and Pancho Villa once roamed this area. Violent death has been no stranger over the centuries to this rugged region near the border of Old Mexico where the jagged peaks of the Organ Mountains are burnished red with each sunset, a fitting blood-red for what has happened here over the years.

Even the modern-day violence of nuclear warfare hangs ominously over the far-stretching desert and mountain ranges, which contain the White Sands Missile Range. Here, most of the nation's rockets have received their first testing. To the north is Trinity Site, where the first atomic bomb was exploded in 1945. Beautiful and bizarre is the land, a strange blend of violence and death, old and new.

On the brilliantly warm Saturday morning of February 11, 1990, Las Cruces was to experience its most terrible and violent episode in many years. Geronimo, known for his inherent savagery and sadism, would have reveled in what took place at the city's only bowling alley that horrible February weekend.

Officially it began to unfold at 8:33 a.m. that day, when a hysterical young female—screaming and crying with pain—called the Las Cruces Police Department to report a wanton act of cold-blooded murder that would shock the nation.

The almost incoherent girl babbled and sobbed that people had been shot and badly hurt in the bowling alley, which was on fire. She was calling from the Las Cruces Bowl at 1201 East Amador Avenue.

Fire trucks, ambulances manned by paramedics and city police units converged on the popular bowling alley that almost everyone knew had been scheduled to host a junior league bowling tournament at 10:00 a.m. Firemen, upon reaching the scene and seeing smoke pouring from the bowling alley, rushed inside and headed for the apparent source of the smoke, the bowling alley's office.

Amid the thick and choking smoke that was boiling from a pile of burning papers on a desk, the firefighters found several people, including small children, sprawled on the floor of the office. Some of the victims were not moving, but one woman groaned and tried to raise herself as help arrived.

The firemen dragged the people from the smoke-filled office to the adjacent lobby of the building. When they did so, they made a shocking discovery. All seven victims had been shot! At least three of them, a man and two children, appeared to be beyond any human help, dead from the gunshot wounds. Paramedics gave what aid they could before loading the four survivors into ambulances and speeding toward the hospital with sirens wailing and red lights flashing.

Police Sergeant Phil George was the first police officer to reach the scene. Rushing inside with the firemen, he was stunned by the gruesome scene in the office. He helped to remove one of the victims, who was moaning and groaning, from the office filled with the dense smoke. Later, the obviously shaken policeman would tell newsmen, "I've never been involved in a crime so gruesome. In seventeen years, I've never had a day like this."

When he was able to return to his police unit, George radioed the dispatcher to send everything available and to contact Captain Fred Rubio, chief of detectives of the department's criminal investigation division. Like many of the officers, Rubio was off duty and at home on this Saturday morning. But he was at the scene some 10 minutes after receiving word of the murder horror at the bowling alley. He began immediately to call in off-duty detectives and other investigators.

The scene of pandemonium at the bowling alley was almost unbelievable to the spectators who began to throng the area as word of the crime spread. The bowling alley was cordoned off with yellow crime scene tape and the crowds were kept across the street to prevent any loss of possible evidence.

While investigators were assigned to go to the hospital to get any statements they could from the shooting survivors—if they were able to talk at all—Captain Rubio and detectives who joined him tried to sort out the hellish events.

From quizzing employees of the bowling alley who had come to the scene and other persons in the immediate area, the lawmen learned that the bowling alley had opened at 8:00 a.m. to get ready for a junior league bowling tournament in which youngsters age 10 to 14 took part. The tourney had been scheduled for 10:00 a.m.

Shortly after the bowling alley was opened, the seven victims, including employees and their children, apparently had been herded into the office by a gunman or gunmen who robbed the safe, then coldbloodedly set about executing all witnesses, even the young children. Within a short time, the lawmen learned enough from talking briefly with those victims at the hospital to know that two armed robbers had been involved. The gunmen grabbed money from the safe as it was being counted when they entered, shot the victims, then piled papers on the office desk and set them afire in an apparent attempt to destroy any evidence.

Within an hour, the victims had been identified. Three were dead when rescuers arrived; a tiny girl had died after being taken to the hospital. Three others were in serious or critical condition from gunshot wounds.

Killed in the fusillade of bullets fired in the office were Steve Saenz Teran, 26; his two-year-old daughter, Valerie; his six-year-old stepdaughter, Paula Holguin; and a 13-year-old girl, Amy Houser. Valerie had been pronounced dead on arrival at the hospital.

The wounded who were fighting for their lives at the hospital were identified as a cook at the bowling alley, the daughter of the bowling alley owner and her 12-year-old daughter. Apparently it had been the youngster who had phoned the police department to hysterically report the mass shootings and fire.

Detective Chief Rubio contacted the state headquarters of the New Mexico State Police at Santa Fe, the capital, and requested that its well-equipped mobile crime lab van be dispatched to Las Cruces. Some months earlier, Rubio had arranged with the state police to provide a much smaller satellite crime lab at New Mexico State University for analysis of crime scene evidence. However, the scope of the bowling alley murders and attempted murders led to his calling in the highly trained crime scene technicians and their equipment from the state headquarters.

The crime scene itself, Rubio knew, would be a tough one to process for evidence, since the victims in the office had been dragged to the lobby by firemen. It was possible, he theorized, that the emergency removal of the people from the densely smoky office, plus other firefighting efforts, could have obliterated or damaged evidence.

Because of the distance the crime lab squad had to travel from Santa Fe and the time it took to process the scene—the taking of still and video photographs, the dusting of the office and other areas for possible fingerprints and the careful probe of the scene foot by foot in a search for evidence—the removal of the slain victims was delayed until midafternoon.

Meanwhile, teams of officers scoured the neighborhood where the bowling alley was located in search for witnesses who might have seen the gunmen or the vehicle in which they were riding. From two residents living in the area, police were able to put together partial descriptions of the killers. They also obtained information that the pair had probably fled in an older-model, green vehicle that could have been, from varied witness stories, a van, truck or pickup. No one had gotten a license number.

As best as could be pieced together, the killers were described as Hispanic men. One was said to be about 45 to 50 years old, 5 feet 6 inches tall, of medium build, weighing 135 to 140 pounds, with a dark complexion, black hair combed back and brown eyes. When last seen he was wearing a green-and-white plaid sport coat, dark green or brown pants and black cowboy boots.

The other suspect was younger, thought to be 29 or 30, about 5 feet 10 inches tall, weighing 170 pounds, with a dark complexion and dark, kinky hair. He was last seen wearing a dark jacket and trousers and possibly a red shirt. He was believed to be armed with a blue steel revolver with a barrel six to eight inches long. Detectives said that the condition of the victims who were being treated at the hospital prevented lengthy questioning. Thus, the information on what happened and the descriptions of the killers were sketchy at best.

But with what they had to go on, city, county and state lawmen, augmented by federal agencies, set up 10 roadblocks on all roads and highways out of Las Cruces. More than 100 officers launched a massive manhunt for the killers, aided by six small aircraft and helicopters that took to the air.

As the investigation proceeded, Captain Rubio met with newsmen who were pressing for details. He admitted that lawmen had little to go on.

"What we have here is a very vicious crime," he said grimly. "You're talking about the assassination of kids, and a whole family almost was assassinated."

He related that the seven victims had been placed in one concentrated area, ruthlessly shot and left for dead after a fire had been started on the desk.

About $5,000 had been taken in the robbery, it was estimated. One of the victims, thought to have been the bowling alley owner's daughter, apparently had been counting the money from the safe when the bandits entered the office only a few minutes after the bowling alley opened.

Based on the descriptions, a police artist using a computer quickly assembled composite sketches of the gunmen. Later, the drawings were shown to one of the victims at the hospital, the 12-year-old girl who seemed to be less seriously wounded than the others. She looked at the sketches and nodded her head. The drawings were reproduced in large numbers. They were distributed to all of the agencies taking part in the massive search and investigation and circulated widely by the news media.

The wife and mother of three of the slaying

victims — Steven Teran and his two small daughters — was attending a class at a local beautician's school when the shootings happened. The distraught young mother was able to tell officers little, except to provide the background of her family and their activities prior to going their separate ways Saturday morning.

Her husband, Steve, had been graduated from New Mexico State University last December with a degree in criminal justice. He wanted badly to become a law enforcement officer, and his application for employment was on file with the Las Cruces Police Department at the time of his death.

"He wanted to go into law enforcement," his tearful young wife said. "He talked to the Border Patrol, Customs, anything. He wanted to use his college degree."

Steve served in the Army and National Guard, and among his wife's treasured photographs was a portrait of him in uniform. Another, with Steve in uniform, was taken with his wife and the two little girls who were shot to death by the robber-killers. One picture showed a Christmas tree in the background with the smiling and happy Teran family.

Steve and his wife had known each other in high school in the little community of Bayard, New Mexico. The wife said Steve worked weeknights at the bowling alley and on the day shift during the weekend, operating the pin machine in the busy bowling alley.

On Saturdays, Steve usually took their small daughters with him to the bowling alley because the couple couldn't find a babysitter to leave them with. But it was a cozy arrangement because the girls and their father were very close, the tearful young woman said.

"They have peace now. They are happy. They'll never cry, no pain. I'm going to miss them to my dying day. But they are in God's hands. I could not ask for more," the distraught mother cried.

And she sobbed in anguish at the brutality and senselessness of killing the children: "What can a two-year-old girl do? Why my little girls, my babies? This whole thing is senseless!"

Captain Rubio, a graduate of New Mexico State University who has been with the police department for 28 years, rose to his present job through the ranks. For 15 years, he was a uniform patrolman who gained an invaluable on-the-job education through his tough work as a street cop. He was promoted to the detective division some 12 years ago and with his combination of a college degree, enhanced by graduate work, and the lessons that the street taught him, he rose rapidly to the post of chief of detectives. A native of Las Cruces, he has watched the city grow from a town where violent crime was minimal to a modern and progressive city where the burgeoning population is pushing the crime rate up.

Located on Interstate 10 only 48 miles north of El Paso, Texas, and its twin border city of Juarex, Mexico, Las Cruces is visited by tourists and transients. Interstate 25 also runs through the city.

"Twenty years ago somebody would get killed and the whole community probably knew who did it," Rubio said. "Then the area started to grow and I've been watching it change. We have drugs, we have transients, we have good highways coming in here from four directions. I don't know if these guys are from another town or another state or another country. But they were mobile when it happened and are probably mobile now. What shocked me when I went to the scene was the magnitude of what happened. What in hell could a six-year-old and a two-year-old do to these individuals?"

With a force of only 19 detectives, investigators who do it all from crime scene processing to affidavit-taking and pursuing all possible leads, Rubio knew his personnel was spread thin. But they worked around the clock, canvassing the neighborhood for witnesses, taking their statements, manning special phones that were set up to receive tips. And the community was responding to the horror of the mass killings. Calls poured in and all of them had to be checked out.

Rubio believed the killers had cased the bowling alley previously. The detective chief said, "I have a gut feeling they were here prior to Saturday morning. They knew ahead of time where the money was."

As happens in all such massive probes, tips on possible suspects came to the Las Cruces police from different locations in the Southwest area. Two men resembling the bowling alley killers were arrested in Deming, New Mexico by sheriff's officers there. The pair was arrested on illegal drug charges. Deming authorities notified Las Cruces when they noticed the suspects looked like the composites of the bowling alley gunman. Rubio sent two detectives, Rickey Madrid and Leo Borunda, to Deming.

He instructed them to get pictures and fingerprints of the suspects so that the prints could be checked against the random prints found in the bowling alley and witnesses could look at the photos in a so-called "six pack" — a photo lineup consisting of six pictures to be shown to the witnesses. Later, the two men were eliminated as suspects when the prints and photos were checked.

Another tip came from officers at Anthony, Texas, where police said they had received information from employees at a local car dealership. The employees said that two men had stopped there three hours after the Las Cruces killings, asking directions to Mexico. They were riding in a green van similar to the one in which witnesses said the gunmen fled after the murders. But this was just another lead among the many that lawmen would have to check out in their efforts to solve this crime.

Three days after the slayings, police updated the composite drawings of the suspects when the survivors had improved enough to be questioned further by detectives.

The new sketches were distributed to all agencies who had received the first drawings, especially border authorities. Las Cruces detectives went to El Paso to brief border agencies on the investigation, since it was believed the killers might have headed into Mexico.

Theories and speculation abounded in the once-quiet New Mexico city, now stunned by the shocking mass murder. A psychologist at New Mexico State University offered her theory to police about the type of men who had pulled the triggers and snuffed the lives of even the smallest children.

"They have a reason—in their minds—that neutralizes their actions, to rationalize what they are doing," she said. "Violence is always easier to do if the one committing the violence distances himself from the victim, or doesn't feel a great deal of empathy toward the victim."

The psychologist added that the killers didn't think about getting caught and being punished, so the severity of the penalty didn't matter to them.

Meanwhile, relatives and friends buried Amy Houser on February 13th. Final rites were conducted in Immaculate Heart of Mary Cathedral, which was packed beyond its normal capacity of 800 people by relatives, police, fire department and paramedical personnel, and scores of the girl's schoolmates and teachers. When the small casket was wheeled into the church, some of Amy's cherished possessions were on top—two stuffed animals from her younger years, a soccer team trophy she won in 1982 when she was the only girl on the school team, her favorite perfume and her library cards.

During the emotional service, the clergyman said, "Shock, outrage, disgust, anger, pain are a few of the words that describe the emotions of all of us here and indeed the city of Las Cruces is experiencing over the events that occurred this past Saturday."

When the funeral procession reached the cemetery and the flower-laden casket was lowered into the ground, the eighth-grader's classmates filed slowly by, dropping final blossoms on the casket and then bursting into tears. A strong and cold wind that was blowing made the overcast day even worse.

The following day, ironically Valentine's Day, Steven Teran and his two small daughters were laid to rest in the cemetery near the little town where he and his wife had been high school sweethearts. Steve Teran was dressed in his National Guard uniform and a U.S. flag was draped over his casket.

The estimated 700 people who came to the funeral were more than the small pink adobe church would hold. One of the floral wreaths bearing the names of the three victims was in the shape of a valentine heart. The solemn words of the Roman Catholic bishop fell on the hushed church.

"There are no healing words," he said. "There is no healing wisdom that can help us answer our questions. Why did this have to happen and why did it have to happen to these innocent people who became the victims of such a heinous and horrible crime? . . . The power of evil, the power of darkness, the power of death was there, but my dear friends, our faith tells us that a more powerful presence was there. . . . We cannot blame God for what happened. This was an act of evil men. . . ."

Even as last rites were held for the massacre victims, the residents of the town were busy raising a large reward to be paid for information to bring the two killers to justice. Information would be accepted on a confidential basis, the reward raisers announced. Almost immediately the reward money was soaring into the thousands of dollars. The president of the Chamber of Commerce told newsmen, "We want to show these type of individuals who would commit these crimes that our community will not put up with it. We will put our money where our mouth is."

Four separate memorial funds also were set up for contributions that would pay for the hospital and funeral costs of the victims, it was announced.

Although police were receiving hundreds of calls from people with tips or information they thought might be helpful, no new leads had been uncovered. Detectives had considered the possibility that the mass slaying motivated by robbery might have been linked to another murder in the city less than a month earlier.

A 22-year-old employee of a service station was found with his hands tied behind his back and fatally shot in the head in the gas station on January 15, 1990. But police had information that seemed to indicate the attendant's death was not related to the bowling alley shootings.

Trying to cover all possible ways of tracking down the mass murderers, Chief of Detectives Rubio assigned two of his detectives to fly to Washington, D.C., and confer with FBI experts on what kind of criminals might be involved. The detectives met with a 10-member panel of experts. Based on the detailed information unfolded by the investigators, the FBI team compiled psychological profiles of the two men who gunned down seven victims and started a fire to try to cover up the crime.

Rubio later told reporters, "They mentioned that we have a very complicated crime with very complicated criminals." He declined to disclose details of the profiles prepared by the FBI. He also disclosed later that it was definite that both men fired shots during the killing spree and that ballistic experts had determined what kind of guns fired the shots. The detective chief did not reveal the ballistic information, wishing to protect information that would verify guilty knowledge if an arrested suspect was involved in the crime.

"But both of the men definitely were shooters," the captain said.

The Las Cruces police received offers of assistance from law enforcement agencies throughout the nation. An expert police artist from Texas' Houston Police Department came to Las Cruces. Working with the survivors of the shootings and a clinical psychologist, he prepared new composite drawings of the suspects. These differed from the earlier drawings that were hampered by sketchy information from witnesses.

Chief of Detectives Rubio said upon release of the new composites, "We have been working very patiently and very sensitively with the survivors because of the extent of their injuries. This is the first time that we have been able to do this at such great length and intensity."

The detective chief also disclosed that the events that preceded the execution-type shootings appeared to be somewhat different from the initial reconstruction of the crime, which had been based on very limited information from the victims who had survived.

It appeared that Steven Teran and his children had walked in on the robbery already in progress, rather than having been there when the gunmen first arrived. This was based on one of the survivors' statements, he said.

Hard pressed for new leads although some 150 suspects had been checked out, Detective Chief Rubio decided that national publicity was needed to crack the brutal case. With this in mind, he contacted the producers of the national television program "Unsolved Mysteries" and requested that a segment be filmed for broadcast.

"I honestly don't know if that will help or not," said Rubio. "It's only a tool. They have, I think, thirty million viewers out there in the United States and Canada. That's what I'm counting on. Hopefully, someone out there will give us the right information."

A field producer for the TV show, who came to Las Cruces to arrange details for the filming, told reporters the multiple slaying was one of the worst cases the show had ever recorded.

"It's a senseless crime in which seven people were shot," she said, "It's incredibly tragic whenever children are involved." The filming crew, director, actors and technicians arrived in Las Cruces on March 19th to film the massacre segment.

Among those who were interviewed was the badly wounded cook who had survived the shootings. For the first time, the emotionally distraught woman gave her version of the massacre to reporters and the TV filmmakers.

She still had two bullets in her body, one in her shoulder and one in her brain, that doctors did not intend to remove because, said the physicians, it would be more dangerous to remove them than to leave them. Saying she still was haunted by the faces of the two killers, the cook said: "I can't understand why they had to shoot. They already had the money. Why did they shoot?"

The woman related that she already had been shot by the gunmen when Steve Teran and his daughters arrived at the bowling alley.

"He said, 'Oh, my God! No!' I recognized his voice." She said she still was conscious even after being shot three times.

The tearful survivor recollected, "I was coming and going, coming and going. I felt myself drowning. I was drowning in my own blood, drowning in my own blood. After the second bullet, I just started praying, I prayed hard."

As the gunmen calmly went about firing shots into the other victims, the woman said she believed that she would die.

"I heard a scream. I started getting really scared. I started thinking those guys are going to kill us. I don't think they are just going to take the money.

"They took a lot from me, because I don't feel the

same. I'm just not the same person."

As a result of the bullet wounds, the woman's vision is blurred and her coordination is poor. But even with one slug still lodged in her brain, the doctors say she will survive.

The cook said that the gunmen forced the victims to kneel before firing the shots. When she later was placed in the ambulance, the victim said, "I knew I was alive."

The woman related that she still sees the faces of the gunmen before her and would have no trouble identifying them. Weeks after the shootings, all of the surviving victims were being kept under close police watch.

Besides the "Unsolved Mysteries" program, Las Cruces police also have asked the readers of this magazine to come forward if they have any knowledge that would help solve the crime. Although investigators continue to work intensely and follow every tip or piece of information, the murders remain unsolved.

But Chief of Detectives Rubio believes that someone, somewhere in the United States, Mexico or Canada, has some vital information that can lead to the identity and arrest of the killers. All information received by the police will be kept confidential. Anyone supplying the information that breaks the case also will be eligible for the thousands of dollars in reward money that is being offered by the citizens of Las Cruces.

Anyone with information can contact the Criminal Investigation Division, Las Cruces Police Department, Las Cruces, New Mexico 88804.

# "4 VICTIMS IN THE TRAILER OF BLOOD!"

by Bob Carlsen

BAYOU BLUE, LA.
JANUARY 4, 1985

When word of the murders reached the sheriff's office it was almost too much to believe. Things like that just didn't happen in the normally tranquil parish. Most of the notorious crimes occurred closer to New Orleans, a couple of parishes away. Lafourche Parish, 86 miles in length, is located in the southern portion of Louisiana and borders on the Gulf of Mexico. Murders don't occur there often, and multiple slayings are even rarer.

Bobby Todd's trailer was located near the small community of Bayou Blue in the northern half of Lafourche Parish. It was almost on the line separating Lafourche and Terrebonne Parishes.

What detectives found in the trailer was a scene of carnage. The linoleum floor was so coated with blood one could have skated. They had to be careful not to slip while checking the victims for some sign of life. Once it was confirmed that they were all dead, the trailer was cordoned off and they awaited the arrival of crime scene experts.

Sheriff Duffy Breaux put his chief of detectives, Olin Terry, in charge of the case. A team of five detectives worked with Sheriff Breaux and Terry on the murder, the first of its kind in their jurisdiction.

The two male murder victims were identified as Bobby Todd, 33, the owner of the trailer, and Terry Hebert, 27. Two female victims were naked. Their clothing was found in a back room. The identifications indicated that one was Sandra Brake, and the second was Anne Tierney, both 19.

Todd, manager of the popular Black Gold Lounge, had been shot twice. Hebert was shot five times in the side and back. Sandra Brake, who was Hebert's pregnant girlfriend, was shot twice in the heart. Anne Tierney had been shot once in the chest, four times in the abdomen, and once in the face.

It was obvious to Detective Terry that this was more than just a robbery. A great deal of hatred and passion was involved in the crime. A robber probably wouldn't have put so many slugs into his victims. All the evidence indicated the killer fired with a frenzy. He must have in order to gun down all the victims before one could jump him.

"He would have had to reload twice," Terry said to other detectives. "Whoever did this hated these people."

Shells found on the floor of the trailer indicated that the killer had reloaded his gun. Empty wallets revealed that money had been stolen. But considering the isolation of the trailer, Terry figured the killer or killers had to be somebody who knew Todd. But then, that could include a lot of suspects, since Todd had been rather well known because he was the manager of the Black Gold Lounge.

The bodies were hauled away and the trailer was gone over with a fine-tooth comb. Technicians couldn't find any bloody fingerprints or other clues to indicate the identity of the person who could have done such a horrible thing.

Detectives fanned out through the Bayou Blue area to question anyone who may have seen a stranger lurking in the area. They doubted that they would find anybody who actually saw or heard the multiple murder because of the isolation of the trailer. But perhaps a distant neighbor had noticed a suspicious character hanging around the area recently. It was a long shot, but investigators were willing to try anything. But as they suspected, nobody in the area had seen a thing.

Detectives questioned persons at the lounge which Todd had managed, and also friends and relatives of the other three victims. The sleuths figured that Todd was the key man in the murders, because they had occurred in his trailer.

It was a sickening thought, but maybe Todd had been the primary target and the other three were just gunned down because they were witnesses. All kinds of theories were kicked around by the detectives, as happens in every case, and each promising idea was pursued.

Whenever you manage a business, you make enemies of some type, detectives realized. Especially when you're the manager of a lounge or tavern there's the possibility that a disgruntled bounced patron might one day return to seek revenge. Also, such nightclubs are prime targets of extortionists who are trying to muscle in on the business. Sleuths had to consider the possibility that organized crime, which flourishes in New Orleans and the other larger cities, could be expanding its operation to include smaller businesses in nearby parishes.

Detectives compiled a list of possible suspects, persons who for one reason or another held a grudge against Bobby Todd or one of the other three murder victims.

They learned of a man, a former street preacher and drug-abuse counselor, who had been behaving suspiciously before the murders occurred. The sleuths learned that the suspect had borrowed a car on the day of the murders. They got the name of the car's owner and received permission to examine the sedan. They found some minute traces of blood on the driver's seat. Unfortunately, the amount was too small to determine anything other than that it was human blood. Typing it was impossible.

Detectives questioned the preacher's friends and learned that he had borrowed bullets for a .357 magnum just prior to the murders.

When the sleuths got the autopsy report back, they learned that the murder weapon was a .357 magnum.

"Do you know where he got the gun?" the witness who had helped his friend obtain the bullets was asked by Detective Terry.

"Nope," the witness replied. "I'd never known him to own a .357 magnum. He didn't tell me where he got it, either."

"Why didn't he just buy some bullets at a gun shop?"

"That's what I wondered. When he first approached me about it, I told him that those cartridges weren't hard to buy. He told me he already had been to the local dealers and they were all out. So that's when I told him I knew where we could get some. I know a guy who owns a .357 magnum. He was a good friend, and he had no problem about giving me some of the bullets."

"About how many bullets did he give you?" the detective asked.

"I'd say around 20. Maybe not quite that many. I can't say for sure."

Detectives questioned more persons and found one who claimed the street preacher had talked about how he had murdered Bobby Todd and the others. The suspect had made the classic mistake of not being able to keep his mouth shut about his deed.

From statements the killer had made to others, detectives pieced together the events leading up to the slaughter. On August 14, 1977 the man prepared himself for the kill by drinking a pitcher of beer and smoking some marijuana. Then he went to the isolated trailer, knocked on the door of the man who had been bedding down his woman, and waited for 33-year-old Bobby Todd to answer.

At gunpoint, he forced his way inside. Todd and another man he didn't know were entertaining two naked women. Todd had told the assailant to stay cool and that he could have the money. But it wasn't money he was after. Todd didn't have the foggiest idea what was going down. And that annoyed the assailant. He wanted to make sure Todd and the others knew his name. He wanted them to know who was about to turn the aroma of sex games into bedlam and the smell of gunpowder.

When the assailant introduced himself, the lounge owner didn't recognize his name. But the realization slowly came just as the man pulled the trigger on the already cocked magnum. The explosion ripped through the trailer and the force of the bullet's impact threw Bobby Todd against the wall.

The women screamed in terror. Before the second man in the room could make a move, the assailant turned the gun on him and put a slug into the guy's side. He crumpled to the floor. The killer knew he had to make every shot count so he could disable all the victims before finishing them off.

He next turned the magnum onto one of the naked women and fired a shot into her stomach. Then he plugged the second woman in the chest. All of the victims were on the floor dying within 10 seconds.

Except for the woman who'd been shot in the heart and died instantly, the victims were lying on the floor moaning.

"Please help me," the gunshot woman said as the blood poured from her gaping wound onto her hands as she tried to hold her intestines inside of her body. "Help me!"

"I'll help you," he said as he stepped over her body and cocked the revolver. Her attention had been focused on her wound. When he spoke, she looked up to see the barrel of the revolver pointed at her face. She screamed. It was cut short as he pulled the trigger.

In all, the killer fired 15 shots into the bodies. Other bullets missed their targets. He had to reload the gun twice. Once he had to stop to unjam it.

Then he took Bobby Todd's money, put it in a paper bag and fled the trailer.

Revenge was his motive. The money meant nothing. But he knew the cops would think robbery was the motive. So he threw the gun and the money into a nearby bayou. There would be no way detectives could link him to the crime, he knew. They wouldn't be able to check the ballistics, because they'd never find the gun.

Detectives checked recent sales at gun shops to no avail. Then they mined recent police reports of burglaries and thefts and learned that a man who lived near the suspect had recently reported that his .357 magnum Colt revolver had been stolen. The theft occurred two days before the trailer murders. And although the guy couldn't prove it, he told detectives he had a sneaky feeling that a recent acquaintance by the name of David Dene Martin, 25, may have been the guy who ripped him off.

The man explained that he hadn't shown his guns to very many persons. Martin had been one of the privileged few to view his small collection. The theft victim figured it had to be somebody who knew where the Colt was kept.

Then the man said something which perked Detective Terry's ears up. He mentioned that the gun wasn't loaded at the time it was stolen. He didn't like keeping loaded guns at home, and he kept all the bullets separate from his guns.

"I keep all the bullets down in the loading room," the man said.

"The loading room?" Detective Terry asked.

"I load my own slugs," the man explained. "I don't buy them. Too expensive. In fact, when I even target practice in hay bales I scavenge through the bales at the end and retrieve the slugs. If they're still in good shape, I reuse them. If they're distorted, I melt them down and mold them again."

The significance of what the witness said did not escape the intelligent police officer. Detective Terry knew that the suspect had been bragging about how he ditched the murder weapon in a place it would never be found. The sleuth believed that was probably true, and without the gun, a ballistics comparison would be impossible.

But if Detective Terry could prove that Martin had stolen the .357 magnum, then maybe there was still a way to get a ballistics comparison. The gun's owner said he had scavenged slugs fired from the Colt .357. The sleuth figured those slugs fired during target practice would have the same ballistics markings as bullets found in the victims' bodies.

"Do you have some of those .357 slugs fired from the Colt?" Detective Terry asked the man.

"I sure do," the witness responded. "You really think they'll do you any good?"

The detective smiled broadly. The witness knew his answer without a word being spoken. He fetched the slugs for the detective, who thanked him and informed him that it probably would be necessary for him to testify in court regarding the manner in which the slugs were found and preserved during and after the target practice sessions.

"That is, if these match up with the other ones," the detective added.

Good news came from ballistics experts at the crime laboratory. The striations on the bullets fired from the Colt .357 magnum during target practice sessions matched perfectly with the bullets extracted from the murder victims. Now all Detective Terry had to do was prove that David Dene Martin had been the one to steal the Colt.

Detectives learned that after the murders, Martin had given some empty shell casings to a woman and told her about how he had plotted the murder of Todd, stolen the Colt .357 magnum revolver, burst into the trailer and gunned the lounge manager down. He killed the other three simply because they'd gotten in the way.

After Detective Terry had talked to all of the persons who knew Martin, he had enough evidence and statements to prove that Martin had stolen the Colt revolver which had been used as the murder weapon.

Martin, who had been arrested during the course of the investigation, was officially charged with four counts of pre-meditated murder.

The trial got underway in April of 1978. The thoroughness with which detectives had done their job was evident to the jury. A parade of witnesses painted a clear picture of how Martin plotted Todd's murder and then bragged about all of the gory details and how he'd been smart enough to dispose of the stolen money and murder weapon.

The defense consisted of this: "I didn't do it." Martin contended that somebody else shot the victims elsewhere and then took them to Todd's trailer.

Nobody believed his story and on April 10, 1978 David Dene Martin was found guilty on all four counts of murder. He subsequently was sentenced to death in the electric chair.

A series of appeals successfully delayed his execution for seven years. But toward the end of 1984 it was apparent that Martin's time was running out. His appeals to the various courts had been exhausted, and his last chance was to go before the state's Pardon Board, which set his hearing for January 3, 1985 just hours before he was scheduled to be executed.

John J. Erny, the assistant district attorney at the Lafourche Parish, had originally prosecuted and now asked the Pardon Board to let Martin die.

"I'm going to tell them what happened. I'm not going to change my mind," Erny said prior to the board hearing. "It's like everything else. In my business you've got to keep an open mind. If they come up with new evidence or some reason to suggest he didn't commit the crime, I'd have to look at it and examine it in good conscience. Absent that, I'm going to have to ask for the death penalty."

The Pardon Board denied Martin's plea for clemency. The ruthless murders of four persons by the jealous lover could not go unpunished. Many citizens felt that to let Martin off with a life sentence without possibility of parole would be to let him win. Others felt that life in prison was an equally cruel punishment as the death sentence.

On January 4, 1985, eight years after the quadruple murder, it was time for execution. David Martin had finished a fine last meal prepared by the prison chef earlier and had spent the last couple of hours consulting with his spiritual counselor. Every appeal had been exhausted. He'd been given every consideration by the state and courts.

Eight years earlier his crime had been a monstrous one. Everybody who knew the one-time preacher and drug counselor still found it difficult to believe that he could have committed such horrible murders.

Even the killer, at times, felt that all of it had to be a bad dream, that he didn't possess such hatred inside him to do such a thing. But when Martin's final walk began, he knew it was all true.

Shortly after midnight burly guards at the Louisiana State Penitentiary at Angola ushered the killer out of his cell on death row and to the pea-green, cinder block execution chamber. There sat "Old Smokey," as some death row inmates had christened the electric chair. It was cold, forboding and loathsome to the man who had murdered four persons. David Dene Martin also knew that this date had been inevitable.

At 12:05 a.m. Martin was shackled at the wrists and ankles. He was wide-eyed and obviously nervous at first. He looked to witnesses to be on the verge of tears.

The warden stepped up to the glass that separated the witnesses from the massive oak electric chair. He leaned over and, looking down, clicked on a microphone.

"He has said he will have no final statement," Warden Frank Blackburn said. He glanced up at the witnesses. "Ya'll hear me in there?" The newsmen, a state judge, a state senator and a reverend nodded.

The killer's anxiety ebbed for some minutes. He wore a long-sleeved white T-shirt. The left leg of Martin's blue jeans had been cut off and his leg had been shaved. An electrode was strapped to his bare skin. A second electrode was then placed on his shaved head, which was damp with his own sweat.

He grimaced once. He appeared to be angry. Martin looked down at his feet and then at the guards. The strap around his leg was causing him some pain. He knew it would all be over in a few more minutes, so he didn't bother to complain.

Martin closed his eyes and the execution hood was placed over his head. The hood smelled musty to him. It smelled like death. Other death row inmates had smelled it before him. Others undoubtedly would follow.

To the right of the killer was a cinder block wall, through which an unseen executioner was able to see the warden. Warden Blackburn stood to the front and left of the killer in front of a large window covered by closed Venetian blinds. Behind the multiple murderer was a large white cabinet, nearly eight feet tall. It housed some of the electrical equipment that would soon cause the killer's death.

A clock hanging over the cabinet door indicated that it was 12:07. Warden Blackburn signalled the guards to leave the room. Thirty seconds later he nodded toward the executioner. David Martin could hear the muffled clunk as the electrical switch was thrown, and his body almost immediately tightened with a jolt. The thumb on his right hand was jammed between the two middle fingers. His left ankle lifted.

Four jolts of electricity ended the story that had begun on August 14, 1977 when he had ruthlessly used a Colt .357 magnum revolver on four persons.

The first electric shock was 2,000 volts and 10 seconds long. Then a 500 volt, 20 second jolt; another 2,000 volt, 10 second jolt; and a final 500 volt 20 second jolt coursed through his body. It was finished within a minute.

Warden Blackburn, a stout, silver-haired, balding man with a mustache, obviously was agitated. He did not enjoy supervising such things. But it was part of his job. He paced to and fro in the execution chamber for five minutes to make sure the body didn't move. When he was certain the condemned man was dead, he signalled for guards and the doctor, who made the official pronouncement at 12:16 a.m.

The story that left five persons dead and had caused an inestimable amount of grief for family members finally was over. As Lafourche Parish District Attorney John Erny said, it was a monstrous tale, "a monstrous tragedy that grows."

# "THE PIZZERIA BLOODBATH"
## by Dan Buttaro

Jeanette Kilmer sensed something was wrong as she and her husband drove past the Domino's Pizza store in Vero Beach, Florida. Jeanette had once worked there, and she thought it strange for the lights to be off at 11:45 p.m. It was Tuesday, May 17, 1988, and the store should still have been open. Jeanette turned to her husband and expressed her concern as the pair continued up the road.

When the couple arrived home, Jeanette phoned Domino's. She got no answer. She hung up and dialed the pizza shop the couple owned. To her surprise, Jeanette discovered their business had become exceptionally busy around 11:30 p.m.

In the meantime, another Vero Beach resident drove to Domino's Pizza. Phil Taylor had phoned in his pizza order around 11:00 p.m. When it hadn't arrived shortly thereafter, Taylor drove over to the eatery located in the 900 block of 20th Place. The business, about a block from a four-lane highway, is situated in the business district of the small coastal community. Taylor parked his car and walked toward the door around 11:35 p.m. That's when he sensed something amiss.

The front store lights were out, but the glass door, normally operated by an employee-controlled electric bolt, was open. Taylor forget about his pizza, now fearing that something was very wrong.

Taylor returned to his car and drove the block and a half to the Vero Beach Police Department. He reported his suspicions. The dispatcher asked Lieutenant John D'Agosto to investigate.

Lieutenant D'Agosto entered the pizzeria 12 minutes later, while the concerned Taylor waited outside. A minute later, the officer ran through the door holding his weapon. He yelled to Taylor, ordering him to get across the street, as he dove into his police cruiser. D'Agosto grabbed the mike from his car radio and announced that he'd discovered a multiple "Signal 33" and possible "Signal 5."

The codes — police jargon for a multiple shooting and possible homicide — immediately alerted other officers. Inside, surrounded by a sea of blood, the veteran officer discovered three bodies, two men and a woman.

Within minutes, police cruisers converged on the scene to back up D'Agosto. The lieutenant, assisted by other officers, entered the pizzeria again. Knowing that emergency medical teams would disrupt the original crime scene, the lieutenant remembered he had a camera in his patrol car. D'Agosto grabbed it and quickly shot a series of photographs.

As the severity of the situation unfolded, officers relayed further instructions to the police dispatcher. They requested that the chief and a team of off-duty officers be called to the store, in addition to the criminal investigators who were already en route.

When paramedics arrived, the officers at the pizzeria quickly balanced lifesaving measures with investigative procedures to seal off the crime scene. They carefully guided the medical technicians to the victims, who were located at the rear of the store. There, the medics found the three people huddled on the small bathroom floor.

One man was in a leaning position against the

back wall. His shirt, trousers, and shoes were missing. Directly in front of him were the two others. The woman, lying face down in a prone position, was nude except for her white socks. The fully clothed man along her left side was in the same position. All three victims had each suffered at least one head wound.

Detective-Lieutenant Ronald B. Blanton, of the Vero Beach Police Department's Criminal Investigation Unit, arrived at the scene within 15 minutes. The dispatcher never advised the detective of the number of victims. She only told Blanton, a 17-year veteran, that he was needed immediately at Domino's Pizza because something serious had happened there. After being briefed on the available information, Blanton went to view the carnage in the bathroom. It looked like a slaughterhouse, the sleuth thought to himself with a shudder.

The detective returned to the front of the pizzeria. There Lieutenant Blanton found the store's safe open. The blue vault, located under a stainless-steel counter, contained no money. It appeared to Blanton that robbery had been the motive behind the murders.

Paramedics rushed the female victim to Indian River Memorial Hospital. As the siren faded in the distance, a second ambulance left with another casualty. The third victim was dead.

Investigators identified the remaining victim as William E. Edwards, 28, the store's manager-in-training. He had been shot at close range. One bullet had penetrated his chest, another his forehead. The sleuths searched for obvious clues while they awaited the arrival of forensic specialists.

In the meantime, the detectives received a tragic update an hour later on the second victim. The female, Frances Edwards, had apparently died at the hospital. The 28-year-old woman, wife of the store manager, had worked at the pizzeria. The couple, sleuths learned, were originally from Tampa and left behind a 2-year-old daughter, who was at their home with a babysitter when the crime occurred.

As probers accepted the grim news, a police captain spotted two males on bicycles about seven blocks from the crime scene. They were hiding in the woods near a lumber company. When the officer approached, the pair fled. One man vanished, but the captain managed to capture the second suspicious male. During the chase, the officer saw the suspect toss a gun into the bushes.

The weapon, a .38-caliber revolver, was recovered after the 26-year-old suspect was captured. Police ran a records check on the suspect and learned that he'd recently been found guilty of burglary. They charged him with being a convicted felon in possession of a firearm, night prowling, and loitering.

In the meantime, word of the capture spread to reporters who were waiting outside the pizzeria. Vero Beach Police Chief James Gabbard said, "He is being considered as a possible suspect at this time. But we are also treating this case as if we had no suspects at all."

By 2:00 a.m. Wednesday morning, it was evident to residents surrounding the pizzeria that something had happened inside. Even during the height of the tourist season, weekday nights were usually quiet and uneventful in this small community.

Vero Beach, nestled along the Atlantic coastline of Florida, is a town noted for its peaceful atmosphere. Sabal palms and pine trees line the quaint streets. Except for the tourists, everybody knows each other. Middle-class families share their picturesque surroundings with their wealthier counterparts—most of whom live on the barrier island separated by the intercoastal waterway. It's the kind of community that looks good on a postcard.

Nevertheless, crime in Vero Beach was not unheard of. But a vicious multiple homicide was. Lieutenant Blanton, during his lengthy career, could only recall a handful of homicides that had occurred in the community.

At the crime scene, officers cordoned off a two-square-block area. A 30-member team consisting of off-duty police officers, forensic technicians from neighboring Fort Pierce, and assistant state attorneys swarmed over the gruesome site.

Even a criminologist from the regional crime lab was summoned for his assistance and expertise. Sleuths searched the pizzeria for clues, while the police photographer recorded each room from every possible angle. Another technician used a state-of-the-art laser beam to locate any fingerprints.

Authorities phoned the Domino's security manager in Pompano Beach. The corporate security specialist rushed over to the Vero Beach store to assist investigators. Forensic technicians processed the crime scene while detectives took notes. Outside, uniformed officers scoured the area for evidence while others canvassed for witnesses who might have heard or seen something.

Lieutenant Blanton was still at the pizzeria when hospital officials sent word that the third victim, 27-year-old Masoud Matthew Bornoosh, was in intensive care—clinging by a mere thread to life. Bornoosh underwent several hours of emergency surgery as doctors attempted to keep him alive. Outside his room, a Vero Beach patrolman stood guard.

A few witnesses told police they saw an auto parked in front of the pizza shop around 11:00 p.m. They described the car as a four-door sedan with a sloped or slanted trunk. The car was red and white.

Blanton was piecing together a possible scenario of what happened on that fatal night when he received word of another double homicide in neighboring Okeechobee County, west of the city. In that incident, a man and woman were found slain in a quaint rural restaurant. The man, owner of the diner, had been bound hand and foot. The woman, who worked as a waitress there, had also been tied up. Both victims had their throats neatly slashed.

The veteran sleuth's initial thoughts told him the crimes were not related. The Domino's victims had been shot and had not been tied. But Blanton didn't want to take any chances. After his preliminary investigation, he would double-check to make sure that the crimes were not connected. In the meantime, Blanton concentrated on the pizza shop.

Word of a car found by the Indian River County Sheriff's Department reached investigators at the pizzeria. According to the report, deputies had discovered the remains of a burnt car at the western end of the county on State Route 60. Deputies said the car, a Cadillac sedan, had a slanted trunk. It also appeared to be red and white.

Since the description and color matched the car that witnesses had observed at the pizzeria earlier the night before, Lieutenant Blanton dispatched a team of Vero Beach officers to the scene of the burnt hulk.

The sedan, a 1983 Cadillac, was located on a desolate stretch of road that runs east and west across the county. Outside the vehicle, technicians photographed partially burnt bank money bags, coin wrappers, and a few empty beer cans. They also found one other potentially significant item: an orange and blue Domino's T-shirt.

A motor vehicle records check traced the Cadillac to a car dealer in Jacksonville, more than 200 miles north of Vero Beach. Apparently, the vehicle had been reported stolen. According to the owner, a handgun was inside the vehicle at the time of the theft.

Lieutenant Blanton was on the phone arranging to fly north to interview the dealer when he received another report from the St. Johns County Sheriff's Department, located just south of Jacksonville. Deputies in that county said they had recovered a bunch of car keys, papers, and other items along a dirt road. The items, evidently tossed from a moving vehicle, had been traced back to the Cadillac stolen in Jacksonville. This new information prompted Vero Beach investigators to fly into St. Augustine first.

Blanton and his partner met St. Johns County officials at the St. Augustine airport. After a brief meeting detailing the circumstances surrounding the discovery, the deputies turned over the recovered items. The Vero Beach sleuths then proceeded to Jacksonville to interview the owner of the burnt Cadillac.

Back in Vero Beach, Chief James Gabbard spoke with the press. He emphasized that a forensics team had worked 14 hours at the downtown store searching for clues and evidence. Gabbard said detectives were waiting for autopsy results before they could release more information. However, he offered a few details about the way the crime had gone down.

"They were herded into a back room and killed," the chief said. "It was beyond description back there. It shocked even us veteran officers."

Gabbard didn't elaborate on the gruesomeness of the crime or wounds. He only said each victim had been shot in the head or upper body. The chief said one man was being held as a potential suspect, but investigators still had no solid leads.

"Robbery is the apparent motive because some cash was missing from a secure area," he explained.

The chief, along with the Domino's security manager, declined to say how much money had been taken from the shop. Gabbard added that investigators were searching for the victims' identification papers, which he believed were taken during the robbery. The chief also made a public appeal for information from anyone who may have seen anything suspicious around the pizza shop between 10:30 p.m. and midnight that Tuesday.

Domino's, a national pizza chain, immediately backed the chief's plea by offering a $10,000 reward for any information leading to the arrest and conviction of the person or persons responsible.

Officials emphasized the Domino's shootings had no obvious connection to the slayings of the restaurant owner and waitress found in Okeechobee County. What they didn't reveal was that they weren't taking any chances. The Okeechobee County sheriff had sent a deputy to Vero Beach to compare facts gathered in both cases.

The slayings in rural Okeechobee County were just as shocking as the murders in Vero Beach. So much so, in fact, that the *Miami Herald*, a regional newspaper more than 90 miles away, would run a story on both incidents in its next edition with the headline: "2 Die In Domino's Shootings; Eatery Owner, Waitress Slain."

Back in Jacksonville, Lieutenant Blanton questioned the owner of the Cadillac. The car dealer said that on the day of the theft, he remembered a particular person on the lot attempting to distract him, apparently while someone else made off with the car. After he realized the car and gun were missing, he immediately reported the theft to the police.

Vero Beach investigators left the meeting with the owner shaking their heads. Stolen vehicles were common. But this car was stolen with a *gun* in it, and that was peculiar, Blanton thought. He decided to stay overnight and ask the owner to submit to a polygraph test the next day.

When asked, the car dealer readily agreed. He

passed the test, thus eliminating himself as a potential suspect.

Lieutenant Blanton was preparing to return home when he received word of yet another homicide. His partners back in Vero Beach told him that the body of a large unidentified white female had been discovered along State Route 60, just west of where the burnt car had been recovered. She had also been shot once in the back of the head.

It was just two days since the Domino's slayings. The detective thought about a possible connection. His instinct told him the killings were probably connected somehow.

"Highly unusual," he remarked.

When Blanton returned to Vero Beach, he told the press, "We believe that the car that was burnt . . . found west of town, was involved in the Domino's slayings."

Initial newspaper stories about the pizzeria shootings were sketchy. While police withheld some details, they weren't withholding any hard evidence. The forensic team went over the scene with a fine-tooth comb. There wasn't anything to be found.

Again, officials asked the public to report anything suspicious they may have seen that evening. With this second plea for help issued to the press, investigators waited for a response. They hoped that someone would come forward. After all, the only witness to the slayings that police had lay in a hospital bed clinging to his life — and unconscious.

Lieutenant Blanton sat in his office studying the medical examiner's reports on William and Frances Edwards.

William Edwards, who'd died at the scene, was found fully clothed and had been shot twice, once in the upper chest and again in the forehead.

His wife, Frances, found beside him, was also shot execution-style. From the trajectory of the bullet, the medical examiner was able to determine that she was probably shot while in a kneeling position. The pathologist also discovered semen in the slain woman.

The hospital report stated that Masoud Bornoosh had suffered two gunshot wounds. The bullet had not penetrated his head on one shot but, instead, had shattered the bone. The other wound was caused from someone shoving the gun's barrel into the victim's left ear before pulling the trigger.

According to the reports, two of the three victims felt the cold steel barrel of the .38-caliber weapon against their bodies prior to its discharge. Lieutenant Blanton couldn't help but think that whoever had committed this crime must have had a heinous criminal history.

The shootings were obviously cold and calculated—designed to eliminate all witnesses—the lieutenant concluded. Other investigators agreed with Blanton about another important aspect: more than one person had taken part in the robbery turned rape and homicide at the pizza shop.

Investigators were sifting through reports when they received their first solid break in the case. A trucker read the newspaper's request for information and wanted to speak with detectives. He drove a route along the rural state highway where the burnt car and woman's body had been discovered. He remembered something odd on the night of the Domino's shootings, he said.

The driver told investigators that he regularly drove his rig on State Route 60 between Vero Beach and Lake Wales, which is located in the central portion of Florida. He remembered that on the night of the murders, other truckers kept their CB radios humming with talk about two white males jumping in and out of traffic. Apparently, the two men were hitchhiking just west of Vero Beach. When the trucker reached the area, the two were still there.

Officials sat and listened as the witness told them how he decided to stop and give them a lift. He recalled that the pair was carrying heavy bags, and one had a funny smell. He also noticed that the men were hot and sweaty, as if they had been walking fast. He drove for a while and then stopped at a small store in Yeehaw Junction — just across the county line.

After the brief stop, the trucker continued his journey, finally dropping the duo off in Lake Wales. Not only did the truck driver remember exactly where he'd picked up and discharged the men, he was also able to assist a police artist in preparing composites of the two.

Armed with this information and the sketches, Lieutenant Blanton assigned a team of investigators in Yeehaw Junction and another team to Lake Wales.

"Try to pick up from where the truck driver had let them off," the lieutenant instructed.

While the teams of lawmen set out to track the two suspicious hitchhikers, hospital officials notified Blanton that Masoud Bornoosh had died. The Iranian commercial flight student, who had worked part time delivering pizzas, never regained consciousness.

Blanton sat back in his chair and read another report. The suspect who had been captured near the lumber company shortly after the discovery of the Domino's shootings had passed his polygraph test. In addition, a ballistics test concluded the gun he'd tossed was not the firearm used at the pizzeria. So another potential suspect had been cleared.

The Lake Wales team began canvassing the town. The owner of a little motel stared at the composites. He told detectives he remembered the pair checking in on the morning after the homicides. They'd only spent two or three hours in their room, he recalled.

The owner checked his files and produced the registration card.

It was signed, "John Whitmore."

The detectives left the motel and eventually found a cab driver who remembered taking the two men to Brandon, another small town on State Route 60, just east of Tampa. He gave the officers directions to the vicinity where his fare departed.

In Brandon, the sleuths located another motel where the pair had apparently stayed. Again the owner produced a desk card. This time the twosome had registered under another name. Slowly, the detectives were tracking the path of the lethal hitchhikers. The two stayed here and ate there. But who were they?

In Vero Beach, the Federal Bureau of Investigation (FBI) told Lieutenant Blanton the weapon used in the Domino's shootings was the same weapon used to kill the woman on State Road 60. It looked like the detective's hunch was wrong. The two crimes were apparently connected after all.

Upon hearing of the connection, the Indian River County sheriff and the Vero Beach police chief formed a task force. The group comprised members of the State Attorney's Office, the Vero Beach Police Department, the Indian River County Sheriff's Department, the Florida Department of Law Enforcement, and the FBI.

In the event the restaurant slaying in Okeechobee County might be related to the Vero Beach homicides, the Okeechobee County Sheriff's Department attached a deputy to the task force. The group was rounded out with the addition of security personnel from Domino's Pizza.

Pizza franchise security persons acted as a support group. The company offered to supply anything that the task force needed to solve the case. The firm's offer included rental cars, aircraft, telephones, and even office help. Corporate executives promised investigators that at least one Domino's security specialist would be connected to the task force office at all times.

In all, a total of 15 full-time investigators were assigned to crack the case.

Blanton and Lieutenant Sidney Dubose of the Indian River County Sheriff's Department were put in charge of the group, which made its headquarters at the state attorney's office in Vero Beach. It had been nearly three weeks since the triple homicide at Domino's, and lawmen still hadn't identified the two mysterious hitchhikers the trucker had picked up on the rural road at the western end of the county.

Investigators assigned to the case began formulating a theory based on the facts they'd acquired to date. According to the Domino's security manager, the store's safe had a 15-minute time delay. The mechanism was designed to thwart robbers. Detectives reasoned that the assailants entered the store intending to rob it. When they discovered the delay on the safe, they forced the manager to punch in the code, deciding to stay until it opened. At some time during the waiting period, the intended robbery escalated.

The robbers probably then herded the three employees into the rear of the store. There they must have ordered Bornoosh into the bathroom and held William Edwards in the store's office. The sleuths based this part of their reconstructed chronology on the fact that Bornoosh had removed his wedding ring and tucked it under some paper in the bathroom's wastebasket. The sleuths reasoned that Bornoosh would have done this alone and not in the presence of an assailant.

Because the man's shirt and trousers had been removed — and were missing from the crime scene — probers deduced that one of the robbers must have forced Bornoosh to undress. Donning Bornoosh's Domino's uniform, the perp then probably posed as an employee in case a customer arrived.

While one robber held William Edwards at gunpoint in the office, another assailant apparently took Frances Edwards to the rear storeroom, forced her to undress, and raped her.

Police figured that at some point William Edwards may have attempted to help his wife and was struck as a result. This segment of the theory was based on the discovery of bloodstains in the office.

The only thing the detectives didn't know was whether Frances Edwards was raped more than once. For that information, they had to await the results of the DNA tests on the semen found inside her.

During or after the rape, the safe opened. The robbers then most likely grabbed the money bags, which contained about $1,143. Realizing they were in the store longer than they should have been, the assailants elected not to leave any witnesses behind. So the bandits eliminated the three employees in the store's bathroom, shooting each victim one at a time.

The first item on the task force's agenda was to contact the state of Florida's Department of Corrections. Investigators wanted a list of prisoners who'd been released or had escaped during the past year and who had served time for homicide, rape, or robbery. Because the burnt car found shortly after the homicide was originally stolen from Jacksonville near the state's northern border, the same request for released or escaped convict information was forwarded to Georgia and the Carolinas.

While Lieutenant Blanton waited for the prison lists, he reviewed reports from the original investigative teams sent to Yeehaw Junction and Brandon. One report from the team sent to Yeehaw Junction said they'd located the motel registration form of a man who was driving a red and white Cadillac. The man used one of the same names that other detectives had found in Brandon.

The lieutenant sent the two investigators back to the motel to fetch the desk registration. A few hours later, they returned with the registration card—and more.

"Same name," Blanton said. "Used the same address—Ten-Twelve Boulevard—that was used in Brandon."

In addition to the registration, the motel manager gave investigators some clothing the two men had left behind. One of the items, a T-shirt, had the name of a restaurant in Greenville, South Carolina, printed on it.

The investigators phoned Greenville authorities and were told a man who worked at that restaurant had been robbed. Officials there added that the perpetrators had also forced the man to surrender his shirt. Lieutenants Blanton and Dubose had discussed the possibility that their quarry may have come from out of state. Now this new tidbit of information from Greenville amplified that hunch.

The detectives looked at each other and spoke about the address listed on the two motel registrations—1012 Boulevard. It had to mean something because it had been used twice.

"If that didn't mean something to him, what's the chance of him remembering what he wrote on a previous motel card?" Blanton wondered.

The prison release and escape lists began arriving. Lieutenant Dubose's job was to review each name, address, and method of operation. The sheriff's deputy remembered his conversation with Blanton about the mysterious boulevard, so he made it a point to check each address.

The deputy's search for 1012 Boulevard ended when he scanned the list sent by North Carolina prison officials. Apparently, the boulevard address was that of a 30-year-old convict, Michael Gene Lovette, who'd escaped from a minimum-security prison on May 13, 1988.

Dubose immediately called the prison. Officials said Lovette had escaped with another prisoner, 24-year-old Thomas Anthony Wyatt, while he was working on a prison road crew in North Wilkesboro. The deputy requested a data sheet and mugshot on each subject. When the material arrived, the Florida investigators compared the photos with the trucker's composites. It was almost a perfect match. Lieutenants Blanton and Dubose now knew who they were stalking.

The task force updated North Carolina officials about Lovette and Wyatt being possible suspects in four homicides. One prison official suggested that the team sit back and wait, believing the convicts would eventually return home to North Carolina.

Blanton and Dubose knew the official was probably right. But they weren't about to sit idle. They wanted to question the two escapees before they left Florida.

To hasten their capture, the task force leaders sent more investigators to western Florida. Blanton didn't want to lose their trail.

While the teams plodded toward Tampa, the FBI acknowledged an error. The woman found on State Road 60 had apparently *not* been shot by the same weapon used in the Domino's slayings, they now said. The victim had been identified as 23-year-old Cathy Nydegger of the Tampa area.

Blanton wasn't concerned about the error. The mistake actually helped investigators. Because of it, the west-coast teams had already tied the woman to Lovette and Wyatt. They were seen at a bar in Brandon also frequented by the victim. Furthermore, Nydegger's car was found in Clearwater on Florida's west coast. The only question Blanton couldn't answer was, why did the suspects bring the girl back to Indian River County to kill her?

Lieutenants Blanton and Dubose decided to pull out all the stops. A wanted poster was printed showing photos of the two suspects, Thomas Wyatt and Michael Lovette, and all pertinent information. Armed with the fliers, teams of sleuths were dispatched to western Florida, Georgia, and the Carolinas. Domino's security distributed the posters with instructions to paste one on every pizza box.

In addition, telephone bills from the suspects' relatives were subpoenaed. The office came alive with officers and assistants checking and cross-checking each and every report. Blanton and Dubose wanted to be able to piece together a chronological sequence of the suspects and their alleged crime spree.

After days of intensive field investigation coupled with criminal report research, detectives pieced together the movements of the fugitive duo. Lovette and Wyatt had managed to escape from the prison road gang in North Wilkesboro, North Carolina, by stealing a canoe. The duo had paddled to the other side of a lake, broken into a house, and swiped two guns. They then walked down the street and stole a car.

In Greenville, South Carolina, the fugitives entered a restaurant, ordered a man working there to remove his shirt, and then robbed him. The convicts forced the victim into his car trunk and then drove a block away. There the suspects left the restaurant worker until he was found later.

Investigators also discovered that the car Lovette and Wyatt stole in North Wilkesboro had been recovered at the airport parking lot in Atlanta.

Once in Jacksonville, the pair stole the Cadillac with the gun inside. From there, they headed south. Eventually, the suspects stopped in Yeehaw Junction, where they got a motel room. Later they drove to Vero Beach, robbed the Domino's store, raped Frances Edwards, and shot her, her husband Billy, and Masoud Bornoosh.

For some reason, the detectives deduced, the suspects abandoned the Cadillac on State Road 60. They set fire to the car and hitched a ride with the trucker. When the pair arrived in Brandon, they stayed at a motel and then went to a bar. There Lovette and Wyatt met Cathy Nydegger. For some reason, the girl drove them back to Indian River County. Before Lovette and Wyatt left, they shot her. The pair then drove west and abandoned her body in Clearwater.

Blanton and other investigators reasoned that the pair of convicts separated in Clearwater. The lieutenant believed the escapees did too many things while together and stood a better chance of eluding the law by traveling solo.

If that's what Lovette and Wyatt were thinking, they were wrong. To the detectives the hunt was a slow process, but to the two men on the lam, time was quickly running out.

Wyatt was driving a stolen truck on July 8th when he made a turn in front of a state trooper in Lancaster, South Carolina. The trooper drove behind the vehicle and put his lights on. Wyatt pulled over to the side of the road, jumped out of the cab, and fled into the woods.

Authorities cordoned off the area. A few hours later, the escaped convict was spotted walking down the highway. When confronted, Wyatt replied that he was the one they were searching for.

Blanton and another investigator, hot on the trail of Wyatt, were in Myrtle Beach, South Carolina, when word of Wyatt's capture reached them. The team quickly chartered a plane and flew to Lancaster.

When the Vero Beach investigators arrived, authorities informed them that Wyatt had asked an odd question prior to their arrival. He wanted to know if Florida's death penalty was by lethal injection or the electric chair.

The suspect agreed to talk with Lieutenant Blanton, but he denied any involvement in the crimes.

Police captured Michael Lovette six days later in Statesville, North Carolina. A relative had rented him a room. The motel clerk recognized the escapee and notified local authorities.

During initial questioning by North Carolina officials and an FBI agent, Lovette admitted knowledge of the Domino's shootings. However, the details of his participation in it remained sketchy.

When Lieutenants Blanton and Dubose questioned him, Lovette began to open up. Even after advising the convict of his rights a second time, he remained eager to talk. His rendition of the twosome's multi-state crime spree paralleled the police scenario. He was surprised at how much the police uncovered.

The suspect said he and Wyatt left a motel in Yeehaw Junction and drove to Vero Beach. The two stopped at a popular night spot for a few drinks. They robbed the pizzeria shortly after they left the bar.

Lovette and Wyatt decided to rape the woman at the pizza shop when they were told the safe wouldn't open for 15 minutes. During that period, one victim was in the bathroom and Lovette held the other at gunpoint in the pizzeria office. Lovette denied any involvement in the rape, but admitted to wearing Masoud Bornoosh's shirt.

After the safe opened, Lovette asserted, Wyatt herded the victims into the bathroom and killed them. Lovette said his partner didn't want to leave any witnesses behind.

Once outside, they drove west on State Road 60 when their car overheated. They emptied the vehicle and set it on fire to destroy any evidence. The gun they'd used in the Domino's slayings was tossed by the roadside. A short distance down the route, Lovette continued, the two fugitives stashed some things under a highway bridge.

Lovette's recollections of their movements corroborated the trucker's statement and other evidence accumulated by the detectives. He also explained why Cathy Nydegger was found shot.

According to Lovette, the pair met her at a bar in Brandon. The two men coaxed her to drive them back to the bridge to fetch the hidden stash. Again, Wyatt didn't want a witness, so he shot the girl. Then they drove her car to Clearwater and split up, Lovette added.

From Clearwater, he began working his way back to North Carolina. Lovette had been in the state a short time before his capture.

As much as Lovette wanted to talk, there was one thing he refused to do: look at the crime scene photographs.

"This told me the reason he didn't want to see them is because he's already seen them," Lieutenant Blanton remarked. "He's already seen what happened."

On July 20th, the task force received the report of another homicide. Sheriff Frank Powell of Richland County, South Carolina, said a warrant was issued for the arrest of Thomas Wyatt. Authorities now implicated him in a fifth homicide.

According to the sheriff, Thomas Wyatt was charged with the robbery and bludgeoning death of Henry "Sparky" Dorrill, a 43-year-old mute man. His body was found June 30th in Columbia. The arrest stemmed from investigators matching tire tracks found near the murder scene to tire treads on the truck Wyatt was caught driving. In addition to the tread marks, authorities showed witnesses a photo lineup that included Wyatt's picture.

The sheriff told the task force that at least a half-dozen agencies from the Carolinas to Florida had been tracing the pair's route since their escape on May 13th.

The legal machine ground out the paperwork that eventually extradited Thomas Wyatt and Michael Lovette back to Florida. While prosecutors prepared their cases, the task force disbanded. Domino's Pizza hosted a dinner for officials involved in the investigation. Plaques, citations, and letters from the corporation's president were presented to the officers.

"It surprised all of us," Blanton would later say. "I have never been involved in an investigation with a store or company where they bent over backwards to assist you in any way they could. You couldn't ask for any company to be any better."

Blanton left the affair knowing the task force had done a super job. Now the legal battle would begin. Two suspects were going to be tried for the three Domino's homicides.

Task force leaders met with prosecutors to discuss the evidence. Blanton walked into the office confident that the group had left no road untraveled during their walk behind the suspects. The officials went over the litany of incriminating evidence.

Investigators had researched the movement of the suspects from the time of their escape until their capture. Motel receipts, witness identification, and telephone bills from relatives positively placed Lovette and Wyatt at each location.

The sleuths even accumulated documentation proving that one of the suspects received a package of clothes and money sent to Florida by a relative in North Carolina.

Although the gun used in the Domino's slayings was not recovered, detectives were able to recover two other weapons alleged to have been stolen by the duo. One of the weapons, a Charter Arms .38-caliber revolver, was believed to have been the gun used to kill Cathy Nydegger.

Detectives retrieved a scrap of paper left in St. Augustine by Lovette. The scrap contained a fiber. Another fiber, which was an exact match, was found on the shirt Lovette had forced the victim, Masoud Bornoosh, to remove while at Domino's.

Lawmen had two confessions from Lovette, who said he and Wyatt entered the pizzeria with the intention of robbing it. Lovette fingered his partner as the shooter.

Probers located a witness who offered to testify against Wyatt, saying the suspect had admitted the Domino's crime to him. But the final element of evidence was the clincher.

DNA tests of the sperm found in Frances Edwards matched exactly with the sperm of Thomas Wyatt. It placed him directly at the scene, implicating him in the rape of the slain woman.

During the session, State Attorney Bruce Colton said the evidence could stand on its own. No deals would be made. Prosecutors were going to seek the death penalty for Thomas Wyatt and Michael Lovette.

Lieutenant Blanton walked out of the meeting exuberant. He wanted it that way.

Wyatt was the first to go on trial. Because of massive pretrial publicity, the judge ordered a change of venue. The trial started in Sarasota, on the west coast of the state, in January 1991.

The prosecution unfolded its case against the accused killer. Of all the testimony and evidence presented, two items were most incriminating. Prosecutors offered the results of the DNA test performed on the sperm recovered from the body of Frances Edwards. The tests proved that it positively matched the sperm of Thomas Wyatt. The state also produced a fellow prisoner who testified against Wyatt.

The witness, who'd met Wyatt after his arrest for the Domino's slayings, said Wyatt had admitted the pizza shop murders to him. He detailed the contents of Wyatt's conversation to the jury. At one point, he said the defendant told him about a comment Wyatt had made prior to shooting Bornoosh. The witness testified that Wyatt bragged about shoving the gun into Bornoosh's ear and telling the victim, "Listen real close and you'll hear it coming." Then he pulled the trigger.

Thomas Wyatt eventually took the stand and denied any involvement in the crime. He said Lovette had left him at the bar for several hours. Lovette later admitted he had killed three people during the time he was gone, Wyatt added.

Even with the DNA tests against him, Wyatt steadfastly denied taking any part in the rape or shootings.

After two hours of deliberations, the jury returned with guilty verdicts on all 13 counts against Thomas Wyatt, including murder, rape, kidnapping, armed robbery, grand theft, and arson. The defendant, smiling and chewing gum, displayed no emotion as the verdict was read.

On February 22nd, the judge sentenced Wyatt for the murders of the Domino's employees. He imposed three death sentences on the convicted killer, in addition to six consecutive life sentences plus 20 years. With Wyatt convicted and sentenced, the state attorney and his assistant set their sights on the next suspect.

Michael Lovette was also granted a change of venue. His trial started May 13, 1991, in St. Petersburg — again on the state's Gulf Coast. Defense attorneys, armed with the knowledge of his partner's trial and subsequent conviction, planned a unique strategy. They conceded Lovette was at the Vero Beach pizza store on the night of May 17, 1988.

Although, according to Florida trial procedures, the defense could not tell the jury that Lovette's alleged accomplice had been convicted, they asked the jurors to remember that it was Thomas Wyatt who was the shooter.

"Michael Lovette's intent that night was to steal the money at gunpoint, and that's what he did," said Chief Assistant Public Defender Clifford Barnes, during his opening statement. ". . . Michael Lovette is guilty of armed robbery. He is also guilty of grand theft of the car and the gun and of arson, because he helped burn the car."

Although the defense admitted that while under the law, a person can be held responsible for another person's actions during the commission of a crime, they tried to convince the jury this was not that type of a case.

"He did not know anybody was going to die," the defendant's attorney pleaded on behalf of Lovette. "He did not help Tommy Wyatt kill anybody. Those deaths were the consequences of Tommy Wyatt's crimes."

Assistant State Attorney David Morgan fired back, contending that Lovette was right beside Wyatt when the crimes were committed.

"We're going to show you why Lovette and his partner Wyatt, partners in fun, ought to be treated as partners under the law when it comes to paying the piper," Morgan stressed.

The prosecutor then unfolded the evidence.

During the half-hour the suspects were in the store, Lovette put on Bornoosh's shirt to pose as an employee in case someone came in. Lovette held a gun on William Edwards while Wyatt raped

Edwards' wife. And when the pair left the store, they made sure no trace evidence, such as fingerprints, hairs, or fibers, were left behind, the prosecutor concluded.

In the end, it took the 12-member jury only three and a half hours to find Michael Lovette guilty of three counts of first-degree murder, sexual battery, and multiple counts of armed robbery, kidnapping, grand theft, and arson. After a post-trial proceeding, they recommended the death penalty.

The judge scheduled sentencing, moving the proceedings back to the Indian River County Courthouse in Vero Beach.

On June 7th, the small, dark, wood-paneled courtroom was packed. Family members and friends of the three Domino's victims, along with investigators, filled the nine rows of bench seats. News reporters, photographers, and television crews saturated the jury box.

Ten minutes before the scheduled 1:30 p.m. sentencing, Lovette walked through the double doors, surrounded by a half-dozen Indian River County sheriff's deputies. The convicted killer was wearing a maroon prison uniform, white socks, and blue sneakers. The stainless-steel chain of his leg restraints rattled as it trailed across the carpeting.

The prisoner's hands remained immobile, cuffed to a brown leather strap fastened around his waist. Lovette's eyes were fixed on the crew of photographers who focused their cameras directly at the defense table.

Prior to sentencing, Lovette's attorney read a short note written by his client. Lovette wrote that he was sorry for the crimes and had remorse for the victims' families. He was especially sorry for the orphaned child left behind.

Circuit Judge Thomas Walsh, who held the option of life or death, asked Lovette to approach the bench. The convicted killer stood up and walked about 10 feet. His attorney stood to his left, while the contingent of deputies formed a semicircle around them. The judge then sentenced Michael Lovette to three death penalties for the Domino's murders.

The prisoner stood with his head down. The judge continued, describing how one day Florida's governor would sign a black-bordered death warrant setting the time and date for Lovette's execution. Judge Walsh said the warrant would authorize prison officials to run a current of electricity through Lovette's body until he was rendered dead.

Michael Lovette's last-minute plea for mercy fell on deaf ears.

In addition to the death sentences, Judge Walsh sentenced Lovette to six consecutive life sentences plus five years. He then ordered the county sheriff to remand the condemned man to the state prison. The judge rapped his gavel and deputies quickly whisked the prisoner away.

Under Florida law, Thomas Wyatt and Michael Lovette's death sentences will be automatically appealed to a higher court before any death warrant can be signed.

Wyatt and Lovette have yet to be tried for the shooting death of Cathy Nydegger. Wyatt has not been tried for the bludgeoning death of Henry Dorrill. The convicted killers now reside on death row — next to "Old Sparky," the state's infamous three-legged electric chair — at the Florida State Prison in Starke.

About 40 minutes after Lovette's sentencing, a journalist walked into the Vero Beach Police Department. Lieutenant Blanton, now a captain, offered the writer a seat and offered a comment about the senseless Domino's murders as he closed the door.

"This is the worst crime," he said. "You've got

three people that were just blown away for a thousand and one-hundred dollars."

Captain Blanton sat back, gazed at the two massive boxes containing the Domino's case file at the other end of his office, and remarked, "It's been a long three years. Now it's over."

EDITOR'S NOTE:
*Jeanette Kilmer and Phil Taylor are not the real names of the persons so named in the foregoing story. Fictitious names have been used because there is no reason for public interest in the identities of these persons.*

# "5 VICTIMS OF THE TICKING TIME BOMB!"

## by Bud Ampolsk

The last-quarter moon drifted low in the eastern sky, casting an eerie pattern of light and shadow over the opulent, well-kept homes and gardens of the wealthy suburban community.

A group of impeccably dressed young people were laughing and joking as they departed a synagogue where they had spent a happy Saturday evening helping to toast the attractive bride and groom at a joyous wedding reception.

The group's laughter suddenly melted away into the surrounding silence of the unusually cold October night as they watched a young man emerge from the darkness and stagger toward them. The man's face was distorted by the excruciating pain that lanced through his body. As the young man collapsed on the sidewalk before them, the horrified celebrants rushed to his aid.

The scene could have been the opening sequence of a horror movie. But, there would be no dissolving to the screen credits that night.

The blood pumping from the man's critical wounds was not the product of a Hollywood makeup artist. It was thick, viscous, nauseatingly sticky to the touch.

The time was 2:29 a.m., Sunday morning, October 13, 1991. The place was the affluent New York City bedroom community of Little Neck, which stands practically on the border separating Queens from Nassau County.

The desperate drama was tragically for real. It had begun days before and it would grip scores of New York City and Nassau County police officers in life-and-death confrontation with a 47-year-old eccentric who had earned the neighborhood nickname of "Crazy Andy." It would bring waves of numbing terror to residents of an area that had long enjoyed a reputation for peace, security, and civility.

Within five minutes of the receipt of the "man-down" call, units from the 11th Precinct were converging on the neatly kept, two-story home, located at 53-42 254th Street, from which the wounded man had emerged. Disregarding their own safety, the first on-scene officers fanned out to surround the structure and move into the moonlit backyard.

Summoned to the scene from his home was veteran Detective-Sergeant John Russell, along with several detectives. Detective Phil Massi would be the sleuth to "catch the case" in what would turn out to be a very long night.

Neighbors, who had been awakened by the growing commotion, would later give graphic eyewitness accounts of the valiant police action.

One man would recall how he and his wife had been startled out of their sleep by the sound of "pops," followed about a half hour later by the crash of shattering glass. Then the man saw the back door of 53-42 254th Street swing open. He watched as police officers, with their guns drawn, began shouting for anybody inside the besieged building to come out.

A voice inside the darkened structure cried, "I can't move!" One of the cops replied, "Crawl out!"

As the neighbor watched in stunned disbelief, a police officer began searching a tool shed in the home's backyard. Moments later, the cop emerged and announced, "We've got two more."

"Two more what?" another cop asked.

The grim reply came quickly. "Two more bodies."

As more and more police officers responded to calls for backup and more and more wide-eyed Little Neck residents took to their lawns to stare in growing horror at the unfolding scene, it became all too evident that what had happened on 254th Street was much more than the serious wounding of one young man. It added up to a mass killing that had claimed the lives of one elderly man and three younger ones and had critically wounded two other young men who had somehow managed to survive the hail of bullets.

The list of the dead included Andrew Brooks, Sr., the 75-year-old owner of the house. Brooks, a retired firefighter and school teacher, lived at the 254th Street residence with his wife, Marion, and his 47-year-old son, Andrew Brooks Jr.

Brian Ducker, another victim, was a 29-year-old driving instructor and close neighbor of the Brooks family. He had been an acquaintance of Andrew Brooks Jr., whom he met while giving lessons to one of the Brooks' relatives. Ducker had recently moved from Little Neck, but he had returned for a few days to house sit his mother's home while she was on vacation.

A third victim, 23-year-old Daniel Gantovnik, had been working in his family's garment business. He had been a close friend of Ducker's.

The fourth victim was 23-year-old Michael Zarabi, a friend of Gantovnik's. The two had worked together in an auto parts dealership. Zarabi lived with his family in the Great Neck area.

The two bodies discovered in the tool shed were those of Andrew Brooks Sr. and Brian Ducker. Gantovnik's body was found in the living room. Zarabi's body lay on the kitchen floor.

The two men who were wounded were rushed in separate ambulances to Booth Memorial Medical Center in

Queens and North Shore University Hospital in Manhasset.

All of the victims had one thing in common linking them to their fate: All had been long-time associates of the now-missing Andrew Brooks Jr., who was suddenly the prime suspect in the shootings.

As members of the New York Police Department searched the Brooks residence, they recovered a 12-gauge shotgun that Brooks Jr. had either overlooked or left behind when he fled the scene. But this discovery was small comfort to the investigators. The numerous shell casings found at the crime scene, as well as a close examination of the victims' wounds, showed that the victims had been dispatched by a .22-caliber rifle with a sawed-off barrel and stock. Police immediately feared—and their fears soon proved warranted—that Brooks had armed himself with the .22 when he had taken off.

With growing dread, sleuths, led by Sergeant Russell and Detective Massi, now began a search for the Brooks' family car, which had disappeared from the home. Putting together the bits and scraps of evidence and statements from witnesses, Sergeant Russell and Detective Massi recognized that a potentially catastrophic situation was developing, one that could reach far beyond the confines of Little Neck. Though they preferred not to think about the final outcome, they understood that there could be many more casualties before things were brought under control.

By now scores of helmeted and flak-jacketed officers, bearing shotguns and other material designed to cope with the pursuit of a mass killer, began moving through the area, on foot, in police vehicles, and aboard helicopters. Lawmen gave terse orders for worried neighbors to stay in their homes, lock their doors, keep away from windows, and repair to basement areas in order to remain out of harm's way.

In the pre-dawn hours, as Little Neck was kept under

a virtual state of siege and police patrols crisscrossed its tree-lined streets, there was one development that made the posse's job all the more difficult. The missing Brooks vehicle had been abandoned by the fugitive only a few blocks from his home. More disturbing, the automobile contained no sawed-off rifle. Brooks, apparently had taken the weapon with him and had decided to proceed with his flight on foot.

Although there were reports through the early-morning hours of doors being rattled by some shadowy figure seeking to enter homes in Little Neck and Great Neck, no trace of Andrew Brooks Jr.'s whereabouts had been discovered.

However, from what detectives had learned from those who knew Brooks over the years, they knew they were dealing with a human powder keg. The wanted man was likely to erupt into acts of unbridled violence at any moment.

The 47-year-old fugitive was described as a heavyset man with long, grayish-brown, slicked-back hair. He frequently favored a filthy black and white plaid shirt, and usually appeared unkempt.

Brooks had not been regularly employed, but he eked out a living by running a clandestine loan-sharking and porno tape business from his father's home. It was said that he rented XXX-rated videotapes from retail stores, bootlegged copies of them, and sold them to young people who lived in the area.

Occasionally, he would watch homes of residents who were away on vacation and receive nominal sums for his services. However, for all intents and purposes, Brooks never held a responsible job. Police learned he spent much of his time prowling local streets, a golf club in hand, sometimes taking practice shots on neighbors' lawns. At other times, he would go through a ritual of casting a fishing hook and line into the street.

The eccentric had also been known as a Peeping Tom who would peer through neighbors' windows. He was also known to stare at and follow young women on the streets. Brooks, sleuths learned, had three prior arrests, one of which was for lewd behavior.

One woman who had grown up on the same block as Brooks said that he had always acted strangely, but lately his actions had become even weirder. She said he had told her that he was under medication for allergies and was being damaged by the treatment.

The neighbor quoted Brooks as saying, "The damage is irreversible; it's in my blood." According to this source, on the Wednesday before the killings, Brooks told her, "You won't be seeing me around." He had also blamed his mother and father for "bothering him" and preventing him from getting the treatment that would relieve his allergies.

Said the woman, "You never could really believe what he said. I knew he was going to snap."

Another woman added, "We knew he was dangerous, a time bomb." She reported that her 21-year-old daughter and some of the young woman's friends had been spooked by Brooks when he followed them in his car while brandishing a knife.

Corroborating this report was still another woman who stated, "He would just stand there and stare at you, try to scare you. We told our kids not to talk to him. We told them to come into the house when he'd walk by."

Despite his unseemly ways, Brooks had not been a recluse. According to one man, the fugitive had enhanced his reputation as an "odd ball" with his desire to associate with men who were much younger than he was. Commented the man, "He always tried to associate with the younger guys." The man told of Brooks' unsuccessful attempts to enter the street games of boys who were 20 years his junior.

Although they taunted him and sometimes teased him by calling him "Stench" because of his body odor, they did not shun Brooks. As a matter of fact, they had kept up an acquaintance with him over the years.

It was significant that four of the younger men who had been shot at the Brooks home had arrived there after midnight on the fatal night.

Although Brooks had frequently engaged in violent verbal confrontations with his father and 73-year-old mother, Andrew Brooks Sr. had made light of his son's erratic behavior.

Recalled a neighbor, "I told Andy [Sr.], 'He's going to kill you and Marion one day.' And Andy would say, 'He's not that bad. Just stay away from him when there's a full moon.'"

Others also felt that it was just a matter of time before "Crazy Andy" would snap. Noted one woman, "He was a very strange man. If it was cold, he was always in shirt sleeves. Everyone was waiting for something to happen with him."

But there were those who disagreed. Commented another woman, "I had seen him walking around, talking to himself. Nobody thought he was dangerous. Everyone thought he was harmless."

But nobody thought Andrew Brooks Jr. was harmless now. The terror that gripped Little Neck and Lake Success was well founded. That Andrew Brooks Jr. was capable of further violence in the early morning of Sunday, September 14th became alarmingly apparent when a 911 emergency dispatcher received a call from a man who was obviously distressed over an experience he had just undergone.

The man, a gardener, had reported for work a little before 9:00 a.m. at a redbrick and white-shingle home owned by an elderly physician and his wife on Bates Road in Lake Success, Long Island. Instead of being greeted by the elderly couple, the gardener had become the target of four shots fired in rapid succession from one of the expensive home's windows.

With that call, it became evident that Andrew Brooks Jr. was not only holed up in the Lake Success home, but had taken the elderly couple hostage. So what until that moment had been an all-out search for a suspected mass murderer now became something even more perilous. Two more innocent lives were on the line. All of the police expertise and the force's most delicate and sophisticated equipment would have to be brought into play if more bloodshed was to be prevented.

With the determination that Brooks had indeed been the one to shoot at the gardener, legal jurisdiction over the attempt to capture the wanted man was now in the hands of Nassau County authorities. But operating in close consultation, it was decided that the operation would be a joint one between county and city police squads.

Sergeant Russell and Detective Massi rushed out to the Lake Success house on Bates Avenue, which took on the guise of a military battleground as scores of helmeted, flak-jacketed, and gun-toting officers took up their various positions around the home where the crazed gunman was holding his two frail captives.

The first police move was to make sure that nobody outside the besieged home would become a target for Andrew Brooks' sawed-off, .22-caliber rifle. To prevent such a tragedy, cops went door to door, evacuating the eight houses nearest to the one occupied by the suspect.

Inspector James G. Courtney, executive officer of NYPD's Queens detectives, Deputy Chief Edward Doughty, the chief hostage negotiator for the Nassau County Police Department (NCPD), and Inspector George Davis of the NCPD, would play key roles in the seemingly endless hours of tension that lay ahead. Sergeant Russell of the 111th Precinct Detective Squad in Queens would also be involved in the negotiating with Andrew Brooks, whom Russell tried to calm down throughout the tense standoff. The decisions the lawmen would make in leading the extremely delicate operations could well spell the difference between life and death for the people inside the home and for the police personnel who were putting their own lives on the line outside of it.

Although every effort would be made to keep Brooks from becoming excited enough to fire his weapon, those mapping the operation recognized the responsibility they had for insuring that the fugitive not make good an escape.

With this in mind, sharpshooters from handpicked S.W.A.T. teams were placed in strategic positions behind trees, police shields, and parked cars. Their high-powered rifles zeroed in on the windows and doors of the hostage house, ready to respond to any hostile action by Brooks.

Having established a command post in the home next door to the one where Brooks was holding out, the cops brought into play one of their most prized and sophisticated high-tech devices. A 700-pound remote controlled robot waddled up to the house's door, its closed circuit videocamera poised to relay pictures to an emergency squad monitor.

But surveillance would not be enough. Voice contact was a must between the police and the crazed gunman. To make verbal contact, the hostage negotiators used the command post phone to call the hostage dwelling.

At 10:30 a.m., after tense and critically delicate negotiations, Brooks agreed to release the retired physician. Under the stress of his ordeal, the doctor had begun to suffer chest pains and there were fears that he might be undergoing a heart attack.

According to Inspector Courtney, the doctor was placed on a gurney and taken to Long Island Jewish Hospital where he was reported in stable condition.

From the rescued doctor, police learned that Brooks had gained entry into the Lake Success home by smashing his way through a glass door in the rear of the home at 5:30 a.m. Once inside the luxurious house, the murderer made his way to the second-floor bedroom where the physician and his wife had been awakened with a start to discover a total stranger waving the barrel of a weapon in their faces.

Any hope that Brooks' release of the ailing doctor was a sign that he would follow up with the release of the doctor's wife and his own surrender were to prove shortlived.

Although conversations between the hostage negotiators and the killer remained constant, they were unavailing as the morning gave way to early afternoon. Brooks stayed inside the house with the 61-year-old wife of the released physician. The crazed man cradled his rifle in his arms before an open second-floor window, his eyes fixed on the intensive police activity taking place on the street below him.

At one point, Brooks asked for a can of soda and it was provided to him. Later on, the cops came up with a six-pack which was hoisted by rope to the second floor by the elderly captive.

At one point in the standoff, tension mounted when Brooks became falsely convinced that some officers had gotten inside the house. He became frenzied, wildly running from room to room, holding his captive in front of him as a human shield.

During this violent outbreak, Brooks began sniping at the police who surrounded the house. He got off five rounds, one of which passed through the uniform sleeve of an officer, luckily without wounding him.

The situation remained deadlocked throughout Sunday afternoon. The police strategy was to exercise supreme caution to prevent Brooks from committing some irrevocable act against the woman he was still holding hostage. That Brooks had been awake for over 30 hours gave police reason to hope. Strong as Brooks seemed to be, there would come a time when fatigue would have to overtake him. Their own patience might prove the lawmen's ultimate weapon against the man who had already killed four and wounded two.

Although she had not communicated with the police, the resourceful hostage was instinctively searching for the same signs of weariness in Andrew Brooks that the police were.

At 5:40, the plucky lady noticed that the gunman's head was nodding. Despite his efforts to stay awake, he was dozing off. This was the opportunity she had been waiting for. She knew that if she didn't take it at this instant, there might not be another chance.

As silently as possible, fearing that any sound of a footstep or creaking of a floorboard might give her away, the woman inched her way down the staircase and to the house's front door.

Suddenly, she was spotted by an equally tense police officer. The cop recognized the peril the woman faced standing there with the gunman still commanding the house's upper areas and evidently possessing ample supplies of ammunition. The cop shouted, "Come on! Come on!"

Spurred by the officer's warning, the woman made her final dash into his arms and freedom. The woman was treated for trauma and released.

Later, Nassau County Deputy Chief Andrew Mulrain would say of the courageous woman, "She had an opportunity to get out and she ran." He added, "She was in good shape and fine, excellent demeanor."

With the last hostage's escape, Brooks became the only occupant of the Bates Road home he had invaded.

If police had been willing to exercise great caution before, they were even more dedicated to the need to spare further bloodshed now that the last hostage had been freed.

Chief negotiator Doughty would sum up his feelings and those of his fellow officers in these terms: "It was important to wait a substantial amount of time for a peaceful resolution that would possibly save lives."

The decision was a tribute to the iron self-discipline of those officers participating in the nerve-wracking confrontation. Throughout the agonizing hours before and after the woman's escape, Brooks had peppered the surrounding lawmen with at least nine shots. There was no telling when he might opt for taking out as many cops as possible in one final burst of desperation.

As night fell over the Lake Success section of Great Neck, brilliant searchlights played over the red and white house. A decision was made to cut off the heat and water inside the dwelling.

At 11:00 p.m., on Sunday evening, the cops took over the ground floor of the house. They brought with them the robot that had been introduced into the confrontation earlier in the day. They hoped to guide the device up the stairs so that it could spy electronically on the crazed man who roamed the upper regions of the home.

Apparently, the move backfired. Andrew Brooks became agitated as he discovered the plan. Shortly after midnight, he used his .22 rifle to shoot the robot up. He managed to knock out listening microphones and its motorized treads. But Brooks was unable to blast away the Cyclopian camera eye, which still remained functional. It continued to provide the negotiating team and the S.W.A.T. sharpshooters who now crowded the living room with views of Brooks as he paced through the four bedrooms and two baths on the second floor.

At 3:00 a.m. on Monday morning, Andrew Brooks found what was to prove his final refuge. He entered the west front bedroom and shut the door tightly behind him. There was more talk between the hostage team members and the barricaded gunman. When the negotiators asked Brooks whether he wanted anything or wished to talk to anybody, his answer was negative. Nor would he give any definitive reply to the only demand by the cordon of police engaged in the exhausting standoff. The police asked only that he drop the rifle out the window and promised Brooks safety in return for his surrender.

By 8:30 Monday morning, the standoff remained where it had been all night.

Said Chief Daughty, "He is fearful, and he's not entirely lucid. He's concerned about going to jail. He's concerned about getting hurt."

A half hour after Chief Doughty made his statement, a shot rang out. The sound was missed by a number of cops in the house. Other members of the S.W.A.T. team who had made their way halfway up the stairs and were now only a few feet from the west front bedroom were taking nothing for granted. There had been other shots followed by prolonged periods of silence during the night. They had no guarantee that the same thing was not happening once more.

Four hours went by without any further sound from the second floor. At one o'clock Monday afternoon, those in charge of the ongoing police operation decided to take the next step. They fired six rubber bullets into the room's side window in an attempt to knock down the venetian blinds that were blocking their view. When the move failed, they used a pole to knock down the blinds and then hoisted a TV camera to the window.

"Raise the camera a little higher," the operators were directed by those manning the monitor. The camera scanned the room and came to settle on a still object on the floor. "We have a picture of a leg at the bottom of the bed," the monitor watchers announced.

As the scores of cops listened over their receivers, the police band radio crackled with the following report made by one officer who had actually entered the bedroom. "Interior to command post. We're in. Subject is here on the ground. Apparently, victim is dead . . . apparently a self-inflicted gunshot wound."

Having heard the laconic message, Deputy Chief Doughty commented, "It was a tragic way to end a situation, but it was a tragic situation to begin with." Doughty and the other officers could take pride from the fact that since the first units had arrived from the 111th Precinct in the wee hours of Sunday morning, no one — not any of the police officers, not the neighbors, not the hostages — aside from Brooks, had come to any harm.

Now that the ordeal was over, Inspector Davis had time to review the chronology of the terrible day and a half. He felt that during the hours of Sunday night, Brooks had lost hope. The inspector said the gunman's last conversation, held at 8:30 a.m. Monday morning, "was of someone whose temperament was going down. His mental condition seemed to be deteriorating. Basically, he was saying, 'It's all over.' He didn't say, 'I'm going to kill myself because . . .' but he seemed to be saying through the night that he had done such a terrible deed, there was no way out."

Neighbors who had lived in terror throughout the bloody weekend were much less forgiving.

As Brooks' corpse, wrapped in a plastic body bag, was removed from the Bates Road house at 4:35 p.m. Monday, some in the crowd of spectators broke into applause. Some shouted, "Thank God it's over!" One added, "Get that lunatic out of here!"

Only in the calm of the aftermath were detectives able to begin piecing together the sequence of events that led to the four murders, the siege, and the suicide.

It was believed that Andrew Brooks Sr. and Brian Ducker, whose bodies had been discovered in the tool shed, were the first to be slain by Andrew Brooks Jr. The best estimate was that the two were killed sometime on Thursday, October 11th. Andrew Brooks Jr. had been seen driving his family's car on Friday. His father and mother had never allowed him to drive the vehicle. The police theory was that the elder Brooks had been slain prior to the automobile junket.

Brian Ducker had last been heard from at 8:00 p.m. Thursday. At that time he had promised to call his girlfriend at 10:00 p.m., according to a relative.

"He never called, and the next morning the girlfriend called his office and he had missed all his appointments," the relative noted.

Later, the young woman went to the house Ducker had been taking care of for his mother and found the door ajar. Other relatives reasoned that Ducker had been coerced to leave the premises. They maintain that he never would have been with Brooks otherwise.

It was thought that Daniel Gantovnik and Michael Zarabi had been murdered on Saturday, October 12th. Sources close to the situation reported that they had gone to Brooks' house at the time because one of the men owed Brooks money, either for a business deal or on a personal loan. That the Saturday evening meeting had been a short one was indicated by the fact that when the vehicles were recovered outside the Brooks' house, the keys were still in the ignition of both cars the men had driven there.

One mystery that continued to defy the best efforts of detectives assigned to the case was the whereabouts of Marion Brooks.

Sergeant Russell believed that something happened to her on the first day. It was on that day that Brooks had been spotted driving the woman's Chevrolet, something she would never have allowed him to do had she been in a position to prevent it.

Russell noted that during the 30 hours of dialogues between the hostage negotiating team and Brooks, the mass murderer had ignored all queries concerning his mother's whereabouts.

Said Inspector Courtney, "He may have taken the secret to his grave."

Mrs. Brooks' car was found near the scene of the siege, but detectives said they found no signs of foul play.

Inspector Courtney thinks Brooks' lethal rampage might have been triggered by the eccentric man's worries over his own health.

Flushing Hospital records show that one week before the killings, an ambulance was dispatched to the Brooks' 254th Street home at 7:49 a.m. by the Emergency Medical Service. The paramedics found Andrew Brooks Jr. bleeding from the gums and from the rectum. He was also suffering from discolored stools. Brooks had refused to go to the hospital and hospital officials refused to discuss his physical symptoms.

There were no indications of emotional disturbance, but the ambulance crew was "on a nonpsychiatric visit" and not looking for signs of emotional distress.

Inspector Courtney did not believe that the man had a fatal disease. Although investigators theorized that Brooks' fear that he was terminally ill had prompted the killings, they did not know how he chose his victims.

Said the inspector, "Over the years he had substantially a hostile relationship with his father, and often his mother acted as an intermediary in an attempt to protect him."

Meanwhile, dogs specially trained to smell out decomposing cadavers were being employed in the search for Marion Brooks. In October and November 1991, Sergeant Russell and his team of detectives were checking sanitation department landfills, trying to find out whether any dumpsters had been recently picked up and where the contents had been taken. Russell hoped the missing Marion Brooks would be found in a barge or dumpster, but he had to admit that detectives had no clues to the missing woman's whereabouts.

Then, on November 21st, a surviving family member went to the Brooks residence to shut off the water in the abandoned building and discovered a foul odor emanating from the basement. Police tracked the odor to its source—a 3-foot-deep hole housing the sump pump—and found the body of 75-year-old Marion Brooks stuffed inside. She had been shot in the back and dumped in the hole head first. The killer had then covered the hole with a metal plate and piled tires on top.

The discovery brought an abrupt end to the six-week-long search for Andrew Brooks Jr.'s fifth murder victim, but it didn't bring police any closer to understanding why the rampage had occurred. Even if the killer had survived his final fatal blast, it isn't likely that the police would ever have had a satisfactory answer to that question.

# "7,000 YEARS FOR THE FREAKED-OUT GUNMAN!"

by Gary C. King

OKLAHOMA CITY, OK.
NOVEMBER 15, 1986

It was approximately 6:45 a.m. on Thursday, January 30, 1986, just before dawn, when the first of a series of calls began pouring into the Oklahoma City Police Department's switchboards. The calls were reports of shots fired in the 1700 block of North Cairo, located in the northeast section of the city.

One of the callers was a nearly frantic, unidentified woman. She said that she and a male companion had been chased by a man with a gun while driving down Cairo Street, and that he had fired shots at them. She told the dispatcher that she had escaped by jumping from the car, but her companion had been shot. Officers were immediately dispatched to the scene on this cold, gray morning, not really knowing what to expect when they got there.

When they arrived, they found the car parked at the location described by the woman, but there was no sign of anyone inside it or near it. Where was the wounded man? they wondered. And where was the woman who had called police? As they approached the car, their questions were partially answered when they heard loud, thumping noises coming from the trunk. Someone was inside, apparently trying to get out or draw attention to that fact.

"Police went to the location, and they heard some banging noises coming from the trunk of the car and found a shooting victim there," police spokesman Captain M.T. Berry would later tell the very eager press corps.

After police opened the truck, they quickly determined that the man inside had been seriously wounded. They immediately allowed paramedics, who'd followed them to the scene, to attend to the man's wounds. Because of his condition and state of mind, the victim was unable to provide many details of the shooting at this point. He was, however, identified as Craig Martin, and was quickly taken by ambulance to a nearby hospital for treatment of multiple gunshot wounds.

Minutes later, at 6:51 a.m., a second series of calls reporting shots fired was received at the Oklahoma City Police Department. The shots had been fired this time in the 1800 block of Northeast 20th, not far from the scene of the earlier shooting and just east of Martin Luther King Boulevard. This time the shooting had occurred at a residence.

When officers arrived at the house, they noted that a large plate-glass window at the front of the home had been broken out. A dog initially kept police from getting inside the house, but it was eventually subdued and police entered the residence. Inside they found a large amount of blood on the floor, and a crimson trail that led out the back door. Following the long, gruesome trail of blood to the backyard, they found a black woman, in her late 20s to early 30s, lying face down in a large pool of blood, clad in a yellow sweater and blue slacks. It appeared she had been shot several times, and she was pronounced dead at the scene.

Nearby, a young black girl was found lying on the ground, alive but very seriously wounded from what appeared to be gunshot wounds to her chest. Unconscious, she was treated by paramedics at the scene and whisked off to Oklahoma Children's Memorial Hospital.

Detectives were sent to the scenes of both shootings, and all available personnel were called to duty to investigate what had occurred that morning. Among those present at the death scene were Homicide Lieutenant Bob Jones, Detectives Eric Mullenix and Bob Bemo, and Oklahoma County District Attorney Robert H. Macy. Crime lab technicians Frank Carr and Mel Thee were also summoned to the scene, as was a representative from the medical examiner's office.

The dead woman was identified as Teresa Thomas, who, according to relatives, would have turned 30 years old had she lived only two more days. The young girl shot was Teresa's six-year-old daughter. Police said they had no idea what had prompted the attacks on the woman and her daughter.

"We're trying to put all that information together and trying to put a logical sequence of events together," said Captain Berry, a process, he pointed out, that could take some time. "There's no need to rush the investigation. What we're concerned with right now is building a good solid case and making sure we are factual about everything."

One neighbor told police that she had heard several gunshots about 7 a.m., but she thought they came from another neighborhood. "It's getting to be a bad world to live in." She added that she did not know the victims.

Police weren't giving out much information at this point because they didn't want to hinder their investigation and because they didn't know all the details yet themselves. However, another neighbor talked to reporters and said he watched the police investigate the backyard murder scene through his binoculars.

He said he observed a great deal of blood from a large wound near the dead woman's spine, and speculated that she had been shot by a large-caliber weapon.

"I could see it wasn't any wound from a .22. There was too much blood." This neighbor, like the others, said he didn't know the victims. "Everyone works around here. There's not much time for socializing." The neighbor added, "I've got a friend who was shot three times. Another who was stabbed. They are always doing it to each other around here."

Yet another resident told investigators that he had lived in the neighborhood for the past six years, and said Thomas and her daughter had moved in about six months earlier. He said he thought another woman also lived at the house.

"You know how family is," he said. "There was a lot of coming and going. But this is a peaceful neighborhood," he added, his view of the neighborhood clearly conflicting with that of other residents. "Nothing like this has ever happened."

"Was it her husband who shot her?" asked another neighbor, serving only to annoy the busy investigators. "She used to have one, you know." The detectives assured the neighbor they would check out every possibility.

Minutes later, at approximately 7:25 a.m., while patrol officers were searching for the gunman witnesses had described as young, black, and of medium build and height, Oklahoma City police received a third series of telephone calls. This time a gunman at the Consolidated Freightways terminal, located in the 1400 block of South Skyline, had gone on a shooting spree and had shot several people.

The police couldn't believe what was happening in their city on this winter morning, and at this point, they didn't know if they were dealing with three unrelated shooting incidents or if the shootings were somehow tied together. Because of the lack of details, they chose to treat each incident as a separate case.

By the time police arrived at the trucking terminal, two people were dead, two had been wounded, and dozens of others were literally frightened out of their wits. Lawmen quickly discovered that the gunman had also left the area.

The dead were identified by co-workers as James L. Rider, 44, described as a "gutsy little guy," and Carl D. Lake, 34. Both had been shot numerous times. The two wounded men were identified as Bruce Richardson, 38, and Mark Hunter, 48.

Investigators immediately rounded up all the eyewitnesses to the shootings and took reports from each. The story, they said later, was a shocking and disturbing one, one of the most violent cases in Oklahoma City's history.

It was 7:15 a.m., police were told, when Roger Adams, a driver-salesman, placed his timecard in the clock and punched in for work on the trucking terminal dock before joining several others in a nearby breakroom for morning coffee. The room, said Adams, was just east of the office used by terminal dispatcher and operations manager Carl Lake, who was being groomed for the position of terminal manager. The room was connected by a door that could be opened only from Lake's office.

"I was in the breakroom when I heard two shots," said Adams. "POW! POW! Then I heard a metal chair scraping over the floor, and Carl Lake said, 'Goddamn it!'" Moments later, said Adams, another employee opened the door from Lake's office and ran into the breakroom. Adams told investigators that he then asked the employee what had happened.

"'Carl's been shot.'" Adams said, quoting the other employee. Adams said he then went into Lake's office and knelt down beside him to see if he could help. "There was blood all over his face. He looked as if he had been shot right between the eyes."

"He just happened to be in the wrong place at the right time," interjected another person about Carl Lake. "It's pretty hard to understand why sometimes."

Adams continued with his story and told police he quickly looked out the other door of the office, the one that opens to a hall and leads to the main office and front door of the building.

"I saw a bunch of people crawling and running toward me down the hall," he continued. "They were shouting for someone to call the police and an ambulance. A man was right behind them firing a handgun." Adams said a bullet came so close to him he heard it as it passed his ear.

Adams said he ran back into Lake's office and left through the door that opened into the breakroom. He and another employee then ran onto the loading dock and into a nearby office to call police. However, they had been unable to get the telephone to work in all the excitement and panic. "We didn't know you had to dial nine to get an outside line," he said. Unable to call police, Adams ran back toward the breakroom and saw the gunman, described as a black man in his early to mid-20s, "run from the south to the north side of the dock. Then I heard four more shots . . . the four that killed Jim Rider." Rider was also an operations manager.

Backing up Adams' account of the shootings, another witness told investigators that when the gunman initially drove into the terminal yard, he called Bruce Richardson, 38, an account sales representative, over to his car. The gunman got out, forced Richardson onto his hands and knees, and said, "I've taken all the crap that I'm gonna take from you sons-of-bitches," then shot Richardson three times, once in the face. Richardson was unconscious for a few minutes, and woke up a short time later in a pool of blood. He was helped by a co-worker to one of the waiting ambulances and was taken to Presbyterian Hospital, where he was admitted with gunshot wounds to the forehead, shoulder, and rib cage. Despite his wounds, he was listed in good condition following surgery.

When the gunman walked in the front door of the terminal building, said yet another witness, he stopped at the front desk where two female employees were working and asked to see the assistant terminal manager. At this point, his gun was not visible. As one of the employees called the assistant terminal manager on the intercom, the gunman left and walked down the hall toward Lake's office. Moments later, shots were heard. Following the gunshots, the man walked past the main desk and one of the women asked him what had caused the loud noise.

"He had a big smile on his face and said that he didn't know what caused the noise," said an employee. He then walked down the stairs toward the front door, as if he were going to leave. But he turned around and came back up the stairs, at which point he began shooting at people and driving them down the hall toward Lake's office, "herding them like cattle."

One employee told police he saw the gunman reload his gun before going to the north side of the dock, the location where Jim Rider was shot.

Before the gunman left, police were told, he reloaded his gun again and continued to shoot at anything that moved. At one point, the gunman spotted a young man hiding behind a truck.

"The gunman saw him, walked up to him and pointed the pistol at him to shoot him," said an official close to the investigation. "This man was begging the gunman not to shoot him, saying, 'I'm a young man, my wife's pregnant . . . I've never seen my baby, and I wanna live to see my baby." When the gunman started to squeeze the trigger, he suddenly realized he needed to reload. As he grabbed bullets from his pocket and flipped open the cylinder, the young man saw his chance and bolted away, running through the trucking lot. The gunman fired at him after he'd reloaded, but fortunately missed his target.

From interviews with witnesses and victims at Consolidated Freightways, the gunman was identified as Cyril Wayne Ellis, 24, a former employee who had filed workman's compensation claims against the company over a foot injury. Company officials described Ellis as a malingerer who would do just about anything to avoid working. He was regularly absent from work with claims of being sick or injured. According to records, Ellis had fought with the company over the on-the-job injury in which his foot had been run over by a forklift, and officials said he had missed several months of work over the prior year and a half.

An APB was issued immediately, and law enforcement officers all over the city, county, and state were provided with a photo of the dangerous suspect.

As the detectives began to put the pieces of the case together, they soon learned that Ellis was the former lover of Deniece Brooks, the formerly unidentified woman who had first called police to report that she and a man were being shot at early that morning. She and Ellis had been engaged to be married, but they had recently split up after a longstanding domestic dispute.

As the investigators delved deeper into the case, they learned that, the night before the shootings, Ellis and Brooks had another fight. Ellis, Brooks said, had been distraught over his foot injury and the disputes over his workman's compensation claims. She, however, talked him into checking into the psychiatric ward of St. Anthony Hospital.

"She was going to leave him," said D.A. Robert Macy. "They were having all kinds of domestic problems. We considered it a ploy to try and get her back."

After a very short stay at St. Anthony, which consisted of only a few hours, Ellis left with Brooks in her car, against medical advice. As they were driving they became embroiled in another dispute, and Brooks jumped out of the car at one point and ran inside the Sheraton Century Center Hotel and called police, pleading for help. When police arrived, however, Brooks refused to sign a complaint and Ellis drove away in her car.

In the meantime, Brooks called a relative and asked to be picked up at the hotel. When they arrived at Brooks' home a short time later, they found it had been ransacked. They discovered that a television set had been taken, among other things.

Police were again called by Brooks, and they went to her home to investigate. Because of the missing television and because police were concerned about ownership of the car Ellis had driven away in earlier, officers subsequently went to Ellis' apartment in the 4500 block of Cherryhill Lane. Ellis, however, refused to answer his door despite repeated attempts by police to get him to do so. Nearly an hour later, he opened the door after pleas from a relative who had been brought to the apartment. After talking with him, the relative told police that Ellis seemed "emotionally distraught."

"Ellis explained that he was under a lot of stress," said Captain Berry, "because of an injury on his job and his problems with his fiancée (Ms. Brooks)." However, "he was reality-oriented at the time . . . he wasn't talking about spaceships or little people hiding in the basement."

The problems had been resolved by the time police

left, and because Brooks again refused to sign a complaint, Ellis could not be held. Brooks said "she only wanted him to go back to the hospital," according to Berry.

"The problem is," said Homicide Lieutenant Bob Jones, "you can't hold a man there against his will if he's not court-committed."

Afraid to stay home that night and fearful that Ellis would come back, Brooks stayed with a relative, police were told. Early the next morning, she was being driven back to her home by Craig Martin, Teresa Thomas' fiancé, to get some clothes for work when they suddenly met Ellis driving down the street. When he saw them he immediately turned around and started chasing them, firing shots at Martin and Brooks, with one of the shots hitting Martin. The account of what happened was confirmed by Martin from his hospital bed.

At one point, Martin pulled into a driveway as another driver was attempting to back out. Ellis pulled up behind, blocking Martin's car. Seeing the gun, the other driver backed out of the driveway and sped away. Brooks, meanwhile, jumped out of the car and ran away, leaving Martin to face Ellis alone.

Holding the gun on Martin, Ellis ordered the injured man from the car, led him to the car's trunk. Holding the gun to Martin's head, he ordered him to open the trunk and climb inside. Martin complied, and Ellis closed the trunk.

As Ellis began looking for Brooks, Martin started shouting and beating on the inside of the trunk, trying to get out. Hearing the noise, Ellis walked back to the trunk and opened it.

"So you don't want to live, huh?" Ellis asked Martin. Ellis then shot him twice more. He closed the trunk to Martin's car and left in the car he had been driving, in pursuit of Deniece Brooks. Martin told authorities that he kept quiet after that.

Investigators could only speculate as to why Ellis drove to the home of Teresa Thomas, but they believe he did so because he thought Deniece Brooks had gone there. Although Ellis and Martin were described only as "superficial acquaintances," Ellis was said to have known Craig Martin and Teresa Thomas through Deniece Brooks. Brooks, police soon learned, was a close relative of Thomas.

Meanwhile, evidence gathered at Thomas' home and studied by lab technicians Frank Carr and Mel Thee indicated that the gunman shot Teresa Thomas first inside the house, then chased her and her daughter out the back door, firing off rounds as they moved.

"We had no witnesses," said D.A. Macy, "because Teresa was murdered and her daughter was very critically wounded. But we were able to trace their paths by blood patterns. . . . Wounded, Teresa was crawling on her hands and knees and he kept following her, shooting her until he killed her. . . . As the daughter crawled along the sidewalk behind the house, he shot her three times. For a considerable period of time we didn't expect her to live," Macy added. Listed in critical condition, Teresa's daughter was breathing with the aid of a respirator following extensive surgery.

Police received a telephone call from a woman in nearby Del City who reported that Ellis had come to her home in the 4100 block of Meadowview Avenue. The woman was a relative of the suspect, who showed up at her home unexpectedly and announced that he was "tired of running" and wanted to turn himself in. The relative agreed to call police, but made Ellis remain in the yard until police arrived.

When Del City Officers John Smith and Mike Brown arrived, Ellis was still waiting outside. He offered no resistance as he was taken into custody, and was not carrying a gun at the time of his arrest. A

1975 brown and tan Pontiac was, however, impounded by authorities.

Cyril Ellis was subsequently transferred to the Oklahoma City Jail, where he was booked. He was charged with three counts of first-degree murder and four counts of shooting with intent to kill. Ellis appeared barefoot and handcuffed before Special Judge James B. Croy in Oklahoma County District Court. Ellis only stated his name, age and birth date before the judge, who ordered him held without bail.

On his way out of the courtroom, Ellis was stopped by a radio station newsman and was asked if he had anything to say. Ellis responded that he was "just sorry."

In doing additional background on Ellis following his arrest, detectives learned that he had been feuding with officials at Consolidated Freightways since June 3, 1984, the date of his on-the-job accident, which he alleged had caused a permanent disability. In August 1984, Ellis received a warning letter from the company, stating that he had not been performing his job at 100 percent efficiency.

In the month that followed, Ellis' left foot was operated on twice. He missed several months of work while recovering. On December 16, 1984, he was released by his doctor, who stated that Ellis could go back to work.

"The patient went to work but by the time his shift was over, the foot was really bothering him," wrote a doctor in a subsequent report, who also stated that Ellis suffered from 35 percent permanent impairment to his left foot. By that time, Ellis had already received more than $10,000 in disability workman's compensation payments.

Between December 16, 1984, and January 17, 1985, the date on which Ellis filed a claim in state Workers Compensation Court for alleged permanent disability stemming from the earlier accident, he continued to see doctors and underwent mental tests. The tests indicated "some psychological disturbance . . . that seems to be related to this injury and its effects on the patient's ability to function at work," said one doctor.

"The patient states he is depressed from worrying that he will not be able to perform 100 percent at his job and will lose the job, but the patient has such pain in the left foot that he is not able to work at 100 percent efficiency," wrote one of the doctors in a statement attached to Ellis' claim.

Because of defense questions regarding Ellis' sanity at the time of the shootings, the court ordered that the defendant undergo additional psychological testing to determine his competency to assist in his own defense.

Oklahoma County District Judge Leamon Freeman said the examination was warranted "under the bizarre circumstances and severity of the crime," and ordered Ellis sent to Central State Hospital in Vinita.

Meanwhile, District Attorney Robert Macy said he would seek the death penalty in the case.

"It is the worst shooting since I've been district attorney," said Macy. He added that evidence showed the killings were premeditated.

"We can clearly establish that he knew each individual that he shot and that, in his own way of thinking, he might have had some motive for shooting each of them," continued Macy. "Apparently, it started as a domestic dispute with his girlfriend, accelerated from there to her family and then from there on down to his place of employment."

Ellis was soon judged competent to stand trial and assist in his own defense. With regard to his sanity at the time of the shootings, Macy said the prosecution "will meet the sanity issue head-on should they (defense attorneys) raise it."

It was revealed later that, shortly after his arrest

and after being advised of his constitutional rights, Ellis talked with investigators briefly about the crimes for which he was charged. He described the shootings to some degree, and after he had shot Teresa Thomas and her daughter said to himself: "While I'm at it, I might as well take care of all my problems." He told investigators that he then went home to get additional ammunition.

According to Captain Berry, a .38-caliber pistol believed used in the shootings was found at a location near Northeast 10th and Vicki in Oklahoma City. Additional ammunition was found inside Ellis' apartment and, along with the pistol, was turned over to ballistics and forensics investigators. They subsequently determined that the pistol was indeed the one used in all of the shootings allegedly committed by Ellis.

But where did he get the gun? detectives wondered. People interviewed earlier by sleuths had said that they didn't think Ellis owned a gun, and none of the local gun shops had a record of a recent sale to him.

However, as they probed deeper on this subject, the detectives soon learned that the night before the shootings Ellis had gone to a local gun shop to make a purchase. However, the store clerk, whom Ellis knew personally, told investigators that Ellis didn't have enough money to buy a gun. Ellis told the clerk that he was running some sort of "drive-in" stand and that some strange people had recently been hanging around watching him. Fearing they were planning to rob him, Ellis explained that he needed a gun to protect himself and his business. The clerk referred Ellis to a friend, who agreed to loan him a .38-caliber pistol until he could raise enough money to purchase his own. Ellis bought a box of ammunition from the store and left. Investigators determined there was no wrongdoing on the part of the gun shop clerk or the person who loaned Ellis the .38, since Ellis had not provided them with even a clue as to his actual intended use of the gun.

Cyril Wayne Ellis' trial began on November 15, 1986. A jury found him guilty of three counts of first-degree murder and four counts of shooting with intent to kill. He received three death sentences plus 7,000 years. This is believed to be the largest sentence ever meted out by a jury in Oklahoma.

EDITOR'S NOTE:
*Deniece Brooks, Craig Martin, Bruce Richardson, Mark Hunter and Roger Adams are not the real names of the persons so named in the foregoing story. Fictitious names have been used because there is no reason for public interest in the identification of these persons.*

# "ENRAGED LOVER MASSACRED A FAMILY OF 5!"

by Bob Carlsen

MARRERO, LA.
MAY 29, 1983

The man was nervous as he walked into the large department store. There was a security guard at the store's entrance who gave him a brief glance.

The man walked back to the firearms department to purchase some type of weapon. He wasn't sure exactly what he would come away with, but knew it had to be of sufficient caliber to kill somebody.

He decided on a .22-caliber rifle. It was cheap yet effective at close range. And that's what he would do. Blow them away at close range.

He threw the money on the counter and left in a hurry after the transaction. He went to his apartment and got the .38-caliber revolver. Then he haled a taxi.

It was about 5:25 when the cabby left him off at the intersection of Fourth Street and Robinson Avenue in the city of Marrero, Louisiana, which is in Jefferson Parish near New Orleans.

His destination was one block away, a house on Robinson Avenue. He had a plan. He knew he could get away with murder without being caught.

He made sure nobody in the neighborhood saw him as he skirted up the street to the house. In a nearby lot eight men were playing cards. They'd been there a good portion of the afternoon, and had no reason in the world to think that their game would be broken up by a deadly tirade.

The killer burst into the house and caught all who were inside by surprise. The eyes of the off-duty sheriff's deputy widened when she noticed that the intruder was brandishing a rifle. Without giving any of them a chance, he started firing.

Sheila Thomas, the 27-year-old sheriff's deputy, fell to the floor dead after receiving a bullet from the rifle in the brain and another in the left arm.

Sheila's four-year-old daughter, Shantel Osborne, was shot with the rifle in the right forehead. The bullet tore into her brain. He had fired at point blank range.

The little girl's father, Carl Osborne, received a rifle shot that entered his right ear and shattered his brain. He, like his daughter, was shot from a mere six inches away.

Myrtle Griffin, 44, Sheila's mother, died of two bullet wounds to the upper front of her chest. One bullet passed through her heart and the other through her lung. Both were fired at close range and both exited out her back.

The slayings occurred so quickly that nobody had a chance to do anything. The screams were brief, for the slugs were pumped into the victims in rapid succession. The expended shells dropped to the floor.

When the shooting erupted, Owen Griffin, 45, one of the eight men playing cards near the house, rushed towards his home. His wife, stepdaughter and her husband and child were inside, and he knew he had to protect them. He ran to the side door, looked inside but saw nothing; then he ran around to the front door.

As he plunged into the house, the killer fired a bullet into the right side of Owen Griffin's face. It shattered his backbone, and he died instantly.

Only the little four-year-old girl was alive as the killer quickly hid the .38-caliber revolver in an air duct vent, and then placed the .22-caliber rifle under Sheila's bed covers. She had been living with her mother and stepfather in the house during this time.

As quickly as he'd burst in, he was gone. And not one of the other seven men who'd been playing cards with Owen Griffin saw what the killer looked like.

Four persons were dead. A little girl lay bleeding to death inside the house on Robinson Avenue. It was the worst slaughter in recent Louisiana history. And the killer had gotten away without being spotted.

Jefferson Parish Deputy James L. Johnson was one of the first lawmen to arrive on the scene. Captain Kevin Smith wasn't far behind, followed by 28 more.

It was 5:30 p.m. Nobody had seen the killer flee, and it was believed he might still be in the house. Deputy Johnson called for a K-9 unit, which arrived within minutes.

The dog cautiously entered the house and, after a few minutes, again appeared at the door. It was safe to enter, the officers now knew.

When Deputy Johnson and Capt. Smith entered the house, they were appalled at the carnage. The five bodies lay around the dining room table. Expertly, so as not to disturb evidence, the officers checked the victims for a pulse.

"Nothing here," Capt. Smith said as he gently placed the arm of a victim down.

"Wait a minute," Johnson said. "I've got something."

Deputy Johnson was holding the limp arm of four-year-old Shantel Osborne. She had been found in a chair near the table. She was rushed into an ambulance and then to the hospital.

Little did the investigators realize that she would be their only eyewitness to the killing. Despite the fact there were many people nearby, nobody had seen the killer. Only Shantel knew his identity, and she would never be able to tell, for she was dead soon thereafter.

Crime scene investigators descended upon the death house along with hordes of newsmen. Marrero had never seen anything like this before. This kind of crime rarely happened in Louisiana or, for that matter, the entire deep south. A family massacred in broad daylight while others were nearby but helpless.

Bullet fragments, blood, brains, and shell casings were found on the floor of the house. The bodies of the two men, Carl Osborne, Shantel's father, and Owen Griffith, 45, were slumped together. Apparently when Griffin charged into the house, he was shot and fell on the already dead body of Osborne.

Sheila Thomas, Shantel's mother, and Myrtle Griffin, were found on the floor.

As technicians carefully poured over the house in search of any evidence such as fingerprints, other detectives busied themselves by questioning the neighbors and the seven men who had been playing cards with Griffin when the mass murder occurred.

"He rushed into the house and never came out alive," one of the men told detectives. "It was just before 5:30 when we heard the shots," he said. The witness related that he first saw Griffin run across the vacant lot to his house, going first to the side entrance and then entering the front door.

"I heard more shots after Owen went in the house," the witness told investigators.

When hiding the guns, the killer had not only been careful, but meticulous. He knew the air duct vent cover could be removed and the .38-caliber revolver easily stashed in there. It would be difficult to find once the vent cover was replaced.

When he went into Sheila's bedroom to hide the rifle under her bed covers, he was careful not to step in any blood or brain particles. By not tracking anything into the bedroom, the cops wouldn't suspect he'd gone in there. And he was right.

There wasn't a speck of evidence in the house to indicate that the killer had done anything other than enter the home, blow his victims away, and then quickly leave. Naturally since no weapon was found near the crime scene, the assumption was the killer took the murder weapon with him.

There was no evidence to cause the investigators to start tearing into such things as the air vent or mattresses.

If the sleuths would have found the weapons stashed away in the house right after the crimes, they would have had a vital clue.

The detectives worked into the evening. An officer had been sent to the hospital to guard Shantel Osborne and talk to her if at all possible. The disappointing news came back that she was dead. The detectives' job would be that much harder.

After the seven card players were questioned, the search for witnesses branched out to other neighbors. Nobody saw the suspect. Nobody even saw or heard a car roar off after the shootings.

It seemed logical to the detectives that the killer would have wanted to make a quick getaway, if he'd had a car. Perhaps he'd parked it just a couple blocks away.

Detectives expanded their search into nearby neighborhoods in their effort to find a witness who'd seen a strange car speeding away from the murder scene. Although some leads were checked out, none proved fruitful. It just seemed like the killer appeared out of nowhere, and vanished in broad daylight just as quickly.

That left open several possibilities. Perhaps the

killer lived in the neighborhood, or maybe he'd gotten a ride to the crime scene area from a friend, or maybe he'd gotten there in a cab. The first and third possibilities could be checked out. The second couldn't be worked on until a suspect was located.

Detectives contacted area cab companies and learned that shortly before the murders, a female cab driver had dropped a man off at the corner of Fourth Street and Robinson Avenue, just a block away from the murder scene.

Detectives pounced on the clue and learned that the man the cabby had dropped off had been carrying a .22-caliber rifle. The West Bank cab driver said the rifle looked relatively new to her.

Detectives reasoned that a man fleeing a murder scene while carrying a rifle would certainly be conspicuous. Perhaps he'd stashed the weapon somewhere in the house.

A relative of Sheila's was contacted, and the day after the murders another search was made in the house. The relative found the rifle under the covers of Sheila's bed.

It was a .22-caliber, and on its stock, the detectives noticed, Sheila's name had been written several times with a felt tipped marker.

Also in Sheila's bedroom was an incriminating 30-page notebook found in her closet. The notebook, in large, crude print, contained obscenities and threats to Sheila Thomas, the slain 27-year-old deputy.

The notebook didn't have the author's name in it, but detectives surmised from its contents that it was penned by a jealous ex-boyfriend.

The notebook spoke of their relationship, and how Sheila took advantage of it. At least that's how the author had perceived the situation.

"And now you want to go and f--- around," the notebook stated on pages five and six. "It do not work like that you and me will have, to bouth be dead bitch."

The improper punctuation and misspelled words in the notebook indicated to the detectives that its author had little education. Later in the notebook it stated: "But God know I made my life streight and now Sheila want to mess it up but no, she have to go to the wormes she took all I work for then leave to go and be with Carl but I just cannot take it eany more."

Detectives checked into the background of Deputy Sheila Thomas and learned that she did have a former boyfriend who would have fit the profile of the person who penned the crude notebook. His name was Leslie O. Lowenfield, detectives learned after questioning relatives and friends of the victims.

Lowenfield had come from Guyana and was not well versed in the use of the English language, especially the written word, the detectives were told.

As the investigation continued, Dr. Alvaro Hunt performed autopsies on the five victims. All were shot at close range with a small caliber weapon, Dr. Hunt told the detectives. In some of the cases it was possible to determine the caliber of the weapon used.

Detectives already had determined that the weapon was some type of automatic .22, as shell casing had been found at the murder scene.

Dr. Hunt said that some of the wounds didn't appear to be consistent with a .22, and that a second weapon might be involved, but it was impossible to determine its caliber from bullet fragments found.

Detectives obtained a photograph of suspect Lowenfield, put it in a montage, and the female taxi driver picked him out as being the man she'd dropped off at the corner near the murder scene shortly before 5:30 p.m.

Det. James Trapani, who spearheaded the investigation, knew that Deputy Thomas and Carl Osborne were probably the primary targets of the killer, if it indeed had been Lowenfield.

Det. Trapani learned that Deputy Thomas had, for the past two years, been assigned to jail and courthouse duties. She was a guard and escorted prisoners to court. She was well known and well liked at the Jefferson Parish courthouse. She was present daily in at least one of the court's 15 divisions.

For that reason, detectives questioned her work associates and learned that Deputy Thomas had a very good friend, also assigned to prisoner escort. The friend told detectives that she knew Leslie Lowenfield; and that five days before the mass murder, Lowenfield had said he was going to kill Sheila Thomas or "blow her brains out," as he put it.

Detectives learned from one of Sheila's cousins that on the evening of August 29, 1982, Lowenfield had appeared at her (the cousin's) apartment and said he was gong to kill Sheila Thomas and Carl Osborne, the father of Sheila's baby, as well as Myrtle Griffin, Sheila's mother.

Det. Trapani and other investigators learned Lowenfield's address and descended upon the apartment. Nobody was there, and neighbors said they hadn't seen Lowenfield since the afternoon of August 30th.

An all-points bulletin was put out for the suspect but he was nowhere to be found in Marrero, Gretna, or New Orleans. Leslie O. Lowenfield, 28, had simply vanished after committing the murders.

The search for Lowenfield dragged on with no results. But Det. Trapani had his men working on several fronts, and while the search for Lowenfield was on, detectives were trying to trace the rifle which was one of the murder weapons.

Their hard work paid off when they turned up the department store clerk who had sold the gun. The clerk said she probably could remember the man she'd sold the gun to because not too many sales were made on August 30th.

Detectives showed the store clerk the photo montage, and she picked out the photo of Leslie O. Lowenfield as being the man who had purchased the murder weapon.

Another link in the chain of circumstantial evidence was in place. Det. Trapani knew that he would have to build the case on circumstantial evidence because there was no eyewitness to the five murders. He knew it would have to be an air-tight case if he was going to bring in Lowenfield and get a murder conviction.

The hours ticked by, the days passed, and still there was no sign of Lowenfield. It was a week after the murders that Lowenfield's second murder weapon was found.

By then another relative had moved into the house to tidy things up and take care of the property preparatory to the settling of the estate.

He found the .38-caliber revolver in the air vent. He turned it over to a deputy sheriff, who in turn gave it to detectives.

The fact that the killer knew enough to hide the revolver in the ductwork indicated to detectives that the slayer had to be somebody familiar with the home. Again, Lowenfield met the qualifications.

Ballistics experts studied the bullets that had killed the five victims and determined that all the shots were fired from either the automatic rifle or the .38-caliber revolver.

No fingerprints had been found on either gun to link Lowenfield to the weapons.

The search for Leslie O. Lowenfield dragged through September when the FBI got into the act because it was believed he had fled the state.

Lawmen got reports of Lowenfield surfacing in different parts of the country, and every lead had to be checked out. They all proved false.

For awhile it was believed Lowenfield had gone to Florida, but no trace of the suspect could be found in that state. Florida appeared to be the most promising possibility because while checking airline, train and bus depots, detectives learned that Lowenfield had purchased a bus ticket for Florida for August 29th.

But that was the day before the murders, and detectives learned that the ticket wasn't used. As they would eventually find out, the purchase of the bus ticket by Lowenfield was just part of a plan to fabricate an alibi for himself for the time of the murders.

It was October 5, 1982 when FBI agents Michael J. Henehan and Thomas F. Sinnott were working the Brooklyn, N.Y. area at 11:30 a.m. The agents had familiarized themselves with Lowenfield as well as other fugitives wanted by the bureau.

When they spotted him walking down the street, there was no doubt in their minds who he was. The agents followed Lowenfield for a short distance and called for other backup units. When they determined it was safe to make the arrest, it was done without incident.

The month-long manhunt for Leslie O. Lowenfield had finally come to an end.

Lowenfield was held at Riker's Island Prison in New York pending his extradition to New Orleans. During his stay at Riker's Island, he wrote several letters in which he said he didn't intend to shoot the four-year-old child. In the letters, he described how Carl Osborne had grabbed the tot and tried to use her as a shield just before the girl and her father were shot.

The letters were turned over to detectives, who realized that they were just as good as a confession. Lowenfield apparently didn't expect the letters to be used as evidence against him. If he'd known they would be given to detectives, he probably wouldn't have penned them.

A handwriting expert compared the letters, the notebook that had been found in Sheila's closet and other known samples of Lowenfield's writing, and determined that the same hand had penned them all.

Detectives learned that Lowenfield planned to use as part of his defense the story that he'd taken a bus trip to Florida 21 hours before the murders and that he was in Jacksonville at the time of the slayings, looking for work.

Det. Trapani knew that because his case against Lowenfield was strictly circumstantial, he would have to disprove Lowenfield's alibi.

Detectives set about tracking Lowenfield's movements from the time he left New Orleans to his arrival in New York. It was a time-consuming task but their efforts finally paid off.

Detectives found a witness who said that Leslie Lowenfield had telephoned her after the murders from a location in Alabama.

"This was the day after the killings," the witness told detectives.

Leslie Lowenfield claimed he left for Florida on a bus 21 hours before the killings. That being the case, how could he be in Alabama the day after the murders?

He couldn't, was the logical conclusion. He'd lied about leaving on the bus, detectives knew from the start, but now they had proof that he couldn't have been in Florida as he'd claimed.

Leslie O. Lowenfield was eventually extradited to Jefferson Parish from New York, and he went on trial in May of 1984.

Assistant District Attorneys Arthur Lentini and Greg Gremillion sought the death penalty and presented the case in much the same manner as detectives had unearthed evidence. They did battle with two highly competent court-appointed attorneys who defended Lowenfield.

Testifying at the trial were the department store clerk who sold Lowenfield the .22-caliber automatic rifle, the cab driver who dropped him near the murder scene, the seven men who had been playing cards with one of the victims, and witnesses who knew Lowenfield had threatened to kill Sheila Thomas and Carl Osborne.

Dr. Hunt told of the grisly manner in which the five victims were killed. The defense made a great deal of the manner in which the two murder weapons were found in the house after the crime investigation was completed.

"You had all the police rank out there that night," one defense attorney said at the trial. "You had everyone from Sheriff Harry Lee on down and all those police overlooked the two guns," the attorney criticized.

The attorney also argued that it was incredible to think one man could have hidden the two guns so quickly and effectively and fled the scene before police arrived one minute after receiving the 5:30 p.m. telephone call at headquarters.

The attorney suggested that more than one person would have to be involved, and that Lowenfield was not one of the individuals.

Lowenfield took the stand and called all of the state's witnesses liars. He said the cab driver was lying, the department store clerk was lying, and he denied writing the threatening notebook which had been found in Sheila Thomas's closet.

But the most damning state witness against Lowenfield was the woman who testified that she'd received a telephone call from Lowenfield from Alabama the day after the murder.

"I never met her," Lowenfield said on the stand about the witness. "I never saw her before she came in this courtroom Saturday and testified. I guess someone coached her on what to say."

The woman had testified that she had met Lowenfield in the spring of 1982 and had been in his apartment and he had telephoned her frequently that summer. Lowenfield denied it all.

He had to deny it, because it shot holes through his alibi that he was in Jacksonville, Florida looking for work in the shipyards at the time of the murders.

Lowenfield insisted he left New Orleans at 8 p.m. on August 29th, arrived in Jacksonville on August 30th where he couldn't find work, and caught a bus to New York. He arrived there September 1st. He said a cousin showed him a story in the newspaper about the Louisiana mass murder.

The jury was faced with the task of either believing all the state's witnesses or else believing Lowenfield. There was no middle ground; no chance that facts were confused. Lowenfield simply called all the state's witnesses liars. One of his attorneys contended that the department store clerk who had sold the gun identified Lowenfield because she was hysterical over the fact that she'd put the murder weapon in the killer's hands. She would have identified anybody the police suggested, the defense attorney told the jury.

In closing arguments, the defense urged the jury not to rush to a judgement. The defense said it was a rush to judgment which had brought the case this far and had put an innocent man on trial.

On Monday, May 14, 1984 the jury got the case and deliberated for eight hours without reaching a verdict. Judge James Cannella dismissed three alternate jurors.

The jury began deliberations on Monday at 11:50 a.m., and at 8 p.m. sent Judge Cannella a note stating that the panel was weary and wanted supper and rest.

The sequestered jury took the rest of the night off, and resumed deliberations Tuesday.

The whole while defendant Lowenfield remained in the packed courtroom and chatted amiably to a capacity crowd which at times even laughed at some of his jokes. Deliberations dragged on Tuesday, and Judge Cannella called attorneys into his chambers to tell them he was about ready to declare a mistrial because the jury obviously couldn't reach a verdict. But he gave it more time, and about an hour later the jury returned with its verdicts.

They found Leslie O. Lowenfield guilty of three counts of first-degree murder in connection with the deaths of his former girlfriend, Sheila Thomas, Carl Osborne, the father of Sheila's daughter; and Myrtle Griffin, Sheila's mother.

Those three persons, the jury determined, were the primary targets.

The jury found Lowenfield guilty of voluntary manslaughter in connection with the shootings of four-year-old Shantel Osborne, the daughter of Sheila and Carl, and of Owen Griffin, who had burst onto the scene to help.

After returning the verdicts, the jury began deliberating at 8:20 p.m. about whether to recommend death in the electric chair or life in prison for the first-degree murder convictions.

After deliberating seven hours, the jury decided Lowenfield should die. As jurors were discharged Wednesday and led out of the Gretna courtroom, Lowenfield, in handcuffs and leg irons, was led back to the Jefferson Parish jail by three armed deputies.

He smiled at his two court-appointed attorneys and said, "Hey, see you guys later."

On May 29th, Judge James Cannella sentenced mass murderer Leslie Lowenfield, 30, to be executed three times in the electric chair.

It was not an easy task for the judge, and his voice

cracked during the proceedings. His judicial aides even left the courtroom. They didn't want to hear the sentences three times.

He told Lowenfield three times that an electrical charge will be sent through his body "until you are dead, dead, dead."

Judge Cannella admitted after the sentencing that it was one of the hardest things he ever had to do in his life. He was shaken by the experience.

"That is an enormous emotional experience," Judge Cannella said, "to read that and then to read it three times. I'm just glad that under the new state law, the jury determines life or death in a first-degree murder conviction, and I just make the formal pronouncement."

The triple death penalty is believed to be the first of its kind in Louisiana.

"I know there are some inmates in Angola currently under a single death penalty and life sentence for multiple murder convictions, but I have not heard of a triple death penalty," an assistant to the state's Secretary of Corrections said.

Under Louisiana law, the case will be automatically appealed. Lowenfield is currently awaiting the outcome of that appeal.

# "HE BUTCHERED 3 WITH A MEAT CLEAVER!"
## by Gary C. King

It was windy and overcast on Monday morning, December 14, 1987, in Portland, Oregon, the crime capital of the Northwest. Pretty 17-year-old Chou Muy Aing, a Cambodian refugee, no doubt felt the winter chill as she got off the bus with some 40 other children at Cleveland High School, located in the southwest part of the city.

Donning a raincoat and carrying an umbrella and a knapsack filled with her books and lunch, Chou, along with other youths, hurried down the long sidewalk and into the front entrance of the school. Despite the burgeoning crime rate in the City of Roses, Chou, like most people, never figured she'd become a statistic.

It was the last week of school before Christmas vacation and Chou, naturally, was happy and excited. The Christmas tree was already up, but she had more decorations to help put on it. She had presents to make and buy for loved ones, and family and friends to visit during the holidays. As was customary, there would be much food to eat. Chou would enjoy both the American and Cambodian religious rituals her family observed at Christmas. But most important of all, at least to Chou and other kids her age, Christmas vacation meant that there would be no homework for more than two weeks.

Unfortunately, none of those things became a reality for Chou and her family that Christmas season. Instead, violent deaths, many tears, and a throng of homicide probers filled their holidays.

According to school officials, Chou Aing left school at her usual time that day, shortly after 3:00 p.m., taking the bus back to her own neighborhood just as she always did. It was approximately 3:40 p.m. when she arrived at the home of Jane Hall, a neighbor who cared for Chou's two young cousins for a short time every day after school.

Chou, as usual, was happy to see Kiry Aing, 7, and his brother Chantha, 6. Likewise, they were delighted to see their older cousin. Since she lived with the boys' parents, responsibility for picking up the children was hers, a duty she didn't mind. She was so close to the boys that she considered them her brothers. Chou had always had a lot of fun with Kiry and Chantha after school, and this day likely would have been no exception.

When the trio approached the blue-trimmed one-story house, everything appeared normal. With no reason to think about their safety, Chou and her cousins entered the front door with the key Chou always carried. Once inside, one of them turned on the television after apparently deciding it was too wet and gloomy to play outside. Another child plugged in the Christmas tree lights.

Seconds later, an attacker appeared out of nowhere. With the mirror image of the Christmas tree lights twinkling off the sharp, shiny objects he held in each hand, the attacker struck without hesitation or warning, burying a meat cleaver deep into each of the children's heads, at the same time stabbing each with a large knife again and again. Investigators would later theorize that the killer must have been lying in wait for the children.

Less than half an hour later a close relative also

walked up the front sidewalk, just as she did every day after work. The relative, like Chou Aing and her two cousins, had no reason for fear or concern. As she reached for the doorknob, she could hear that the television was on. As she opened the door, the TV tube's brightness spilled outward through the dusky doorway. As far as she knew, the kids were watching afternoon cartoon shows.

It wasn't until the woman opened the door all the way that she saw the horror. Gasping in disbelief, her knees became weak and she nearly collapsed when she saw the spattered blood and shattered bodies of the children she loved so dearly. When the reality of the gory scene set in and she realized all the children were dead, she began to shriek.

A few minutes later, a team of officers out on routine patrol from the Portland Police Bureau were instructed by the emergency dispatch center to respond to a report of dead bodies at a home in the 5600 block of Southeast Ogden Street. Even though both officers had seen a lot of blood in the line of duty, nothing could have prepared them for what they found when they arrived at the small home that afternoon.

The living room, where the bodies lay, was drenched with blood. The walls, the ceiling, and the furniture were shrouded with crimson spray and spatters. There were many splotches where blood must have spurted from the victims' wounds as the killer attacked each of them with his sharp weapons.

As the officers moved carefully around the room, they observed that the carpet beneath the bodies was saturated with blood. There were also trails of blood, suggesting that at least one of the victims had made a feeble attempt to escape the attacker after being mortally wounded.

The officers checked for signs of life but, as they had expected, found none. The victims, they observed, had suffered what appeared to be multiple chopping and stabbing wounds over much of their bodies. The victims were still warm to the touch.

Although it wasn't the first time the officers had been called to the scene of a grisly killing, both were visibly moved by the awful tragedy that had occurred inside the house. These were, after all, children who had been butchered, and no cop finds child killing easy to endure. The officers found themselves wondering aloud about who could commit such an atrocious act against these innocent and helpless victims.

After they notified headquarters of their grim discovery, the first officers to arrive attempted, ever so gently, to obtain a statement from the distraught, nearly hysterical relative who had found the bodies. They could get little out of her at this point, however. They spent most of their time trying to comfort her while waiting for assistance to arrive.

Minutes later Homicide Detective Susan Hill arrived at the crime scene, accompanied by Detective David Simpson. Duane Bigoni, a deputy Multnomah County medical examiner, was also sent to the site, as was a deputy district attorney and a team of criminalists from the Oregon State Police (OSP) crime lab.

As the Photographic Unit did their work by taking numerous pictures of the victims and their surroundings, Detectives Hill and Simpson looked around the house. Except for the gruesome, unsightly mess in the living room, the house was clean and well kept. It was apparent, however, that someone had been in the kitchen prior to the killings. Some of the drawers and cabinets had been left open, and there was evidence that someone had eaten rice. At this point, however, there was no way the lawmen could tell when the rice was eaten or by whom.

As they went through the house, room by room, Detectives Hill and Simpson could find no signs of forced entry. They did discover a bathroom window that had been left unlocked and slightly raised. They noted that it could have been used as the perpetrator's point of entry. It was also possible, they knew, that the children might have known the killer and had willingly let him or her inside the house.

While the home was being processed for clues, Hill and Simpson made inquiries throughout the neighborhood. One of the first persons questioned was Jane Hall, Kiry and Chantha's babysitter.

Hall, after recovering from the initial shock of learning about the horrible killings, told the sleuths that Chou Aing had picked the two boys up between 3:40 and 3:50 p.m., her usual time for doing so. Hall explained that they normally stayed at her house for about an hour in the afternoon, until Chou got out of school and picked them up. She said she had not noticed anything unusual that day in the neighborhood.

Between tears and sniffles, Hall described the children as "very polite" and said they were "good kids." She also described their family members as responsible and caring neighbors who always picked the children up on time and paid their babysitting bills promptly.

Other neighbors, also saddened and appalled by the savagery in their neighborhood, told the detectives they saw Chou, Kiry, and Chantha arrive at their home shortly before 4:00 p.m, but none had heard or observed anything unusual. They had seen no strangers in the neighborhood. Some of the neighbors said that the family members were friendly, although they were quiet and kept to themselves most of the time.

By the time the detectives returned to the house, the relative who found the bodies had been placed in the care of another relative. None of the officers, the detectives were informed, had been able to get anything other than a possible identification of the bodies from the distraught family members. Detective Hill made a note that another attempt to question them would have to be made as soon as possible.

Since the victims' bodies were still warm to the touch when found, Hill knew that the killer could not yet be far away. And since he or she had left such a hot trail, Hill wanted to make certain that she followed up every lead before the trail had a chance to get cold.

Meanwhile, criminalists informed the sleuths that they had found the suspected murder weapons — a large butcher knife and a meat cleaver. Since there were other knives of varying sizes similar to the suspected murder weapons in the kitchen, they surmised that the butcher knife and meat cleaver had likely been taken from that room.

The murder weapons were bagged and sent to the crime lab, where an attempt to lift bloody fingerprints would be made. Detective Hill also requested that blood on the weapons be typed for purposes of comparison and ordered that fingerprints be lifted from every room in the house. She instructed technicians to pay special attention to the kitchen and the bathroom window areas.

Responding to hungry news hounds, who had heard about the butchery while monitoring police radio frequencies, Detective Simpson said he had little to offer them at this point. He provided reporters with only the sketchiest of details and said he had not yet arrived at any theories concerning the motive for the "senseless" killings. He said it was not yet known if anything had been taken from the house.

"The deaths are to be described as very violent," Simpson said, as he turned and walked back inside the house.

Duane Bigoni, deputy Multnomah County medical examiner, told reporters the victims had multiple injuries. In keeping with the morgue's and the Portland Police Bureau's longstanding policy of remaining tight-lipped about cases under investigation, Bigoni would not reveal the specific nature of the wounds.

"It was a mess," said Bigoni. "There was lots of blood." He added that the cause of the victims' deaths was obvious, but he would not disclose anything else.

A short time later, Detective Hill contacted an official at Woodmere School, where Chantha Aing was enrolled in kindergarten and Kiry Aing in second grade. The principal was at home that evening, but, considering the seriousness of what happened, readily agreed to meet with Hill.

The principal described Kiry as "a bright and gifted boy. You couldn't ask for a nicer child." She added that although she did not know Chantha personally, she had heard he was a "bright and delightful" child.

In response to Hill's questioning, the principal said the children were taken to school each morning by one of their parents or by someone designated as a guardian. The parents were very interested in their children's education, made evident by their regular participation in parent-teacher conferences.

The principal added that there was nothing unusual about the youngsters' last day at school; they had left at their usual time. She emphasized that they had not been released to any unauthorized person.

Similarly, interviews with officials at Cleveland High School, where Chou Aing was a senior, revealed that Chou was a very good student who had overcome the language barrier through hard work. According to a counselor there, she received all As and Bs.

"She worked extremely hard and had aspirations of going to college," said the counselor. "Education was of paramount importance to her family. She was a joy to work with. She eventually wanted to become a lawyer and was doing very well. She had also started to blossom socially, and that was a pleasure to watch."

He told detectives that Chou planned to attend Portland Community College for two years and then transfer to a four-year college, after which she planned to seek admission to a law school. The counselor told detectives that Chou would have turned 18 on January 1st.

The detectives soon began to theorize that maybe Chou Aing had made an enemy at school, perhaps a jilted boyfriend, and that Kiry and Chantha had been killed simply because they were in the way and could serve as witnesses if left alive. It was a longshot and lawmen knew it, but it was better than having nothing on which to focus their probe.

The sleuths interviewed several of Chou's closest friends along those lines, but their theory was soon shattered. They learned that she was well liked by everyone and, much to their dismay, had no known boyfriends. As they wound up each interview, probers were left with no clues of who might have had a motive to kill Chou and her cousins.

In the meantime, fear and shock overwhelmed Portland's Cambodian community. Nobody could understand how something so terrible could happen to such innocent children.

"They [residents of the Cambodian community] don't know what to think," said an official of the group Sponsors Organized to Assist Refugees. "They are wondering, 'Who could do this to children? Why? Why come all the way from the terror of Cambodia to have this happen?' This is supposed to be the country of freedom, and look what happened.

"Everyone knows everyone else," continued the group's official. He added that members of the association are brought together not only because of their ethnic backgrounds but because of the hardships that most of them have had to endure. "They have been trying to reconstruct in their minds and reconcile why anyone would do this."

The next day Dr. Larry V. Lewman, the Oregon state medical examiner, performed autopsies on the three victims. He concluded that the cause of their deaths was multiple stabbing and chopping injuries to their heads, necks, and torsos. He said all the victims had wounds on their hands and arms, which suggested they had attempted to defend themselves from the chopping and stabbing blows.

After reviewing the autopsy reports, Detectives Hill and Simpson continued with their attempt to learn as much about the victims and their family as possible, hoping for anything that might point them toward a suspect. Because of her age and gender, they continued to concentrate mostly on learning what they could about Chou Aing.

Additional background on Chou revealed that she arrived in the United States in 1981, after fleeing Battambang, Cambodia. The detectives learned that Chou also had another cousin, Narin Aing, 16, a junior at the same high school, who had also fled Cambodia. The investigators were told that at one time Narin lived with Chou and her relatives at the Southeast Ogden Street house, but was not living there at the time of the killings. It was a lucky thing for him, they recalled thinking at the time.

According to the Portland Cambodian Association, Chou and her cousin arrived in Portland with their relatives after being sponsored by other family members who were already living in the United States. The sponsorship split Chou's family. It allowed Chou to move from a refugee camp in Thailand, but forced her to leave her mother and father behind.

Her parents, however, were later allowed to emigrate to Australia, where they obtained work in a doughnut shop. It had been their wish, detectives learned, that Chou go to the United States where she could obtain a better education and have a brighter future. Chou had been making plans to visit her parents the following summer.

Additional interviews with friends and neighbors revealed that Chou's social maturation had caused problems between her and her relatives. About three weeks before the killings, detectives were told, Chou moved into a neighbor's home after having a dispute with one of her legal guardians.

According to her friends, Chou had complained that her relative insisted she study hard at school, then come directly home. Chou, on the other hand, had wanted to date, go to movies with friends, and go shopping in downtown Portland. Her relative forbade her to do such things, saying he feared for her safety. It was after the relative refused to allow her a social life that Chou Aing moved out.

Could this be a potential lead? The detectives explored the possibility. It was possible, they reasoned, that Chou and her two young cousins were killed by an angry family member who temporarily went berserk.

Sleuths soon realized, however, that their theory had too many holes in it. Both adults in the household had airtight alibis. Each was at work at the time of the murders, and they could both prove that they hadn't left their places of employment for even a few moments that day.

Furthermore, family members were described as respectable. They were said to be loving and nurturing toward all the children despite their cultural differences concerning discipline.

As far as the dispute between Chou Aing and her guardian was concerned, the detectives were unable to directly link it to the killings. Witnesses described the dispute as a clash between the freedom of the teenage way of life in America and the strict tradition of Cambodian discipline. After they had finished interviewing family members and others from the Cambodian community, it was easier for the detectives to understand how such a clash could have developed.

A few days after Chou moved out, the sleuths were told, she received a telephone call from her mother in Australia. Her mother gave her an ultimatum: either move back into her relatives' home or face being permanently cast out of the family. Chou obeyed and moved back in with her relatives. The dispute appeared to have been resolved after her guardian allowed her to go to a movie with a boy Chou had met through a friend. The outing had been her first date with a boy.

Leaving no stone unturned, Detectives Hill and Simpson checked out the boy. But the sleuths established that Chou's date had nothing to do with the murders.

As they continued their investigation, Detectives Hill and Simpson learned that a similar dispute between Chou's cousin, Narin Aing, and one of their legal guardians erupted one Sunday the previous April. Much of the dispute involved the amount of time Narin was allowed for a social life and for watching television. Narin, who carried a heavy class load and worked part time, wanted more time for himself but wasn't allowed it by his guardian.

Unwilling to live by his guardian's rules, Narin packed his bags and moved out of the house following a heated argument. He went to the home of a friend who lived only a few blocks away, where he was invited to stay. Unlike Chou Aing, Narin never moved back.

"I told him he could live with us until things got worked out," said Narin's friend's father, Paul Gage. But things apparently never were ironed out, and a few months later, Gage became Narin Aing's legal guardian. Narin's former guardian willingly signed the new guardianship papers in front of a school counselor.

"I told Narin we all had to pitch in and help," said Gage, and Narin agreed. He turned over to Gage half of his $80-per-week earnings from a grocery store job to help pay for his food.

Narin was described as "shy, quiet, hard working, and reliable," with an interest in electronics and mathematics.

In the meantime, fingerprints lifted from the interior of the house where the victims were murdered failed to yield any significant leads. Most of the prints were matched to the victims, family members, friends, other relatives, and police officers. One set was questionable, but the detectives figured those prints likely belonged to Narin, which would soon be verified or refuted. Results from the murder weapons were inconclusive.

While sleuths were still looking for a lead that might point them toward a prime suspect, they decided it might prove useful to interview Narin Aing and check his fingerprints as part of their continuing process of eliminating suspects. Detectives Hill and Simpson went to his foster home, located in the 6300 block of Southeast Duke Street.

The detectives were met by Narin's legal guardian, who said he had been expecting the lawmen to show up sometime. Narin was at home, Gage said, as he ushered the investigators into the living room.

Narin Aing made no attempt to greet the detectives. Dressed in a light blue sweatshirt over a white T-shirt, faded blue jeans, and tennis shoes, Narin looked up briefly as he ran a hand through his bushy, medium-length black hair. He then looked down, placing his hands in his lap. He simply sat in a chair, quiet and subdued. It appeared to the detectives that he was depressed. They thought it best to approach the slightly built youth in a low-key manner.

He looked terrible, they observed. Narin's eyes were swollen and red, as if he had been crying, and he appeared tired. Both detectives surmised he hadn't slept much since the killings. They told him how sorry they were to hear about his cousins' violent deaths and explained that they had to ask him some questions.

At first Narin didn't respond much, and the sleuths thought it best to continue to take it easy with him. They began by asking him general questions about himself, which they hoped would make him feel more at ease with them.

They learned that Narin was a good student. He had a tough class load, but his grades ranged from A to C. He told the detectives that he was enrolled in advanced electronics, algebra, geometry, physics, English, and a government class. He liked to ride his bicycle to and from school.

They asked him questions about his relationship with his former guardian and why he moved out. They were hoping to learn as much as they could about the conditions at the home where the victims had lived just in case they had missed something important earlier. Narin explained in detail how he had wanted more freedom to do things he liked to do, such as watch television and go out with friends. However, he said that his requests were always denied.

The probers turned the interview toward the subject of his cousins' murders by asking Narin if he was feeling depressed over what had happened. He responded that he was and added that he was depressed much of the time. In fact, he said he had skipped school the day after the murders.

As the interview wore on, Narin began to talk more and more freely about the murders. Before long he began to reveal intimate details surrounding the gruesome crime, information that had not been made public and could only be known by the killer and the police.

Although the detectives would not reveal what Narin had told them or what evidence, if any, was found in his possession, he apparently provided sufficient details to cause Detectives Hill and Simpson to arrest him at about 9:00 p.m. on three charges of murder. He was lodged in the Multnomah County Juvenile Detention Center. It was the first time in Portland's history that a juvenile had been charged with a triple homicide.

Until their interview with Narin Aing, Detectives Hill and Simpson conceded that he had not even been considered a suspect in the case. They had been focusing their attention mainly on sorting out the clues they had already uncovered, not knowing where they would lead, and both were shocked at the outcome.

However, as they delved deeper into their probe following Narin's arrest, they realized that those clues would have sooner or later pointed toward him.

On the day of the murders, they learned, Narin left school at 2:00 p.m. after deciding to skip his last class of the day. He had complained about having a headache that afternoon and said that he felt depressed.

In tracking his movements of that afternoon, Detective Hill and Simpson learned that Narin rode his bicycle from school through the streets of Southeast Portland. At one point he stopped at a store to buy soda, after which he rode to Joseph Lane Middle School, a few blocks from where his cousins lived.

From there, the detectives believed, Narin went to the Ogden Street house. In the scenario they prepared for the district attorney's office, the sleuths said they believed Narin entered the residence through a bathroom window. Once inside, they alleged, he looked around the house to see what had changed since he left eight months earlier. He stopped in the kitchen to eat some rice, they theorized, which is when he found a butcher knife and a meat cleaver.

The motive behind his actions was still not clear, but they believed it was revenge against his relatives over the strict discipline handed out at their home.

Details of Narin Aing's past began to emerge soon

after he was seen by a Seattle psychiatrist who has worked extensively with Southeast Asian refugees. Among the things that came out during the psychiatric interviews was that Narin had experienced recurring violent daydreams in which he saw faceless killers with enormous hands strangling people. He also expressed recurring thoughts about committing suicide, but had never made an actual attempt to kill himself.

Narin told the psychiatrist and others that his fantasies would often pass after he talked with friends about them or simply watched television. He also said that he sometimes had difficulty remembering his past in Cambodia.

Despite the difficulty Narin had in recalling his past, the psychiatrist learned that when Narin was about four years old, he and his natural parents were displaced by Cambodian dictator Pol Pot, who evacuated cities and towns following the rise to power of the violent, Communist-backed Khmer Rouge (literally, Red Cambodians) in 1975. Nearly everyone, Narin said, was ordered to work clearing jungles and forests, which covered much of the country. More than one million people died or were executed because of the forced labor and resulting hardships of displacement.

During the next four years, Narin's life got worse and became more than the living hell he had become accustomed to. He was placed in a camp where children were not only subjected to inhuman living conditions, but were also forced to perform severe physical labor. Although he didn't witness any of the numerous killings perpetrated by the Khmer Rouge, Narin claimed he saw many dead bodies that had been mutilated. He also witnessed much sickness and saw many children and adults die of starvation.

According to a psychiatric report provided to authorities, Narin's mother died of starvation when he was quite young.

In 1979, shortly after the Vietnamese invasion of Cambodia, Narin fled his homeland with other children and crossed the border into Thailand. It was there, police learned, that he met his "adoptive parents," who would, two years later, bring him to Portland, Oregon, along with Chou Muy Aing and their infant Kiry. Narin was 10 years old at that time.

After their arrival in the City of Roses, Narin and Chou Muy picked berries in their new country to help earn money for their adoptive family. Later, Narin took a job at a local fast-food restaurant and, later still, he was hired as a courtesy clerk at a story.

Soon after Chantha was born, Narin began to feel that his adoptive parents were paying more attention and showing more love to their natural children than to him. Narin began to be subjected to harsher disciplinary measures, but the discipline was consistent with his culture's tradition.

While the disciplinary measures exceeded typical American standards, the psychiatrist concluded that Narin's treatment was "harsh but not unacceptable. . . . He feels there has never been anybody on his side," a feeling that may have contributed to his thoughts about suicide. Although the psychiatrist only interviewed Narin for approximately 12 hours over several sessions, she said she had found no evidence of physical or sexual abuse.

One of Narin's high school counselors told the detectives there was nothing in his behavior that even hinted toward his impending outburst of violence. The counselor described Narin as a "highly motivated student" and "a very good student who worked hard."

"He was quiet and reserved," said the counselor, "but he did have friends and a social life." He said Narin had complained about not having enough freedom at home, that he was not allowed to watch much television or take part in social activities. But, added the counselor, those were typical objections among high school students.

"I work with a lot of kids who are unhappy at home," the counselor told detectives. "But I never observed any evidence of Narin being physically abused."

Detectives Hill and Simpson probed the question of possible abuse by questioning the victims' family, as difficult as it was.

"Narin insisted on a lot of freedom," said one of his adoptive family members. "I didn't understand what kind of freedom it was . . . I come from a culture where everything is very tight, very strict. But I learn about American society, too. I explained to him a lot about teenage freedom . . . I did not really want him to go [move out of the house]. It was his choice. I begged him sometimes, 'Please stay until you are eighteen. Then you can fly where you want.' "

At a hearing before Multnomah County Circuit Court Judge Stephen B. Herrell, a psychiatrist and a Portland psychologist testified about Narin Aing. They said he suffered from post-traumatic stress disorder and from continuing intermittent depression because of his horrible experiences as a child in the refugee camps of Cambodia. Both said that his mental problems required long-term therapy, longer than he would receive during the four years he could be held in custody if tried as a juvenile.

After agreeing that Narin Aing suffered in Cambodia "under a political system about as inhuman as can be imagined," Judge Herrell ordered Narin to stand trial in adult court.

On Wednesday, September 21, 1988, Narin Aing agreed to testify to the facts of the case without a jury before Multnomah County Circuit Court Judge Philip T. Abraham. Deputy District Attorney Helen T. Smith outlined a possible motive of revenge against his adoptive parents for being too strict. She said the three victims had sustained more than 100 wounds from an attack with a knife and a meat cleaver.

Judge Abraham found Narin guilty of three counts of aggravated murder. Because Narin was a juvenile at the time the murders were committed, a possible death sentence was never an issue under Oregon statutes.

On Tuesday, October 18, 1988, while awaiting sentencing, Narin was found unconscious in his cell at Portland's Justice Center Jail despite an around-the-clock suicide watch. He was rushed to Oregon Health Sciences University Hospital, where he remained in a coma in critical condition.

A short time later it was determined that Narin Aing had obtained, by trading cigarettes with other inmates, enough of the antidepressant drug doxepin for an overdose. Although the authorities were unable to determine precisely how many pills Narin had ingested, it had been enough to effectively cut off oxygen to his brain. The doxepin was in addition to the medication Narin was already taking under extremely controlled conditions for his chronic depression.

"In a jail, things like cigarettes and medicine are used as currency," said Sergeant Jim Davis, public information officer for the Multnomah County Sheriff's Department, which has jurisdiction for the operation of the jail. "The only thing that came out of this one was that these inmates are 'con wise.' They know how to get and to keep the medicine. Some of the ways they do it are not very pleasant. It is obvious that Narin knew what he was going after."

Three days later, Narin Aing died as a result of his drug overdose without ever regaining consciousness. His death left his adoptive family grief-stricken and perplexed.

"We wonder, and we don't understand why, it [the murders] happened," said a family member. "We don't have any exact answer why Narin came to kill

[Kiry, Chantha, and Chou Muy] . . . We think Narin had been influenced by something or fueled by somebody. But we don't know."

Narin's former guardian said he visited Narin at Oregon Health Sciences University Hospital a short time before his death, but Narin remained unconscious, unable to hear or speak.

"I just told him I forgave him," said the former guardian. "But that's not enough for me. I wanted to know why. . . . I know he knew he made a mistake. That's why he committed suicide."

The answers, said the family member, died with Narin.

EDITOR'S NOTE:
*Jane Hall and Paul Gage are not the real names of the persons so named in the foregoing story. Fictitious names have been used because there is no reason for public interest in the identities of these persons.*

# "THE HUNTER'S QUARRY WAS A FAMILY OF 5!"

by Ed Barcelo

PORT HURON, MICH.
MARCH 1, 1983

The death clock was set and running a countdown for slaughter.

The place? Not a likely setting for wholesale massacre, more of a place for hunting and trapping, an outdoorsman's paradise known as Brockway Township, Michigan, about 80 miles north of Detroit, and some 20 miles west of a point where Lake Huron flowed into the St. Clair River. Beautiful, rugged country, but the fierce winters were legendary and not for the faint-hearted. Remote country, too, for the nearest town of any size was a place called Yale, a two-mile rocky-road drive to the east.

At 4:00 a.m, April 7, 1982, a bathroom light went on in a brick one-story ranch home on Carson Road. The man-of-the house was readying himself for another grueling 60-mile drive to work. And what a hell-raising ride it was going to be, the man might have thought. A freak, post-winter snowstorm was belting the countryside, and the weather bureau had issued a traveler's alert, a warning of hazardous driving conditions throughout the state. Serious enough to warrant area school closings.

But treacherous as the drive might be, some 30 minutes later the man backed his car out of the snow-covered driveway and headed for his job in Warren, Michigan. The time: 4:30 a.m.

Horror lay fours hour away, shortly after daybreak.

But dawn crawled in. And a bleak morning it was in the Michigan outback, with night's darkness desperately hanging on, compromising, finally admitting a cold, grayish light to the east as bleak as death's pallor.

Approximate time: 6:00 a.m., and the man who had made the long drive to Warren, Michigan was now at work. In the man's home, 60 miles away, Mrs. Bette Giuliani and her four children, unaware that the schools were closed, squeezed out the last hour of sleep. Soon, they would stir. Soon, the mother would rise, robe herself and awaken the children.

But on this bleak, cold April morning, the out-of-bed-and-off-to-school routine was a preparation for death.

At 7:40 a.m., 100 minutes later, Ellie Burns, a Brockway Township housewife, phoned her neighbor, Bette Giuliani. The two women were members of a four-woman bowling team, and each Wednesday morning, after the children were off to school, the women made the several-mile drive to a Port Huron bowling alley. Following the league play, Ellie and Bette would coffee-klatch in a nearby restaurant. Today's routine would be no different, except for the closing of the schools.

As usual, Bette Giuliani was in good spirits, though neither of the two women thought favorably of the inclement April weather. But Ellie hadn't phoned to talk about the weather; she wondered if her bowling partner would mind if she brought her pre-schooler to the bowling alley.

Mrs. Giuliani doted on the youngster and said it would be fine.

That was the end of the conversation. Except that Ellie told Mrs. Giuliani that she'd be there to pick her up at about 8:30 a.m.

Less than 45 minutes later—promptly at 8:30—Ellie Burns parked her car in the Giuliani driveway. With her in the car was her 13-year-old daughter, Carol Ann, and a younger daughter, four-year-old Patricia. While the mothers bowled, Carol Ann would visit Mrs. Giuliani's daughter, Cindy Jo, (Cynthia) also 13.

Caught in a brisk wind, hair flying over her shoulders, Carol Ann ran to the Giuliani side door. She pounded on the door and shouted her friend's name.

Shivering and getting no response, the teenager rapped again, harder. But still no answer. Now she tried the doorbell. And no answer.

Puzzled, shrugging her shoulders, the 13-year-old returned to her mother's car. "There's nobody home," she said.

Mrs. Burns frowned. "That's impossible. I just spoke to her on the phone 30 minutes ago and told her I was coming over."

The teenager slid back into the car. "Well, nobody answered."

Resolutely, Ellie Burns climbed out of her car and went to the side door. Her daughter trailed after her. Mrs. Burns rapped once, then tried the knob. The door was unlocked.

"Bette?"

Silence. Only the howl of the wind.

Above that howl, Mrs. Burns exchanged puzzled glances with her daughter. The lights were on. Where were they? She repeated her friend's name, then tentatively crossed the living room. Her daughter followed.

Reaching the hallway, which neatly bisected the ranch-style home and led to the kitchen, bedrooms and bathrooms, Ellie Burns couldn't immediately comprehend what she saw.

Three of the Giulianis, Bette among them, were stretched out on the floor. In that instant, a thought flashed through Ellie Burns' mind: "What are they doing sleeping in the hallway?"

And then she saw the blood, the shot-up faces, the empty shell casings, and she screamed, "Oh my God!"

Instinctively, she turned away and herded her daughter into the Giulianis kitchen. Seconds later, she lifted the wall phone and called the sheriff. As she spoke, her eyes fell on a kitchen clock. The time was 8:36 a.m., she would later remember. A time for tears.

Then, with the call completed, Ellie Burns lost control of her emotions. Sobbing quietly, held protectively by her daughter, she sank to her knees and prayed.

For St. Clair County Sheriff Deputy Barry Lang and Detective Bruce E. Lindke, who arrived at 9:00 a.m., the moment was akin to walking in on a massacre. The place was a slaughterhouse, a sight that churned the investigators' stomachs.

Bodies and blood and shell casings were everywhere. Nearly every wall in the house was blood-spattered and much of the carpeting was stained in crimson. In all, the lawmen counted five bodies: Mrs. Bette Giuliani and her four children, two boys and two girls. All had been shot to death. All had been struck by one or more bullets. And all had been shot in the head.

A small Blood City, the Giuliani home. A study in scarlet.

Minutes later, Detective Robert V. Quain, a 19-

year veteran arrived. No less shocked than his two fellow investigators, Quain discovered the lifeless body of nine-year-old Dean Giuliani, dressed except for his shoes, in a bathroom shower stall. The little boy had been shot twice in the face at close range.

Tears crowded Quain's eyes. The kid had been trying to hide from the killer—that was his later impression. A kid without a face.

Gingerly stepping over the fallen bodies, the investigators inventoried the scene.

The body of 50-year-old Bette Giuliani lay sprawled on the hallway floor near the kitchen. Also in the hallway, a few feet away, was the body of a daughter, 17-year-old Kathleen Giuliani. Eric Giuliani, 19, had been slain in his bedroom. The youngest girl, Cynthia, who was 13, was found dead in a second bathroom, next to her parents' bedroom.

The late Giuliani family. Five human beings shot to pieces and turned into inanimate matter. More grisly than the veteran lawmen could stand. Incredible horror without meaning. And the apparent instrument of that horror—a .22-caliber rifle—lay on the hallway floor near the bloodied, bullet-riddled bodies.

Speechless, chilled by a gruesome scene they would never forget, the officers tried to unglue themselves from their personal emotions. In years to come, the men would be unable to recount the exact words they exchanged. Nor would they want to remember. But on April 7, 1982, after senses were collected, the lawmen did the things they must: Phone their office, then contact the St. Clair County Coroner's Office.

Almost as dazed as the two witnesses who had unwittingly walked in on the multiple-slaying scene, the detectives questioned Mrs. Burns and her daughter.

Questions and answers came with difficulty. Mrs. Burns, ashen-faced, blank-eyed with shock, was in no emotional state to answer questions. Nevertheless, she provided lawmen with the names and ages of the Giulianis. She also recounted the earlier phone conversation with her late friend, Bette Giuliani.

When the officers asked her where Bette's husband was, Mrs. Burns explained that he was at work. A General Motors plant in Warren, Michigan, she said, and because it was so far away, he left before daybreak.

The lawmen exchanged glances.

Then, they wanted to know how Bette Giuliani had sounded on the phone that morning. Was there any indication that something was wrong? Did she sound nervous?

Pausing to wipe her tears and speaking in a voice that threatened to crumble, Mrs. Burns said Bette sounded fine. She gave no impression that anything was out of the ordinary.

This told the lawmen something about the time element. If Mrs. Burns' recollection was correct, it could then be assumed that the faceless killer or killers arrived at the Giuliani home sometime between 7:40 and 8:30 a.m.

Was the family having troubles?

None, she said quickly. Nothing out of the ordinary. The family got along just fine.

Mrs. Burns said she'd known the Giuliani family for nine years, ever since the latter had moved here from Capac, Michigan. They were an active, pleasant family, popular in the rural community, churchgoers, hard workers. The children helped their father toil the family's 40-acre farm, which produced much of their food.

In the face of Mrs. Burns continuing praise for the Giulianis, the lawmen found the slayings all the more baffling. For if the family had no known enemies, why this senseless multiple horror?

The answer, if one existed, was knotted in its own paradox; that is, the assumption that the Giulianis had no enemies. Clearly, they had one enemy. A very deadly enemy.

In the minutes that followed, the yard filled with police vehicles of every description. St. Clair Sheriff David J. Doktor and more deputies arrived. Detectives and police officers from nearby Yale, Michigan were on hand to assist, and lending the gruesome scene its forensic officialdom, was Yale assistant medical examiner, Dr. Benjamin C. Clyne.

In later court testimony, Dr. Clyne would say, "I didn't touch the bodies, but I could see evidence of bleeding from the head, mostly.

"The oldest boy was on the floor in a bedroom, the mother and a girl were in the hallway, and the other girl was on the floor in the bathroom. The youngest boy had got into the shower.

"The rifle wasn't real close to anybody. It was near the bedroom where the oldest boy was found, about three or four feet from the girl and her mother in the hallway.

"The mother was dressed and the little boy was dressed except for his shoes — some were in night clothes. I don't really remember."

And while the coroner's people would need autopsies to accurately determine how many times each victim had been shot, it was obvious that four of the slaying victims had multiple gun shot wounds in the head, and one of them had been blasted three times.

In all, the investigators counted 14 empty shell casings, and it appeared that each bullet had struck its mark. But something peculiar was noted by the lawmen. The Giulianis apparently hadn't offered any resistance to the killer's attack. There was no sign of a struggle, no evidence of forced entry.

This seemed to say that the killer or killers was someone known to the Giulianis. The facts also hinted that the slaughter happened too fast for any resistance. The assailant had entered the home, destroyed an entire family—maybe all in less than two to three minutes.

But again, why? While the lawmen exchanged conjectures, other law enforcement agents tramped to neighboring farmhouses to ask questions.

In the blood-splattered Giuliani murder home, police technicians photographed the slaughtered victims, while other specialists dusted the home, inside and out, for fingerprints. The carpeting was studied for trace evidence: dried mud, weeds and any other foreign particles. Most important, the apparent murder weapon, the .22-caliber rifle and empty shell casings were bagged for the ballistics experts.

But none of this would come quickly. In fact, the specialists would spend the entire morning and afternoon in the Giuliani home, searching for clues that might lead to the identity of the killer. Thirty minutes later, at 1:00 p.m., with the victims' bodies still exactly where they'd fallen, state police lab technicians from Madison Heights arrived at the Giuliani home to search for clues.

While this was taking place, Detective Lindke and a Giuliani neighbor drove to the General Motors plant in Warren, Michigan, and confronted Mr. Giuliani with tragic news.

Later, the neighbor said, "We took him to a friend's home. He's better off down there. He wanted to come back home, but he stayed down there. He's in shock. He doesn't believe it's happened. Now they're wiped out. Why? It's so unreal. It just scares you so."

But the mind-reeling family massacre was equally traumatic for the investigators, each of whom was now emotionally committed to finding the killer. To that end, seeking a motive, the detectives had to know more about the Giulianis.

Friends described 17-year-old Kathy Giuliani as an extraordinarily talented singer. "Music was her life," said her high school music teacher. "Out of all the kids that I have seen at Yale in the last ten years, if anyone could have made it professionally in music, she could have."

But there was nothing in the blonde high school senior's background to suggest a murder motive. With music as her all-consuming passion, Kathy did not attend parties or hang around in local teenage haunts. She simply preferred to stay home and practice her music.

However, her older brother, Eric Giuliani, 19, was more outgoing, according to friends. "Everybody knew Rick (nickname). He was a nice guy, very athletic," said one acquaintance.

A 16-year-old girl who occasionally dated the handsome murder victim said, "He liked going to movies and parties. But I don't know who would do a thing like this."

Said the high school athletic director, "He was a real nice kid—well-mannered."

Others characterized Eric as a person who loved to hunt and trap animals. He also loved cars and motorcycles, several friends said. "I saw him at a lot of parties," another friend recalled. "Everywhere there was a party, he'd be there."

But Eric Giuliani was also interested in his future. Following high school graduation, he had worked in an auto factory. But he soon decided he was not cut out for factory work and enrolled at a local town college. He didn't drink much, his friends said, and one friend had seen him as recently as the night before.

"He was playing pinball in the arcade," the friend said. "But there was nothing suspicious looking."

But where was the motive? investigators asked themselves.

Of 13-year-old Cynthia, the youngest Giuliani daughter, the road was equally blind. Nicknamed Cindy Jo, the dark-haired junior high schooler had many friends, did well in school and was popular with both boys and girls. One youth boasted that he had gone with pretty Cindy Jo when they were in the sixth grade, a romance that lasted two days.

"She had a lot of boyfriends," an eighth-grade classmate said. "She was real nice and real easygoing."

But less was known of nine-year-old Dean, affectionately called Dino. A teacher described him as "likeable — just a neat little fourth-grade fellow."

Mrs. Bette Giuliani? Extremely liked and respected by school officials for her many volunteer efforts. Active in community affairs, a teacher of religious education classes in their parish church — a fine person.

So there were no known skeletons in the family closet, and their church pastor of six years said, "The Giulianis were a close family. They came to church every Sunday, and they'd come together as a family."

But who had killed them, and why?

Yale police and St. Clair County sheriff investigators worked feverishly throughout the early afternoon seeking the answers. But residents had become shocked, afraid and confused by the slayings. The helplessness and insecurity that gripped these people was mirrored by everything they said.

At the same time, authorities commented that this was Michigan's third multiple killing of a family in the last six weeks.

Seven members of the George Post family of Farwell were found shot to death at their home, February 16, 1982. Robert Lee Haggart, 31, had been charged with murder in those deaths. He was soon to have been divorced from his wife, Garnetta, one of the victims.

On March 13, 1982, five members of the Robert Paulsen family, of Allendale, Michigan, died also in their home. The Paulsens were shot to death, and a fire was set.

Now, April 7th, and another one . . . and the killer still at large.

But in Brockway Township, things were suddenly happening. In their Carson Road house-to-house questioning of Giuliani neighbors, detectives turned up two witnesses who might have seen the killer that morning. The witnesses described a youth riding past their homes on a ten-speed bicycle, a rifle on the handlebars. One of the witnesses recognized the youth as 16-year-old James Porter.

With controlled interest, the lawmen asked more questions. Porter, a 5-foot-8, 145-pound Yale High School junior, lived only a mile from the Giuliani home, according to the witnesses. More than that, the high school youth reportedly was a long-time friend of the Giulianis; in fact, one witness said Porter and Eric Giuliani had been bosom pals until a few months ago, when a disagreement ended that friendship.

What kind of disagreement? the lawmen wanted to know.

An acquaintance said, "Rick (Eric) and Jim (Porter) were in business together, trapping muskrats and selling the pelts to a dealer. But in November, Rick accused Jim of sneaking into the family's basement and stealing pelts. Jim Porter felt the pelts were his, and it made Rick mad."

The acquaintance said that things weren't the same after that, and the relationship cooled.

"Supposedly they had been in a fight this past week — at a party is what I heard — but I don't know."

Collectively, the information might be meaningful and Porter a hot suspect, the detectives thought. But tips were often worthless and much of this might be readily explained away. For instance, teenage boys frequently had a falling-out with each other, so Porter's differences with the older Giuliani boy could perhaps be nothing. As for Porter being seen carrying a rifle, nothing so unusual about that, not in this part of the country, where teenage boys regularly hunted.

Still, routine demanded the detectives pick up the youth and ask him a few questions. Just to clear the record.

Only, Porter was not at home, and by midafternoon his whereabouts were still unknown. Which called for a choice: The lawmen could let time slide, wait for the boy to return home. Or they could act now. Following a hasty conference, the investigators decided not to wait and an APB was issued for 16-year-old James Porter.

Meanwhile, in the gloom of late afternoon, with a bitter wind sweeping across Carson Road, saddened neighbors stood in front of the Giuliani home and watched the eerie procession of blanketed stretchers being carried to waiting ambulances.

In the neighborhood and in nearby Yale, investigators probed for more information on Porter. The words they heard were not praiseworthy.

The Yale High School principal said James had been disciplined for fighting in school. "The fact of the matter is, he was known as a fighter," the principal said.

Students who knew Porter described him as a rowdy who liked to flirt, drink and play the macho man.

"Let's put it this way," said a mother whose daughter befriended Kathy Giuliani, one of the murder victims. "There have been problems with the boy . . ."

Several residents in the area reported recent petty thefts in their yards. There were suspicions but no investigation or charges.

The pelt dealer, who had had many transactions with Eric Giuliani and James Porter, remembered an incident during a hunting trip up north in which Porter and Eric got into a shoving match in a store. The dealer described Porter as "pretty—light blond hair, blue eyes. He looks like the all-American boy, really. He was all right until he opened his mouth."

But while friends and casual acquaintances were generally in agreement that Porter was a cocky bully who liked to fight and intimidate people—a young kid with a mean streak toward people and animals who would try to justify his misdeeds, none could conceptualize the 16-year-old turning the Giuliani home into a slaughterhouse. He was bad, it was said. But not that bad.

Then, at about 6:00 p.m., April 7th, Yale Police Chief Randall Packard cruising on Main Street, spotted a red late-model Chevrolet with two youths in the front seat. Thinking one of them might be Porter, Packard turned on his flasher lights, gave chase and pulled the car over to the curb. Perfunctorily, he radioed for a back-up. In a matter of seconds, a St. Clair County Sheriff Department patrol car sped down the street from the opposite direction and squealed to a stop. Deputy Ray Gleason jumped from the car and drew his service revolver.

Gleason ordered both occupants of the car to freeze, then told the passenger, a young man with blond hair, to get out and put his hands on the car roof. Then Gleason placed a pair of handcuffs on the youth and put him in the rear of his patrol car.

An unmarked police car arrived, followed by two Sanilac County Sheriff Department patrol cars, driven by Sergeants Daniel Dundas and David Hall.

Chief Packard ordered the driver of the Chevrolet out of the car and put him in his patrol car.

The passenger was blond-haired James Porter, and

his driver-companion was 18-year-old Henry Willis, of Yale.

Willis was later released, but Porter, a juvenile, was taken to the Yale Library. With a family member present, detectives questioned Porter for four hours. The youth denied any knowledge of the Giuliani shootings and insisted he'd been home all morning except for a short time when he went to check on some of his animal traps. Later he'd joined with his friend Henry Willis, he said, and the pair had driven to Port Huron. But authorities, uncertain of the youth's alibi, lodged him in the Port Huron Detention Center, pending further investigation.

Meanwhile, one of Porter's arresting officers commented on the youth's arrest.

"Jimmy wasn't scared. Anyone stopped by a police officer, even if it's for a traffic violation, gets a little nervous. Not Jimmy, he wasn't nervous—he was real cool. His buddy was petrified, but Jimmy showed no signs of any emotion.

"It just wasn't . . . normal . . . ," the officer said. "He was calm, unusually calm. When I was patting him down for a weapon, he asked, 'Are you going to tell me what this is all about?' I told him, 'no, that in a minute detectives would talk to him.' A short time later he asked the same question—just before we took him over to the library where he was questioned."

To bolster their suspicions, the authorities now focused their attention on the apparent murder weapon used in the mass murders—the .22-caliber rifle found in the hallway near the bodies. But the Michigan State Police Crime Laboratory in Michigan Heights quickly determined that this was not the murder weapon. The tracings on the ejected shell casings did not match test firings of the rifle found in the Giuliani home.

Subsequent questioning of Giuliani acquaintances

revealed that Eric Giuliani did own such a gun. But teenager James Porter also owned a .22-caliber rifle, and a family member searched the house, found the gun in a rear-bedroom closet, and turned it over to the detectives for ballistics and fingerprint studies.

Michigan State Police Crime Laboratory specialists Detective Sergeant J. Bullock and Lieutenant Robert White quickly went to work. Provided with a bullet taken from the body of 17-year-old Kathleen Giuliani and 14 empty shell casings found in the murder home, the crime experts determined that the fatal bullets had been fired by Porter's .22-caliber rifle. The sleuths further determined that a left thumb print found on the rifle matched that of the juvenile suspect.

While detectives searched for more evidence and tried to tie in a motive, authorities charged the 16-year-old youth with five counts of aggravated murder and five counts of possession of a firearm during the commission of a felony. Appearing in court, Porter calmly pleaded innocent to all charges.

Meanwhile, St. Clair County Prosecutor Robert H. Cleland petitioned Probate Judge Robert R. Spillard to designate jurisdiction in the case: Would Juvenile Court retain jurisdiction or would James Porter be tried as an adult?

Ultimately, Judge Spillard ruled that Porter would be tried as an adult, which elated the investigators. Tried as an adult and convicted on the charges, Porter would face a mandatory sentence of life in prison without parole. But if Judge Spillard had ruled that Probate Court would retain jurisdiction, Michigan law mandated that Porter, if found guilty, would have to be released from custody at age 19.

Despite their satisfaction with the ruling, the detectives and prosecutor knew the investigation was far from complete. Their case, such as it was, was based solely on ownership of the murder weapon and the statements of two witnesses who on that fatal morning had seen the Porter boy, armed with a rifle, riding his bicycle past their houses. More was needed — a motive; information from other witnesses; facts to lend credibility to police charges against the high school junior. And without this additional information — a St. Clair County Grand Jury indictment notwithstanding — the case would be weak.

In the quest for more damning evidence, detectives requestioned the witnesses who had seen Porter on his bicycle that morning. One, a housewife, said:

"He was out here on his bike in front of our house — my daughter saw him. He was riding on his bicycle toward his house. He wasn't going fast. He was just riding home — he didn't appear to be in any hurry.

"It was about 8:15 in the morning. We know that for sure, because my daughter had gone next door to her grandmother's and woke her up. My mother-in-law looked at the clock, and it was 8:14.

"My daughter didn't see any gun, but our neighbor did. He said he saw Jimmy on the bicycle with the gun when he rode by his house. His dogs were barking and when he went to check on them he saw Jimmy."

The neighbor, also requestioned, reaffirmed his earlier statement. He told detectives he'd seen Porter riding his bicycle west on Yale Road, and some time later he'd seen the youth riding east on Yale Road, back toward his home. The witness said he was certain Porter was carrying a rifle.

Meanwhile, sources close to Porter said the youth now claimed he remembered little of what happened before 9:00 a.m., April 7th, the morning of the murders. The sources said Porter did not remember being there, going to the Giuliani home. Porter also told a source that he had been plagued with blackouts before April 7th, including once when he awakened to find himself in a field near his home, with his .22-caliber rifle in his hands. He said he didn't remember how he had gotten to the field.

Skeptical of these reports, detectives continued their investigation. Again, the authorities fielded statements of Porter neighbors. One neighbor said, "I know Jimmy Porter killed our dog—but I don't know what he did with the Giuliani family."

The neighbor told police that Porter was seen firing a gun on her property. The next day she found her 9-year-old dog shot to death at the rear of her home. "I didn't see him shoot the dog, but I know he did it. And last summer he pointed a gun at one of my six children—we reported that to the police."

Others, noting that Porter was always hunting with his rifle, reported they'd frequently complained to police about shot-up signs and buildings in their yards. The residents thought Porter was the culprit, but they couldn't prove it.

Still searching for a motive, detectives quizzed a Giuliani relative. "Jimmy never had to knock to come in the Giuliani house," the relative said.

But the relative noted that Eric Giuliani suspected Porter of stealing money from their home on several occasions, which ultimately led to a fight between the two teenagers in the family driveway—this on March 21st, less than three weeks before the mass murders.

Digging for facts of a possible burglary angle, detectives requestioned Porter's friend, Henry Willis, who had been driving the car on the evening that Porter was arrested.

Following intense questioning, Willis cracked. He confessed that Porter had taken Eric Giuliani's bank book in March—a month before the murders—forged Eric's signature and withdrawn $300 to $400 from Eric's account. Willis also stated that Porter again had Eric's bankbook on April 7th, the day of the murders. This time, Porter withdrew $1000.

Willis, at the time unaware of the Giuliani murders, stated he picked up Porter at the Porter home about 1:30 p.m. that day. Then they drove to the bank.

"Jim was filling out the withdrawal slip. He wrote Eric's name and the amount . . . $1000. Jim went into the bank to get the money. We were going to split it."

"Did you reach this agreement together?" Willis was asked.

"Yes," Willis answered. Then he said Porter came out of the bank and handed him $500. "I didn't have to ask him for the money, he handed it to me and I put it in my pocket—tens, twenties, fifties—maybe fifteen bills."

Willis said that he and Porter then drove to Port Huron and went on a spending spree. On their way home, Porter tossed Eric's bankbook in a creek, Willis said.

So police now had a motive for the horrible murders—a cheap robbery that had left people dead. And the prosecutor was now ready to do battle.

As expected, James Porter, who had now turned 17, pleaded innocent to the crimes, and innocent by reason of insanity. To that end, Porter's lawyer, Dennis Smith, solicited the services of Dr. Emanual Tanay, a psychiatrist renown for his frequent testimony in court proceedings.

Following his examination of the defendant, Dr. Tanay testified, "He described to me what happened. He got up that morning between 7:30 and 8:00, went outside and saw a pheasant. He had a gun in a case, and he told me rode a relative's bicycle. He said he had a strange feeling. He knew he was moving. He saw people. He saw a neighbor plowing snow.

"He said he was in a trance. He came to the

Giuliani residence. He used a side door. He just simply kicked in the door.

"He said he saw Kathleen. He fired right away at her. Then he saw Mrs. Giuliani come out of the bathroom; he shot her. Then Cindy; he shot her. He made a few steps forward to a bedroom where Eric was in his underwear and shot him. He walked into the utility room and heard some sound. It was nine-year-old Dean and he shot him. He said he got on his bicycle and rode home.

"He fixed himself two pieces of toast, and he said everything was like nothing had happened. He has a clear memory as to what happened, but he was in a depersonalized state. He was there, but he wasn't there. He was there in a dreamlike state. He said, 'The whole thing took maybe sixty seconds.'"

Tanay said he asked Porter why the Giulianis didn't resist. Porter told him, "Because it was all so quick. There wasn't any movement."

But the Circuit Court jury was unaffected by Tanay's "dreamlike, depersonalized" description of the defendant. The jury had heard psychiatrists, a psychologist and three people from the St. Clair County Juvenile Detention Center testify that Porter admitted killing the Giulianis. They also had listened to the testimony of several crime lab experts—33 prosecution witnesses in all. In summation, that jury was convinced of James Porter's guilt.

Unanimously agreed that the youthful defendant was mentally competent when he planned the robbery and cold-bloodedly executed the five Giulianis, the jury found James Porter guilty of five counts of aggravated murder and five counts of possession of a firearm during the commission of a felony.

Subsequently, St. Clair County Circuit Judge James T. Corden sentenced the convicted blond killer to life in prison, with no provision for parole.

But while observers note that justice has been

served, those same observers are mindful that the Giulianis are forever dead.

EDITOR'S NOTE:
*The names Ellie Burns, Patricia Burns, Carol Burns and Henry Willis are fictitious and were used because there is no need for public interest in their true identities.*

# "HIS TEMPER FLARED . . . AND 87 BURNED!"

## by Bud Ampolsk

The first alarm rang in firehouses at 3:41 a.m., March 25, 1990.

Three minutes later, at 3:44 a.m., firefighters from Engine Company 45 and Ladder Company 58 were among the first to arrive at the Happy Land Social Club at 1959 Southern Boulevard, off East Tremont Avenue in the Bronx.

One firefighter of Engine Company 45 said, "There was someone in the street who was telling us there were loads of people trapped inside. Yet we couldn't hear anybody screaming. We didn't hear any yelling; there was no one hollering.

"As we made our way up to the second floor, it was just layers of bodies. They were intertwined and contorted and fused together from the heat. We had to untangle them.

"You can't imagine what went on in there, you can't imagine what those people did to try to survive."

Another Engine Company 45 firefighter said, "These people didn't have a chance. They just died and fell."

Said a fireman from Ladder Company 58: "Some looked like they were sleeping. Some looked horrified. Some looked like they were in shock. There were some people holding hands. There were some people who looked like they were trying to commiserate and hug each other. Some people had torn their clothes off in their panic to get out."

Another fireman from the same company said, "You see the first body and you say, 'You didn't get there fast enough.' Then you see the second body, and the third body, and the fourth body, and after that you can't talk anymore. There's nothing to say."

Five minutes after the firefighters' arrival, the blaze had been knocked down. The frantically mobilized emergency rescue and emergency medical service units were at the scene.

Said one EMS worker: "When I got there, there were already nineteen people piled up outside on the sidewalk. Some looked like they had tried to get their coats over their heads to protect their faces. There was one woman who looked like she was trying to hold onto her boyfriend for dear life. There was a woman holding onto the hand of a man she was with. There was a man lying over a woman as if he was trying to shield her with his body.

"I had to count and tag every one of those bodies. My head is still spinning."

Over the scene of mass carnage, the pungent stench of gasoline hung like an evil cloud. Its presence gave clear indication that the task of crack city detectives was just about to begin.

Lieutenant James Malvey of the 48th Precinct was awakened from a sound sleep in his Orange County home at 4:30 a.m. by the insistent ringing of a telephone. Later he would recall, "The dispatcher told me we had eighty dead—eighty victims of a homicide. I asked her to repeat it. She did. I said, 'I'm on my way.'"

Lieutenant Malvey dressed hastily in a pair of gray

flannel slacks, a light blue button-down shirt and a striped tie. As he sped toward the death scene, he thought that there had been only 12 homicides reported to the 48th thus far in 1990. The figure was just about average for the territory. Now this.

The veteran police officer tried to steel himself for what lay ahead. But nothing prepared him for the shock he felt when he arrived at the Happy Land Social Club: "After twenty-five years on the force, I'd seen just about everything. But I'd never seen carnage like this."

As the firefighters, the medical workers and representatives of the city's medical examiner's office went about the horrifying business of tagging bodies and preparing them for removal, stricken relatives and friends of the dead gathered behind police lines set up on Southern Boulevard and East Tremont Avenue. Lieutenant Malvey gathered the detectives of his command around him and set the strategy for what would be the longest and most soul-shattering day of his career as a police officer.

That day would take its place among the worst in New York City annals. Indeed, the final toll of 87 dead reached in the Sunday, March 25, 1990 blaze would be second only to that of the 146 workers incinerated in the tragic Triangle Shirtwaist Company fire of March 25, 1911. By a macabre twist of irony, the date of the Happy Land conflagration marked the 79th anniversary of the Triangle fire. It had occurred just as preparations were being finalized to commemorate the historic Triangle blaze with solemn ceremonies to be held at the 10-story Asch Building, where the 146 young garment workers had met their deaths. The building is now a part of New York University's Washington Square campus.

While the Triangle fire had been kindled accidentally, the Happy Land holocaust was suspicious from the start, and marshals from the New York City Fire Department immediately began a probe.

First, there was the smell of gasoline. A number of firefighters reported that they had noticed the odor on their rubber boots after having entered the graffiti-streaked, decrepit, two-story building that housed the clandestine, unlicensed gathering place.

Then there was the speed with which the fire had spread up the narrow stairway and into the second-floor dance area of the club.

Third, there was the quickness with which the flames had been doused once firefighters were on the scene.

To bolster the arson theories, authorities brought in specially trained dogs that had been schooled to react to chemical odors. According to their handlers, the dogs' reaction was what might have been expected were there some accelerant still soaking the premises.

Now the detectives under Lieutenant Malvey's command began to move among the crowds of onlookers who had been drawn to Southern Boulevard by the commotion. The sleuths were seeking to piece together a chronological scenario of the events leading up to the kindling of the lethal fire.

From a bouncer who had been on duty near the club's entrance, police learned that there had been an altercation of a personal nature between a woman who worked at the social club and a man. The bouncer had intervened, ordering the man to leave.

A number of witnesses saw and heard the dispute. One witness described the man who had been involved in the arguments with the woman and the bouncer as having been thick-chested and bearded with long hair. During the finger-pointing wrangle, the witness alleged, he heard the bearded man shout, "Don't push me, don't push me!" Then the combatant yelled, as he was being bodily ejected from the ground-floor entrance, "I'll be back!"

Other witnesses claimed they heard the bearded man threaten, "I'll shut this place down."

From a college student working on his first night on the job at a neighborhood self-service gas station came the account of a bearded man approaching him shortly after 3:00 a.m. on the morning of March 25th. The part-time employee sold the man one dollar's worth of gasoline, the transaction taking place through a protective bulletproof glass designed to protect workers from potential robbers in a crime-ridden neighborhood.

The student was badly shaken because of his horrified realization that he had inadvertently provided the fuel which caused the deaths of the 87 revelers.

He was quoted as saying, "I don't know why this happened to me. It's the worst that I have ever experienced. It's such a coincidence because it was my first day on the job and it was the anniversary of that terrible fire (the Triangle Shirtwaist Company blaze).

"I'm a simple guy. I just want to study and make some money for myself. I'm trying to explain to myself what happened. Because it's eighty-seven people. It's incredible."

While this phase of the probe was going on, the full extent of the horror was beginning to be felt throughout the neighborhood of Honduran nationals who had frequented the Happy Land Social Club. Many of those gathered at Southern Boulevard stood in stunned silence as they waited for word of loved ones who had perished in the blaze.

In time, they would learn that 26 of the dead were women. Sixty-one were men. Only five people had managed to get out of the club alive. This was shown, according to New York Mayor David N.

Dinkins, by the fact that 68 of the victims' bodies were discovered on the upper floor of the two-story structure and 19 on the narrow stairway to the ground floor.

There were indications that a number of the victims had been crushed under the weight of others who had fallen on top of them in their panicky attempt to flee.

In order to cope with the terrible business of informing next of kin about the identification of casualties, American Red Cross workers arranged to have Public School 67 opened. In the schoolhouse, situated just a block away from the gutted social club, Salvation Army, Red Cross and other social workers circulated among the crowd, showing them hastily taken photographs of the victims for identification purposes.

For many, the viewing of the Polaroid snapshots meant the end of all hope. A number of people were seen leaving the school building, sobbing bitterly.

An angry Mayor Dinkins vowed, "Anybody who had an opportunity to view eighty-seven bodies will know we will not tolerate it." The mayor ordered that immediate measures be taken to shut down the hundreds of unlicensed clubs throughout the city where violations of the fire and building codes were found.

Typical of the mental agony felt by one group who huddled around the photographs, which had been spread across a table in the school, was one man who spotted the images of the dead faces of his wife's three brothers, a teenage niece and a cousin. He recalled the unheeded advice he had given the victims.

"I told them not to go," the man wept, "but kids are kids. I knew it was dangerous."

One woman had come to the school because her two sons had not come home after a Saturday night on the town.

One man worried about the fate of five teammates on an ethnic neighborhood soccer team. Indeed, many young habitues were members of various soccer teams. Another hoped that having seen his friend's car parked near the Happy Land did not mean the worst.

Many said the social club had served as a gathering place for young people. While there had been occasional fights there, they maintained that the Happy Land had been for the most part peopled by hardworking and law-abiding neighbors who had just sought a little fun to break the bleak realities of life in the economically deprived Honduran community.

One woman who waited with the others for word spoke bitterly of the life she had found in the United States. She commented, "We came looking for a better life and we just found disappointment and disgrace."

Another waited for information on her boyfriend's fate. She noted that he had wanted her to accompany him to the Happy Land, but that she had been too tired. Also, there had been nobody to watch over her three small children.

Of her missing friend, she related how the construction worker had been making plans to return to his native Honduras, having lived in the Bronx for the past three years.

She declared, "He did not like it here. He used to say there was too much violence here. He said his land (Honduras) was so peaceful and his family was there, he has no one here except for me."

At 8:30 a.m., the first of the trucks bringing the dead to the New York County morgue arrived at Manhattan's East 30th Street facility. A group of uniformed police recruited from various precincts throughout the city stood side by side with medical examiner's office personnel. As gently as possible, they lifted the blue or green body bag-shrouded corpses onto gurneys.

It would take over four hours for the complete delivery of the 87 cadavers. Once inside the morgue, the victims were placed so that their heads pointed to the waiting refrigerators. Throughout the area there was the suffocating stench of antiseptic mixed with the smoke clinging to the seared flesh of the bodies.

In all, it would take over three days to complete the grim work of conducting autopsies and making positive IDs of those who had died.

As this was going on, Lieutenant Malvey and the detectives under his command were making swift progress in their search for the thick-chested and bearded man, the prime suspect in the 87 arson slayings. From witnesses who had gone all out to cooperate with the police, they now had a name and address.

The wanted man was 36-year-old Julio Gonzalez, who was said to be living currently at Buchanan Place in the Bronx.

At 4:00 p.m. Sunday, March 25th, Lieutenant Malvey, two detectives and a fire marshal rapped on Gonzalez's door. A moment later, the door swung open and the bearded Cuban national, appearing sleepy-eyed, stood before the lawmen.

Malvey and his colleagues asked Gonzalez to accompany them down to the stationhouse of the 48th Precinct to answer some questions.

Later Malvey would say of the meeting, "He (Gonzalez) acted like he was being picked up on a traffic warrant, like it was nothing."

The detective lieutenant recalled that on the way to the precinct stationhouse Gonzalez reportedly even asked one of the arresting officers for a cigarette.

Once in the squad room of the 48th, detectives began questioning the suspect slowly. Said Malvey, "We asked him who he was and what he did last night."

According to the police, Gonzalez then told the officers that he had left his apartment at eight o'clock on Saturday evening. He had arrived at the Happy Land sometime between midnight and 1:00 a.m., Sunday. He had ordered an eight-ounce beer at the bar.

Gonzalez is alleged to have stated to the questioning detectives that he had gotten into a fight with his ex-girlfriend. They had begun shouting at each other. At this point, the bouncer had asked Gonzalez to leave the club.

According to the police account, Gonzalez told the bouncer, "I'll be back!"

In the statement he gave the detectives, Gonzalez was reported to have admitted that he had returned to the Happy Land approximately a quarter of an hour later. He was carrying one dollar's worth of gasoline with him in a plastic container. He tossed the accelerant into the areaway, then threw several lighted matches into the puddle. The suspect said he left the club after setting the fire, but later came back to watch.

Lieutenant Malvey noted that Gonzalez showed "hardly a trace of emotion" during the interview. However, when detectives read back their notes to him, the suspect appeared to be overcome with the enormity of his act of arson.

Said Malvey, "He choked up. Tears welled in his eyes."

It was also reported that at no time during the stationhouse proceedings did Julio Gonzalez request an attorney.

After making a videotaped statement (recorded in Spanish), the accused man appeared in several police lineups where he was identified by various witnesses. Later he was taken to Bronx Central Booking for processing.

Talking of Gonzalez's behavior at the 48th Precinct headquarters, Lieutenant Malvey commented, "He couldn't have been more cooperative. If they were all like that, we'd solve every homicide."

At a news conference where New York City Police Commission Lee P. Brown announced that a suspect had been taken into custody and his name was Julio Gonzalez, police spokesman Lieutenant Raymond O'Donnell summed up Gonzalez's confession this way:

"He's been away from her (his former girlfriend) for a while. He's drinking at the club. He wants to get back with her. She says, 'Leave me alone.' The bouncer ejects him. He comes back and sets the place on fire."

On Monday, March 26th, Julio Gonzalez was formally charged with having committed the biggest mass murder in United States history. In all, he was arraigned on 87 counts of murder committed in the course of arson, which is felony murder, 87 counts of murder by depraved indifference to human life, one count of attempted murder and two counts of arson.

He was ordered admitted to the psychiatric ward of Kings County Hospital for evaluation and was placed under a 24-hour-a-day suicide watch.

Among the key points in the case Bronx prosecutors were preparing against the suspected mass killer were these:

His tearful videotaped confession.

Gasoline-soaked sneakers and clothing allegedly found in his possession at the time of his arrest.

Eyewitness accounts and the statement of the young gas station attendant who sold Gonzalez the dollar's worth of gasoline.

Gonzalez's ex-girlfriend was quoted as saying, "He told me, 'You won't be here tomorrow!' Then he walked out."

The fact that the woman had appeared at the emergency facilities at Public School 67 caused something of a furor among those who were still awaiting final word on their missing relatives and friends.

In a voice choked with fury, one man demanded, "May I ask what you are doing here?"

The woman replied, "I lost people too. I lost friends."

As the crowd's mood grew uglier, two police officers moved in to escort the woman out through a back entrance of the school.

Now new details of Gonzalez's checkered past began to surface. It was said that the Cuban refugee had been one of the Mariel boatlift people—a group that included some with criminal or psychopathic backgrounds in Cuba—who were allowed to emigrate to the United States under an amnesty arranged with Fidel Castro.

It was said that Gonzalez had been serving time in a Cuban prison after his conviction as an army deserter.

Upon his 1980 arrival in the United States, Gonzalez had been housed in detention camps established in Wisconsin and Arkansas. Released from these institutions in 1981, he then traveled to New York City to live with a sponsor family. It is said he never applied for permanent residence status in the United States and could have been subjected to deportation.

Those who knew him said his association with the erstwhile "girlfriend," who had survived Gonzalez's rage, had covered a span of six years and had been a happy one until recently.

Then, three months before the fateful Happy Land confrontation, something had turned sour between the couple. There was talk that the woman, who was some nine years older than Gonzalez, had been angered over the attention he had been paying to one of her nieces.

It was then that the woman had ordered Gonzalez out of the home they shared. It was also said that Gonzalez had been unemployed for about six weeks, having left a job in a lamp factory.

The picture presented by those who had known Julio Gonzalez while he had lived at Buchanan Place was entirely different from that of a raging jilted suitor who caused the deaths of 87.

A woman who lived across the hall from the sparsely furnished, 10-foot-square room Gonzalez had occupied said, "He was a good person. He caused no problems. He never fought with anybody."

The building manager declared, "He's a nice, quiet, clean guy."

Lieutenant Malvey reported that interviews with other tenants at Buchanan Place had given Gonzalez's behavior there a clean bill of health. Not only had he been quiet and mannerly, he had shown no signs of drug use.

Whether Gonzalez had ever been a drug abuser remained somewhat in doubt. According to a spokesman for the United States Immigration and Naturalization Service, Julio Gonzalez had told Cuban authorities that he trafficked in drugs before leaving the Caribbean island. In making the statement to American INS officials upon his arrival in the United States, Gonzalez had pointed out that he had confessed to drug dealing in Cuba in order to qualify for inclusion among the 125,000 people who were exported from Mariel to Florida. At the time, Castro was reported to be giving priority to people who had been incarcerated in Cuba for mental or criminal problems.

The immigration spokesman said he had no way of verifying Gonzalez's statements about drugs or his relations with the Cuban authorities. The official also noted that there was no record of Gonzalez having engaged in criminal activities while he was a resident of the United States.

Meanwhile, word filtering out of the psychiatric ward where Julio Gonzalez was being held for mental evaluation had the accused killer in a state of extreme depression. One inmate, who claimed to have spoken to Gonzalez, reported that the suspect was alternately weeping bitterly and reviling the woman who had spurned him.

Said the other inmate, "He seems very, very depressed. He is so emotionally distraught that tears keep coming down."

The inmate added that Gonzalez was enraged that his ex-girlfriend was still alive. The man noted that he and Gonzalez had met while they were both being held at Bellevue Hospital. Ruby Riles, a spokeswoman for the Department of Corrections, reported that Gonzalez was transferred to Bellevue when it became apparent that the psychiatric analysis might be protracted. Said Ms. Riles, "Since they admitted him, it looks like he might stay for an extended period."

Those mourning for slain loved ones had little time or inclination to worry over the suspect's emotional status. They were preoccupied with the terrible task of claiming their dead and making arrangements for their burial.

On Wednesday, March 28th, hundreds of mourners followed the line of metal coffins — 16 blue, one pink — as the caskets were carried from the Rivera Funeral Home in the Bronx to nearby St. Joseph's

Church. Once inside the church, 11 coff[...] placed end to end down the middle aisle, [...] other six were aligned along the altar, form[ing] improvised cross.

The only words of comfort the clergyman could offer his parishioners were, "Sudden death for the Christian is also sudden mercy.

"We pray this evening that the Lord may strengthen our understanding. We hope the Lord eternal will lead them home."

There were those in the church who remained inconsolable.

As the cortege of caskets was being returned to the funeral home to await shipment to Honduras for burial, a choir of 30 women lined the steps of St. Joseph's singing the "Ave Maria."

The hymn was almost drowned out by the cries of a 17-year-old classmate of 19-year-old Israel "Tony" Bulnes.

"*Porque? Porque?*" the hysterical youngster screamed. "Tony, take me with you. *Porque? Porque?* He's not dead. Tell him to come out to speak to me."

Bulnes had been a senior at Evander Childs High School. His dream, which would now remain forever unfulfilled, had been to study medicine.

In the funeral home, Bulnes' family knelt by the casket weeping.

Remembered one grief-stricken relative, "The last time I saw him, he was happy and going to pick his girl up to go dancing. Now he is inside a half-open coffin. I can only see half of him."

Noted a teenager who mourned a favorite uncle, "I try to be strong. How can I? I want to hide."

A young woman stood sadly over the open casket of her girlfriend. The dead girl had been dressed in very soft and feminine pink. Rosary beads were

...ined around her fingers.

Gently, the grieving woman placed her own hands over her friend's. She stood there for long moments in silence. Then she said softly, "My dear friend, this is the last time we hold hands."

The auxiliary bishop presiding at the mass talked of having counseled the widow of a man who had died in the fire. He said, "I didn't see her crying. I told her you have to cry to let out the pressure."

The 66-year-old clergyman noted that the Happy Land fire had reawakened his memories of the horrors of the Spanish Civil War, which he had experienced as a young boy.

"The thing is you don't know how to react. It takes in all your being."

The bereaved were being given emotional and physical support by a veritable army of social workers. Operating side by side were priests, members of the Red Cross and mental health counselors. One of the urgent needs was for the immediate distribution of emergency funds to defray funeral costs.

Governor Mario Cuomo, members of Congress and representatives of the International Red Cross were working feverishly to arrange free transportation to Honduras for those who would accompany their dead to their final resting place. It was expected by Honduran officials that at least 75 of the 87 victims would be buried in the small villages that line the northern part of the small Central American nation.

The New York State Air National Guard was working with the Defense Department to obtain permission for troop carriers which had been turned into airborne hearses to gain right-of-way into international air space.

As the week-long period of mourning continued, the New York City Human Resources Administration was providing $900 toward funeral expenses for each victim. The New York State Crime Victims Board was offering $2,500 for the same purpose. The Roman Catholic Archdiocese was providing free burial sites and had waived fees for funeral masses. The American Red Cross was donating two round-trip tickets free to any two family members who would be accompanying their dead kin back home.

While all of these acts of compassion were going on, the Bronx County District Attorney's Office was going about the grim business of presenting the results of its investigation to a Bronx grand jury.

On Friday, March 30th, just five days after the deadly fire had erupted at the Happy Land Social Club, the grand jury acted. Assistant Bronx District Attorney Eric Warner reported to Judge Efraim Alvarado that the grand jury had voted the indictments against Julio Gonzalez.

The list of charges and the possible sentences should Gonzalez be convicted of them were:

—Second-degree murder "under circumstances evincing depraved indifference to human life." 87 counts. Maximum penalty 25 years to life in prison.

—Second-degree murder "in the course and the furtherance of the commission of a felony." 87 counts. Maximum penalty 25 years to life in prison.

—First-degree arson. "Charge alleges defendant knew people were in the building and the fire caused physical injury. One count. Maximum penalty 15 years to a life term.

—Second-degree arson. "Charge alleges defendant had reason to believe people were in the building when the fire was set." One count. Maximum penalty eight and one-third years to 25 years.

—Second-degree attempted murder. One count. Maximum penalty eight and one-third years to 25 years.

—First-degree assault: One count. Maximum penalty five years to 15 years.

If Gonzalez were found guilty on all counts and the sentencing judge were to rule that he serve maximum time on each of the 178 counts consecutively, the sentence could possibly add up to 2,000 years in prison.

Following release of the grand jury findings, court-appointed Defense Attorney Richard Berne said he would have his client examined by a psychiatrist of his choosing. However, he would not comment further on the strategy he planned to employ in representing Gonzalez.

In other court action the same day, two Puerto Rican families filed suit in the United States Federal Court in Manhattan, charging that the city of New York and several businessmen were responsible for the deaths of their relatives in the Happy Land Social Club fire.

The city was cited in the civil action because of what one lawsuit described as "a negligent failure to warn of the hazardous and dangerous conditions" at the social club and "to take actions necessary for the regulations of such premises."

The first suit was filed by family members of victim Carmen Delia Hernandez Pizarro. The suit, filed jointly by firms in New York and Puerto Rico, sought $57 million in damages.

The second suit was filed by family members of two of the victims, Marisol Martinez Rodriguez and Aida M. Martinez Rodriguez. The suit, filed by the same two law firms, sought $100 million in damages.

Neither suit named Julio Gonzalez.

The reason for petitioning the federal courts was that the lawsuits involve people from different states.

Therefore, the cases must be decided in federal, rather than state, courts.

Jurisdiction was also claimed on constitutional grounds. It was charged that the city, through its alleged inaction, had an "official policy" of indifference to the constitutional rights of the public.

Commenting on the 178 felony counts facing Julio Gonzalez, A.D.A. Warner reported the Bronx District Attorney's Office was not considering any plea bargain.

Said Warner, "I am very confident that we have a good case against Mr. Gonzalez. No case is open and shut. We have a good case. The evidence is strong."

On Saturday, March 31st, a blustery cold and threatening early spring day, 50 coffins lined a huge hangar at Kennedy International Airport. They rested atop standard pine shipping crates and were decorated with arrangements of roses and carnations provided by the Retail Florists Association.

In the hangar identified as Building 14, a small group of officials and reporters gathered at 10:30 a.m. They heard a clergyman representing the Archdiocese of New York tell them, "The tragedy is incomprehensible. And without diminishing the pain the families have experienced, we come here with hope after witnessing the coming together of a community this week to deal with the crisis."

"They came here seeking hope and opportunity," Deputy Mayor Bill Lynch told the assembled journalists and bureaucrats. "We hope this will never happen again. We will do everything possible to make sure the city will remain a place of opportunity."

After the brief ceremonies, Red Cross and Pan American Airways volunteers placed each of the coffins inside the crates, then loaded them aboard a chartered red, white and gold DC-8 for the flight to

San Pedro Sula, Honduras. There, Honduran President Rafael Leonardo Callejas waited to receive the bodies of his fallen countrymen and countrywomen.

A mass was scheduled for Monday morning, April 2nd, followed by transport of the coffins to hometown cemeteries for interment.

At the time of this writing, Julio Gonzalez was being held without bail in the prison ward of Bellevue Hospital for further psychiatric tests. He remained under a round-the-clock suicide watch.

As Gonzalez awaits further court action on the felony charges against him, it should be remembered that under the Constitution of the United States, he has the right to be presumed innocent of all charges unless, or until, proved otherwise under due process of law.

# "4 BLASTED IN POSTAL BLOODBATH!"
## by Gary C. King

ROYAL OAK, MICHIGAN
NOVEMBER 14, 1991

Thursday, November 14, 1991, started out as a normal, crisp autumn day for most people in Detroit. Workers commuting from the Motor City's suburbs jammed the major arteries on their way to jobs at the Fisher Building, General Motors, the Burroughs Corporation, Ford, and a number of other major businesses in or near the downtown area. Others were heading out of the city to their jobs in the suburbs, and for them the commute was much easier. Regardless of where they worked, most of the workers in this city of more than a million people felt reasonably safe in their workplaces. Because Detroit is a city known for crime, some actually felt safer at work than inside their own homes. But all that was about to change . . .

None of the morning drivers could have known about the heavily armed young man who was heading out of the city toward the middle-class suburb of Royal Oak, some 12 miles north of downtown Detroit, or that he was about to add another grim chapter in the history of mass murder in America.

The man parked his vehicle near the Royal Oak Post

Office, a 1,000-employee mail-processing facility that occupies a full square block of Royal Oak's downtown area and services 50 other post offices in the Detroit metropolitan area. The loading dock at the back of the building was buried waist-deep in mail sacks, many of which had been loaded onto four-wheeled carts. Trucks were coming and going with efficient regularity, picking up and dropping off sacks of mail, while the mail carriers were reporting in to pick up their day's worth of deliveries. It's little wonder, then, that nobody noticed the man calmly walking through the wrought-iron gate with something deadly beneath his jacket.

It was 8:50 a.m. when the man pulled the sawed-off semiautomatic rifle out of his jacket and opened fire. He began spraying bullets at the workers on the loading dock, shooting at least three employees before he entered the building through a rear door. Many potential victims hit the deck when they saw what was happening. Others hid behind mailbags and prayed that their number hadn't yet come up. Survivors reported later that the gunman seemed calm as he moved through the building and walked up a flight of stairs to a complex of offices, where he shot three more people in rapid succession. Leaving many others alive and fearing for their safety, the assailant walked back downstairs to a mail-sorting area at the opposite end of the building from where he'd begun shooting on the loading dock. There he fired off several more rounds.

It was all happening so quickly that no one knew where the gunman might strike next. Those who realized what was happening remained hidden, afraid to come out and warn others or to summon help.

A letter carrier who was arranging his mail when the gunman came into the sorting area recognized him from 25 feet away. The carrier dropped to the floor just as the gunman saw him and opened fire. Fortunately, the spray of bullets missed its target. Taking advantage of the momentary reprieve, the letter carrier yelled out to the gunman and pleaded with him to show mercy. But the gunman was apparently lost in his own world and didn't seem to hear the terrified man's pleas.

"No, Tom, no!" the mailman cried out. "Don't do it!" He pleaded for his life repeatedly, suddenly afraid that his life was over as the gunman continued firing. Finally, after what seemed like eternity, the gunman turned and walked away, sparing the letter carrier's life.

Seconds later, however, additional shots were fired in a nearby office. By that time, customers on the first floor had heard some of the gunshots and were scrambling to get out of the building and to their cars. At the same time, several employees began jumping out second-floor windows onto the parking lot below in order to escape the mad gunman's bullets. One, who had been injured in the fall, saw a man parking his car and yelled for help: "Please! Call the police! Somebody's shooting inside!"

Several more shots went off inside the building, followed by a few moments of silence. Then, a single gunshot shattered the peace. Afterward, the post office was momentarily enveloped in an eerie calm. Employees and patrons alike were quietly lying flat on the floor or crouched behind office furniture and machinery for cover from the madman's bullets. Each person hoped and prayed that the gunman's bullets would not find him or her.

Moments later, the silence was broken as people began to realize that the shooting spree was over and cautiously came out of hiding. Many cried openly, and others shook from intense fright. Sirens wailed as police cars and ambulances converged on the scene. Police marksmen surrounded the post office, their own rifles trained on the windows and doorways, while uniformed officers sealed off the block in all directions. The normally peaceful locale suddenly looked like a war zone, with "soldiers" ready to return enemy fire. But no more shots were fired.

Finally, several postal employees came out from the far end of the building and announced that the violence was over. The gunman, they said, had shot himself in the head. He was still alive, someone said, but he was unconscious, and could do no more harm to anyone. The employees then directed the police and paramedics to the dead and the maimed. Paramedics did what they could at the scene for those who had been injured, and then wheeled them out on gurneys. Six waiting ambulances whisked the wounded off to area hospitals. One of those rushed into surgery was the gunman himself, who had suffered a severe self-inflicted head wound.

According to a local television station, the American Red Cross began announcing that it was "in desperate need of blood" to treat the wounded. Beaumont Hospital in Royal Oak, which had received four of the injured, including the gunman, pleaded for at least 90 units of blood. Oakland General Hospital, which was treating three wounded, announced that it needed blood, too—as much as it could get. Although there were conflicting reports about the number of victims, there appeared to be at least 10. Three of those were dead at the scene. Three additional victims—two women and a man—were listed in critical condition. Officials would not name the victims at that time.

Police officers struggled against chaos as they blocked off the area and began their search for witnesses who might be able to explain what had triggered such a tragedy. It was the second such incident to hit the U.S. Postal Service in a month, and the fifth in as many years. Reporters from local newspapers and television and radio stations tried to get past police barriers, also eager to learn what happened and why, but they were held back along with the curious onlookers.

"There's been a shooting, that's all we can say," said

a Royal Oak police spokesperson. "When we find out what happened, we'll issue a statement."

Although there was no official statement yet on the fatalities, word spread quickly that there had been three deaths. Little did anyone know that the death toll would rise before the day was over.

Meanwhile, as police investigators sidestepped blood puddles and passed by blood-sprayed walls, they evacuated the building and cordoned it off, establishing it as a crime scene, to prevent confusion and further contamination of the evidence. It was imperative that they get the scene organized and under their control as quickly as possible.

Soon, according to Royal Oak Police Officer Joseph Hill, postal employees identified the gunman as 31-year-old Thomas McIlvane, of Oak Park, another Detroit suburb only a short distance from Royal Oak. McIlvane had been fired a day earlier after being brought up on charges of time-card fraud. He had apparently fought a year-long battle to save his job. Finally, he had threatened to come back with a gun, according to witnesses. One witness said she wasn't surprised by what happened.

"Tom felt like he was pushed out," said the witness. "Desperate people do desperate things."

Another witness, Dan Lee, told investigators that McIlvane was "crazy" and a "walking time bomb." Lee, who said he had served with McIlvane in the Marine Corps in the early 1980s, told investigators that he heard McIlvane say he would return to work with a gun.

"He was a kick-boxer," said Lee. Lee said that McIlvane had been a lance corporal in the Marines, adding, "He had made previous threats. One time at Twentynine Palms Marine Corps Base, there was a guy he was mad at, and he drove a tank over his car." McIlvane had also apparently joked about the mass shooting at Luby's Cafeteria in Kileen, Texas, which occurred in October, and said he would do the same if he was not reinstated in his job. When it was decided that his firing would stand, McIlvane kept his promise to get vengeance by committing mass murder.

Another employee who witnessed the killing spree told detectives that he thought the shooting was "kind of fake, at first." But he quickly changed his mind, he said.

"Somebody said it was firecrackers," he said. "It sounded kind of like that. Then I smelled the gunsmoke and I knew it was for real. I heard five or six shots in the mail-sorting area, and I started running. I saw one supervisor lying on the floor, covered with blood."

Another witness told police that he had arrived outside to mail a letter and heard four or five shots fired from inside the building, followed by a short pause and several more shots. Bewildered at first, the witness soon realized what was happening.

"As I was pulling into the parking lot, I saw a lot of people running out, screaming," said the witness. "They were screaming, 'Someone call the police!'

"I heard eight or ten shots and I'm sure he must have fired eight or ten shots before they ran out. People were jumping out of windows. People were stumbling, falling over things and each other. People were running out the back door."

Another customer told police that he talked to some of the employees who had escaped.

"They were just really freaking out," he said. "They said they knew this guy was going to do it."

"I don't think anyone can characterize something like this except chaos," said Royal Oak's fire chief. "When something like this happens, you don't believe it. I don't know what the world is coming to." He told reporters that the gunman had opened fire in at least three different areas of the post office, but that all of the shootings had occurred in non-public areas.

In light of the poor morale at post offices nationwide and the high incidence of disgruntled employees seeking vengeance over being fired or for being reprimanded by their superiors, the news of a prior warning and previous threats was of great concern to the police and served to open yet another can of worms for the already besieged and troubled postal service.

On October 10, 1991, authorities alleged that a fired postal worker armed with two machineguns, grenades, and a samurai sword, killed a former supervisor and her boyfriend at their home in Wayne, New Jersey. Afterward, he went to the Ridgewood Post Office, where he formerly worked, and killed two mail handlers when they arrived at their jobs. Following a four-and-a-half-hour standoff with police, the man surrendered and is now awaiting trial.

On August 10, 1989, postal service employee John Merlin Taylor of Escondido, California, shot his wife to death in their home. Afterward, he drove to his workplace, the Orange Glenn Post Office, where he shot and killed two fellow employees and wounded another before committing suicide.

On December 14, 1988, a postal worker in New Orleans shot and wounded three people and held his girlfriend hostage for 13 hours before surrendering. Fortunately, there were no deaths in that case.

The worst massacre in the history of the postal service occurred on August 20, 1986, in Edmond, Oklahoma, when Patrick Henry Sherill, a part-time letter carrier, shot and killed 14 of his colleagues before killing himself. Like Thomas McIlvane, Sherill had a history of work problems and had faced the possibility of being fired.

What was happening within the postal service to cause such massive waves of violence? Were the postal service's troubles just beginning? Many investigators found themselves wondering what was yet to come, especially considering that all of the post office violence seemed to stem from disgruntled employees seeking revenge. Shootings and acts of violence occasionally occurred at other workplaces across America, they knew, but never was a single employer so besieged with violence as was the U.S. Postal Service.

Postal service officials and police investigators alike hoped that the investigation would reveal what steps could be taken to ward off possible future attacks. But what they uncovered in Royal Oak proved only more disturbing, as employee after employee told authorities that they had expected just such an attack by Tom McIlvane. Apparently, rumors of an impending shooting had been circulating for some time.

"Everybody said if he didn't get his job back, he was going to come in and shoot," said postal employee Jake Wheeler, who added that McIlvane's threats were often discussed at the post office in Royal Oak. "Everyone was talking about it. They said he was mad, that something was going to happen."

Wheeler also told the investigators that the stress level at the post office was high, due mainly to poor working conditions. "They just drive you," he said. "People are upset. They even made the routes longer."

When asked why McIlvane had been fired, one worker told detectives that it was over "something they made up, something they trumped up on him." But another employee told investigators that McIlvane had been fired for time-card fraud and insubordination. He had altered his time card, said the employee, and regularly mouthed off at his superiors and at customers.

When asked by investigators why McIlvane hadn't been prosecuted for making threats following his dismissal a year earlier, a top-level postal official responded that an internal investigation had not uncovered anything sufficient for which to prosecute him.

"We were aware of a concern by employees about

Mr. McIlvane's behavior," said the official. "He was profane and abusive. But none of these complaints were of the magnitude for us to prosecute him. . . . We don't have the answers to all the different questions that may be posed. Indeed, we may never have the answers. All of us are looking for logical answers to a very illogical event."

In May 1989, said the official, McIlvane used profanity in dealing with a difficult customer. "We investigated, but he never exhibited that type of behavior when we were around. He has a history of contact with the investigative arm of the postal service." The incident triggered a hearing, but no action was taken against McIlvane.

According to postal service records, McIlvane once called a supervisor obscene names to her face. He had also been involved in "pushing and shoving" incidents with other employees.

Another official told investigators that the postal service took preventive actions after learning about McIlvane's threats, including the installation of doors with combination locks. At one point, the postal officials had even considered placing a security guard on the premises, but the idea was ultimately rejected.

"We simply don't have guards guarding the doors," said the official. "This is a mail-processing facility. There are so many mail carriers coming in and so many vehicles, it's impossible to keep the back of the post office sealed."

"These are public buildings," said yet another high-ranking postal service official. "I don't think you can make them hermetically sealed. We can't make forty thousand post offices armed camps. . . . When you look at each one of them, you don't find a threat. Let me be brutal: If we had a police officer at the back dock in this case, we would have had one more dead."

Another witness, who requested anonymity out of fear of retribution by postal authorities, said that postal workers generally had been under tremendous pressure in recent years.

"If you don't return to the post office after your route, there are repercussions," said the witness. "You can't keep up on the heavy mail days unless you skip your lunch and your break."

"They ride you all the time," said another employee. "You can't even use the bathroom unless it's your break. They sent a guy home this morning for whistling. For *whistling*! You could almost feel it there — the tension was building almost every day. You can't laugh, you can't talk to your neighbor. It's just ridiculous."

Such sentiments were expressed by postal workers across the nation in the wake of the Royal Oak shootings.

"I just think things should get better," said one postal worker. "Maybe this tragedy will make a difference, but I just don't know. You never know from one day to the next whether you'll have a job. . . . The only thing I can say is, I'm not surprised."

Another postal worker who didn't want to be identified told police that only two days before, McIlvane had threatened one of the people he killed. "He has been threatening for over a year." The employee said that postal officials had placed combination locks on the back side of the building and on the gates and sliding doors a few months earlier to prevent such a tragedy, but it was to no avail.

"We talked about the potential danger quite a bit," said another employee. "He said he was going to do it, but I guess they just didn't take it seriously."

The employee described how she had been working in the mail-sorting area when she first heard the gunshots.

"I hit the floor," she said. "I looked out in the hall and I saw him running down the hall with a coat over the gun."

She was unable to identify the type of weapon she saw McIlvane carrying, but she believed it was a rifle. "It was something that he could fire a lot of shots at once," she said.

McIlvane had four "banana" clips of ammunition, which consisted of approximately 100 rounds taped together "commando-style," when he entered the building. Police identified the weapon as a .22-caliber Rugur semiautomatic rifle whose barrel McIlvane had apparently sawed off.

Still other witnesses told police it appeared that McIlvane had a "hit list" and was shooting only those with whom he'd felt he had a score to settle.

"There's no doubt this employee had intended to get at the people responsible for his being fired," said one postal service official.

One of those people was 33-year-old Christopher Carlisle, manager of station branch operations at the Royal Oak postal facility. Carlisle, police were told, was the person responsible for firing McIlvane in 1990 for swearing at his supervisor and for insubordination.

The probers learned that Carlisle had a reputation for being quite tough. Prior to taking his post at Royal Oak, Carlisle had been a delivery supervisor for eight years in Indianapolis, where he was known to be an authoritarian manager. No one, however, was happy to hear that Carlisle had become a victim of an assassin's bullet.

Carlisle was identified as one of three victims pronounced dead at the scene. The two others were 32-year-old Mary Ellen Benincasa, an injury compensation specialist, and 37-year-old Keith Diszewski, a labor relations specialist. By midday, six other victims were still alive, three listed in critical condition and one listed as serious. McIlvane was also still alive, despite the self-inflicted gunshot wound to his head, but he was not expected to survive.

"[McIlvane] had been declared brain dead," said a

Beaumont Hospital nursing supervisor. "But he is not legally declared dead and he is still on life support."

It was obvious from the outset that McIlvane wouldn't be able to shed any light on why he had chosen such a severe course of action in response to his firing. Most people would either pursue further legal action, or simply get another job and move on with their lives. But police reasoned that McIlvane's troubles were much more deep-seated than simply getting fired. The firing had unquestionably been the triggering factor. But something else—perhaps a mental imbalance—must have caused him to resort to extreme violence. However, the investigators knew that the complete answer might never be known.

Meanwhile, Royal Oak homicide detectives ran a background check on Thomas McIlvane. They learned, among other things, that he was a 1979 graduate of Berkley High School in Royal Oak. According to a relative, he was given an "undesirable" discharge from the Marine Corps following the episode at Twentynine Palms, when he drove a tank over a car, despite having served four years. An undesirable discharge is one notch short of being dishonorable. They also learned that both of McIlvane's parents were dead and that he was unmarried. He'd been living with two roommates at the time of his deadly shooting spree.

McIlvane's criminal record was not extensive, the detectives learned. A year earlier he had been charged with making threatening telephone calls to a supervisor, but he was acquitted. His ongoing dispute with supervisors and employees, however, led to the revocation of a concealed weapons permit for hunting and target shooting, according to Oakland County Prosecutor Richard Thompson. Aside from the aforementioned, McIlvane's criminal record was clean.

"No matter what law you have on the books," said Thompson, "you can't stop these events from occurring."